Cognitive Therapy for Command Hallucinations

Auditory hallucinations rank among the most treatment resistant symptoms of schizophrenia, with command hallucinations being the most distressing, high risk and treatment resistant of all.

This new work provides clinicians with a detailed guide, illustrating in depth the techniques and strategies developed for working with command hallucinations. Woven throughout with key cases and clinical examples, *Cognitive Therapy for Command Hallucinations* clearly demonstrates how these techniques can be applied in a clinical setting. Strategies and solutions for overcoming therapeutic obstacles are shown alongside treatment successes and failures to provide the reader with an accurate understanding of the complexities of cognitive therapy.

This helpful and practical guide will be of interest to clinical and forensic psychologists, cognitive behavioural therapists, nurses and psychiatrists.

Alan Meaden is a consultant clinical psychologist working for Birmingham and Solihull Mental Health NHS Foundation Trust and is the lead for the Trust's Assertive Outreach and Non-Acute Inpatient Services. He has been involved in research on command hallucinations and the development of theory and practice for their treatment for over a decade. Most recently he has been the supervisor and trainer for therapists on COMMAND: the recent multicentre randomised controlled trial.

Nadine Keen is a chartered clinical psychologist on the COMMAND trial (CBT for command hallucinations) and at the Psychological Interventions Clinic for outpatients with psychosis, South London and Maudsley Trust.

Robert Aston is a cognitive behavioural therapist at Birmingham University.

Karen Barton is a clinical psychologist at Birmingham and Solihull Mental Health NHS Foundation Trust.

Sandra Bucci is a lecturer in clinical psychology at the University of Manchester.

Cognitive Therapy for Command Hallucinations

An advanced practical companion

Alan Meaden
Nadine Keen
Robert Aston
Karen Barton
Sandra Bucci

Routledge
Taylor & Francis Group

LONDON AND NEW YORK

First published 2013
by Routledge
27 Church Road, Hove, East Sussex BN3 2FA

Simultaneously published in the USA and Canada
by Routledge
711 Third Avenue, New York, NY 10017

Routledge is an imprint of the Taylor & Francis Group, an informa business

British Library Cataloguing in Publication Data
A catalogue record for this book is available from the British Library

Library of Congress Cataloging in Publication Data
Cognitive therapy for command hallucinations: an advanced practical
companion/Alan Meaden . . . [et al.].
    p. cm.
    Includes bibliographical references and index.
    1. Auditory hallucinations – Treatment.   2. Cognitive therapy.
    3. Auditory hallucinations – Treatment – Case studies.
    4. Cognitive therapy – Case studies.   I. Meaden, Alan, 1961–
    RC553.A84C64 2012
    616.89'1425 – dc23
    2012014253

ISBN: 978-0-415-60234-1 (hbk)
ISBN: 978-0-415-62528-9 (pbk)
ISBN: 978-0-203-08654-4 (ebk)

Typeset in Times New Roman and Gill Sans
by Florence Production Ltd, Stoodleigh, Devon

MIX
Paper from
responsible sources
FSC® C004839
www.fsc.org

Printed and bound by CPI Group (UK) Ltd, Croydon, CR0 4YY

Dedication

This book is dedicated to the memory of Janey Antoniou. Janey was one of the most respected campaigners for the support of those with mental illness. She died tragically on 23 October 2010 at the age of 53. Diagnosed with schizophrenia in 1985, Janey spoke about her experiences of stigma, and hearing taunting and commanding voices. She was a high profile and powerful advocate for people using mental health services both nationally and internationally. Janey worked to raise awareness and combat stigma of schizophrenia with major government, NGO and academic organisations in the sector, such as the Royal College of Psychiatry, Institute of Psychiatry, Rethink Mental Illness, Mind, ISPS UK, and was the service user representative on the panel reviewing the NICE guidelines for the treatment of schizophrenia published in 2009. On a more personal level, Janey described her experience of living with schizophrenia in poetry, which won a number of awards. This book was written with the intention of broadening the practice of cognitive therapy for command hallucinations by providing those in the helping professions with a detailed practice manual. It is hoped that one day all service users such as Janey who experience distress as a result of command hallucinations will be able to access this effective evidence-based therapy.

Michael Antoniou and Alan Meaden
November 2011

Knowledge is merely a collection of perspectival illusions which, while necessary for the preservation of the human species, stands as a function not of truth but of power.

Alan Schrift

Contents

Appendices

Figures

Tables

Notes on the cover art

For me the buildings represent being at peace and controlled. I can see things more clearly than I used to see them. The buildings are tall, strong, robust and stable and the voice is less overwhelming. When I painted the picture I felt calm and this is shown in the colours I used. They are lovely and bright, these are a far cry from the dark pictures I paint when I am not well.

The different words on the wall (mad, crazy, love) are how I see myself, what the voice says and how others might view mental illness. Sometimes things are chaotic. The words are all confused and overlapping. But I am loving myself more and see others as loving me. My confidence has definitely grown. The words on the wall are not the main part of the picture. They are words on a wall and the wall itself acts as a barrier to protect the buildings behind.

Alice
Service user and artist

Preface

Cognitive therapy for command hallucinations (CTCH) is not an all together novel enterprise. John Percival (cited by Peterson, 1982), the son of English Prime Minister Spencer Percival (1762–1812) at the age of 27, began seeing visions and hearing voices that commanded him to act in harmful ways. His behaviour subsequently became of concern and a 'lunatic doctor' was called who proceeded to strap him to his bed and feed him broth and medicine. Percival gives a vivid account of his experience which captures several of the key features of our approach:

> Those voices commanded me to do, and made me believe a number of false and terrible things. I threw myself out of bed – I tried to twist my neck – I struggled with my keepers. When I came to Dr Fox's, I threw myself over a style, absolutely head over heels, wrestled with the keepers to get a violent fall, asked them to strangle me, endeavoured to suffocate myself on my pillow, threw myself flat on my face down steep slopes . . . and upon the gravel walk, called after people as my mother, brothers, and sisters, and cried out a number of sentences, usually in verse, as I heard them prompted to me – in short for a whole year I scarcely uttered a syllable, or did a single act but from inspiration. On another occasion being desired to throw myself over a steep precipice near the river Avon – with the promise that if I did so, I should be in heavenly places, or immediately at home, I refused to do so for fear of death, and retired from the edge of the precipice to avoid temptation . . . but this last was not till after repeated experiments of other kinds and proved to me that I might be deluded. For I was cured at last, and only cured of each of these delusions respecting throwing myself about and so on, by the experience that the promises and threats attendant upon each of them were false. When I had fairly performed what I was commanded, and found that I remained as I was, I desisted from trying it. I knew I had been deceived – and when any voice came to order me to do anything, I conceived it my duty to wait and hear if that order was explained, and followed by another – and indeed I often rejected the voice altogether: and thus I

became of a sudden, from a dangerous lunatic, a mere imbecile, half-witted though wretched being: and this as the first stage of my recovery.

Unfortunately not all individuals who experience command hallucinations are able to develop such insights or to challenge their voices in this way. What we now term CTCH is the result of nearly two decades of research clearly establishing the mediating effects of beliefs (Chadwick and Birchwood, 1994) and the important role of perceived social rank (Birchwood *et al.*, 2000), central to understanding the role of power beliefs in harmful acts. Our purpose in developing this model is twofold. First, we wish to offer an evidence-based cognitive therapy that is clearly focused on reducing distress and harmful behaviours. Second, and perhaps most importantly, our aim is to empower the individual to take control of their lives, to enable them to make decisions when they want to and to resist acting in harmful ways.

Following the first book on this topic (Byrne *et al.*, 2006), this second text introduces the key developments in theory and practice that have occurred over the past 5 years. A second aim of this new work is to provide clinicians with a much more detailed guide illustrating in depth the techniques and strategies developed and adapted for CTCH. These are placed within a clear formulation driven eight-stage process that has been utilised by therapists actively involved in the current development and evaluation of CTCH.

Each chapter is illustrated by reference to two key cases which are woven throughout the book. These and other clinical examples, taken from the routine work of clinicians investigating CTCH, are used to clearly demonstrate how CTCH techniques and strategies can be applied. Problem-solving strategies and solutions are presented for overcoming therapeutic obstacles with clients who experience command hallucinations. Importantly, treatment successes and failures are described to provide the reader with an accurate understanding of the complexities of applying the approach.

Those taking part in our recent trial work of course have their own view of CTCH. In line with the emerging literature on the importance of considering therapy from the client's point of view, Jenny and Angel provide their own accounts of CTCH as they experienced it.

My story: Jenny

My community psychiatric nurse (CPN) suggested that I do the project (the current CTCH RCT). I was doing some really stupid things before I started to work with the therapist. I was walking in front of cars and cutting myself. I was doing lots of stuff that the voices wanted me to do. I remember thinking that if I did what they wanted, things would get better – but they didn't. They just kept going on. When I harmed myself, this upset me and my family, and my CPN was worried as well.

I was really nervous, before I started therapy I didn't think anything would help me. At first I just didn't feel it would help me. Nothing seemed to help other people who heard voices, so how would it help me? I'd never really talked to anyone about my voices in any detail. I have difficulty trusting people and I just thought the therapist would ask me lots of questions which I might not feel comfortable answering.

When I first met the therapist, I thought he looked like Wayne Sleep. I really didn't think I would be able to talk to him. I struggled to trust people anyhow and he was a man which made it even more difficult for me. I remember thinking that I would never be able to keep seeing the therapist – it was so scary. I was very frightened. I didn't think I could see him on my own, so I asked if I could go to the first appointment with Christine (this name has been changed). She is someone who I have recently started to talk to about my past. I trusted her a little bit and it helped having her come along with me. This did help me feel a bit calmer and get to know him a little bit.

When I went to the next appointment on my own, this was really difficult for me. The voices wanted me to harm the therapist. They kept swearing at me and kept going on. I was very confused. I just wanted to run out of the room. I did manage to stay in the session and the therapist went really slowly and I felt a bit calmer.

I had lots of questions going through my mind – 'will it help?', 'will it make a difference?' and 'can I cope?' I remember thinking that I had the support of family and friends and should use this to help me get through things. Maybe it would help me.

Once therapy got going, we talked about lots of things. The therapist encouraged me to use some strategies to distract myself from the voices. I noticed that when I did art work (which I really enjoy doing), I didn't hear the voices so much. They went into the background. I also found the same thing when I went to my support group. Both helped me a great deal.

Me and the therapist talked about the voices a lot. I learned so much. I came to realise that the voices only new the things I did. They didn't know anything else. I can't express how powerful this was. I felt so good. The voices weren't magical. This was an eye opener. It made me realise that they weren't as powerful as I had thought they were. They were not magic. Although I still get low at times and the voices can get worse. This is something I still remember and it makes me realise that they are normal like me. They are not special.

In my past, quite a few different things have happened which have been upsetting and difficult for me to deal with. I learned from the therapist that when I had flashbacks, nightmares or thought about all these bad things, it would be very upsetting. This meant I tried not to think about these things. Over time I have sorted out what the voices bring up about my past and have filed them away. This means I am upset less of the time now. The mixed up bag that represents the past is being sorted and filed. This will take a while but I have made a good start.

I have now stopped cutting myself. I realise I don't need to do what the voices tell me to do. I realise that even if I did what they wanted me to they wouldn't stop going on – they never did. I also recognise that I can resist them if I want to and when I go against them nothing bad happens. I also remind myself of the value of not doing what they want: I stay in control and I don't upset any of my family – this is really important to me.

It was difficult to stand up to them the first time. I guess I had listened to them for so long. I was very nervous. But I began to question them and challenge them. I won, I had control and I had the power – they didn't! They lost their power when I realised that they only new what I did. This was such an important moment for me.

I used to listen to them so much and do a lot of the things they said, but I just don't now. I don't think I have any kind of relationship with them now. It's wonderful. I do swear at them now and then but I just ignore them most of the time. I've got used to them now. I guess I accept them. They might not go away but I accept them. I have contempt for them not for myself. I am the one in control.

I think I am a braver person now and more confident. I do have some days when I don't do so well, I lose confidence a little and can get low. But I am able to stay positive. Things don't seem to affect me so much. What they say to me doesn't take hold as much. Their comments don't grab me anymore. The work with the therapist is making a difference even if I can't really pin down at the time what I am doing. What I do know is that I am doing so much better – I don't cut myself, I'm not walking in the road and feel more positive about things.

If I was to advise someone else who was hearing voices, I would say to them that I do know what they are going through and it is a scary experience. Getting help was one of the best things I did. It helped me learn lots of things. In particular it made me realise that the voices only know what I do and that although it seems as if it would be difficult to resist them, I did and they can as well.

It was a good job the project came along when it did. I was very nervous doing it but it was worth it. It really paid off. Without it I might be six-foot under.

I now accept the voices. I don't know whether they will stop or not. Whether they do or not I can still live my life and have a positive future. I am confident about things now and this will help me get the most from my life.

My experience of the COMMAND trial therapy: by Angel

I had very mixed feelings when I was accepted on the COMMAND trial as I feared that the voices would punish me for doing so. I also thought that

I would be made to do things that I would find uncomfortable and to discuss things that would distress me and that I would feel worse than ever. Would I be forced to alter the way I thought? When my therapist phoned to make our first appointment, I was encouraged by the gentleness of her voice; it was most welcome and in such stark contrast to the harsh voices that I experienced.

When we first met, I was assured that I could pull out at any point and that I would not be made to do anything that I did not want to. I was told that the purpose of the therapy was to make my experiences less distressing which was an appealing thought and seemed so much more achievable than the expectation that 'at the end of this therapy you will be cured and if not you will be deemed a failure'. The pressure was off.

Therapy involved concentrating on the voices which I had actively avoided doing so before for fear of them overpowering me. I kept diaries of when I experienced the voices, times when they were more distressing and times when they were less distressing. We also looked at what was going on in my life and how this had an impact on the severity of the voices. This gave me an awareness that was empowering and a realisation that there were times when I did not actually hear the voices (watching TV programmes which were both visually and audibly beautiful). We looked at how I could use various coping strategies and what worked best for me. Looking back on my diaries, I could see at a glance how things were improving for me even though at times I would become overwhelmed by a situation and I would feel there was no improvement.

Challenging the voices by not complying with the voices was a frightening thought but in practise was very powerful. By using the resistance diaries I could see at a glance how non-compliance over a period reduced the frequency of the commands and tested the voices threats and questioned their power and transferred power to me. Initially I could not have done this without the therapist's support and encouragement, but I now was equipped with the tools to challenge the voices myself.

Considering other possibilities and explanations for the voices' existence made a lot of sense and gave some kind of order to my thoughts and feelings.

In the course of therapy, we did discuss some distressing incidents from my childhood and the beliefs I had about myself. We looked at how this could have an influence on the voices. This discussion did make me sad but the therapist and the angel I envisaged embracing me made me feel comforted, strong and unashamed.

I was always encouraged to email or phone the therapist if I felt distressed between sessions and required additional support.

At the end of therapy I felt that my confidence and self-esteem had really grown. I felt more comfortable expressing myself and asking for support. I felt much more in control of my life and the voices. I felt that the therapist and I worked collaboratively and this approach has helped in my relationship with other professionals whom I no longer see as the enemy in difficult times, to be avoided at all costs, but rather as support to help me get by. I resist jumping to conclusions and internalising others' comments or actions but try to think of other reasons for their behaviour and take ownership of my own feelings. For the most part I have learnt to accept myself and have stopped blaming myself all the time

I feel very fortunate to have taken part in this very personalised, customised therapy; I gave it my all and got so much back in return. It was mentally exhausting at times but so rewarding and has provided me with a toolkit to draw on and to use in every aspect of my life.

Acknowledgements

We would like to acknowledge Max Birchwood, Paul Chadwick and Peter Trower for their pioneering work in developing the original model and particularly to Max Birchwood for leading the team and getting the research grant that has made this book possible. We would also like to acknowledge Peter and Angel for allowing us to describe and share their journeys to recovery alongside all of the other clients we have worked with who have taught us so much.

> Alan Meaden, Nadine Keen, Robert Aston,
> Karen Barton and Sandra Bucci
> November 2011

I would like to express my personal thanks to the trial therapists and co-authors of this book for whom I have learned a great deal and had the pleasure of training and supervising. I would also like to express my gratitude to my wife Dr Ann Meaden for bearing with me on yet another book.

> Alan Meaden

I would additionally like to thank the trial supervisors and other therapists in the trial for their continued inspiration, support and guidance. A huge thanks also to Ollie for being an unwavering rock always.

> Nadine Keen

I would like to acknowledge Professor Paul Gilbert and Dr Sarah Major who have independently inspired me to try new ideas and work with clients who ceaselessly amaze me with their courage and determination. I would like to thank Peter and Alice for giving me the support and space necessary to pursue my goals.

> Karen Barton

Abbreviations

ABC	Activating Event, Beliefs, Consequences
AOT	Assertive Outreach Team
CBTp	Cognitive Behaviour Therapy for Psychosis
CDSS	Calgary Depression Scale for Schizophrenia
CMHT	Community Mental Health Team
CPN	Community Psychiatric Nurse
CSE	Coping Strategy Enhancement
EE	Expressed Emotion
MDT	Multidisciplinary Team
MI	Motivational Interviewing
NICE	National Institute for Clinical Excellence
PDA	Personal Digital Assistant
PTSD	Post-traumatic Stress Disorder
RCT	Randomised Controlled Trial
REBT	Rational Emotive Behaviour Therapy
RPW	Relapse Prevention Work
TAP	Treatment Adherence Protocol
TBCT	Team-Based Cognitive Therapy

Introduction and overview

Auditory hallucinations rank among the most prominent of the treatment resistant symptoms of schizophrenia, with command hallucinations being the most distressing, high-risk and treatment resistant of all (Nayani and David, 1996; Shawyer *et al.*, 2003). Command hallucinations occur at a high rate in both adult psychiatric and forensic populations; however, the exact rate may vary considerably. In a review, Shawyer *et al.* (2003) found that incidence rates across eight studies ranged from 18 to 89 per cent with a median rate of 53 per cent. Command hallucinations are clearly an important target for treatment, particularly (as we describe below) given their link to harmful behaviours. In this chapter we describe the development of our approach and summarise its key stages, providing an overview of subsequent chapters.

The development of the CTCH model

The core model we have drawn upon in our work over the past decade on command hallucinations draws heavily upon an amalgamation between cognitive behavioural therapy for psychosis (CBTp) and rational emotive behaviour therapy (REBT) pioneered by the late Albert Ellis and first practised by him more than half a century ago (Ellis, 2004). The first development of the cognitive model of voices (Chadwick and Birchwood, 1994) made clear its explanatory structure to advance both theory and practice highlighting in subsequent studies (see below) the role of key beliefs concerning identity, omniscience, omnipotence and purpose and how these could be effectively targeted in therapy. Chadwick *et al.* (1996) used the activating event, beliefs, consequences (ABC) model adapted from REBT, where A is the activating event (e.g. the voice), B the beliefs about that voice, and C the emotional and behavioural consequences of the beliefs. In contrast to previous psychiatric models, whereby voices are a symptom which need to be removed, auditory hallucinations conceptualised within this model were seen in a new way. Delusional symptoms were now viewed as inferences: guesses or hypotheses about the past or predictions about what is or may be happening that go beyond the evidence. Inferences can be true or false, either as secondary to voices (voice-related inferences or beliefs) or in their own right (delusional inferences or beliefs). Two key principles arise from this cognitive model:

1 Voice activity (frequency, loudness and content) is an anomalous experience and is an activating event (A) which is appraised and given meaning: it activates the person's belief system (B).
2 Distress and problematic behaviours are a consequence of this belief system (control, power, omnipotence and omniscience, compliance, identity and purpose) and are the focus of intervention.

Utilising this simple yet elegant model enables us to remain clear about the targets of our therapeutic efforts. The problems that clients present are located firmly at 'C' (consequences). In cognitive therapy for command hallucinations (CTCH) terms, voice-related distress and compliance or safety behaviours are viewed as posing a risk to others or the person themselves. The aim of CTCH is not to reduce symptoms, since these are the 'A' in cognitive terms and the domain of the psychiatrist or other members of the multidisciplinary team: to treat biological factors and help to reduce social adversity factors which have been implicated in the development of psychosis (Morgan and Fearon, 2007) and possibly its maintenance. In focusing on distress we argue that CTCH is a true cognitive therapy. This cognitive conceptualisation proposes that voices are a psychological problem only when they are associated with emotional or behavioural problems. Support for this focus comes from a recent meta-analysis (Wykes et al., 2008) clearly showing that CBTp is most effective when it is targeted at belief-related distress and behaviours (Trower et al., 2004).

Our central notion, 'power', concerns the voices' ability to harm (sometimes referred to as omnipotence) but is also a broader concept, incorporating other voice beliefs (e.g. identity and intention to harm; sometimes expressed as malevolence) which imply power. For this reason we have adopted the term 'voice-power schema'. The perceived need to comply with seemingly powerful voices is crystallised in this power schema. A key target of therapy is to deconstruct it.

In common with other cognitive approaches, CTCH is a formulation driven approach (discussed in detail in Chapter 3). In brief, our formulation proposes that voice activity at 'A' is appraised within an existing belief system comprising dominate–subordinate schema, person evaluations, dysfunctional assumptions and other interpersonal rules (B). Beliefs about voices in CTCH are conceptualised as arising from attempts to defend against negative person evaluations (Chadwick et al., 1996) or underlying rules and assumptions regarding, for instance, the mistrust of others (Chadwick and Trower, 2008) rather than being purely a misinterpretation of anomalous experiences. These give rise to beliefs about the power of the voice (B), which in turn elicit emotional distress and safety behaviours (C); the latter serving to maintain the beliefs by preventing their disconfirmation. Disappointingly, formulation is not part of current NICE recommendations for CBTp (National Institute for Health and Clinical Excellence, 2009), yet we believe that it is key to a number of important stages in the therapeutic process. First, it allows therapists to identify which As lead to which Bs and ultimately which Cs, thus providing a guiding framework for targeting intervention within the levels of CTCH as well as serving as a focus for supervision. Second, the ABC model encapsulated in our formulation template (see Chapter 3) identifies those aspects of the client's difficulties that are most pertinent. Third, the formulation is a helpful tool for subsequently socialising the client into the CTCH model.

Although we have attempted to manualise our work (as summarised in our Treatment Adherence Protocol or TAP shown in Appendix 1, and also in the CTCH therapy flow chart shown in Appendix 3) in order to subject CTCH to further systematic randomised control trial (RCT) evaluation, it remains a pragmatic approach. That is, therapy is adapted to the individual and their changing case-specific needs. We have found that while some clients progress through the eight CTCH levels in a step-wise and systematic fashion, the majority of clients do not fit a linear therapeutic model. Rather, some appear to benefit more from focusing on levels 1–5 (Chapters 1-5), while others respond better to a focus on level 6 (Chapter 6) where the emphasis is on broader interpersonal social rank factors. Therapeutic work may even be at levels 7 and 8 (Chapters 7 and 8) from the outset of therapy. Our formulation is particularly helpful here because it highlights these case-specific needs, and CTCH therapists must be very mindful of this. In addition, more time may need to be spent on some levels (e.g. engagement) before progress can be made to other levels. In our current trial work (a multicentre RCT) clients average twenty-four sessions, though for some the number required is much longer, as many as forty-two sessions. Ideally clients will progress to levels 7 and 8 (Chapters 7 and 8). Indeed, REBT practice and theory (Walen *et al.*, 1992) assert that such higher level work is vital in consolidating enduring change, as clients might not respond to interventions which solely target inferences (e.g. power beliefs). Core belief work in REBT terms involves addressing the person's core 'demands' and 'musts' which people make of themselves and others. CTCH draws on this work and case vignettes are provided in Chapter 8, which explore the challenges and value of reaching higher levels in the CTCH approach. In line with social rank theory, the core beliefs targeted in CTCH are focused around dominate–subordinate schemas (I am weak, others are more powerful/confident than me), negative self or person evaluations (I am bad and others are worthless) and interpersonal rules and dysfunctional assumptions (in order to be worthwhile I must always do things perfectly/be liked by others/others are not to be trusted), which are most likely to give rise and serve to reinforce negative person evaluations and beliefs about voices (Chadwick *et al.*, 1996). How the person responds emotionally and indeed behaviourally reflects interplay between person evaluations, rules for living, assumptions and inferences. It is important for therapists to be mindful; however, it is not always possible to achieve these higher levels and meaningful work can still be carried out by focusing on the lower CTCH levels.

More recently we have found it necessary to incorporate further aspects of REBT theory and practice, namely the concepts of low frustration tolerance (typically expressed in terms of 'I can't stand it'; Dryden, 1995) and what we have termed 'discomfort intolerance' ('If this happens then it will drive me mad'). We explore this further in Chapter 5 on safety behaviours, as such concepts are especially useful in cases where voices actually deliver on their threats (e.g. by keeping the person awake all night).

Relapse prevention work (e.g. Birchwood et al., 2000a) is not routinely incorporated into the CTCH approach since we view this as a broader psychosocial intervention that may move us away from our focus on the client's distress and problematic behaviour and into more generic illness management work. Much has been written on the subject of relapse prevention, which includes work around psychoeducation (e.g. the 'stress vulnerability' model), self-monitoring (for cognitive, behavioural and physiological signs), and identification of triggers and warning signs of relapse. In some instances, however, it may prove useful to incorporate some of these principles so that the client feels more empowered and in control over their symptoms, thus addressing the client's beliefs about control. For those clients who currently do not experience command hallucinations, relapse prevention principles can be utilised alongside the CTCH model enabling clients to recognise and manage potential As and Bs should they re-emerge.

While formal psychoeducation is not explicitly used in the CTCH approach, psychoeducation in terms of the ABC approach and explanations on theories regarding the possible origins of voices (e.g. the inner-speech loop, stress-vulnerability models and the brains capacity to make 'mistakes') are drawn upon and incorporated as an important element of CTCH. On occasion it may be necessary to provide education, for instance helping a client to understand anxiety rather than attribute bodily symptoms to the direct actions and abilities of powerful voices. This continuing focus of therapeutic efforts at 'C' enables us to more clearly establish that it is belief change which mediates reductions in distress and harmful compliance (Trower et al., 2004).

Coping Strategy Enhancement (CSE; Tarrier, 1992) is used in the CTCH approach. CSE may best be described as an applied behavioural analysis tool whereby the person's coping repertoire and triggers and antecedents for individual symptoms are systematically reviewed. Effective coping strategies can then be identified and enhanced and unhelpful ones discarded. New strategies, such as relaxation or distraction, may then be taught to extend the person's coping repertoire. CSE is frequently employed as a component of CBTp interventions to promote engagement (improving a sense of control and optimism for change) and lessen the impact of residual symptoms. It may also be used as a discrete intervention or used as part of a larger relapse prevention program. This intervention is an important part of CTCH (Chapters 2, 3, 4 and 5) in terms of helping to address and change control beliefs, weaken power beliefs and foster engagement. Subsequently it can serve to build distress tolerance and is often a recurring theme in all stages of CTCH, helping to build a sense of self-efficacy and power.

CTCH: theory and research

Research has shown that clients respond in a wide variety of ways to their voices. Chadwick and Birchwood (1994) observed that if clients' appraised their voices as belonging to someone with power and authority, they would be likely to respond with a degree of anxiety or fear. They also tended to accept that authority and comply with the perceived wishes of their voices. Having established this mediating role for beliefs these researchers conducted two further studies, systematically identifying and categorising the types of belief and voice hearer's behavioural, cognitive and affective responses (Chadwick and Birchwood, 1995; Birchwood and Chadwick, 1997). In these studies all clients viewed their voices as omnipotent and omniscient, while beliefs about the voice's identity and meaning led to voices being construed as either benevolent or malevolent. Cogent reasons were given for these beliefs which, importantly, were not always linked to voice content (e.g. what the voice actually said). In 31 per cent of cases, beliefs were incongruous with content, as would be anticipated by a cognitive model. This was a strong demonstration of cognitive mediation; beliefs about voices were at odds with voice content. It suggested that meanings were constructed by individuals rather than being directly derived from content. Furthermore, voice hearers often reported what they considered to be compelling evidence for their beliefs. Only occasionally did this draw upon voice content. Voices believed to be malevolent consistently provoked fear and were resisted, whereas those perceived as benevolent were courted. However, in the case of imperative voices, the primary influence on whether commands were obeyed was the severity of the command.

Close and Garety (1998) provided further empirical support for this cognitive formulation by demonstrating that people who hear voices construct meaning from the experience. Four beliefs emerged as having particular importance: identity (who is the voice?); its purpose (why is this voice talking to me, what does it want?); omnipotence (how powerful is the voice?); and control (can I influence its frequency, severity or content?). Voices believed to be malevolent in their purpose were associated with resistance and high distress, while those believed to be benevolent were associated with engagement and lower distress or even pleasure. The importance of such beliefs have been highlighted in a recent systematic review; Mawson *et al.* (2010) reviewed twenty-six studies investigating the relationship between appraisals of voices in influencing different emotional reactions. They found several types of appraisals which were linked to higher levels of distress. These included appraising the voices as malevolent, being high in supremacy (which we have termed 'power'), having a personal acquaintance with the individual and attitudes of disapproval and rejection towards voices.

In their seminal, though small scale work, Chadwick and Birchwood (1994) illustrated how these beliefs about voices could be targeted in treatment using an adapted version of REBT. Four participants who heard voices were asked about their beliefs about their voices' omnipotence, identity, and purpose; these were systematically tested and disputed. Large and stable reductions in belief conviction were reported. Perhaps most significantly these changes were associated with reduced distress, increased adaptive behaviour and a fall in voice activity. In a larger scale proof of principle study (Trower et al., 2004), CTCH was compared against treatment as usual (TAU). Thirty-eight participants all reported two or more commands from their 'dominant' voice, at least one of which was a 'severe' command. Participants were considered at high risk of compliance on the basis of their risk histories, use of the Mental Health Act (1983) and hospital treatment. Over 12 months, compliance within the treatment group dropped from 100 per cent to only 14 per cent compared to a drop in compliance from 100 per cent to 53 per cent for the TAU group. There was also a similar change in conviction in voice-power schemas with the treatment group. When the effect of the power beliefs was statistically removed the treatment effect disappeared. In keeping with our focus on change at 'C', the other main target of this study, consequential voice-related distress, was also significantly impacted upon. Conviction in omniscience beliefs also fell significantly in the CTCH group and there was improvement in perceived control over voices compared to the TAU group. These benefits were maintained at 12 month follow-up. Although significant, the numbers recruited to this trial were small and therefore warranted further investigation in our recent multicentre RCT.

While our first study clearly demonstrated the effectiveness of CTCH, its durability is an ongoing question. There is a strand of psychiatric opinion that treatments for schizophrenia are only effective as long as they are active (McGlashan, 1988). An important question is therefore 'how much further intervention is required to maintain the effect of treatment?' This is an issue we address in Chapter 9.

A second development of our cognitive therapy model was the incorporation of social rank theory (Gilbert, 1992; Gilbert and Allan, 1998). Gilbert and Allan propose that evolved mental mechanisms (developed as part of the evolution of group living) encourage people to 'attack the weaker and submit to the stronger'. Such mechanisms we have argued (Birchwood et al., 2010) are played out internally in those who hear hostile voices. In response to their perceived weakened social position, the person experiences these internal signals in the form of derogatory and controlling voices requiring submissive behaviour including appeasement and compliance in order to avoid punishment. Voice hearers subsequently develop beliefs about these experiences which can be understood in terms of an interpersonal relationship. That the voice hearer constructs such an interpersonal relationship is self-evident when one considers the fact that they personify the voices they hear. Benjamin (1989) noted earlier how voice hearers construct a link between themselves and their voices, similar to an intimate interpersonal relationship, which is often one that is inescapable. To further support this theory, in a cross-sectional study, Junginger (1990) found that recent compliance was more likely where the individual personified the voice (e.g. attributed it to an identity).

The existence of a relationship helps to explain why beliefs regarding voice power (omnipotence) and intent (malevolence and benevolence) are very important. Social rank theory is particularly suited to explaining this relationship since it provides a general theory of how humans respond under conditions of dominance and entrapment by another. Studies have shown (Birchwood *et al.*, 2000b, 2004) that this tendency to see voices as powerful and the self as weak and powerless to resist reflects a core self-perception of low social rank. In other words they see themselves as being inferior and subordinate and in a stigmatised position not only to the voice but also to other people, particularly family, peers and the community at large.

Voice power can be viewed within this model as emanating from hostile–dominate and threatened–subordinate interactions (e.g. commands, orders and instructions) and/or through delivering verbal attacks (e.g. negative labelling, criticism and shaming). These patterns can be seen in families of people with schizophrenia where these behaviours (often referred to as high expressed emotion) are common (e.g. Wearden *et al.*, 2000). We suggest that just as these types of relationship (hostile attack–subordinate defence) can be played out between individuals, they are played out internally. In essence, people can have a high expressed emotion relationship with themselves: getting angry and critical for violations and failures, and shaming and negatively labelling themselves (Driscoll, 1989). In other words, the evolved mechanisms for vigilance to violations and the necessary control of a society, derogating subordinates and issuing commands, are directed at the self and they activate submissive defences (Gilbert, 2000b). Submission in the face of a powerful 'other' may be viewed as a very effective defence since it secures the protection of the other and guards against rejection from society and potential disaster. A further power mechanism may be seen in another symptom of psychosis, namely thought broadcasting (often experienced as an inability to keep one's own thoughts, experiences and feelings private). Voice hearers perceive their voices as omniscient (e.g. knowing the person's present thoughts and past history, being able to predict the future, etc.); this is frequently seen by voice hearers themselves as evidence of the voice's power. In essence, malevolent voices appear to have many of the properties of a dominant hostile 'other' seeking out wrongdoing and deceptions, and threatening to reveal these shameful aspects of the person to others or punish the person themselves. This aspect of the voice hearer's relationship with their voice is crucial to understand since the greater the perceived power and omnipotence of the voice, the greater the likelihood of compliance (Beck-Sander *et al.*, 1997). This relationship is not linear, however, and is moderated by appraisal of the voice's intent and the consequences of resisting. Those with benevolent voices virtually always comply, irrespective of whether the command is appraised as 'innocuous' or 'severe' (Beck-Sander *et al.*, 1997), whereas those with malevolent voices are more likely to resist. Resistance increases if the command involves major social transgression or self-harm (Chadwick and Birchwood, 1994). However, when voice hearers predict that the malevolent voice would inflict harm if resisted, appeasement behaviours may be used and carried out as an alternative less harmful act (Beck-Sander *et al.*, 1997). The act of committing such a social transgression may subsequently serve to keep the person in a subordinate position or reinforce negative person beliefs about the self. Voices often draw on such experiences reminding the person of their deeds or threatening to shame or humiliate them publicly by revealing them.

The importance of integrating social rank theory into cognitive therapy approaches is further supported by Mawson *et al.* (2010) in their review. As others have recently reported (Wykes *et al.*, 2008), results from CBTp trials do not consistently report significant improvements in voice-related distress post-intervention. One explanation proposed by Mawson *et al.* (2010) is that mediating variables, such as social schemata, were not targeted in these studies.

To summarise so far, the ABC model offers a valid explanation of the role of beliefs in producing emotional distress, while social rank theory elucidates the meaning and function of the emotion and behaviour in terms of a dominate–subordinate relationship with the voice. However, neither of these aspects of the model account for why beliefs and consequent distress and behaviour are maintained over such long periods of time and are so resistant to remission. As part of our ongoing research efforts and clinical practice we noted how behavioural 'C's' not only result in various types of risk behaviour that are harmful and potentially lethal to the person and others but also served to maintain the individual's beliefs about their voices. In this sense, they functioned as a type of 'safety behaviour' which kept the voice hearer seemingly safe and reduced anticipated negative consequences from powerful voices. Safety behaviours thus serve to prevent disconfirmation of voice beliefs. The notion that safety behaviours are linked to distress in schizophrenia has been demonstrated by Freeman *et al.* (2001) who found that individuals with persecutory delusions used safety behaviours, particularly avoidance, to mitigate threats from persecutors. Freeman *et al.* (2001) suggest that delusional distress is associated with delusional threat and that safety behaviour use is associated with anxiety. Freeman *et al.* (2007) subsequently replicated these findings in a larger sample. Predictions derived from the cognitive model suggest that distress and safety behaviour use would follow from beliefs about the power and malevolence of the persecutor, but this was not specifically tested by Freeman *et al.* (2001). Clearly, this would be the prediction for voice hearers, and in the case of those who have command hallucinations, the prediction would be that safety behaviours would include compliance or at least appeasement to mitigate the perceived threat. Hacker *et al.* (2008) subsequently carried out a cross-sectional study of thirty individuals with hallucinations. Three sources of threat were identified: fear of physical harm, shame and loss of control. More than half the sample scored 5 or more (on a 0–10 scale, 0 being no threat and 10 very much so) on all three threats. Twenty-six reported using safety behaviours to minimise this threat in the last month. The extent to which these safety behaviours were used was strongly associated with beliefs in voice omnipotence. Mood and voice characteristics did not account for this relationship. Furthermore, the association of safety behaviour use and distress was found to be mediated by beliefs about voice omnipotence.

Power and the therapeutic relationship

Engaging and retaining individuals in a therapeutic alliance is fundamental to any form of therapy. Clients are active participants in therapy and should be seen as partners in the formation of the therapeutic alliance. Therapeutic alliance influences successful outcome, accounting for as much as 30 per cent of the outcome (Norcross, 2000). For those experiencing command hallucinations, building a therapeutic alliance can be especially difficult due to the very distracting and distressing nature of the experience and the need to consider reprisals from their voices or professionals for disclosing the content of their experiences. In applying Rogerian principles to working with clients with psychosis, Chadwick (2006) notes the primacy of the therapeutic relationship and the importance of good counselling skills. These skills incorporate the notion of 'unconditional acceptance' involving accepting the client's attitudes, feelings and beliefs and not judging but understanding their needs. Additionally, in CTCH we must also acknowledge that social rank theory applies to the therapeutic relationship and that the therapist is often automatically placed in a position of power. Power relationships and social rank phenomenon are part of the process of therapy. In practical terms this may mean ensuring that the client feels free to disagree, may choose to remain silent at times or withdraw from therapy. The use of a symbolic 'panic button' gives the client some control over the process of therapy, with the option to change topics at any point. This might mean that the client and therapist talk about something different that carries less emotional intensity or end the session completely, checking out first that the client is safe. Such strategies (discussed in Chapter 1) are designed to model increasing the power of the client] through the therapeutic relationship and process of therapy. This can subsequently be applied to the relationship the person has with their voice and more broadly to relationships they may have with other people.

Reducing distress and harmful behaviours (Chapters 4 and 5) along with early attempts to improve coping (Chapter 2) are further key processes for building alliance. We never dispute that the client actually hears voices; however, we do challenge their power and the need to act on them as therapy progresses. Engagement beliefs are explicitly formulated in CTCH (e.g. 'this will make my symptoms worse' or 'if I talk about this I will be sectioned or punished by the voice'). These are explored in a sensitive manner and often take time to address.

Managing and taking risks

Individuals who experience psychosis have been found to be more likely to engage in acts of violence (Brennan *et al.*, 2000; Wallace *et al.*, 2004) and to be at high risk of deliberate self-harm. Of particular concern to clinicians are command hallucinations that stipulate harmful or dangerous actions. These represent 48 per cent of command hallucinations (Shawyer *et al.*, 2003) rising to 69 per cent among patients in medium secure settings (Rogers *et al.*, 2002). Over 30 per cent will comply directly with commands (Shawyer *et al.*, 2003) and a further 30 per cent will attempt to resist but will 'appease' the powerful persecutor, usually by complying with less serious commands (Beck-Sander *et al.*, 1997), but nonetheless placing themselves at risk of later compliance (Shawyer *et al.*, 2003). Compliance rates among forensic samples are some-what higher (Shawyer *et al.*, 2003). However, predicting which, and under what circumstances, individuals will act on their voice's commands has proved difficult to establish despite the apparent wealth of epidemiological data. Results of the MacArthur study (Monahan *et al.*, 2001) found no link between the presence of command hallucinations and violence. A recent secondary analysis of the study, however (Rogers, 2004, 2005), found that the perceived need to 'obey' significantly increased risk. Our research has demonstrated that cognitive mediation is one of the key processes in understanding and managing risk in clients with command hallucinations and not experiencing commands per se. This reflects our own clinical experience that it is compliance beliefs (e.g. 'I must do what my voice says or I will be punished/terrible things will happen to others I care about') which are a key factor in driving risk behaviours. As previously noted, believing that voices are benevolent in their intention (Beck-Sander *et al.*, 1997) is also linked to the likelihood of acting on commands. However, as Thorndike (1911) noted over a century ago, "The best predictor of future behaviour is past behaviour." A past history of acting on commands is therefore important to consider along with the client's ability to resist. Recent support for this is reported by Freeman *et al.* (2007) who note how the use of safety behaviours is (retrospectively) predictive of risk behaviours.

A further important distinction to draw when considering the management of risk concerns the nature and function of these behaviours in the past. The following are important considerations in this regard:

- Were all of these past behaviours driven by commands?
- Was this behaviour a safety behaviour or was it secondary to the experience of hearing a commanding voice: as a means of managing the distress resulting from the frequency or intensity of the voice or their beliefs about the voice?
- Was there some other function to the behaviour?

A careful ABC analysis of all specific harmful behaviours should help to unpick this and identify the function. To restate our aims, CTCH is targeted at harmful compliance where such behaviours are clearly linked to compliance beliefs.

Therapists will also have to consider other relevant risk factors (see Blumenthal and Lavender, 2000; Douglas and Skeem, 2005; Meaden and Hacker, 2010) when working with clients who experience command hallucinations. Personality disorder and substance misuse are particularly pertinent to consider as they have been consistently found to be predictive of risk (e.g. Monahan *et al.*, 2001). Substance misuse is now universally accepted as being strongly associated with the risk of violence and raises the risk regardless of diagnosis or symptoms (Monahan *et al.*, 2001). Other idiosyncratic triggers (such as financial pressures or relationship difficulties) that are known to tip the person into a risk state should be routinely monitored in conjunction with the responsible care team. Knowing and understanding how these triggers operate in a given individual along with their relationship to command hallucinations will help to facilitate positive risk taking. Having a shared understanding of the person's risk (Meaden and Hacker, 2010) can help to reassure other team members and enable additional support to be initiated at more vulnerable times. Issues of lone working will also be important to consider. Co-working is one way of minimising risk while simultaneously generalising skills and effective strategies for a given individual to others in the team. We return to and expand on this point in Chapter 10.

CASE STUDIES

Peter and Angel are our major case studies used throughout the book in order to provide an illustration of the key aspects of the complete CTCH process. Of course, no one client presents with the complete range of complex problems we encounter in those experiencing command hallucinations and we have therefore also drawn upon additional case material to illustrate other key aspects of our work. We have anonymised these as far as possible to maintain confidentiality while preserving the integrity of the clinical features of each case.

Peter's Case

Peter is a 41-year-old man who at the time of therapy lived on his own in a small flat. He had never been married and had no children. He was however in a relationship and had been with his partner for over 6 months. He described this relationship as being up and down and it had at times been quite acrimonious. He did not feel she understood his mental health problems and on several occasions was critical towards him. Peter had a number of friends but unfortunately he tended to isolate himself when he was not coping, and this meant he did not tend to seek help at these times. He had not worked for 2 years after losing his job. Debts had subsequently begun to mount up and 6 months before he was seen by his mental health team, Peter made himself bankrupt. This was a very stressful experience as he had numerous calls and letters from companies asking for payment. He had to keep reiterating that he had been made bankrupt and advise them of what they should do. This made him feel stressed, anxious, depressed and ashamed and led to an increase in his voices.

Peter first became ill when he was 18 years old. He had had a number of admissions to hospital over the past 20 years. He currently has a diagnosis of schizoaffective disorder. Peter has a family history of mental health difficulties. His sister was admitted to hospital during the time he was receiving therapy. His mother died several years ago having committed suicide. He did have some contact with his father but this was a very difficult relationship. They did not get on and when Peter did call him or go round to his house the conversation tended to be one-sided and his father tended to be emotionally distant. Peter reported that his earlier life was very difficult and led to a situation where he did not tend to trust people. While at school he was ridiculed by other children because his mother experienced mental health problems. Peter felt that he and his family stood out and were different. He recounted that when he was growing up he was often insulted by his family and did not feel supported by them. Peter alluded to the fact that he had experienced physical, emotional and sexual abuse but no details were provided.

Peter had recently been discharged from his Community Mental Health Team (CMHT) after he failed to attend several appointments. His only contact was with his GP and subsequently the CTCH therapist (the third author). Peter did not feel that the CMHT had been helpful, supportive or understanding.

At initial assessment, Peter reported hearing one female voice. He did not recognise who it was; she did not sound like anyone from the past or present. He tended to hear her as if she were in external space and also from inside his head. He heard her voice the majority of the time and he could do little to make her go away. When he isolated himself he would hear her more; she would be louder and more aggressive. Peter felt that she had the power to harm him, would materialise if he did not do what she asked and was very knowledgeable about him and his past. She would tell Peter 'to disfigure himself', 'to slit his wrists' and 'to stub cigarettes out on himself'. Peter was regularly insulted by his voice, he was told 'he was ugly, worthless, a failure' and that 'no-one loved him'. At times he found this very difficult, would get very low and was tempted to harm himself; he would regularly think about hanging himself from a local tree.

Angel's Case

Angel is a 35-year-old Brazilian lady who at the time of therapy had been hearing voices for some 20 years. Angel grew up in a large Catholic family and was the youngest of many siblings. She described a difficult childhood during which her mother was highly critical. For example, Angel suffered with severe asthma and, as a child, her mother would chastise her for having asthma attacks, telling Angel that it was a 'sign of the devil'. Angel described having a close relationship with her father whom she felt loved by. At the age of eleven, Angel was repeatedly sexually abused by an adult family friend. At the time the perpetrator told Angel that if she screamed or told anyone, then he would abuse another child instead of her. She felt unable to tell anyone what had happened to her until she was later involved in mental health services.

In terms of her current circumstances, Angel was living in the community with her husband and son. She was actively involved with the service user movement and has been involved in numerous inspiring voluntary projects. She also received support from her local CMHT.

Angel was first involved with mental health services as a teenager when she was admitted to hospital for nearly a year. Subsequently she has had numerous admissions to hospital; the last time being 5 years prior to her starting CTCH. She has received psychotherapy in the past. Angel said when the voices started they were generally manageable but that they had became more distressing after a series of difficult and traumatic events in her family, including a number of serious family illnesses and bereavements. Her father and mother both died from cancer-related illnesses when Angel was in her twenties.

During the initial assessment, Angel reported hearing two voices: a male and a female voice, both of which she did not recognise. These voices criticised her and commanded her to do a number of things ranging from innocuous commands such as 'leave the room' and 'stand up' to more risky commands such as 'walk in the road (in front of cars)' and 'go to the park to sacrifice yourself (set yourself alight)'. Angel reported hearing the voices as if they originated from outside of her head; they spoke more loudly, often lasting for hours at a time. Angel found the voices very distressing and presented as very low and anxious.

Who is CTCH most suitable for?

As we have noted earlier, command hallucinations are particularly treatment resistant, and a symptom for which we have developed an effective therapy (Trower *et al.*, 2004). Our clinical and trial experience has, however, highlighted a number of factors which may mitigate against success and need to be borne in mind when considering suitability:

1   *The potential to develop a good working alliance.* This is clearly the starting point of any therapeutic endeavour.
2   *Motivation to change and the ability to tolerate distress, especially when dropping safety behaviours*, should be considered, since behavioural change is a key target.
3   The hierarchy of needs – where does therapy sit in relation to the person's hierarchy of needs? Many clients with psychosis experience difficult social, relational and financial difficulties, as well as other co-morbidities such as substance misuse. All of these may take priority in the person's life over CTCH.
4   *Positive beliefs about voices and emotional investment in the power schema.* These are important potential cognitive resistance factors to identify. Clients will often have spent a great deal of time constructing a belief system around their experiences. Change may mean letting go of valued beliefs which in some cases are associated with positive emotions but may lead to harmful behaviours.
5   *Cognitive biases.* Several authors have described the role of these in belief formation and maintenance (e.g. Freeman *et al.*, 2002). These may be particularly pronounced in people with psychosis and should not be seen as an exclusion factor per se since they occur in the so-called normal population as well, though arguably to a lesser extent. Instead they highlight the importance of ensuring behaviour change. Assessing their influence in individual cases may nevertheless prove useful.

What might CTCH therapists need?

A sometimes neglected but increasingly relevant question (given the increasing demands on professionals) is what enables clinicians to do this work? Compassion for and the ability to contain client's distress require good support systems to be in place for the therapist, since high levels of contact with those with severe mental illness lowers satisfaction in workers (Oberlander, 1990). The seriousness of the illness, degree of dependency and aggressive hostility displayed towards professionals have all been associated with therapist burnout (Maslach, 1978). Threats of violence and suicide are particularly stressful for health professionals to deal with (Prosser *et al.*, 1996). Additionally, reciprocity (seeing improvement or receiving gratitude; Schaulfeli, 1999) may be lacking when working with clients with longer term complex problems. In such work many authors have written about the impact that working with such individuals can have on clinicians (e.g. Hinshelwood, 2004; Gray and Mulligan, 2009; Hartley and Kennard, 2009). More broadly, Margison (2005) has argued that in order to work with psychosis there is a need for the healthy mental health team, the healthy organisation and the healthy mental health system. He argues that if any of these is compromised it reduces the effectiveness of the system as a whole. Readers can judge for themselves whether this applies to their situation.

In our trial work we have a system of both individual (weekly) supervision and 'Access Grid'. The latter is a form of multicentre group supervision (on a fortnightly basis) and case problem solving facilitated by leading experts in the field. We recognise that this is a privileged position and may be one factor in why translating trial therapies into routine clinical practice is difficult. Good supervision should however be standard. It should enable problem solving and encourage reflection and openness about practice. Chadwick (2006) has also usefully identified the importance of identifying and addressing the therapist's own beliefs which may be especially useful for identifying power issues.

Summary

In this chapter we have provided an overview of the theory, evidence-base and practice of CTCH. In the following chapters we expand on these describing clearly the eight levels of our therapy illustrating them through our main two case studies Peter and Angel introduced here.

Chapter 1

CTCH Level 1

Assessment and engagement

Introduction

The aim of a good assessment process is as much about determining how to offer help as it is about what help can be offered. As a trial-based therapy, CTCH inevitably has a large number of assessment measures which may pose problems for adoption into routine clinical practice given often limited resources and time constraints. In this chapter we are mindful of these considerations in writing a text for clinicians. We describe the measures we have used as well as the general principles and steps of assessment in CTCH. Level 1 work is also about engaging the individual in the process of therapy. Good engagement is the central vehicle for the delivery of other interventions in CTCH and encompasses the concept of therapeutic alliance (Gillespie and Meaden, 2009), a crucial factor in achieving good outcomes. The first and fourth authors have conducted a small exploratory study in the context of ongoing trial work examining the role of engagement in CTCH. While engagement is widely acknowledged as a good predictor of outcome in psychotherapy (Horvath and Symonds, 1991; Martin *et al.*, 2000), it has very rarely been measured in randomised controlled trials of CBTp. This is surprising given that people who experience psychosis can be difficult to engage in mental health services (Sainsbury Centre for Mental Health, 1998). Utilising the Hall *et al.* (2001) scale we rated engagement at monthly intervals for a subset of therapy dyads ($n = 36$). Initial results suggest that engagement with CTCH from the outset was often very high, indicating that the participants found the approach relevant to their needs. Initial analysis further suggests that engagement scores at session 1 were predictive of subsequent engagement, while those who disengaged from CTCH early were very poorly engaged from the beginning. In isolated cases, however, therapist's were able to extend the engagement period and improve engagement overall. Consequently, the Hall *et al.* (2001) measure may prove useful in identifying those most likely to remain engaged in CTCH as well as those clients needing additional emphasis on level 1 work. The key tasks in this level are to:

1 undertake a detailed assessment of the broad experience and impact of command hallucinations;

2 obtain a detailed ABC assessment of the content of the client's voices, which beliefs these give rise to, and their emotional and behavioural consequences, leaving to later stages (levels 7 and 8) the client's beliefs about themselves and others (noting these if they emerge and where relevant);

3 anticipate and address problems with engagement;

4 convey empathy and acceptance and build trust;

5 set initial therapy goals focused on reducing distress and harmful behaviours.

We illustrate these processes in this chapter with reference to our two main case studies Peter and Angel.

Assessment

In order to assess suitability for CTCH, we recommend using a range of measures to assess the defining features of the client's beliefs about their voices, their degree of resistance and engagement with their voices as well as the level of distress and compliance behaviours mediated by their beliefs. In line with forming a strong therapeutic alliance, care must be taken when administering assessment measures in the early stage of therapy. Some clients might find it disconcerting if their initial contact with the therapist is focused on answering a barrage of questions, with little time for them to tell their story in their own time and in their own way. Other clients will respond well to the structure of assessment measures as the pressure is taken off them to tell their story at the outset. This may be the case particularly for those clients who are anxious or even ambivalent about therapy. The therapist will therefore need to tailor their assessment approach to best engage the client. Below is a list of those measures we recommend therapists use as key measures:

1 The Beliefs about Voices Questionnaire-Revised (BAVQ-R, Chadwick et al., 2000) was developed initially as a cognitive assessment of voices to examine the mediating role of voice beliefs in distress and behaviour. The revised questionnaire now includes ratings of Disagree, Unsure, Slightly Agree and Strongly Agree to rate key beliefs about auditory hallucinations, including benevolence, malevolence and two dimensions of relationship with the voice: 'engagement' and 'resistance'. Like its companion assessment, the cognitive assessment of voices interview schedule, it is usually completed on the most dominant and distressing voice.

2 The cognitive assessment of voices (CAV; Chadwick and Birchwood, 1994) further assesses the individual's feelings and behaviour in relation

to the voice, and their beliefs about the voice's identity, power, purpose or meaning, and in the case of command hallucinations, the most likely consequences of obedience or resistance.

3   The Voice Compliance Scale (VCS; Beck-Sander *et al.*, 1997) is an observer-rated scale designed to specifically measure the frequency of command hallucinations and level of compliance/resistance with each identified command within the previous 8 weeks.

4   The Voice Power Differential Scale (VPDS; Birchwood *et al.*, 2000a) measures the perceived relative power differential between the voice (usually the most dominant voice) and the voice hearer, with regard to the components of power including strength, confidence, respect, ability to inflict harm, superiority and knowledge. Each is rated on a five-point scale and yields a total power score.

5   The Psychotic Symptom Rating Scales (PSYRATS; Haddock *et al.*, 1999) measures the severity of and distress associated with a number of dimensions of auditory hallucinations and delusions.

Additional useful measures which we have developed with colleagues over recent years or have drawn upon in our research work with them are the following:

1   The Omniscience Scale (OS; Birchwood *et al.*, 2000a) measures the voice hearer's beliefs about their voices' knowledge regarding personal information.

2   The Positive and Negative Syndrome Scale (PANSS; Kay *et al.*, 1987) is a widely used, well established and a comprehensive symptom rating scale measuring mental state.

3   The Calgary Depression Scale for Schizophrenia (CDSS; Addington *et al.*, 1993) is specifically designed for assessing the level of depression in people with a diagnosis of schizophrenia.

4   The Risk of Acting on Commands Scale (RACS; Byrne *et al.*, 2006) was specifically designed to identify the level of risk of acting on commands and the amount of distress associated with them.

By utilising these measures the assessment process should enable clinicians to identify suitable clients for CTCH. Although not confined to these criteria, we have found that CTCH is most useful for clients who meet the following conditions:

1   an ICD-10 diagnosis of schizophrenia, schizoaffective or delusional disorder under the care of the clinical team (F20,22,23,25,28,29);

2   command hallucinations (PANSS P3 hallucinations score ≥3) with a history of command hallucinations lasting at least 6 months with harmful

compliance (Voice Compliance Scale score ≥3), including appeasement, harm to self and others or major social transgressions;

3   collateral evidence of 'harmful' compliance behaviour linked to command hallucinations (e.g. reported by other professionals or evident from case notes);

4   distress associated with compliance or resistance;

5   be 'treatment resistant' (prescribed at least two neuroleptics without response but on a stable dose of medication for a period of 3 months) or 'treatment reluctant' (refusal to accept optimal medication (e.g. clozapine);

6   *not have* organic impairment or addictive disorder considered to be the primary diagnosis.

Clinicians working in busy routine settings, however, do not always have the capacity to spend two, three or more sessions administering such a comprehensive assessment battery. Nevertheless, we do advocate spending one to two sessions administering the five key measures listed above. In our practice we have found that this can facilitate the engagement process, help identify particular areas that might be more important to focus upon than others and capture change post-therapy, providing evidence of the changes that have been made.

The skilled therapist must strive to strike the balance between asking the questions necessary to arrive at ratings on these measures while allowing the client to tell their story and feel heard and understood. The focus of assessment in CTCH is (at least initially) upon the most dominant voice since this will usually be the one appraised as being most powerful and therefore the one most clearly associated with mediating distress and harmful compliance.

General assessment principles will also apply at this stage and may involve reviewing the client's personal and psychiatric history, interventions received so far and the client's response to them, as well as general stressors, triggers and maintenance factors. The assessment process must also take into account other individual factors (Meaden, 2009) including:

- the current stage of psychosis (e.g. stability, relapse or residual difficulties);
- any attention and concentration problems, requiring shorter sessions;
- social withdrawal or negative symptoms, requiring a slower pace and greater time to reply [Such clients may benefit from a more supportive or gentle conversational style (Kingdon and Turkington, 2005).];
- suggestibility, requiring the use of open questions;
- high levels of suspiciousness and mistrust, suggesting particular attention to therapeutic alliance issues;
- sensory impairment, requiring specialist advice.

Eliciting the As, Bs and Cs

The above measures and assessment processes are designed to cover most aspects of the client's experience of hearing voices. The BAVQ-R and CAV also elicit the general ABC of the client's voice hearing experience. However, this general cognitive assessment does not readily help to clarify which As lead to which Bs and which Cs. This is essential for formulation, goal planning and intervention. The therapist may usefully focus upon a single recent and distressing incident involving the use of a safety behaviour. Such recent events can be recalled and analysed since they will have greater emotional salience. The CAB (Consequences, Activating event and Beliefs) process described by Meaden and Hacker (2010) and summarised below is a useful framework:

1   Ask about the behaviour (obtain the Cb) – if the behavioural consequence is not clear clarify it (this is the safety behaviour in CTCH terms).
2   Ask about the emotional consequence (obtain the Ce) – if the emotional consequence is not clear clarify it.
3   Enquire about the actual A which led to the interpretation or belief.
4   Establish the A–B link: 'So the voice said you are on your way and you took that to mean you were about to be killed?' – eliciting and clarifying the B.
5   Reflect back the information gleaned from the CAB process as an A–B–C chain: 'So the voice said you are on your way (A) and you took that to mean you were about to be killed (B) and understandably you felt very afraid (Ce) and locked yourself in the bedroom' (Cb; a threat mitigation strategy in safety behaviour terms?) This also serves to socialise the client into the model.

Case example: Tony

Tony assaulted his mother (the Cb) – he shouted at her and punched her on the arm.

Tony was distressed (the Ce) – he felt afraid.

Tony heard his voice say 'Kill your mother' (A).

Tony believed that he should act but not fully comply (B; his compliance beliefs) – 'I must do what my voice says otherwise they will kill her' and 'Hitting her will keep them quiet'.

Other ABCs can then be clarified, which may lead to different types of distress and behaviour rather than harmful compliance: derogatory insults (A)

– 'you're a fool' which Tony believes to be true (B) – 'I am a prat' and is distressed about (Ce) – feels low, and may act upon (Cb) – Tony withdraws and stays in bed.

This level of assessment enables the therapist and client to agree which behaviours and distress, and which beliefs, should be the focus of further assessment (e.g. eliciting the evidence for), goal setting and intervention. It also enables the clinician to be clear about whether the harmful behaviour is voice driven: is it harmful compliance or does it serve some other function and therefore require a different type of intervention?

Case example: Ali

Ali hears a persistent voice saying you are worthless and ugly (A). After several hours of abuse from the voices she cuts herself (Cb) as a means of easing the distress that this experience causes her (Ce) but not because of any compliance belief but rather because she believes that this is an effective way of managing her distress (B) since it functions to focus her attention away from her voices and also elicits care from others.

Cognitive work may be aimed at addressing discomfort intolerance beliefs rather than any compliance beliefs she may otherwise hold. Intervention for Ali may further usefully focus upon improving her emotional regulation and self-soothing skills.

Some clients find it difficult to accurately recall incidents of voice activity. Allocating time to log such activity is a helpful strategy in assessment. Using this technique, the therapist gives the client a blank notepad, or a 'voice diary' (see Appendix 4 for an example) and invites the client to log the content of the voices as well as the client's own thoughts, beliefs, fears, etc. in response to their voice activity. Provided the client is in agreement, both therapist and client can then review the diary in session. In this way, the therapist is not reliant on the client's memory of voice activity and may even elicit a much richer exploration of the content of the voice.

Angel's assessment

Information obtained from Angel's general assessment is summarised in the preceding introduction and overview. Here, we report the detailed assessment findings regarding Angel's voices derived from our assessment tools described above.

Angel reported hearing two voices: a male and a female voice, both of whom were equally dominant. As well as criticising Angel, for example by saying 'you're useless', 'you're a fraud', the voices instructed her to do a number of things that she did not want to do. These commands ranged from somewhat innocuous commands such as 'leave the room' and 'stand up' to more risky commands such as 'don't take your medication', 'walk in the road (in front of cars)' and 'go to the park to sacrifice yourself (set yourself alight)'. Angel reported hearing the voices almost continuously, often lasting for hours at a time. She said that they sounded like they originated from outside of her head and that they spoke more loudly than she did. She described their content as always unpleasant and negative; understandably Angel found the voices very distressing. In terms of Angel's mood, she presented as very low and rated in the severe range for depression on the CDSS. Furthermore, Angel described feeling anxious, guilty and bad 'all of the time'.

Angel's beliefs about her voices

Angel believed with 100 per cent conviction that the voices were messengers from God which she felt compelled to listen to because she believed that they were teaching her 'the right way'. She was concerned that if she did not listen, she would miss out on 'warnings' of bad things that might happen. Furthermore, Angel believed that if she did not comply with what the voices commanded, bad things would happen to other people. Consequently, Angel generally complied at least partially with their commands. This led to Angel putting herself in a number of very risky situations, such as going to the park with lighter fluid with the intention of sacrificing herself. On one occasion she tried to set fire to herself but a passerby intervened. Angel also walked out into the road in front of cars on several occasions. When she did this, sometimes oncoming cars were forced to swerve around her or had to mount the pavement so as not to hit Angel. When Angel walked into the road she did so in the belief that no one would be hurt and that the cars would pass through her. The voices told Angel that this would be 'proof' that Angel was special and that she had been chosen by God to stop the pain and suffering in the world. Angel also complied with other commands including not taking her anti-psychotic medication. According to the medical notes and Angel herself, without medication she tended to become very unwell and more consumed and distressed by her voices. Angel believed that the voices were 100 per cent powerful and that she had no control over them at all. On the VPDS, she rated her voices as much more powerful, stronger, more confident and knowledgeable, superior to her and much more able to harm her than she was able to harm them.

Engagement

CTCH has been developed as an individual cognitive therapy typically involving 45 minutes to 1 hour sessions offered initially on a weekly basis. Considerable time and greater multidisciplinary co-working and liaison may, however, be required in order to successfully engage some clients in this work. Sessions may need to be flexible in terms of time and place; they may be shorter in length (25–30 minutes) given the distressing nature of voices and the client's varying tolerance as well as taking into account cognitive factors such as poor concentration. The therapist may need to be persistent and continue to offer appointments if they are cancelled and missed. Initial work may involve joint sessions with others. Engaging other health professionals involved in the client's care and enlisting them in the therapy process are important in building a trusting relationship and also in ensuring continuity of care once therapy has come to an end. Liaison with family members and carers is also likely to be important in some cases to support the aims of therapy and prepare them for any temporary increase in distress the client may experience.

While persistence is important, it must also be balanced with allowing clients space to consider both the pros and cons of treatment so that they have control over the process of therapy from the outset. In situations where initial engagement is problematic, the best strategy is to 'roll with resistance' by being patient and maintaining contact.

Therapeutic style

From the outset of therapy it is important to convey an empathic, trusting and warm relationship with clients. Chadwick (2006) has noted the primacy of the therapeutic relationship and stressed the importance of good counselling skills in working with clients with psychosis. These skills incorporate the notion of 'unconditional acceptance' not judging but accepting the client's attitudes, feelings and beliefs as valid. A meta-analytic review of seventy-nine published and unpublished studies of varying psychological therapies by Martin *et al.* (2000) has demonstrated a moderate relationship between the therapeutic alliance and outcome of therapy. In a further review, Hewitt and Coffery (2005) have suggested that while a positive therapeutic relationship may be necessary, it is not sufficient to enable therapeutic change in psychosis. In a systematic meta-synthesis of ten qualitative studies of CBT (including two studies of people with psychosis), A.C. Meaden (2009) reported two of the key themes which emerged regarding therapeutic relationship issues:

1   *The trusted listener.* This theme concerned the qualities of enabling the client to feel able to talk and that they had been listened to. Having someone listen to and respect the client's point of view was proposed as

being particularly pertinent for those who have psychosis, given that experiences such as voice hearing tended to be classed by the medical establishment as symptoms to be got rid of rather than phenomena that have personal meaning. Focusing on the clients experience and treating that experience as being valid were further important factors identified.

2   *Power and authority.* Many participants in the studies reviewed seemed to be aware that the therapeutic relationship was one in which the therapist had more power than the client, could handle difficult dynamics and provide direction from the therapist (at least initially), which was seen as desirable.

Openly discussing some of the difficulties of entering into a new relationship with the therapist can assist clients in feeling understood, facilitate the establishment of trust and diffuse any fears associated with therapy. Listening to the client's experience of their voices and encouraging them to give a detailed account of their voice hearing experience are essential. The client will have usually evolved a mini theory of their world and the role that they and their voices play in it. The client will usually have a subordinate role in this relationship. In CTCH, we must also acknowledge that social rank theory applies equally to the therapeutic relationship and that the therapist is often automatically placed in a position of power. Lowe (1999) has suggested that calling therapy collaborative does not lessen the institutional power of the therapist but rather enhances it because of the concealment involved. In CTCH, the therapist needs to be aware of this dynamic and learn to use their power benignly until the client is able to take more control and address the power balance with their voices, and other people, including the therapist. Ellis (2005), while clearly advocating collaboration in therapy, also recognised that therapists are experts who should use their knowledge to intervene directly when the client is experiencing difficulties. An example is teaching the client to dispute their irrational beliefs (Walen *et al.*, 1992). This more didactic position is something we advocate as part of the process of addressing beliefs in levels 4 and 7 of CTCH. We know for instance that voices tell lies, are fallible, make exaggerated claims and rarely are able to deliver on their threats. Didactic methods can be used to teach the client these. Didactic disputation strategies involve the use of mini lectures, analogies and parables (Walen *et al.*, 1992). However, while the therapist may be more knowledgeable regarding theories of psychosis and voice hearing and of what interventions may work in general terms, the voice hearer should be acknowledged as the expert on their voices, how they affect them, what is an acceptable pace of therapy and which goals they wish to focus upon. It is also important to note that clients can also use their knowledge about the power relationship in order to pursue their own agenda: talking to the psychologist to get discharged from hospital (A.C. Meaden, 2009). This may constitute compliance rather than engagement in therapy.

Case example: Isaac

Isaac was initially resistant to seeing the therapist. Sessions were scheduled to occur at a local clinic but he failed to attend. The therapist decided to visit Isaac at home but he refused to open the door. A short conversation ensued through the door, which ended in the therapist suggesting that she would return at another convenient time. One further visit resulted in Isaac again refusing to open the door. The strategy here was just to make contact to reassure Isaac that his views were perfectly valid. The therapist also sought permission to visit at another convenient time. On the next occasion Isaac felt more relaxed and allowed the therapist into his flat. The first few sessions were kept brief and covered his general well-being and topics of interest, with the primary focus of engaging him. After three sessions, the therapist felt that she had started to develop a more open and comfortable rapport with Isaac, so asked a few questions to raise the topic of voices and gently introduce cognitive exploration. Given that many people (including health professionals) in the past had dismissed Isaac's experiences, it was important for the therapist to acknowledge as a fact that Isaac did hear voices and to validate his distress. Over subsequent sessions, time was devoted to listening to and eliciting the details of Isaacs's experience of voice hearing.

Anticipating problems in engagement

In addition to engagement issues with those affected by psychosis generally, the particularly distressing nature of the experience of command hallucinations suggests the need to anticipate problems with the engagement process. This will help the therapist develop strategies for keeping the client engaged early on. The process of assessing the client's As, Bs and Cs regarding their voices can be applied here to aid the early detection of unhelpful beliefs about engaging in therapy. We have routinely encountered a number of common obstacles.

Voices commenting on the therapy or therapist

Voices often comment negatively about the therapist. These may represent the client's own anxieties about the usefulness of therapy or trustworthiness of the therapist or may constitute the voices' perception of threat. In working with clients who hear voices, we treat the voice as a real 'other', as in Isaac's case. This fosters genuineness and builds trust. Clinicians may be concerned that this will reinforce in some way the client's symptoms. We would note that the voice is real to the client and considered by them to have its own motives, fears and anxieties. If these are not taken into account, voices can quickly sabotage therapy. This stance also enables an additional strategy to be used: *passing messages to the voice*. Here, in an effort to lessen resistance by voices to the process of therapy, the therapist might consider asking the client to pass a message onto the voice, or, with the client's permission, speak to the voice directly, emphasising that the aim of CTCH is to ease distress rather than get rid of voices. This voice dialogue approach draws on the work of Wilson van Deusen (1971, 1974) who for 16 years worked as a clinical psychologist in Mendocine State Mental Hospital in California, talking directly with the voices of his patients and treating them as real since this is how they were experienced by them.

Actively raising the issue that voices might comment about the therapy or the therapist's credibility can help to overcome client's fears and increase the therapist's credibility. Clients are often relived that the therapist has raised this issue early on and often subsequently feel able to disclose what the voice has said about therapy and the therapist.

Case example: Ralph

Ralph disclosed that his voices had dismissed the therapist's efforts, saying 'don't listen to him, he is useless!' The voice had gone on to threaten Ralph with a heart attack (causing symptoms of anxiety). The therapist stressed his knowledge about working with others experiencing voices and noted that this was not an unusual reaction. The therapist also asked Ralph to pass a message to his voice that the aim of the sessions was to help Ralph cope better and be less distressed and *not* to weaken or get rid of him (the voice). Subsequent work looked at examining alternative explanations for Ralph's symptoms.

Unrealistic expectations of therapy

All clients come to therapy with expectations about what can be achieved and what the therapist can offer. In some cases, clients report that their primary goal is to get rid of the voices altogether. This is often an unrealistic goal and not one we promote in CTCH. On occasion voices do appear to disappear or recede into the background, but this is not an outcome that can be routinely achieved. This expectation needs to be addressed early on, as clients will quickly become disillusioned particularly if the frequency and intensity of their voices continue at the same rate as before, or even increase. Acknowledging the clients' goals while clarifying the aims of CTCH is a key step, and one which is intended to increase the client's motivation to engage in therapy by:

- helping the client understand their experience of the voice in a new way;
- developing effective coping strategies and gaining more control;
- reducing the distress associated with their voices;
- reducing harmful compliance;
- helping them get on with their lives and make choices as they want to.

This will help both the therapist and client develop more realistic, measurable and achievable goals. Asking the question *why now* and *who wants what* are helpful here. Clinicians may wish to embed CTCH goals within a systematic process of goal setting such as SMART (specific, measurable, achievable, realistic and time-limited). Short-term goals can be agreed with clearly defined steps needed to be reached in order to achieve longer term goals.

In some cases, clients will report wanting to hold on to a special voice. This might be because the client feels special hearing voices, or because the voices have warned that there will be awful consequences if their removal is attempted. Examining the benefits of CTCH as in Chapter 3 can be helpful here. If, however, there is no strong emotional C (the client only has positive affect) then there may be no rationale for CTCH. In some cases, this may still mean that there is potential for harmful compliance: Kevin hears the voice of God who wants him to kill himself so that he will go to heaven and fly with the angels. Such clients may require a risk management approach, more focused on monitoring and supervision.

Case example: Asim

Asim heard voices emanating from his tattoos. He believed that his tattoos provided him with supernatural powers. On several occasions, Asim ingested batteries (following the tattoos advice) in the belief that this would provide him with superstrength. He also jumped from a window in the belief that he could fly. Despite the high levels of risk associated with these commands, they were not associated with any distress or negative affect. Furthermore, Asim said that he would be devastated if he were to lose his powers and his source of strength. Although Asim was willing to meet with the therapist, his engagement was very superficial and he had no desire to work towards any change associated with the voices. Consequently, the therapist worked with Asim's team to help manage and monitor Asim's risk behaviour.

Exacerbating symptoms

Understandably, clients have fears about their voices and other symptoms worsening if they talk about them. Indeed this may happen, and the therapist should be mindful of this. Agreeing a pace of therapy that the client feels comfortable with is important here as well as monitoring any changes in distress or symptoms. Introducing coping strategies early on is consequently a key strategy and can be discussed here as an early goal (see Chapter 2).

Socratic dialogue can be used to highlight that the voices are already difficult and are likely to get easier to manage, rather than worse as therapy progresses. It might also be helpful to reflect that the voices may want the hearer to believe they will get worse, in order to keep the person at their beck and call, and highlight the fact that the voices may have something to lose by engagement in therapy, and therefore are likely to encourage the person not to participate. Any previous examples of successful interventions can be elicited and reflected upon here even if they brought only temporary benefit. The therapist also needs to demonstrate that they understand the distress the client feels when they hear voices, and takes it seriously.

Therapy won't help

Clients may understandably be sceptical about the benefits of therapy. This is not surprising since by definition clients referred for CTCH will often have demonstrated treatment resistance to standard care. As noted in our introduction command, hallucinations are the most distressing, high risk and treatment resistant of all symptoms of schizophrenia (Nayani and David, 1996; Shawyer et al., 2003). The therapist must be sensitive to this and be prepared to discuss why this approach is different and may share information regarding research findings as well as most usefully the reports of testimonials of clients who have undergone CTCH. For example, one of our clients stated in an independent qualitative interview:

> It taught me how to handle the spirits (voices). The therapist encouraged me to believe in myself, that I didn't have to do what they said no more. It was really tough but no one is ever bothered to be that interested in me before, it was the best thing that happened to me.

Other more detailed testimonials of CTCH are to be found in the preface to this book.

Disclosure will lead to hospital or more medication

Previous experiences may have led many clients to be wary of disclosing their experiences, especially safety behaviours, since this will often have raised concern in others and may have led to changes in medication, hospitalisation, lack of leave, etc. These are frequently real concerns and the therapist will need to sensitively discuss under what circumstances they will need to contact others and raise any concerns. The fact that clients experience commands does not automatically mean that they are at risk and this should be communicated to the client. It is the presence of compliance beliefs (especially those who appraise their voices as benevolent) along with the frequency of past and current safety behaviour use that should be considered. Therapist and client will need to judge, and ideally negotiate together, when additional support and intervention may be needed and in what form this should be.

Engagement strategies

In addition to addressing concerns about engaging in CTCH, we have evolved a number of specific strategies to further promote good engagement. Though not necessarily unique to CTCH, these can be used as strategies to share power, giving the client some control over the process of therapy and thereby also modelling skills which can be adopted for later use with voices.

The panic button

The use of a symbolic 'panic button' can help the client gain control over the process of therapy (promoting the notion of taking control in other relationships), with the option to disengage at any point, remain silent or withdraw. Here, the client is encouraged to press the panic button in order to either terminate the session or talk about something else. The therapist should enquire, however, why the client has pressed the button and explore the reasons for this if the client is agreeable (possibly at a later time). This technique often has a paradoxical effect, in that the more able clients feel to withdraw from therapy, the more likely they are to engage in it (Chadwick *et al.*, 1996).

Non-voice talk

Commencing CTCH with a gentle, warm and relaxed conversation about a general topic of interest (as in Isaac's case above) can facilitate engagement and build rapport. In the very early stages the therapist might only briefly discuss voices or mention them in passing. As the client becomes more relaxed and at ease with the therapist, information regarding the phenomenology of the client's voices can be elicited.

Some clients continue to find it tiring, draining and distressing to focus in on these experiences for any length of time. In these cases, a useful strategy is to allow the client a period of time in the session where they do not need to talk about their voices. For example, topics of general interest (e.g. music interests, current issues), identification of life goals or a discussion around past experiences of belief change allow the client some 'breathing space'. This may also enable the therapist to understand more about the individual's life experiences which can assist in formulating at the later stages of therapy. Periods when the panic button has been activated provide further opportunity for this.

Agreeing initial therapy goals

Building on assessment and engagement work, a further important component of level 1 work, is to agree the overall focus of therapy. As noted above, the emphasis in CTCH is upon reducing distress and harmful compliance in order to help the client lead their life and make choices as they wish to and not as the voices dictate. The therapist will at this point have begun to develop a collaborative description of the voices and the person's experience of them. Two early strategies are used here. The first is to normalise the voice hearer's relationship with their voice, suggesting that boundaries can be set and some control established. The second is to firmly locate the problem at C, thus setting initial goals around reducing voice-related distress and agreed appropriate safety behaviour reduction goals.

Normalising the voice relationship

In her qualitative meta-synthesis A.C. Meaden (2009) identified the theme 'Others like me', noting how participants in several studies highlighted the importance of knowing that they were not alone in their difficulties. In CTCH, psychoeducation may be helpful in promoting engagement by noting how others share similar experiences (possibly citing famous cases such as John Nash, Jack Kerouac, Syd Barrett, Gandhi, Churchill and Robin Williams) and how this is a problem which is amenable to intervention. In CTCH, attempts are made to also normalise the voice relationship through using everyday metaphors. This encourages the client to take a step back and consider the power relationships with voices in everyday power relationship terms. This can be achieved through using two helpful metaphors:

1   *The nosey neighbour.* This metaphor demonstrates to the client that it is okay to set boundaries with their voice. The important message to communicate is that just like setting boundaries with a curious and nosey neighbour, the client can consider setting boundaries with their voices. The following example, from Romme and Escher (1993), shows this metaphor in action:

> *T*: Let me put the situation to you, it's the kind of thing that everyone will have experienced. Just suppose you had a really nosey neighbour who was always poking his nose into your business. Let's imagine

that you have tried to avoid this person at all costs; you rush indoors when he's not looking, you know, that sort of thing?

C: Ah ha.

T: Let's suppose you wanted to make the nosey neighbour even nosier. What would you do?

C: You'd invite them in during the week, then you'd really have trouble getting rid of them.

T: And if you wanted to stop the neighbour being so intrusive?

C: You'd have to put your foot down, say you're busy, maybe come back when you've more time.

T: Would it be easy?

C: No, because you wouldn't want to upset them, you'd have to say it in a kind way, but stick to your guns.

T: Voices behave like a nosey neighbour I think: they come in when they're not wanted even if you're busy doing something else. You can get apprehensive in case they appear; avoid doing things that invite them in . . . sound familiar? One client I worked with got really fed up with the interruptions of the voice, she sometimes shouts at them and sometimes she gives in and does what the voices ask. If the voices were just like a nosey neighbour, what would you advise her?

C: She has to put her foot down again.

T: How could she do that, what comes into your mind?

C: She could say, 'I'll talk to you later when I have more time'.

T: Should she avoid going places to avoid bumping into the neighbour?

C: No, she'd never be able to relax or be at ease.

T: Say the voice/neighbour got upset?

C: That's the neighbour's problem . . . but it won't be nice getting on with your neighbours, you want a quiet life.

2 *The school bully.* The school bully metaphor nicely demonstrates that the relationship clients have with their voices can mirror other relationships in their life. Using this metaphor, the therapist asks the client if they were bullied as a child, and if so, to think back to that time. Alternatively, they might imagine a family member (son, daughter, niece, etc.) coming to them for help with bullies. The therapist then explores with the client what this was like, what things the bully said, how they coped with the bullies, etc. The idea is that in the short term, standing up to, or ignoring, the bully might mean the bullying gets worse, but in the long term the bullies will probably get bored and give up. The same might apply to the voices.

A cautionary note. In some cases, clients who experience command hallucinations will have been severely bullied and this could have been a very traumatising experience for them. In such cases, the bully metaphor would be contraindicated. The therapist might consider using the nosey neighbour metaphor instead, or alternatively, offering a safe self-disclosure in the following way:

> I remember when I was younger I used to ride this old bike to school and some of the bullies at school used to make fun of me. And so, for a while, I didn't ride the bike because I used to be embarrassed and afraid that they would make fun of me. And then I thought, actually, the more I didn't ride the bike and the more I did what the bullies said, the more they carried on anyway. Then one day I actually thought, 'I like my bike', so I started riding it again and eventually they just stopped bullying me. I realised that once you ignore bullies or you stand up to them, they tend to back down in the end. I used to be so frightened of these bullies, but it was only when I began to realise that they weren't that powerful, that they were all mouth and no trousers, that I was able to get on my bike again. Eventually, they just backed down. What do you think about that?

Another safe metaphor is to think about a telephone that is always ringing (e.g. sales calls or an annoying relative) where the caller wants to sell you something or find out what you are doing. What would the client do in this situation? Would you tell them to call back, put the phone down or ignore the phone so that the caller eventually stops ringing?

Using normalising techniques such as these can often make discussion around the voice experience more accessible and meaningful for the client. Furthermore, it often allows some distance between the client and their experience, making it feel safer to discuss. Through Socratic questioning, the therapist can explore with the client the coping strategies they have used and how it made them feel or what approaches they might use in the future.

Locating the problem at C

At the end of CTCH level 1, the client and therapist need to work towards developing a shared description and understanding of one key idea: that the goals of therapy are to reduce distress and compliance behaviour, and agree that this will be the overall focus of therapy. Earlier ABC formulations are helpful here, using these the therapist highlights how these are the problems that the client is presenting with, not the voices per se. It can be noted that often many people (including the client themselves) at different points experience voices but are not always distressed by them or engage in harmful behaviours. Agreeing that this is the focus can be the first step in socialising the client into the cognitive model.

Case example: Dan

In the assessment, Dan recalled that there had been a period in his life, just after his daughter was born, when the voices were not so distressing or intrusive. He said that although he still heard them (A) he was able to 'push them aside' and not do what they say. He recalled that this was a much happier (Ce) period in his life in which he did not follow the voices' orders (Cb). Highlighting this to Dan instilled hope that the initial shared therapy goal, to feel less distressed and not be obliged to comply with the voices, was feasible.

Tackling difficulties in assessment and engagement

The strategies described so far for assessing and engaging clients in CTCH have proven effective in working with the majority of clients we have encountered in our trial and routine clinical work. Some clients of course require greater attention to level 1 work; typically we would devote up to six sessions on this stage. For some clients, however, difficulties achieving this level persist.

Problems completing measures

Some clients may refuse to complete even the most simple of our measures. This might be for a variety of reasons, including negative experiences of being assessed and consequent treatment or a dislike of being assessed or categorised in any way. For example, Mark flatly refused to complete any measures. He had spent several years in forensic services where assessments were common place. He had also been compulsory sectioned after disclosing that he continued to experience command hallucinations.

For such clients a gentle approach is needed. The CAB procedure can be carefully woven into sessions and key questions from our measures introduced sensitively into therapeutic dialogue. Assessment and engagement may take many sessions with such clients.

Chaotic engagement

For a subgroup of clients, engagement can be particularly chaotic and problematic. These clients often fall under the remit of specialist services but can also be found in generic mental health teams. In such cases an assertive outreach style approach may be needed, characterised by persistent long-term efforts to develop and maintain engagement alongside team working practices.

In several cases, therapists have found it beneficial to use a mobile phone and texts to facilitate engagement and attendance at appointments. In many instances, clients find it helpful to respond to a quick text rather than have a conversation over the telephone. It is important, however, to ensure that certain boundaries are put in place regarding the therapist's working hours and access to the therapist and what the client should do outside of these. This withstanding, texting the client can help maintain contact, encourage the use of CTCH approaches and facilitate homework.

Case example: Lauren

Lauren had developed a problematic relationship with drugs in response to hearing voices. Her flat was known by local services as a place where drug deals were carried out and local gangs would hang about outside, often fighting over the right to do business in that area of the city. It was, therefore, agreed that the safety of the therapist on home visits would be compromised. However, Lauren struggled to make clinic appointments, either at the community base or the GP surgery, and regularly changed her mobile telephone number. Transport was arranged for several appointments, which were not attended. The therapist, therefore, decided to conduct as much of the assessment/engagement process over the telephone, whenever Lauren could be contacted. It was agreed that some of this information would be shared with the care coordinator who reinforced the message given by the therapist wherever possible. This resulted in three appointments being attended at clinic. Lauren, however, subsequently disengaged completely; the community team discovered she had moved to another part of the country.

Case example: Sandy

Sandy was initially seen at home by the therapist as she refused to be seen elsewhere. Despite appearing to engage in initial sessions, Sandy was frequently not at home when the therapist visited on subsequent occasions. When Sandy was at home, she would be 'devastated' that she had missed the appointment saying that she had just not remembered. Sandy did not have a phone on which the therapist could call to remind her of appointments, nor did she have any family members to remind her about the appointments. To overcome this, Sandy and the therapist agreed to meet at the same time each week and wrote the time of the appointment on a large piece of paper which Sandy pinned up in her bedroom. The therapist also wrote to Sandy each week reminding her of their appointment time. Despite this, Sandy's attendance continued to be erratic – she maintained that she had forgotten the appointments, had lost the letters and not looked at the paper in her bedroom. Eventually, it was agreed that on the day of their visits, the therapist would drop by Sandy's flat on her way into work to remind Sandy of their appointment (Sandy refused to meet first thing in the morning but was happy for the therapist to briefly stop by). Although Sandy missed some subsequent sessions, her attendance improved greatly and she successfully engaged in a total of fifteen sessions.

Session summaries can also be useful with such clients (see Chapter 9) to provide some continuity in between sessions. Team-based cognitive therapy may be another such approach (see Chapter 9 and Meaden and Hacker, 2010).

Superficial engagement

Sometimes clients may attend appointments and talk about their experiences but do not appear to be fully engaged in the process. They may talk about their difficulties in a matter of fact way. The client's beliefs about their voices and especially the evidence for them may be unconvincing. A number of potential reasons for this may need to be considered and examined.

For some, discussing their experiences and their personal history may be just too painful. They may find it difficult to tolerate such distress or may be dissociating from painful experiences. As we have noted before, if the client does not identify an emotional C then therapy may not be indicated, at the very least there will be limited motivation for therapy and the therapist will need to be creative in identifying a rational for intervention. Motivational interviewing may help, perhaps linked to the client's own recovery goals with some discussion of how harmful compliance works against these. Alternatively the client may be attempting to please someone else (e.g. a carer) by agreeing to therapy. There may also be compliance rather than engagement for other gains: wanting to get leave from hospital. The therapist will need to link with the team and examine the client's broader goals and needs.

Case example: Ken

Ken, it emerged, wanted to stay in hospital in order to avoid criminal proceedings for a sexual assault which he claimed had been in response to command hallucinations. It was difficult to elicit any compliance beliefs and his beliefs about his voices did not hang together; evidence for them was weak and particularly poorly defined.

Care should be taken not to offer explanations in these cases but to carefully elicit what the client thinks about their experiences. A specialist risk assessment should be considered for clients such as Ken, examining criminal attitudes and character based factors as well as dynamic risk factors and the circumstances under which such behaviours have occurred.

Engagement work with Peter

Peter's experiences with his CMHT were negative and he felt that both his consultant and care coordinator were not very involved in his care and were not 'there' for him. This just added to his sense of alienation and made him feel that he did not deserve help. His voice would add to this feeling, confirming his own negative views of himself. This made him feel lower still; he would ruminate further and think about harming himself.

In the first few sessions with Peter, it was important to show empathy and genuineness and convey understanding. The therapist listened to his story and went at his pace, making him feel as comfortable as possible. This was partly achieved by introducing the idea of a 'panic button'; if Peter felt that things were getting too much he could press an imaginary button on his sofa, the therapist would understand what this meant and they could talk about something different. The session could end at an appropriate point making sure he was calm and reassured. This provided him with control over what was talked about, creating a collaborative working relationship. It also served to model taking control in other relationships including his relationship with his voice. This was very important as Peter felt that others did not care about him or take note of his needs.

Engagement strategies with Peter

It became clear early on that Peter felt that he stood out and that he was different; people he believed knew all about his mental health problems and that he had lost his job and had been made bankrupt. It was accordingly important to normalise his experiences of voice hearing, providing examples of instances where other people hear voices and live their lives despite them. Peter would regularly go on the internet and he was encouraged to look at the work of Romme *et al.* (2009). Many people, it was suggested, hear voices and are able to incorporate voices into their lives and may even find them supportive. Given the right set of circumstances, it was noted that anyone can experience hearing voices (e.g. following a bereavement). Although he felt different, it was suggested perhaps his situation was not as dissimilar as he thought from that of many other people. Peter found this normalising work and other information (e.g. from MIND, 2009) very helpful and empowering. It began to sow the seed that although he saw himself as different, mental health problems were actually very common, and this might allow him to view himself more positively.

It was suggested that the voice he heard might discourage contact with the therapist and that this could be anticipated. The therapist reflected on his work with other clients and that this had happened with some of them. This led to a discussion about why this was the case and that the voice might feel threatened. It was highlighted that the CTCH approach was not about getting rid of the voice but about shaping a different relationship with her, one that was more equal. This enabled Peter to disclose that he was in fact being discouraged from attending sessions by his voice. Peter, however, valued the therapy and understood that the voice felt threatened. Peter was able, with support from the therapist, to identify that it was not what the voice wanted that was most important here, it was about what his needs were, and this motivated him to challenge and continue with the therapy sessions.

Normalising Peter's voice relationship

The idea of a relationship with the voice was introduced. Peter was told he was useless, no good and that he should harm himself. The nosey neighbour metaphor was used to illustrate how the woman's voice he heard was constantly intruding into his life. Peter and his therapist were able to explore how frustrating and annoying it is when someone, like a nosey neighbour, intrudes into your life. Peter's options with his intrusive voice were explored and he was asked what advice he might give a friend in a similar situation. Peter suggested that if his friend focused on other things and became less 'hooked in' to what was happening with the neighbour, he might feel less annoyed and frustrated.

Agreeing initial therapy goals with Peter

The idea of getting his friend to focus on other things was reflected back to Peter in terms of the voice he heard and whether he could apply a similar approach. This provided an opening as to what might help Peter to redirect his attention away from his voice in the future, thereby reducing his distress and compliance. The subsequent goal of developing his coping strategies (level 2 work) was introduced.

Engagement work with Angel

In the initial sessions, the development of a trusting collaborative relationship was key. Angel was keen to let the therapist know about some of her difficult early experiences, including the sexual abuse, but clearly stated that she did not want to spend the sessions 'dragging up the past'. Furthermore, she said that she had received therapy in the past which she felt had helped her deal with those experiences. The therapist reassured Angel that she was not obliged to discuss anything that she did not feel comfortable about. One thing that became apparent to the therapist early on in the sessions was Angel's sense of inflated responsibility and her tendency to feel very guilty about events that were out of her control. Angel clarified that her evidence for this guilt and sense of responsibility was a 'feeling' of intense guilt and responsibility. Identification of her 'emotional reasoning' bias was very important thera-peutically as it emerged that this same cognitive bias was also used as evidence supporting her beliefs about the voices. To facilitate engagement, Angel was given a notepad and a folder, the same as that used by the therapist. Given the importance of subordination schema in this client group, it was hoped that this would pave the way for a more collaborative relationship with both parties taking responsibility for session note-taking.

Engagement strategies with Angel and normalising the voice hearing relationship

During the first session, Angel presented as very anxious, telling the therapist that she was too frightened to talk about the voices. The therapist told Angel that she admired her courage to admit that, and queried whether the voices had tried to discourage Angel from coming to the session in any way. The therapist explained that, in her experience of working with other people, voices often advised clients not to come to the sessions, and not to trust the therapist. The therapist proceeded to ask Angel if the voices had said anything similar to her prior to the session. Angel was reassured by the therapist's comments and was able to disclose that the voices had warned her that she would be sectioned if she spoke about the voices. The therapist compared the voices to school bullies, who might discourage the child that they were bullying from telling the teacher. The therapist normalised how frightening that must feel. Angel found this analogy helpful and added that she thought the voices felt threatened by the therapist because they thought she might try to get rid of them. The therapist then asked Angel if she could perhaps pass a message to them that the aim of the sessions was to help with Angel's distress and not to get rid of them. The therapist also reassured Angel that if the sessions felt overwhelming or if she wanted to stop at any point, she could put her hand out, as if pressing an imaginary panic button, and that they could either terminate the session or talk about things other than the voices. It was agreed that if Angel was to use the symbolic panic button, the therapist would steer the conversation towards a chosen topic that made Angel feel less distressed, for example her son. Subsequently, Angel felt more in control of the sessions and was able to continue with therapy and talk openly about the voices. Furthermore, the fact that Angel was not sectioned after the session was later used as evidence that sometimes the voices can get things wrong – a useful piece of evidence when challenging the omniscience of the voices. Angel also reported that the voices accepted the therapist's message at face value.

Agreeing initial therapy goals with Angel

Angel's initial goals for therapy were agreed as being able to ignore the voices and to not believe what they said to her so that she did not feel compelled to do what they said.

Summary

In this chapter we have highlighted in practical terms how therapists might enter into the process of assessment using different methods. The process of engagement and anticipating and addressing problems is key to building a sound therapeutic relationship and paves the way for agreeing initial therapy goals.

Chapter 2

CTCH Level 2

Promoting control

Introduction

Promoting control is a key concept in CTCH. Mackinnon *et al.* (2004) have reported that those patients in their study who were unable to resist their command hallucinations rated them as intrusive and had fewer coping strategies than those more able to resist, and were prescribed higher dosages of medication. Helping clients develop and build a coping repertoire will not only give them some reprieve from their voices but early successes will help build confidence in the therapy and the therapist, thereby promoting engagement. Improving coping in CTCH is also central to the process of gathering new evidence for reframing this increased control as a power shift in the client's relationship with their voices. In this chapter we describe in detail the process of promoting control and show how we use this to address power beliefs and relationships.

Aims of promoting control in CTCH

In CTCH, promoting control is introduced early on, even before the client is socialised into the cognitive model and more detailed goals for intervention are agreed. The aim is to help the client to develop an understanding of the factors that increase and decrease the frequency, loudness, intrusiveness and content of their voices and develop coping strategies to manage them. This will foster and consolidate engagement and reduce resistance to therapeutic efforts by improving control, since the client will often experience some increase in their distress as a result of talking about their voices and resisting their commands. During the subsequent course of therapy, the aim is to also emphasise the client's strengths in coping with their voices and build evidence against their own sense of powerlessness. In level 2 work, the key tasks are to:

1   systematically review the effectiveness of the client's existing coping strategies;

2   enhance the client's existing coping repertoire for reducing distress associated with voices;
3   introduce new strategies that have been effectively used by other voice hearers;
4   use this increased control to cast doubts about the voice's power.

Reviewing and enhancing clients' existing coping strategies

In most cases, clients have been living with their voices for many years. During this time they will usually have developed different ways of coping with their voices, although they might not view these strategies as a means of coping (Falloon and Talbot, 1981). Farhall et al. (2007) note that the use of self-initiated so-called natural coping strategies appears almost universal among voice hearers. Despite this finding, voice hearers continue to have psychotic experiences. Coping strategy enhancement (CSE; Tarrier et al., 1990) is frequently employed as a component of CBTp interventions (Jones and Meaden, 2012). It is in essence an applied behavioural analysis tool whereby the person's coping repertoire, triggers and antecedents are systematically reviewed for individual symptoms so that coping strategies can be identified and enhanced and unhelpful ones discarded. New strategies, such as relaxation or distraction, may then be taught to extend the person's coping repertoire. Clients' existing coping strategies often vary in their complexity from simple and direct attempts to control cognitive processes to more complex self-directed methods that aim to modify cognitive content and inferences. Falloon and Talbot (1981) uncovered three broad groups of coping strategies:

1   behavioural change: increasing or decreasing interpersonal contact;
2   efforts to lower physiological arousal: relaxation methods;
3   cognitive coping methods: attentional control, challenging thoughts and distraction.

Carr (1988) subsequently elicited 310 strategies and categorised them into five groups:

1   Behavioural control
     i   Distraction
     ii   Physical change (inactivity/activity)
     iii Indulgence (eating, drinking, smoking)
     iv   Non-specific: keeping busy.
2   Socialisation.
3   Cognitive control
     i   Suppression: trying not to think about voices
     ii   Shifted attention: redirection to neutral comforting ideas
     iii Problem solving.

4   Symptomatic behaviours, which tended to reinforce symptoms: acting in an angry manner, shouting, seeking reassurance.
5   Medical care (relatively rare).

During the assessment, it is important that the therapist draws out which coping strategies the client might already be using and reframes them as such, so that the client can identify that they have already been managing their voices over time. When systematically reviewing a client's existing coping strategies, the important factors to consider include discovering when strategies are used, how consistently strategies are applied and how effective the strategies are that are employed. A simple Likert scale can be used to rate the efficacy of each strategy with the client and highlight an ineffective strategy (Tarrier *et al.*, 1990). Nelson (2005) lists some useful questions to help elicit current coping strategies:

1   Do you do anything when you hear the voice?
2   Is it worse in some places than others?
3   Have you ever noticed anything special that helps at all when that happens?
4   In what way does it make you feel better?
5   Do you use it every time, or do you forget sometimes?
6   Would it be helpful if you were to use it more often?

The CAV interview (Chadwick and Birchwood, 1994) can also be used to elicit the client's existing coping strategies. Questions from the CAV that are useful here are as follows:

•   When the voice talks, what do you usually do?
•   Do you listen because you feel you have to?
•   Do you listen because you want to?
•   Do you shout and swear at the voice?
•   Do you do what the voice says willingly?
•   Do you talk to or try to ignore the voice?
•   Do you try to stop talking to it?
•   Is there anything you have found to do that makes the voice go away or seem less intense (e.g. talking, reading and drugs)?

The antecedent and coping interview (ACI; Tarrier, 1992) is a further useful tool specifically designed to identify the antecedents for psychotic symptoms and the efficacy of coping strategies.

Introducing and teaching new coping strategies in CTCH

Farhall *et al.* (2007) propose that the therapist explores with the client what strategies are useful to them and may subsequently use a prompt list to elicit further potentially useful strategies that might not have been previously considered. What is also important is that the role of the different approaches is considered: are they used to stop voices or to help mediate the client's emotional response. This will help the client and therapist work collaboratively and identify the right strategy for the right effect. Clinically it has been identified that clients using the same strategies achieve different responses. The value of employing strategies which function to regulate emotional response rather than remove voices may be usefully emphasised.

To ensure that new coping strategies can be implemented, they must be carried out systematically through a process of over-learning, simulation and role-play until the strategy is internalised by the client. Prompts can be used between sessions (e.g. flashcards) to assist new learning. New strategies should be introduced one at a time so as not to overwhelm the client. Further strategies can be added until there is an effective coping repertoire established. Teaching the client too many strategies may mean that the client is unclear which ones to use when and might confuse the client about the most appropriate or effective strategy to implement when under stress.

Useful coping strategies in CTCH

We have found the following strategies useful in promoting control in clients with command hallucinations:

1   *Switching voices on and off*

Learning to switch voices on and off involves:

- proposing the idea that control over the voices means that they can be turned on *and* off; the analogy of learning to drive a car is helpful in that feeling in control of a car involves being able to start *and* stop the car;
- identifying cues that increase/decrease the frequency and intensity (volume) of voices;
- introducing these strategies within session;
- encouraging the client to initiate or increase voice activity for short periods, then turn the volume down or stop them altogether, with a view to gradually lengthening these periods.

Case example: Laura

Laura found that introducing a visual image of a remote control helped her turn down the volume of her voices. She was able to create this image in her mind's eye by closing her eyes. She saw herself gradually turning the voice down as she did when she adjusted the volume of her MP3 player. She found this really helpful; not only did it work but she also recognised that she could do something about the voices – she had the power to influence and control them.

---

2   *Attention switching*

Cather (2007) and Wells (2000, 2007) have explored the role of problematic thinking patterns in psychological disorders and the value of using attention training to help clients approach auditory hallucinations in a novel way. Modifying metacognitions helps the client recognise the role they play in maintaining psychological disturbance, increase perceived client controllability over voices and reduce distress. Clients are actively encouraged to shift the focus of their attention from one subject or experience to another. The therapist trains the client, in session, to switch attention on cue through rehearsal. For example, if a client becomes anxious when talking about their voice in session, the therapist can invite them to perhaps describe a picture hanging on the wall in order to shift their attention. Alternatively, the therapist might invite the client to focus their attention on a set of positive images, such as recalling a recent enjoyable holiday or other occasion using all the senses. The aim with this latter technique is for the client to continually rehearse this memory until they are able to elicit it at will.

Some clients benefit from the therapist highlighting the point that the more we focus and attend to a noise, the louder and worse it seems. By inviting the client to focus on the sound of traffic noise outside (or any sound that you might be able to hear in the distance from the therapy room), the therapist can demonstrate that the more we pay attention to sounds the louder and more pronounced they seem to become. In this way, the therapist can help the client make the connection that the more they attend to their voice, the more intrusive and distressing it might seem.

Case example: Chris

Chris tended to hear people walking past his flat and sometimes they would hang around having just left the local pub. The voices kept saying that they were planning to 'get him'. As a consequence he became very scared and upset and this tended to increase the voices further.

The therapist introduced Chris to the idea that the more he focused in on something (the people talking outside his flat), the louder they became. In turn, this increased the voices' loudness and led to him becoming distressed.

In session, Chris was taught to focus on a fixed point in the room and begin to move his attention from sounds within the room to sounds outside the room. After some practice he was able to increase his ability to switch between sounds when he needed to. He was asked to practice this as homework starting with a couple of close sounds (e.g. a clock in his room, a radio turned down low) and then to sounds outside the room and further away (e.g. people talking just outside his room or walking down the corridor, cars driving past or birds in the trees).

Over time when faced with people talking outside his flat, Chris was more able to identify that he was focusing on external sounds and his negative voices. He was able to switch to competing sounds within his room (e.g. the TV, music, talking to other residents). Consequently, the frequency with which he heard voices, and the level of associated distress he experienced, reduced. He found using this technique considerably helpful and empowering.

3   *De-arousing techniques*

High levels of arousal have been implicated in the psychopathology of voices and frequently occur as both antecedents and responses to voice experiences. Teaching client's brief relaxation, such as progressive muscular relaxation, or breathing exercises can help reduce this arousal. Such techniques may also be employed in session when a person is becoming agitated and can helpfully illustrate the effect of attention switching: to one's breath. Recording these sessions and giving the taped session to the client further enable them to rehearse the techniques out of session.

Case example: Mike

Mike experienced his voices as extremely distressing to the point where he would have nightmares about the content of their threats. The nightmares were directly linked to his voices saying malicious things prior to him falling asleep and increased their sense of power. Understandably, Mike's sleep was constantly disturbed and was consequently poor in quality.

Mike was taught to use an audio-guided visual imagery relaxation technique that he would listen to at night-time, just before going to sleep. He found that not only did it distract him from the voices, his sleep improved (it was less broken) and he slept overall for a longer period of time. It did not get rid of the voices completely, but Mike did begin to question their validity and power.

While these techniques can be powerful intervention tools, some de-arousing techniques can be adopted as new safety behaviours by some clients and the potential for this should always be borne in mind, a point we will return to later in this chapter and in subsequent chapters.

4   *Increasing activity levels*

Given that people who hear voices are particularly prone to isolation and reduced physical activity, standard activity-scheduling can be a powerful coping strategy. Social isolation can serve to maintain unhelpful beliefs about the subordinate position of the individual and is a common safety behaviour, often a threat mitigation strategy. Increased activity not only fosters more social engagement, thus reducing isolation, but also creates a dual task competing for attentional resources. If such behaviours do indeed function as safety behaviours for the individual, then increasing activity levels may need to be introduced as part of safety behaviour reduction work as described in Chapter 5.

Case example: Lucas

During one therapy session Lucas said that a long-term wish of his was to own a dog. With encouragement from the therapist he bought a dog and it was at this point that he started to venture out of the house more frequently. At first, he walked the dog twice a week, but eventually Lucas was able to walk the dog around the local park daily. He found that, as a result of this, he interacted with other dog owners at the park and this in itself brought about a significant change in his mood, the frequency with which he heard voices and the beliefs he held about others.

---

5 *Distraction techniques*

Distraction techniques help focus a client's attention away from their voices. Verbal distraction techniques are thought to be more effective than non-verbal techniques because the same language areas of the brain which are activated during voice activity are used when implementing verbal tasks (Nelson, 2005) and directly compete with 'inner speech', one of the mechanisms thought to underlie voice hearing (Johns *et al.*, 2001). A common distraction technique used with voice hearers is listening to music or audio books on a Walkman or iPod. As noted by Nelson (2005), there is some evidence to suggest that aggressive pop music can provoke voice activity and agitated behaviour. With this in mind, warning clients about this potential risk is advised. More importantly, however, clients need to feel in control of the strategies they use and if this type of music resonates with the client's mood at the time, then it need not be necessarily discouraged. Other verbal strategies include reading aloud, singing aloud (if socially appropriate), whistling or humming, counting under one's breath and phoning a trusted family member/friend.

Humming is a particular favoured strategy that we use and can be rehearsed in session by asking the client to choose a favourite song or tune and, provided you know it, humming it together or perhaps setting up a humming competition with the client. This can be a fun exercise and potentially down ranking the therapist, helping develop the therapeutic alliance and promoting an equal role in the relationship.

Case example: Donna

During one session early in therapy, Donna reported she was having a particularly hard time concentrating because the voices were so loud and distracting. She felt there was no way to control them, and that this was the way she often felt at home; she had no choice but to listen to them. The therapist suggested that some people found music helpful but given that there was no music system in the room she wondered if Donna might want to sing or hum a favourite piece of music. Donna stated that she felt self-conscious doing this, so the therapist proposed they have a competition: who could hum the loudest. After humming the entirety of Cliff Richard's Summer Holiday, Donna spontaneously beamed and started crying, saying that those 5 minutes had been the only respite she had had from the voices all that day. She was very surprised that the technique had worked and agreed that it would be a useful unobtrusive way of reducing the intensity of the voices at other times. In later sessions she reflected that if she could remove them by simply humming then perhaps she had more control than she initially thought, and indeed, perhaps the voices might not be quite as powerful as they made out.

6   *Other techniques*

Other techniques we have found helpful in level 2 work include non-verbal strategies such as having a bath, pampering oneself (e.g. doing your hair and nails), doing the housework, watching TV, wearing earplugs and so on.

Using cue cards and diaries

In order to help clients identify and practise using coping strategies, a voice activity diary (as shown in Appendix 4) can help identify triggers for the voices and how much control the person had before and after using the chosen strategy. The diary can then be used to illustrate a change in control and shift in power. With some clients, writing things down can be difficult and therefore developing visual representations of how successful the strategy has been can be valuable, using for instance a visual analogue or Likert scale of emoticons pre- and post-strategy. The client can then indicate how effective the intervention was compared with a different one or none at all.

Clients frequently forget when to use their coping strategies, and in many cases they forget to employ helpful strategies when they are most needed. This is not surprising given the highly distressing and distracting nature of their experiences. It is therefore often useful for therapists to provide clients with summary notes, cue cards or other memory aids identifying the key points to prompt the use of strategies known to be helpful. An example is shown in Appendix 4. Such summary notes and coping cue cards are a useful and practical way of engaging the client in the therapeutic process and socialising them into the cognitive model of homework.

Establishing initial boundaries

Drawing on social rank theory in CTCH, we frame the client as being in an interpersonal relationship with their voice(s). Through guided discovery the therapist can help the client consider that over time they have developed a relationship with their voice. Consequently the client can; now that they have developed some coping strategies, consider putting boundaries in place with their voice, just like they might implement boundaries in everyday relationships. This can be linked to the engagement strategies previously described (Chapter 1), using the analogy of the 'nosey neighbour' or a friend who always calls to normalise the boundaries within social relationships. Two useful further strategies are helpful here. The first involves talking back to the voices, a strategy which we extend in level 6 (Chapter 6) to consolidate the power shift. The second strategy focuses on allocating voice time, a negotiation strategy. With both of these techniques, the main learning point is for the client to identify that it is possible to set boundaries with their voices. On occasion, however, this technique can be counter-productive and can increase hypervigilance to voices, requiring careful monitoring.

Talking back to the voices

Inviting the client to engage directly with the voice may seem like a risky strategy for the client (and it can be anxiety provoking for the therapist too). However, it is a powerful technique in disarming the voice of its power and enables the client to take further control. Here, the therapist encourages the client to focus on what the voice is saying, then invite the client to consider talking back to the voice, for example encouraging the client to tell the voice to 'Stop' or 'Go away' in a firm voice, out loud when alone. While in public, clients might consider using their mobile phone as a socially acceptable way of talking back to their voices. Normalising analogies can be used here to illustrate that this would be the approach to take with a person who constantly, and rudely, interrupts someone. Engaging directly with voices is not a technique to push if the client seems anxious, particularly if there has not yet been any shift in the client's sense of their own powerlessness.

The therapist may begin to introduce this technique by rehearsing in session with the client some responses they might make when they hear their voice saying, 'I'm not going to let you control my life' or 'I can't listen now'. Cue cards summarising these can be helpful for the client to support practice out of session when emotions are high and voices are distressing.

Allocating time to listen to the voices

The aim here is for the client to begin to exercise some choice about when to listen to the voice. For example, the client might tell their voice, 'I will not listen to you now because I'm busy. Come back at 3.00 pm and I will listen then'. At the set time, the client chooses how they manage and respond to the voice.

Coping strategy or safety behaviour?

As noted earlier, some coping strategies which the client already uses may also act as safety behaviours. Similarly, in teaching new strategies these too may come to function as safety behaviours (this is discussed in detail in Chapter 6). In these cases the coping strategy while serving to mitigate against the sense of immediate threat maintains the client's belief that their voice could have carried out the feared threat if the behaviour (the new coping strategy) had not intervened to prevent it. In preventing the disconfirmation of power beliefs, these new safety behaviours work against the aims of level 2 work which is to begin to question the voice's power. The therapist must judge whether a coping strategy has the potential to function in this way for the client. This is more likely if the coping strategy quickly reduces distress. In these cases, the client may readily make the link that when they utilise the new strategy (e.g. humming their favourite song) then the voice does not deliver on its threats (e.g. to abuse and insult them). Humming in this case then becomes the new safety behaviour: 'the voice does not punish me because I hum my favourite song', but the power of the voice is not disconfirmed: the voice can still punish. This new belief and its implications for voice power must now be examined.

Case example: Sarah

Sarah said that praying helped her to cope with the voices. She said that when the voices told her to hurt herself, or someone else, she would pray for God's help and forgiveness (she believed that the voices were punishing her for bad things that she had done and could make her harm herself). The therapist initially supported the use of this coping strategy. Further assessment revealed, however, that Sarah believed that the only reason she had not fully complied with the voices commands to hurt herself or others was because God was intervening, rather than because she was gaining any control herself or that the voices had lost some of their power. Hence, praying was serving as a safety behaviour, which was preventing disconfirmation of Sarah's power beliefs about her voices.

Since talking helped, Sarah agreed with her therapist that talking to a friend when she became distressed would be a strategy she could employ. However, it soon became apparent that this too served as a safety behaviour (help seeking) and functioned in the same way as praying. Sarah and the therapist proceeded to examine a number of coping strategies that might prove useful. It was established that listening to music would just *blot them out* and not mean that they could not punish her for non-compliance: cutting herself. Relaxation was something Sarah could do herself (rather than others intervening) and meant that she could cope better with their threats and so they had *less of a grip* over her. The threats were not *blotted out* but she gained more emotional resilience by remaining calmer in the face of these threats.

Introducing new strategies may have other side effects.

Case example: John

At the suggestion of his therapist, John would hum each time he felt distressed by his voices when they threatened him for non-compliance. He would hum while on his own and when in the company of others; any time he found the voices overwhelming (which was often). Humming offered John significant reprieve from the voices. He began to think that if he hummed regularly, the voices might disappear. Over the course of a month, John went from humming occasionally to humming throughout the whole day. People began to notice that John was humming and he found that others seemed to look at him strangely. This reinforced his belief that he was 'weird' and 'mad'. While John found the humming technique helpful in the short term, it became maladaptive in the longer term and had a detrimental impact on his social relationships and functioning.

The therapist and John explored how this strategy had become problematic itself. After some discussion, John was understandably anxious to stop humming as he considered that it was helping him cope with his voices and to gain some control over them. He could, however, see that it was impacting on his friendships and his ability to go out in public. John agreed he would try to hum only when he was alone and when he rated the voices as 8 out of 10 on a distress scale (0 = no distress; 10 = extreme distress).

For other clients, there might be a greater advantage in terms of building engagement by helping the client to cope more effectively even if this becomes a new safety behaviour. Once the voices' power has been questioned in subsequent stages of CTCH (level 4), then the therapist and client may return to examine the implications of the coping strategy/safety behaviour in a new light.

Reframing control and raising doubts about power

Coping strategies can be viewed in terms of cognitive and behavioural methods (Bucci and Tarrier, 2010). Cognitive methods include generating alternative explanations and examining the evidence for beliefs, while behavioural methods involve using behavioural experiments. Once a combination of different coping strategies are built up, the use of attention switching and de-arousing techniques, they can serve to dull the strength of a delusion so that reality testing can be implemented (Bucci and Tarrier, 2010). In CTCH terms this constitutes questioning how much control the voices have and by implication their power, enabling the subsequent dropping of safety behaviours. Coping strategies will also help the client to feel that they have tools that enable them to resist their voice's commands. At this stage, however, the focus is simply on making the client aware, through Socratic questioning or didactic methods that they have some control.

Tackling difficulties in promoting control

An important point to consider is that clients will find it effortful to employ coping strategies when their level of arousal is high. Some clients may simply not have the motivation to rehearse certain strategies, they might not believe that they would be helpful in the first place, or the voices may simply denigrate their efforts. In some instances, clients find that they become depressed when the voices are persistent. At these times it can be difficult for them to initiate strategies. Rehearsing coping strategies within a therapy session can help break this vicious cycle and promote hope that the client can gain some control. Even though the voices might discourage the use of a particular coping strategy, the therapist can gently encourage the client to practice different strategies in the safety of the therapeutic environment. Exploring with the client the positives of taking a chance and doing something contrary to what the voices are saying (e.g. attending therapy sessions when commanded not to do so) is another strategy the therapist can employ. This builds up evidence that the client can make a difference even if it is emotionally challenging.

Other coping strategies (which often constitute safety behaviours) such as substance use, avoidance, or partial compliance may be preferred as they provide temporary relief and have proven efficacy from the client's point of view. Nevertheless, it is important to attempt to build coping strategies in order that clients have the opportunity to examine their beliefs about the control of voices.

Strategies give only temporary relief

As is often the case, clients frequently report that using coping strategies gives only temporary relief. This is not surprising given the often long-term nature of these experiences and the psychological meaning and importance clients may give to them.

For some clients this may reduce their motivation to continue with therapy. As those therapists who work with victims of domestic violence will know, clients often find it difficult to leave an abusive partner. The point we emphasise, however, is that coping strategies are intended to provide some temporary relief and to cast doubt on the voice's power and the client's own sense of powerlessness. In this the therapist should not oversell the use of coping strategies: the aim is to improve coping and not remove symptoms, and to explore triggers for the voices (e.g. times of stress and times of solitude) when the client may need to have their 'repertoire' of coping strategies ready.

Insufficient or inconsistent application

Often clients will report that the strategy has proven ineffective or that they have tried this strategy before to no effect. Before moving on to the next strategy, the therapist should spend some time reviewing the use of strategies:

- Under what circumstances was the strategy used?
- Were there any factors which could have been present which would have reduced its impact (e.g. practicing relaxation in a noisy environment)?
- How consistently/correctly was it used?
- How long was it used for until the client gave up?

It is doubly important that techniques wherever possible are practiced in session to ensure their correct use and that the necessary degree of skill has been attained. The therapist will often have to maintain the client's confidence that the technique has proven to be of benefit for many people and persistence may be needed (while avoiding the potential for the client to experience themselves as a failure).

New coping strategies are too effective

In rare cases, some clients may report that strategies have got rid of the voices altogether, which may also reduce motivation to continue with therapy. Returning to our ABC model and rationale for CTCH, we may consider in such cases whether it is ethical to continue: if there is no emotional or behavioural 'C' then there is not a rational for CTCH. The client may of course relapse in the future and remain at risk of later compliance, and this should be explored with the client with perhaps a pathway back to therapy agreed if the client still wishes to disengage.

Case example: Thelma

Thelma heard the voice of her grandmother who instructed her to stay in bed all day and not eat. In the past this had led to Thelma severely neglecting herself and almost dying through lack of nutrition. She had been hospitalised on a number of occasions. Thelma was supported to develop coping strategies involving listening to music, keeping herself busy around her flat and reading books. She and the therapist worked subsequently to develop boundaries with her voice. Thelma reported that these were very successful and that she was no longer bothered by her voices; she subsequently disengaged from therapy. Thelma appeared to function well for a time and remained out of hospital for some 2 years (breaking her 12 monthly pattern of admissions). However, following a stressful time in her life she relapsed and was admitted again to hospital with severe self-neglect.

Level 2 work with Peter and Angel

Peter

Reviewing Peter's existing coping strategies

Initially the therapist explored what Peter did when he heard voices and how he coped with this. It was clear early on that he was very active and tended to keep very busy. He had a broad range of things that he did that provided opportunities for distraction and socialisation. These included listening to music, playing the guitar, going on the internet, meditating, reading, making art work (painting, sculpture), listening to a relaxation tape, going for a run, going to the gym, swimming and spending time with friends. Peter found that these were reasonably effective as long his mood was stable and he was not dealing with any crisis in his life.

Enhancing his current repertoire of strategies

When Peter was low, he would tend to distract himself less and isolate himself by staying in his flat and lying in bed. This tended to make him more vulnerable and at times led him to focus more on what his voice was telling him; he would begin to believe her more and he would contemplate harming himself.

The therapist initially explored what helped Peter cope and how much he was using these particular approaches when things were more difficult for him. Over time it was possible to explore his maintenance cycle and how he tended to behave when he was low. At these times he tended to think 'what's the point, she won't go away'. Peter it emerged reduced the strategies he used in the flat and how much he went out, the intensity of his voices subsequently increased and this influenced the likelihood of him harming himself.

One of the main elements of working with Peter was helping him to become more aware of this pattern of behaviour and examining what strategies he could use most effectively when things were tough. Highlighting this pattern through a jointly constructed formulation was very helpful. Part of the therapists role was to educate him about how thinking 'what's the point, she won't go away' led to his reduction in using his usual coping strategies. The trick was to ask Peter to suspend his belief in these thoughts and set them aside. For example, initially Peter could focus on strategies he could use in his flat and which drowned out the voice he heard. For Peter the strategies that did this were:

- listening to music;
- listening to a relaxation tape;
- meditation;
- engaging in his art work.

Even if the voices were troubling him and he did not feel well, the therapist emphasised the importance of utilising these approaches. To help him do this the therapist and Peter wrote down on a flashcard the reasons for employing the coping strategies along with a reminder that they were effective and had worked before:

The more I practice these strategies, the better I will become at them
Don't give up!
They have helped me before
I am getting more control and getting my life back
I enjoy doing them

Subsequently Peter reported that the voices lessened and he was then encouraged to leave his flat, whether this was to go for a run or to the gym.

Introducing new strategies

Over the following sessions the therapist and Peter were able to look at him taking back control through the use of strategies he had used in the past but was not using now. In Peter's case, using Carr's (1988) structure of strategies, socialisation and medication were areas that required development and enhancement. He had taken medication in the past but had stopped doing this when his contact with the team had stopped. Medication helped him maintain a more stable mood so that his lows were less frequent. After exploring this and examining the costs and benefits, Peter agreed to try medication again.

Peter used to socialise a lot (with family and friends) but he had stopped doing this as he was discouraged by the voice and his confidence was now a lot lower than it had been previously. Peter acknowledged that isolating himself stopped him using this valuable strategy which tended to quieten down the voice and discovering information that might invalidate what the voice was telling him. Part of the work, it was suggested, involved him taking a chance and doing something that the voices did not want him to do: see friends and family. It was also about him taking a chance and trusting his team again. Seeing them and be represcribed appropriate medication with the support of the therapist enabled him to experience less lows and he was consequently better able to get out of the house and socialise.

Challenging the voice's power

Although in most cases, distraction, socialisation and use of medication did not get rid of Peter's voice, it did help him focus on other things, gather information that invalidated the voice and allowed him to keep his mood stable. Peter began to feel less overwhelmed; it reduced the likelihood he would hang himself and it changed the power relationship. He felt he was taking back control by maintaining strategies even when he did not feel up to it. Similarly he spent time with others and found this really enjoyable. When he made contact with the team, this was a more helpful experience than he had anticipated and conflicted with what the voice had been telling him about them. These experiences added further to his changing belief that he could resist, take control back and that much of what the voice said was incorrect.

Over time a helpful metaphor was developed. At times the voice he heard was relentless; she was very insulting, went on and on and made him question whether things would change/get better. It was suggested that perhaps this was like being at sea in a storm. The storm rages and a consequence of this is that it creates huge waves that could sink any ship at sea. The storm metaphor was explored in terms of what the best approach would be: to fight the sea or to roll with the storm. If Peter was able to use his coping strategies effectively, he could take control and steer his ship to safety.

Peter found this metaphor very useful. While he found it difficult to stop the voices completely, he was able to do things to help the situation when things were really bad. Peter himself introduced another element. He said that it had been helpful looking around when he was at sea; other people too would have their own ships and were dealing with their own storms using their own approaches to get through the situation. This helped to normalise the situation and promoted acceptance of his mental health problems.

Angel

Reviewing and enhancing Angel's existing coping strategies

When the therapist initially met Angel, she believed that she had absolutely no control over the voices and that they were present 100 per cent of the time. She rated her own control as being 0 per cent, and expressed that nothing that she did helped with the voices. Angel was also reluctant about trying any new strategies, as not only was she doubtful that these would work but she thought that employing them might antagonise the voices. The therapist suggested completing a voice diary as a way of assessing when the voices were better and worse during the week. The therapist added that if they could perhaps discern any triggers for when the voices were worse, they could work together to reduce them. Angel was initially worried about completing the diary as she thought that by focusing on when the voices were worse, it would make her feel even more hopeless. Angel then, very insightfully, suggested that she could instead just record times when the voices were better during the week.

When Angel returned the following week, she was keen to show the therapist her voice diary which, very helpfully, indicated that when Angel was watching certain television programmes, and when she was with her son, she barely heard the voices at all. This was a completely new insight for Angel and challenged her initial belief that the voices were there 100 per cent of the time. As a result of this, it was agreed that Angel could increase the amount of time spent watching television and being with her son. She increasingly noticed that the voices were less distressing and less frequent at these times. This produced new hope that there were times when things were a bit better and helped Angel feel more able to explore times when the voices were worse. Such exploration highlighted that the voices tended to be worse after Angel read the newspaper: it emerged that Angel was spending significant amounts of time scanning the newspapers for bad events which she believed she was responsible for (which was confirmed by the voices). Angel was reluctant not to read the newspapers at all as she was concerned that she would miss out on warnings about bad things happening. The therapist suggested that given that the same stories would be in the newspaper no matter how many times she re-read them, perhaps she only needed to read the paper once in the morning. Angel agreed to do this and said that she found it helpful to not feel the need to constantly check the newspapers throughout the day.

Introducing new strategies

Findings from the voice diaries provided Angel with the impetus to try new strategies; perhaps things could get better for her and perhaps she could build on the small periods of respite that she had gained. A session was spent going through a list of strategies that other voice hearers had found helpful from a set of coping cards (see Appendix 5). Angel was interested in the idea of singing to herself. Although she said she was too embarrassed to do this in session or with other people, she said that she would try this when she was at home alone. She said that although it did not completely drown out the voices, singing uplifting songs made her feel better which, she said, seemed to distract her from the voices. Angel also liked the idea of setting boundaries with the voices. Drawing on Angel's expertise as a mother, the therapist asked her how she had managed when her son was small, if, for example, she was busy and her son demanded that she play with him. Angel said that it was important to let her son know that she was busy but to give him a time when she would be free to play with him. The therapist suggested that perhaps Angel could try this strategy with the voices, for example, by saying 'I am busy now, I'll listen to you at 5 pm'. Angel was keen to try this but reported that in practise the voices did not listen to her or go away. In fact sometimes, it would make them even more relentless, which she felt made her anxious and exacerbated the voices still further. The therapist and Angel explored ways to overcome this: Angel had tried relaxation and breathing exercises in the past but as she had not found these helpful she was reluctant to try them again. Eventually, Angel and the therapist developed the idea of imagining herself in a protective impenetrable bubble in which she could not hear what the voices were saying. The therapist asked Angel to describe all the sensory qualities of this bubble: what she could see, hear, taste, smell and feel. Angel was then asked to practise generating this image as a homework task. Angel found this technique very helpful and while it did not work every time, there were times when she was able to envelop herself in the bubble and not listen to the voices.

Reframing control and raising doubts about power

The effective use of these strategies was used by the therapist to reinforce Angel's beliefs about her increasing control over the voices: Angel said that for the first time she actually felt that she had some control over them which she now rated as being 40 per cent (rather than 0 per cent). This finding enabled the therapist to introduce the possibility that perhaps the voices were losing some of their power over her: perhaps this new found strength within Angel was making them back down a bit. Although Angel said that she found this difficult to believe, she said that the increasing control that she had acquired generated an eagerness and a hope to examine this further.

Summary

In this chapter we described our approach to using CSE and how we use this to reframe and dispute beliefs about control and power at an early stage. We build on this work in subsequent chapters.

Chapter 3

CTCH Level 3

Socialising the client into the cognitive model and developing the formulation

In this chapter we describe the three key tasks of level 3 in CTCH, namely socialising the client into the model, developing and sharing the formulation (providing a further mechanism of teaching our cognitive model) and agreeing the beliefs to be targeted. Socialising the client into both our ABC and broader CTCH models (through the shared formulation process) are essential components of our approach regardless of which other levels are the focus of subsequent work or in which order they are addressed. As part of level 3 work we build upon the process of socialising clients into the model by agreeing the beliefs to be targeted in subsequent sessions.

Socialising the client into the ABC model

Generally clients do not separate their As from their Bs in the generation of their distress or problem behaviour. Most commonly problems are located at A: it is the voice or what the voice says, how often and how loudly they talk rather than the client's interpretation of it or beliefs about how they should respond, that are viewed as the problem. This represents an A-C model in cognitive terms. Relocating the problem at B is the key task here since it is these interpretations or beliefs that lead to distress and harmful behaviour. Understanding this opens the possibility of change and subsequently reduced distress and the need to comply. When beginning the process of socialising clients into our cognitive ABC model (as described in Chapter 1) their investment in maintaining their voice-related beliefs, and continuing to see them as facts, becomes readily apparent. For many, they will have heard (and believed) their voice(s) for many years; the voices are persistent and clients believe that they should listen to them either for guidance or to prevent harm to themselves or others. Clients will typically have evolved a mini theory of the world and their role within it in relation to an ongoing dialogue and relationship with their voices and potentially other unusual and distressing experiences and events.

Case example: Keith

Keith had heard his mother's voice for many years. When he was younger, he felt that she favoured his brother over him. He was emotionally and physically abused by both his mother and his father (who also sexually abused him). The voice of Keith's mother would regularly criticise him if he made a mistake or began to trust someone; she would shout and scream that it would not end well. She would also encourage him to attack other people, stating that they were talking about him and they were a threat to him. This led Keith to be constantly on edge when he went out; he scanned his social environment for any signs of threat and would threaten others before they could hurt him. He believed that what his mother said was indisputable, so he should listen to her and that this would keep him safe. However, this led to him getting into trouble with people and the police. He felt constantly under threat by his mother and described how she had dominated his life as a child and continued to do so now (in the form of a voice).

It was important in Keith's case to understand his reasons for listening to the voice of his mother, the impact this had upon him emotionally and how it influenced his behaviour, both positively and negatively (keeping him safe but also leading to him feeling threatened, afraid, and a risk to himself and others).

We never dispute the fact that the person hears voices or what they say, but rather whether what they say, or the client's interpretation of it, is true or indeed beneficial. The therapist may begin by exploring any doubts or uncertainties the client may have about their beliefs. The client may have adhered to what their voice wanted but now question the validity of what they were told.

The therapist's task may be summarised as guiding the client and helping them to explore how their beliefs (e.g. that the voice is powerful and *must* be obeyed) have developed and how they are the client's own beliefs about the voice. The ABC model is used to clarify each of the client's emotional and behavioural consequences along with which As and which Bs precede them. The therapist will have already gained a good sense of these during the assessment and engagement phases and can now draw upon this understanding to explore with the client their experiences and help create a shared understanding. This is critical if the client and therapist are to work together on a shared agenda and agree goals for change.

It is helpful to highlight the processes by which all human beings (including the therapist) make mistakes and sometimes draw the wrong conclusions. If possible the therapist can share their own experiences of instances when their own beliefs have proven incorrect. For example, thinking that their birthday had been forgotten when in fact a surprise party had been planned. It can also be helpful to examine the role physical stressors may play: we do not think as clearly when we are tired, if we are under stress or when we have consumed alcohol. All of these factors can influence how we think and how we process information.

Beliefs are not facts

An important step in the socialisation process is relocating the problem at B, how the beliefs function for the client and how they are the drivers of their distress and behaviour. Time should be spent exploring the idea that beliefs are different to facts, in that beliefs are not necessarily supported by irrefutable evidence. For example, the sun heats our planet is a fact, scientific evidence supports this and the vast majority of people would agree with this view. However, some people believe in ghosts, yet the evidence is less clear-cut here. Beliefs are informed by a variety of factors, such as the client's personal experiences, their normative culture, what they have learned through family and friends, and what they have learned from TV; all will inform their viewpoint.

Case example: Julie

When the idea of facts and beliefs was explored with Julie, she was able to generate examples of a fact and a belief. She stated that she had a partner called Matt who was currently employed. Julie stated that this was completely true: a fact. When she was asked to provide an example of a belief she suggested that the existence of God was a belief. The therapist explored with her the idea that many people believe that God exists, but that there were different views on the form that God took depending upon their religious doctrine. Julie also stated that some people were not sure if God exists and some were certain that there definitely was not a God. This led on to the therapist and Julie exploring the idea that many people will have a strong conviction that their view holds true. But how can everyone be right? It was concluded that these views are not facts but beliefs that are held very firmly. In some cases they can change over time (e.g. a born again Christian) but in others they remain constant.

Beliefs can change

It is likely that all clients will have some experience of changing their beliefs but may not be explicitly aware of or recognise that this process has happened. The therapist's task is, through the use of guided discovery, to elicit these examples. Periods of non-voice talk can be useful, since they not only enable the client to be seen as a person but also to gather information about their personal history, social network, and hobbies and interests. The client's own examples can be developed and explored with them. This can help to understand more fully the client's experiences of their voices and their relationship with them.

Case example: Desmond

Desmond described how he had heard what he thought at first to be the voice of Princess Diana but had come to realise that it could not be her because the sorts of things she said (e.g. that she would take away all of the food from starving children in Africa) were not in keeping with his knowledge of her. Desmond had also believed that Jimi Hendrix (whom he greatly admired) had been involved in various political conspiracies, but later after watching a documentary had concluded that this was just nonsense.

Other non-voice-related examples may be identified from clients. For many people, tastes in music change over time and their once favourite band might be replaced by another. Favourite foods change over time as do the places we once socialised which were perhaps considered to be *the* places. If the client is unable to generate any examples of when beliefs have changed, the therapist can provide examples of their own. Examples we routinely use are as follows:

- Centuries ago the majority of people believed the world to be flat. Subsequent exploration and now pictures of the earth from space show this is not true.
- Santa Claus brings you your presents at Christmas (if you have been good!).
- The Tooth Fairy takes your lost teeth from under your pillow and replaces them with money.

Benefits of beliefs over facts

Having introduced the notion of how facts and beliefs differ, the therapist can begin to explore whether there are advantages and disadvantages of maintaining or holding certain beliefs. Those who comply with their command hallucinations typically hold compliance beliefs: that they (or others they care about) will be harmed or shamed if they do not listen to and comply with what the voice commands. There may (from the client's perspective) be benefits as well as disadvantages to the compliance belief.

Case example: Veronica

In Veronica's case, her voices commanded her to harm herself by cutting her arm and her throat with a knife.

Advantages of holding and maintaining the compliance belief are the following:

1 It (the compliance belief) protects me from being harmed by the voice.
2 The voices become quieter (when acted upon).
3 The voices could really hurt me and my family.
4 The voices will shout more (if I disobey) and it is really scary.
5 The voices will go on and on and not stop unless I listen to them and do what they say.

Disadvantages of holding and maintaining the compliance belief are the following:

1 I will end up hurting myself.
2 I will add to the scars on my arms.
3 I will end up in hospital again.
4 My family will be very upset.
5 I cannot take control of my life.
6 I cannot build up my confidence.
7 The voice persists anyway – even if I do what they say, they just come back.

At this stage of therapy, it is not about directly challenging the beliefs which clients such as Veronica have developed but rather introducing the idea that alternate perspectives do exist and that there might be advantages to adopting a different view. In Veronica's case, there were more disadvantages to maintaining her belief. This helped to build motivation for change. Undertaking this exercise helped Veronica explore the short-term gains of harming herself and how this was short-lived. For her, if she resisted the voices and did not harm herself, she gained more control in the longer term.

Using the CTCH formulation to socialise the client into the ABC model

Once clients are on board with adopting a cognitive approach, work can proceed to socialising them into the ABC model. In practice this means 'selling' the cognitive model (Wells, 2003), educating the client regarding the links between thoughts, mood and behaviour. As Trower *et al.* (2010) note, the task of socialising the client into the cognitive ABC has to be handled with care, because it transfers emotional responsibility to the individual.

The therapist may draw on a number of useful analogies here, both general and voice specific, in order to illustrate the role of beliefs in emotional and behavioural processes. The following are three such examples:

Example 1:

> *Scenario (a)*
> Karen walks home at night through a subway. It is dark and she sees someone walking towards her. She thinks that this person is going to attack her. How is she feeling? What does she do?

> *Scenario (b)*
> Karen walks home at night through a subway. It is dark and she sees someone walking towards her. She thinks that this person is a friend coming to meet her. How is she feeling? What does she do?

Example 2:

> *Scenario (a)*
> David hears a noise in the night. He thinks that a burglar must be breaking in. How does he feel? What does he do?

> *Scenario (b)*
> David hears a noise in the night. He thinks that it is his cat coming in through the cat flap. How does he feel? What does he do?

Example 3:

> *Scenario (a)*
> Tom hears a voice say 'you are on your way'. He thinks that the voice is going to kill him. How does he feel? What does he do?

> *Scenario (b)*
> Tom hears a voice say 'you are on your way'. He thinks that he is on the way to great things. How does he feel? What does he do?

The ABC model can be used with the client to explore the various elements of the above scenarios and show how the same A can result in different responses (emotionally and behaviourally) depending upon their appraisal of it at B. The client can be invited to suggest some of their own conclusions and how they might go about testing them out.

Developing and sharing the formulation: socialising the client into the CTCH model

The preceding steps are aimed at exploring with the client the value of viewing their problems in ABC terms and the benefits of adopting a cognitive model. The ABC formulation is a powerful tool capable of expressing and distilling most aspects of the client's psychotic concerns, distress and behaviour. These are brought together in the CTCH formulation. Initially this may be in a simplified ABC form (as shown in Figure 3.1 for Angel) to highlight how power beliefs in general may impact upon how the client feels and behaves. As the sessions progress, the therapist can incorporate the other relevant beliefs (e.g. control, compliance, omnipotence, omniscience, identity, meaning and purpose).

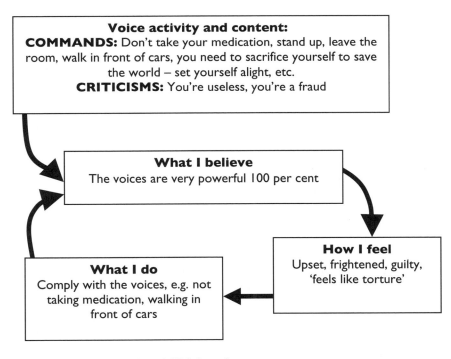

Voice activity and content:
COMMANDS: Don't take your medication, stand up, leave the room, walk in front of cars, you need to sacrifice yourself to save the world – set yourself alight, etc.
CRITICISMS: You're useless, you're a fraud

What I believe
The voices are very powerful 100 per cent

How I feel
Upset, frightened, guilty, 'feels like torture'

What I do
Comply with the voices, e.g. not taking medication, walking in front of cars

Figure 3.1 Angel's initial shared ABC formulation

An important step in the process of developing a formulation is working alongside the client to explore and uncover what beliefs exist and identify their function. Formulation has been defined by Kuyken *et al.* (2007, p. 3) as:

> . . . a process whereby therapist and client work collaboratively first to describe and then to explain the issues a client presents in therapy. Its primary function is to guide therapy in order to relieve client distress and build client resilience.

A formulation helps the client to understand the links between what they are told, what they believe and how it can impact on their mood and behaviour. The process of constructing a formulation in CTCH involves separating out the various As, Bs and Cs, mindful of the fact that there may be several As (e.g. objectively innocuous comments, derogatory comments, commands to harm self, commands to harm others) which may in turn activate different or the same Bs (different beliefs within the power schema). Each of these may constitute separate initial ABC formulations. These are ideally shared with clients as a further strategy for socialising them into the cognitive model. Formulation also serves to guide treatment, provide a structure, look at functional links between different elements, test hypotheses, help motivate and promote hope for the future (Townend and Grant, 2008).

Evidence for formulation

As discussed in Chapter 1, there is good research evidence to support the utility of the ABC model and adopting a social rank approach in the reduction of distress and compliance behaviours. However, considerable debate exists regarding the validity and reliability of formulations more generally, and key questions remain:

1 Are they useful to both the client and therapist?
2 Do they help change take place?
3 Can therapists agree on what should be included in each formulation?

Chadwick *et al.* (2003) have noted that clients themselves appear ambivalent about the process of formulation and it is therapists who find formulations most useful. Clients on the other hand have reported having a better understanding of their problems than therapists do (Zuber, 2000). A number of investigators (Persons *et al.*, 1995; Eells *et al.*, 1998; Persons and Bertagnolli, 1999; Flitcroft *et al.*, 2007) have all identified that, to a certain extent, clinicians find it easier to agree on specific here and now problems, but find it more difficult agreeing on deeper beliefs that the client might hold. Specific frameworks for improving the quality of formulations have been developed (Mumma, 1998; Fotherill and Kuyken, 2005). Our template reflects our model (as described in the introduction and as illustrated in our two main case studies below) and incorporates its key elements. This provides consistency and ties our formulation to the evidence base.

Formulation can also serve as a map that informs the client and therapist about the client's past, present and future. Persons *et al.* (1991) propose that the formulation itself might not bring about change but the process that occurs when it is constructed and developed does help change emerge. During this process, the client and therapist can develop a therapeutic alliance, gain understanding and foster self-efficacy. In CTCH, this is also part of the process of addressing the inherent power imbalance in the therapeutic relationship. It is first and foremost a collaborative venture in which the therapist shares their knowledge of CBT and their scientific understanding of voices, while the client shares their expertise of living with voices as it uniquely affects them. As in all levels of CTCH, the therapeutic relationship remains central to all activity even when more didactic methods are employed. Norcross (2000) proposes that this is the most important factor over and above any specific interventions.

Using formulation throughout CTCH

In CTCH, other formulations are sometimes adopted in order to map specific aspects of client's difficulties (as shown in subsequent chapters) or as a means of sharing key aspects of the broader CTCH formulation if the whole formulation seems overwhelming. Kinderman and Lobban (2000) suggest that formulations evolve over time with more complex layers added as new information emerges, adding greater depth and informational content. In the fostering of engagement, Freeman and Garety (2006) have suggested how it is important to work within the client's frame of reference, not going 'too fast too soon' sticking to the 'here and now' before relating the client's experiences to past events. Some clients may want to discuss and explore past events from the outset of therapy and it is important to consider the benefits of doing so. While this may help with fostering a good relationship and keeping the client engaged, it has the potential to overwhelm the client with past trauma which in turn may exacerbate their voices before effective coping strategies are in place. The therapist must be mindful of this and be open and honest about the potential pitfalls of going too quickly.

Judgments may also need to be made about the impact of sharing all of the formulation too early. The therapist may hypothesise or uncover core beliefs (dominate–subordinate schemas, negative self or person evaluations, interpersonal rules or dysfunctional assumptions) which may form the focus of later work (Chapters 7 and 8). This part of the formulation may be kept back until the links are uncovered in the therapeutic process and the relationship of core beliefs to psychotic experiences more clearly established.

The process of reformulation continues throughout CTCH as new information becomes available and ideas are revised. Reformulation can also be used to demonstrate change to the client (see Figures 8.6 and 8.8). The process of formulation is illustrated in our two main case studies below.

Agreeing the beliefs to be targeted and setting initial therapy goals

Once the therapist and client have arrived at a shared understanding of the client's beliefs and the functional role they play in their distress and behaviour, the next task is to agree which ones should be targeted first. Prior to this level of therapy, the therapist and client will have worked together to develop a set of effective coping strategies in order to gain some control over the voice(s). In this sense, control beliefs are the first target. Subsequent beliefs to be targeted can be agreed using a number of methods. One approach is to rate the degree to which the client holds their belief to be true using a 0–100 scale (not at all convinced to completely convinced). This helps to determine the conviction with which the belief is held as well as offers opportunities to explore what has led to any doubts about the belief, providing support for the notion that beliefs are open to change. Some clients find it difficult to provide a verbal percentage rating of their conviction. In these instances a visual analogue scale can be drawn out, representing the two poles: 'it is false' to 'it is true'. The client is asked to indicate with a cross where they see their belief falling.

A next useful stage is to identify all of the pieces of evidence that support the client's belief and rank order them in terms of least to most convincing. Some useful questions are detailed below:

- Content: what do the voices actually say?
- How do the voices control the person: shouting at them, making threats, controlling their emotions, being able to physically manipulate them (producing somatic symptoms)?
- What gives the voice(s) its power: their frequency, volume, content, other voice beliefs? *Examining the dimensions of the VPDS described in Chapter 1 can also be useful here.*
- Identity (e.g. God, the Devil, bullies or abusers from the past): what makes you think it is X (the way they sound, what they say, claims they make about themselves)? *The cultural significance of such beliefs should also be considered.*
- What makes the voice omniscient: what do they see and know about? What have they predicted and have these predictions come true?
- Does their advice seem sound?
- What makes the voice omnipotent (what can they do/claim to have done)?

- Why must the client comply (either with what the voice directly commands or with what they believe are its wishes)?
- Are there any other hallucinatory experiences that support voice beliefs: seeing the voice (possibly in human form), experiencing bodily sensations?

Of course, belief conviction is not the only factor to consider when agreeing beliefs to be targeted. Brett-Jones *et al.* (1987) have usefully devised a system for rating beliefs across a number of dimensions (including conviction), which may be considered:

- interference (with daily functioning);
- preoccupation (time spent thinking about the belief);
- response to hypothetical contradiction (openness to considering alternative explanations and testing out beliefs).

Some beliefs may also hold greater emotional attachment for clients and may clearly link to more readily to their core beliefs: believing that punishment (a purpose belief) is justified because the person is bad (a negative self or person evaluation). These beliefs may warrant early attention since they may work against change because change would involve working against a moral imperative for the client. Alternatively, these beliefs may be too difficult to address early on for the client, and gaining a sense of control and creating some doubt about other beliefs may reduce the client's distress sufficiently for them to be able to work on such beliefs which often link to past trauma (a point we return to in Chapters 7 and 8) or other difficult experiences.

The aim of this preparatory work is to establish which beliefs are likely to respond most readily to subsequent cognitive therapy, reducing resistance and building motivation (for the therapist and client) for further change. We have termed this the *weakest first principle* (Meaden *et al.*, 2010) and employ it routinely throughout CTCH.

Clarifying the use of safety behaviours

The ABC model helps to tie together the beliefs that the client holds and the emotional and behavioural consequences they lead to. These behaviours we classify as types of safety behaviour:

- full compliance (e.g. taking an overdose of paracetamol);
- partial compliance (e.g. putting paracetamol tablets on the kitchen table ready to take);
- appeasement (promising to buy paracetamol later that day);
- threat mitigation (e.g. not keeping paracetamol in the house, avoiding walking or going past shops selling them).

All of these behaviours serve to keep the person safe (from the voice or the consequences of full compliance with it) but also prevent disconfirmation of voice beliefs (see Chapter 5).

For each individual some safety behaviours will be easier to drop than others. The consequences of not carrying out each safety behaviour will need to be explored. An intervention hierarchy can later be agreed and constructed to target behaviours which the client feels will cause least distress or have fewest adverse consequences if not carried out (see Chapter 5). Clarifying with the client how each behaviour works for them in the context of sharing and agreeing the formulation at this early stage is useful preparatory work. Clients will usually be concerned or distressed about having to engage in the behaviour (leading to a further ABC) and will want to stop. By implication coming to view their problems in ABC terms, the possibility can also be raised that the client's safety behaviour may not be necessary.

Tackling difficulties, socialising clients into CTCH and sharing the formulation

Of course, not all of our clients are readily socialised into CTCH and different strategies will need to be adopted. Several sessions may be needed, and the therapist must be vigilant to look for examples from the client that offer opportunities to highlight the benefits or application of the model. Instances where voices have made false predictions or claims can be very useful. These can be explored and highlighted as not being facts. New information may have emerged that disputes their claims and this might help explore different interpretations of the voice's true power.

ABC formulations from each type of A or content (derogatory comments, ambiguous comments, advice, criticisms, insults and commands) may be shared rather than the whole CTCH template (as shown in Figure 3.1 for Angel). Voice beliefs that are perceived as less important or less strongly held may be the focus of these ABC formulations for which the client may be more open to considering an alternative to their A-C model.

Case example: Ronald

Ronald rejected attempts to socialise him into the CTCH model. As well as hearing them, he saw his voices in ghostly form making them more compelling. They continued to be very distressing and he had tried to hang himself on a number of occasions and cut his throat in response to their commands. Level 2 work was helpful and demonstrated to Ronald that he could take some control back, highlighting that this was a belief and not a fact. An ABC of his control beliefs was formulated before and after coping strategy work and he acknowledged feeling more hopeful.

Case example: Trisha

Trisha's voice often commented on what she was doing. Exploring this with the therapist, she noted that the voice sometimes said things that were inaccurate at such times. Her voice would often say – 'she's going to make tea', when in fact she was getting up to do some other domestic chore. This was reframed in ABC terms.

In some cases, resistance to working at level 3 may be less obvious. Clients may passively resist, appearing to go along with the therapist's attempts to propose the model. Time should always be taken to clarify with the client that they understand the model and can give their own examples. The client's cognitive abilities and any negative symptoms may also need to be considered. The provision of written materials may also be useful here.

Case example: Tyler

Tyler initially appeared receptive to the notion of the ABC model but could not describe it back to the therapist and how it might apply or work for him. At the beginning of each subsequent session, Tyler recalled little of the content of the previous session. He, however, remained distressed by his voices and would seldom leave his flat (a threat mitigation strategy). Level 2 work (Chapter 2) provided a more consistent focus and Tyler appeared to be able to put some new coping strategies in place. However, work did not progress to further stages since Tyler was not receptive to interventions aimed at belief change.

In other cases, clients may be so distressed and in the grip of their voices that any attempt to relocate the problem at B is too difficult. Others may actually welcome the experience and not be motivated to engage in exploring such alternative ways of viewing their difficulties despite acting in harmful ways.

Case example: Anna

Anna rejected the ABC model. She believed that her voice (George Michael) would reward her for obeying his commands, even though these appeared at odds with George Michael's public image. George promised her money and a fine house once they were married, but this could only be achieved if she was in heaven (even though George Michael was still alive). She, therefore, had to harm and eventually kill herself. Anna's voices had warned her about the therapist and that he was trying to 'split them up'. The voice would not be dissuaded from this point of view by the therapist's messages (see Chapter 2). At this point Anna disengaged from therapy. Monitoring and supervision of Anna and her ongoing risk behaviours were suggested to the team as an alternative strategy. Anna, however, disengaged from the team too. It became increasingly difficult to monitor her and she subsequently poured petrol over herself and set herself alight. She suffered third degree burns and is now an inpatient in a rehabilitation service.

Training the inner detective

Building on the process of socialisation and formulation, a useful next step (in preparation of level 4 work) is to train the inner detective. As part of exploring with the client a different view of what is happening, the therapist might suggest that the client adopts the persona of a fictional detective. The client, in collaboration with the therapist, is invited to collect evidence in support of the voice and alternative (less distressing) beliefs. It is useful to agree which detective the client identifies with: Sherlock Holmes, Miss Marple, Poirot, Morse, Columbo, etc. What do they like about them? Why is their approach so effective? Columbo can be an excellent example not only for his tentative manner when questioning but also for the way in which he attends to small inconsistencies. Evidence is collected and analysed following the scientific method and that of the chosen investigator. Logic is applied (as used frequently by both Holmes and Poirot) along with the motives of the voice(s), the consistency of their commands and whether other possible explanations could equally apply.

Case example: Desmond

Desmond noted that his voices had claimed that Princess Diana was involved in starting the Suez crisis. The lack of supporting evidence for this was quickly revealed from a trip to the local library: Desmond discovered that the Suez Crises began on 29 October 1956 before Princess Diana was born, which was 1 July 1961.

It is important to consider cognitive biases when training the inner detective. The most convincing empirical evidence is that a significant proportion of individuals with psychosis are hasty in their data gathering (e.g. they jump to conclusions) which may lead to the rapid acceptance of beliefs even if there is limited evidence to support them (Fine *et al.*, 2007). Findings from studies also indicate that individuals with psychosis have belief inflexibility: difficulties reflecting on their beliefs and in being able to consider alternatives (Freeman *et al.*, 2004). In addition, clients may interpret events as having personal meaning in line with their core beliefs.

Case example: Chris

Chris constantly monitored his environment for signs (e.g. newspaper articles) of tragic events which his voice told him were due to him. For Chris, this just confirmed what he already believed: 'he was bad'. He reported other daily instances: noticing a penny on the pavement and immediately interpreting this as the sign of 'a bed penny turning up'. Chris roundly rejected any alternative explanations for these events.

For clients such as Chris a different approach may be taken: focusing initially on highlighting belief inconsistencies or targeting core beliefs (as discussed in Chapter 8) earlier on.

Level 3 work with Peter and Angel

Peter

Socialising Peter into the ABC model

The ABC model shared with Peter was a way of understanding the links between what the voice told him, how he appraised what he was told and the impact this had on how he felt and his subsequent behaviour. For example, when Peter was told that he was useless and that he should hang himself, he began to think 'she's right, she knows what she is on about'. The voice he heard was persistent, knew things about him and he consequently believed she was right. He would become scared, depressed and angry. When he was most vulnerable, he contemplated acting on what the voice had told him to do. Previously he had cut and burnt his arms. On one occasion he bought items in order to carry out his plan to hang himself. Fortuitously a friend visited him and his plan was interrupted. This led to a great deal of criticism and guilt, criticism of himself and why he listened to the voice, and guilt that he had contemplated doing what she wanted and leave friends behind.

BELIEFS ARE NOT FACTS

At this stage it was important to understand the content of the voices and how Peter appraised them, relocating the problem at B. For example, when he was told he was useless, Peter recounted that the voice knew about his past and the difficulties he had encountered. The voice, therefore, seemed very knowledgeable (omniscient). She was right and he was useless, and this was validated by events that had already taken place. Peter treated what he was told as if it were a fact and not open to question.

Peter would feel ashamed at these times and tended to isolate himself from friends and family. This exacerbated his low mood, creating a maintenance cycle. The more he was told to isolate himself, the lower his mood became and the less control he seemed to have.

When the voice told him to cut himself, Peter would listen because he believed she would go on and on and he would not, he believed, be able to cope (the compliance belief). She would also threaten him, and he wanted to avoid punishment (a further compliance belief). This led to him feeling frightened and low, and this would increase the chances that he would go on to harm himself.

At this point the therapist explored the idea that although Peter believed what he was being told, it might be helpful to consider what were facts and what were beliefs. It was important to explore the difference between these two ideas and how each might lead to different responses.

BELIEFS CAN CHANGE

During the sessions, Peter revealed a great deal of guilt and shame regarding a number of aspects of his life, including the loss of his job, his bankruptcy, developing mental health problems, difficulties in his relationship and a friend killing himself. All provided fuel to support his view that he should have done more to protect himself and that he had let others down. Over time it was possible to explore the role of how Peter might tended to see things in black and white terms (you either have no mental health problems or can't function at all because of them) and how he perceived that he was personally responsibly for all that had happened. It was also possible to introduce the concept of catastrophising and how this process might perpetuate Peter's view that although he had experienced difficulties in his life, his negative predictions about his future might not necessarily be true. Peter found the introduction of these thinking errors (Powell, 2009) very helpful and it provided him with opportunities to assess his thinking style, gather more information and break certain patterns.

There seemed to be a dual relationship between what the voices told Peter and what he believed. He would strive for things to be perfect or would believe that nothing would work out and that the future was bleak. It was agreed therefore that part of the assessment and formulation process was to explore some of Peter's thinking errors more generally, look at the evidence for them and introduce the notion of including these as part of his therapeutic goals. Like his beliefs about his voices, it was proposed that these beliefs were also open to change. It was highlighted how, for instance, while he currently believed that things were bleak and viewed himself negatively, when he was working, earning money and had better mental health he viewed himself more positively. These views of himself and the future were therefore not fixed in stone and it did not follow that he would always see himself in this way.

BENEFITS OF BELIEFS OVER FACTS

Peter and the therapist subsequently explored the different types of thinking errors he was prone to and the value and limitation of holding these and his beliefs about his voice. For example, Peter believed that his voice was very knowledgeable and this led him to listen to her a great deal. There were advantages and disadvantages to holding this view and these were subsequently explored. The therapist noted that treating what the voice said as a fact had become a habit that was difficult to break as she was so convincing, and it was less distressing than challenging her. On the other hand, there might be value to treating what she said as a belief; if it was a belief it was not fixed and an alternate view could be developed.

Developing and sharing the formulation with Peter

Having socialised Peter into the cognitive model and the idea that beliefs are not facts and can change, the therapist collaboratively developed the initial CTCH formulation (shown in Figure 3.2). Peter and the therapist were able together to gather a detailed description of his beliefs and the impact these had on him. Core beliefs and power schemas were held back and introduced in later sessions as part of the reformulation process. Peter found the ABC model a valuable tool that helped him better understand the links between what the voices told him, the role of beliefs and how these led to distress and self-harm behaviours. In some instances, Peter would comply with commands and directly harm himself. In other instances, he tended to appease the voice or isolated himself. As a result, Peter felt subordinate and powerless.

Agreeing the beliefs to be targeted and setting initial therapy goals

At this stage, Peter and the therapist began to explore any doubts he had about his voices and how he might assess in more detail her claims and make changes in his life. All his beliefs (as shown in Figure 3.2) were written down and rated in terms of his degree of conviction in them. It was agreed that a key belief to target initially was the voice's omniscience. Peter's voice said a lot of derogatory things about him: that he was no good and useless. This made him feel down and led to a spiral of low mood, reduced activity and social isolation and self-harm. If, however, the voice was not so all seeing and all knowing, it was suggested this would mean that he did not have to believe everything she said.

Training Peter's inner detective

Once the idea of thinking errors and the advantages and disadvantages of holding beliefs had been examined, Peter and the therapist began to discuss how he could assess the evidence for his beliefs. In the past he had always been vigilant for information that validated what the voice told him. Becoming the detective promoted the idea that he should be on the look out for information that refuted what she said. This was valuable information which would allow him to take control back. As a first step it was suggested that he could start to collect evidence from events past and present regarding predictions that his voice had made (omniscience beliefs).

Angel

Socialising Angel into the ABC model

In the third session, Angel arrived looking very distressed. She explained that her phone at work had not rung for 2 days and she believed that this was

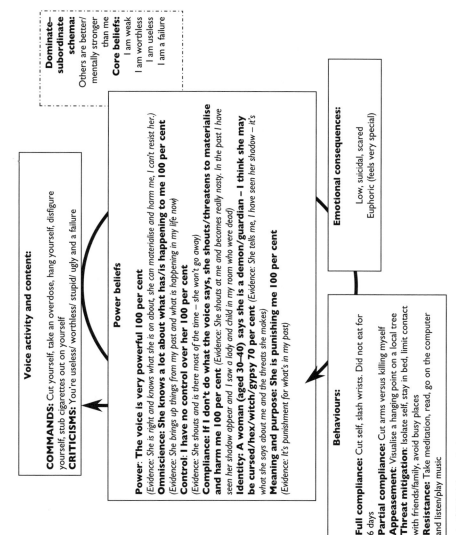

Dominate–subordinate schema:
Others are better/ mentally stronger than me

Core beliefs:
I am weak
I am worthless
I am useless
I am a failure

Voice activity and content:

COMMANDS: Cut yourself, take an overdose, hang yourself, disfigure yourself, stub cigarettes out on yourself
CRITICISMS: You're useless/ worthless/ stupid/ ugly and a failure

Power beliefs

Power: The voice is very powerful 100 per cent
(Evidence: She is right and knows what she is on about, she can materialise and harm me, I can't resist her.)
Omniscience: She knows a lot about what has/is happening to me 100 per cent
(Evidence: She brings up things from my past and what is happening in my life now)
Control: I have no control over her 100 per cent
(Evidence: She shouts and is there most of the time – she won't go away)
Compliance: If I don't do what the voice says, she shouts/threatens to materialise and harm me 100 per cent *(Evidence: She shouts at me and becomes really nasty. In the past I have seen her shadow appear and I saw a lady and child in my room who were dead)*
Identity: A woman (aged 30–40) says she is a demon/guardian – I think she may be cursed/hex/witch/gypsy 70 per cent *(Evidence: She tells me, I have seen her shadow – it's what she says about me and the threats she makes)*
Meaning and purpose: She is punishing me 100 per cent
(Evidence: It's punishment for what's in my past)

Emotional consequences:

Low, suicidal, scared
Euphoric (feels very special)

Behaviours:

Full compliance: Cut self, slash wrists. Did not eat for 6 days
Partial compliance: Cut arms versus killing myself
Appeasement: Visualise a hanging point on a local tree
Threat mitigation: Isolate self, stay in bed, limit contact with friends/family, avoid busy places
Resistance: Take meditation, read, go on the computer and listen/play music

Figure 3.2 Peter's CTCH formulation

because she was not doing her job properly and that people did not like her. Seizing this opportunity, the therapist explored the reasons for this in ABC terms, examining the various reasons for why the telephone might not have rung. Angel, however, said that she remained 100 per cent convinced that the phone had not rung because she was not doing her job properly and was not liked. The following week, Angel arrived at the session looking a little more upbeat than the previous session. The therapist explored the reasons for this:

Angel: I found out that the reason the phone had not rung was because it was broken and so the ringer was not working.

NK: Okay. Can you tell me a bit more about it?

Angel: Well when I looked on the answering machine, I realised that there were some messages that I had not picked up. When I looked into it, I found out that the ringer on the phone was actually broken.

NK: And how has that made you feel about the situation?

Angel: Well, I feel much better. At least it isn't because I've done something wrong and people don't like me anymore.

NK: Well, that's interesting. Isn't it? Because if I remember rightly, you were pretty sure that that was the reason the phone hadn't rung last week, weren't you?

Angel: Yes, I was. Totally convinced.

NK: And if I was to ask you how much you believe that now, what would you say?

Angel: Well, I don't believe it at all anymore because I've found out the phone was broken.

NK: Mmmm, I wonder what that might tell us about the beliefs that we hold?

Angel: Well, I guess sometimes we can get things wrong and sometimes our beliefs about things might change, even if we are really sure about it.

NK: Yes, and it sounds as if this new information has changed not only your belief, but also how you feel about the phone not ringing?

Angel: Completely. I don't feel as bad or guilty anymore . . . like I must have done something wrong. All I need to do is get a new phone (smiling).

NK: I wonder what that might tell us about how different beliefs might change the way we feel?

Angel: Well, I guess it shows that we might not feel so upset if we believe something different.

This experience was subsequently reframed by the therapist in ABC terms in order to socialise Angel into the cognitive model.

BELIEFS ARE NOT FACTS

In the above example, Angel herself had clearly shown how beliefs are different to facts (and can therefore change) and can sometimes be wrong. It was further proposed that beliefs can also change over time, such as beliefs about Santa Claus and the Tooth Fairy. The therapist shared her experience as a child being awoken by her mum in the night trying to delicately exchange a baby tooth left under her pillow for a fifty pence piece. Needless to say, this was the end of the therapist's belief in the Tooth Fairy! Drawing upon this, the therapist tentatively queried whether Angel had any doubts about the beliefs she held about the voices. Angel said that she would like to believe that the voices were not real but that she could never envisage that happening. The therapist introduced the idea of doing a cost/benefit analysis of Angel's beliefs about the voices being true and false. This was a particularly helpful strategy because it highlighted that although Angel found the voices very distressing, and said that she would rather believe that they were part of an illness (rather than because she had been chosen by God), a big 'cost' if she were to find out that her beliefs were false was that it would take away her sense of being special. In view of this, the therapist reassured Angel that she was not questioning Angel's beliefs in whether the voices existed but rather her beliefs in how *powerful* the voices were and therefore whether Angel *must* always comply with their commands. In making this suggestion, the therapist was able to draw upon earlier incidences of when the voices had made mistakes, for example, when they had incorrectly told Angel that she would be sectioned if she came to the session; the therapist referred back to a bully analogy previously used to illustrate what might be happening:

NK: Given that we've already said they are a bit like bullies, I'm just wondering if, like bullies, they might be making out they are more powerful than they really are?

Developing and sharing the formulation with Angel

Having socialised Angel into the cognitive model, along with the idea that beliefs are not facts and can change, the therapist and Angel collaboratively developed the initial CTCH formulation (as shown in Figure 3.3). Beliefs, affect and behaviour were revised accordingly during this process leaving to one side core beliefs and power schemas (these being introduced in later sessions as part of the reformulation process discussed in Chapter 8). Safety behaviours were carefully broken down into full compliance, appeasement or partial compliance and threat mitigation. Angel said that she found drawing out the formulation together very informative. Drawing on earlier discussions about the role of beliefs, it was suggested to Angel that it was her beliefs about the voices that were driving the distress that she felt and her subsequent

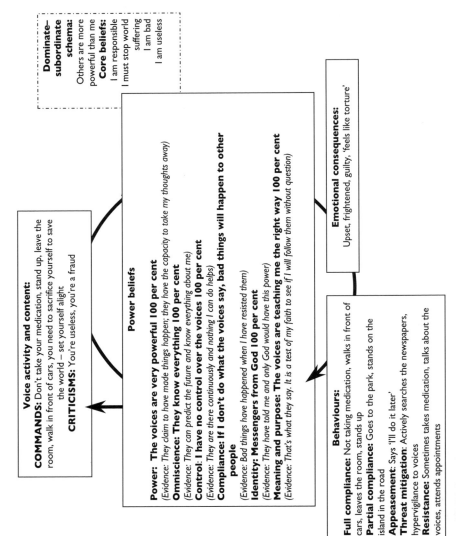

Dominate–subordinate schema:
Others are more powerful than me
Core beliefs:
I am responsible
I must stop world suffering
I am bad
I am useless

Voice activity and content:
COMMANDS: Don't take your medication, stand up, leave the room, walk in front of cars, you need to sacrifice yourself to save the world – set yourself alight
CRITICISMS: You're useless, you're a fraud

Power beliefs

Power: The voices are very powerful 100 per cent
(Evidence: They claim to have made things happen; they have the capacity to take my thoughts away)
Omniscience: They know everything 100 per cent
(Evidence: They can predict the future and know everything about me)
Control: I have no control over the voices 100 per cent
(Evidence: They are there continuously and nothing I can do helps)
Compliance: If I don't do what the voices say, bad things will happen to other people
(Evidence: Bad things have happened when I have resisted them)
Identity: Messengers from God 100 per cent
(Evidence: They have told me and only God would have this power)
Meaning and purpose: The voices are teaching me the right way 100 per cent
(Evidence: That's what they say. It is a test of my faith to see if I will follow them without question)

Emotional consequences:
Upset, frightened, guilty, 'feels like torture'

Behaviours:
Full compliance: Not taking medication, walks in front of cars, leaves the room, stands up
Partial compliance: Goes to the park, stands on the island in the road
Appeasement: Says 'I'll do it later'
Threat mitigation: Actively searches the newspapers, hypervigilance to voices
Resistance: Sometimes takes medication, talks about the voices, attends appointments

Figure 3.3 Angel's CTCH formulation

compliance with them. Although Angel felt cautious about examining her beliefs, she expressed feeling hopeful that things could improve.

Agreeing the beliefs to be targeted and setting initial therapy goals

Following work at level 2, there had already been a shift in Angel's control beliefs:

Old belief: I have no control (0 per cent) over the voices.
New belief: I can gain some control (40 per cent) over the voices by using my coping strategies.

It was agreed that it would now be a good point at which to begin examining the following two beliefs held by Angel about her voices in the context of the evidence she used to support them:

1   The voices are 100 per cent powerful (omnipotence).
     Evidence:
     i.   They claim to have made things happen: the Tsunami, 9/11 and the deaths of family members.
     ii.   They have made correct predictions about bad things happening.
     iii. They have told me that they are God's messengers teaching me the 'right way'.
     iv.   They have the capacity to take my thoughts away.
2.   If I don't do what the voices say, bad things will happen to other people (compliance).
     Evidence:
     i.   Bad things have happened when I have resisted them.

Training Angel's inner detective

Once the idea that beliefs can change had been suggested, the therapist introduced Angel to the concept of thinking errors, in particular the role of the 'confirmation bias' and how this may prejudice and distort the way in which we perceive, select and store information. It was suggested that to overcome this it might be helpful to adopt a more detective-like approach in which one looks for unbiased 'hard evidence'. Angel said that she liked Miss Marple because most of the other detectives on TV were always men. Consequently, it was agreed that Angel would try to look through the eyes of Miss Marple and when situations arose she would ask herself:

What's the evidence for that?
What's the evidence against that?
What conclusions would Miss Marple's draw about that?

These questions were typed onto a pocket-sized coping card that Angel could keep in her purse or pocket.

Summary

In this chapter we have provided an overview of the process of formulation in CTCH and how we socialise clients into our cognitive therapy model. Level 3 work sets out the foundations for a deeper exploration of the client's belief system and opens up the possibility that all the evidence might not fit; other perspectives can be taken and these can hold out hope that the dominant relationship the voices currently hold does not have to remain this way. The culmination of this phase of CTCH is to lead the therapist and client into disputing and reframing agreed aspects of the client's voice-power schema to which we now turn in Chapter 4.

CTCH Level 4

Reframing and disputing power, omniscience and compliance beliefs

In this chapter we describe our key strategies for reframing and disputing power beliefs, showing how we have incorporated and adapted general CBT principles as well as REBT principles into our approach. It should now be clear that our focus is on disturbance at C: voice-related distress and harmful compliance behaviour. In Chapter 3 we showed how the client can be socialised and motivated to engage in CTCH and which beliefs might be targeted first. In level 4 we suggest that the next step in deconstructing the power relationship is to focus on beliefs about power, omniscience and the need to comply. The overall aim of this phase of CTCH is to address the perceived power imbalance which underpins compliance and distress. The aim is to reduce the perceived power of the voice and weaken the conviction that the client is being and will be punished or harmed. Successful change here shifts the power balance and enables clients to act against the voice-power schema.

Belief change strategies in CTCH

From our experience of CTCH over a number of years, we have acquired insights into the ways in which voices maintain their power over clients. We aim to share these insights with the client. We know for instance that voices tell lies, are fallible, make exaggerated claims and rarely are able to deliver on their threats. Didactic disputation strategies involve the use of mini lectures, analogies and parables (Walen *et al.*, 1992) and can be used to teach the client these insights. At other times we employ the Socratic method, exploring and questioning the client regarding their beliefs about their voices and promoting alternative perspectives which are more helpful to them (e.g. 'my voice's predictions are always right' to 'my voice sometimes gets things wrong'). At different times and at different stages of CTCH, both of these methods can be useful tools, skilfully mixed by the therapist to dispute power beliefs. Wells (2003) proposes that Socratic dialogue is about asking a variety of questions and providing summary statements for the client. Padesky (1993) outlines four components in the Socratic dialogue process:

1   asking informational questions;
2   listening;
3   summarising;
4   using synthesising or analysing questions.

The Socratic approach aims to ask questions that the client is able to answer, it is goal driven and questions are phrased so that they open up the subject area, a gentle questioning style is adopted, and the therapist is inquisitive and genuine. This questioning style can help to explore the content and meaning of the client's experiences and promotes understanding; this in itself can potentially lead to gradual cognitive, emotional and behavioural change.

Padesky (1993) suggests that guided discovery is about going on a journey with the client. It is about the process of exploring and guiding the client to discover information along the way. She suggests that the process involves gathering data, examining information from a variety of perspectives and seeing how the client can use this new information to plan ahead.

In CTCH, the therapist draws upon the client's own doubt (past or present) about the validity of their voice beliefs, any contradictory evidence and behaviour (e.g. acting against the voice's wishes without consequence) along with any emerging questions the client raises regarding the possibility that their beliefs may be wrong. Typically we:

- begin by exploring the origin or source of the belief
  How did you figure this out?
  What led you to this belief? How did you discover this?

- tentatively and sensitively seek clarification
  Are you saying that your voice never gets things wrong?

- review, list and critically examine support for the beliefs, including the reasons and evidence for the belief obtained from level 3 work
  It sounds like my abuser (identity).
  I can't start or stop it (control).
  It knows all my secrets (omniscience).

- develop and critically examine the implications and consequences of the belief
  So you believe that unless you do what the voice says, you and your family will be harmed?

- seek and fairly examine conflicting views (alternative points of view)
  So sometimes you can ignore it and choose not to listen (disputing control)?

The *weakest first principle* is our starting point. Having carefully elicited all of the supporting evidence in level 3, we begin the process of eliciting disconfirmatory evidence. This can be built up from anything the client has noticed in the past that seems to be inconsistent with what the voices have said, made predictions about or claimed responsibility for. Using the inner detective, clients are encouraged to collect new evidence of mistakes, fallibility, lies, false claims, unmet threats and inconsistencies.

Highlighting inconsistencies

Inconsistencies are nearly always apparent when clients' belief systems are explored. Highlighting these is a gentle form of cognitive challenge that begins the process of weakening conviction, while allowing the therapist to *back off* if strong resistance is encountered, in order to maintain and not threaten the therapeutic alliance. Common inconsistencies we have encountered are as follows:

- Voices will sometimes tell the client that they are no good, yet also tell them that they are special.
- Voices may have a special purpose in mind for the client (e.g. saving the world) but their commands work against this end (e.g. asking the client to deny themselves food, leaving them too weak to save the world).
- Typically, voices will make mistakes about real events (they of course only know as much as the client knows) and may get the dates of events or details wrong.

The client might be aware of such inconsistencies and bring them up in sessions. However, in other instances the therapist may need to elicit these through guided discovery or Socratic dialogue. The client can be encouraged to reflect on these.

Case example: Nigel

Nigel believed much of what his voices told him; however, he did notice that they sometimes got things wrong. For example, they would tell him the result of a football match and Nigel knew that the information they were telling him was incorrect. They would also say that he was useless, worthless and no one liked him, yet they would also tell him he was special and had special powers. He was unsure himself how these worked together. Over a number of sessions, Nigel and the therapist discovered other instances where they would tell him inconsistent and contradictory information. Together Nigel and the therapist were able to explore some of the possible reasons why the voices might be behaving in this way. Perhaps they did not know everything after all. Maybe they were actually trying to take control by dominating him through making themselves look omniscient. Nigel and the therapist explored whether powerful voices would get things wrong. Furthermore, if they were so powerful why did they need to use words to dominate and not use other more powerful means of gaining his attention (e.g. physically harming him). Although Nigel was not totally convinced by these discussions, he did begin to question more of what they told him: had they truly predicted the Tsunami in 2005 or was that a lucky guess?

By subsequently following a line of logical reasoning, further inconsistencies in the client's belief can be exposed.

Case example: Lisa

Through Socratic questioning, Lisa realised that her voices said things that were contradictory. They made comments about her room being untidy, when it was clearly not, they also said 'you're ugly' one minute and 'you're beautiful' the next.

Addressing omniscience beliefs

In this phase of CTCH, the therapist and client fairly examine (bearing in mind that the therapist is not all seeing and all knowing either) the omniscient quality of the voice(s). Key questions for the therapist and the client to resolve in this process are:

- Do the voices really know everything?
- Can they make accurate predictions?
- Are they fallible?
- Do they tell lies?

Discrediting the voices and revealing that they are fallible (and therefore are just like everyone else) is an important strategy in down ranking them and loosening their hold over the individual. Didactic techniques are often useful here. We aim to teach the client:

- that the voices do not really know everything as they claim or as the client assumes;
- that they make mistakes: get their predictions wrong, and so are fallible;
- that if they do not know everything and are fallible then they cannot be as powerful as originally believed;
- that the voices have and do tell lies.

Further questions may then be raised:

- If they lie about certain things, what else are they lying about?
- If they know everything, why do they need to lie?

Case examples: Joe and Stephen

Joe heard voices that told him that the end of the world was coming in the year 2000 (it did not!).

Stephen's voice commanded him to shave his head and he would get respect from others (he did shave his head but did not get more respect).

Having created uncertainty and weakened beliefs about omniscience, it becomes possible for the therapist and the client to question and investigate whether they can deliver on their threats.

Addressing power (omnipotence) beliefs

Sometimes referred to as omnipotence beliefs (being all powerful or having unlimited power), these beliefs can be expressed simply as 'my voices are very powerful' (conviction rate = 100 per cent). A number of voice characteristics may contribute to this, including the tone and volume of the voices (e.g. loud, angry and shouting voices), how confident and self-assured they sound (all contributing to their sense of authority) and accompanying visual hallucinations. Of course, other voice beliefs (in addition to omniscience) all confer some power (e.g. identity of an inherently powerful entity such as God). In this sense, weakening power beliefs is a process that occurs throughout CTCH. In this stage, the therapist's task is to raise the key question:

- Can they deliver on their threats?
- Are they all mouth and no trousers?

Answering this will open the option of resistance and ultimately behavioural change. In this process, the therapist has foreknowledge:

- Only something physical, like a knife or a bullet, can harm the physical body.
- Voices rely on the client to act for them.
- If they were so powerful, they should not need the client to act for them.
- Voices boast and make great claims about their abilities but are ultimately unable to carry them out.
- Voices make claims for having done things that could equally well be attributed to someone else's actions, or indeed be a naturally occurring phenomenon.

Case example: Desmond

Desmond noted how his voices threatened to kidnap him, take him to a warehouse and torture him. He agreed, however, that this had never happened and also began to assert that just because he was a follower of Jimi Hendrix did not mean that he should be punished in this way for it. He concluded that if they really could do this to him then 'why don't they just get on with it!'

Addressing compliance beliefs

Safety behaviours are adopted by the individual to reduce perceived threat and provide short-term relief. In this they are effective and their value should be explicitly acknowledged as understandable attempts by the client to deal with difficult and distressing circumstances and experiences. However, in the longer term, safety behaviours function to prevent disconfirmation of compliance beliefs: the voice's ability to carry out their threats. Such behaviours serve to keep the client trapped in a subordinate position. This phase of level 4 work is aimed at encouraging exploring with the client whether the feared consequences of non-compliance always follow. Once the client begins to doubt the voice's power and question their omniscience and omnipotence, therapy can proceed to weakening conviction in compliance beliefs. A number of questions can be usefully formulated with the client for this purpose:

- Do I always need to do what my voice says?
- Can I resist without penalty?
- Has the voice delivered on its threats?

Implicitly, the therapist knows that:

- the voices will not have always done something when the client resisted;
- the person can learn to resist.

The therapist's task is to explore this with the client.

Case example: Adam

Adam heard voices telling him to not go out and to harm himself by various means. The voices threatened that he would be struck down by lightening or would be stabbed in the eye, and become blind, if he disobeyed them. The voices had been saying this every day for about 6 years. Early discussions revealed that Adam had sometimes been able to resist the voices: he occasionally went out and had not fully complied with commands to harm himself. Despite this he had never been struck down by lightening or stabbed in the eye. The therapist and Adam calculated roughly how many times Adam had resisted the voices without their threats coming true. As Adam estimated, this was about once per day for 6 years; this equated to approximately 2,190 occasions of resistance. This enabled the therapist to tentatively suggest whether perhaps the voices were 'all mouth and no trousers?'

It is important to help the client identify the perceived consequences of carrying out a command compared with the perceived consequences of resisting it (e.g. the short-term reduction of anxiety compared to being sectioned, causing lasting harm to oneself or others). Work at this level is designed to facilitate a smooth transition to level 5 work and weaken resistance to dropping safety behaviours. The client is supported in identifying and reviewing past and current examples of where they have not acted in accordance with the compliance belief and nothing has happened. Similarly, clients are encouraged to examine instances where the voice might have claimed to have punished them and to weigh this against possible alternative explanations.

Case example: Veronica

Veronica was regularly told that if she did not harm herself her elderly father who she lived with would be killed. Unfortunately, Veronica's mum died a few years previously and her voice told her that they had been responsible. This greatly distressed her and she was understandably desperate to do all she could to keep her father safe and well. In many cases, this involved her cutting herself or taking small overdoses. Over a number of sessions, the therapist and Veronica explored how long she had been doing this for and what impact it had had. Together they examined instances where she had gone against the voices. Initially, this was a process of identifying mini examples where threats of some kind had been made; she had resisted complying and nothing terrible had followed. There had also been occasions when the voices had told her not to see her friends; if she did then her friends too would be harmed. This sometimes dissuaded her from seeing them and she would isolate herself. However, there had been a few instances where she had seen them irrespective of the voices' threats and no harm had occurred to them.

There were other occasions where she was told to harm herself but had been disturbed by her father or did not have time to go ahead with the voices' commands. When these instances were examined, Veronica reported that she had eventually attended to what they wanted but acknowledged that they had not issued further such commands in the interim period and no consequences had followed

At this point in her therapy, Veronica was beginning to doubt her voices' power and their ability to carry out their threats. Further evidence against their power came when Veronica and her therapist examined the consistency of her compliance. When she first started hearing voices, it emerged she tended to comply entirely: this would involve cutting herself and taking a serious overdose. Over time she acknowledged that she had learned that she could take smaller overdoses and draw red lines on her arms (representing cuts) and this would appease the voices. She did not have to completely comply and nothing bad happened. Veronica's changing approach to harming herself and her doubts about whether her voices could deliver on their threats made it possible to subsequently explore her mother's death. Veronica described how she had been diagnosed with lung cancer after years of being a heavy smoker. This was reviewed as a more likely cause, especially since the voices had never claimed responsibility for her mother smoking!

Consolidating the power shift

Having reframed and disputed a number of the client's power beliefs, the therapist can build on this and attempt to consolidate this work by explicitly inviting clients to reflect on the changing power balance. The broad aim of CTCH is after all to raise the power of the individual in relation to both their voice and their interpersonal relationships (described in Chapter 6). Most of the preceding interventions not only address the client's beliefs about their voices power but will also simultaneously and necessarily provide growing evidence that the client has mastery and control, not the voice. Through Socratic questioning this can be explored with the client. Once the client is more aware of what is happening, new powerful interpersonal self-beliefs can be elicited and stated:

- I do not always have to do what my voice says.
- I can resist without penalty.
- We are equally fallible.

Questioning the voice's commands is a further strategy that can be introduced here. This is a form of the behavioural test and can be used once the client is feeling more in control and the power imbalance has begun to shift:

Case example: Rebecca

Rebecca had frequently tried to throw herself in front of moving cars when her voice told her to do so. Working with the therapist she learned to respond more assertively by saying, 'Why should I do that?' and 'Why don't you do it yourself if you want to?'

Case example: Desmond

Desmond eventually grew tired of his voices' threats and when they threatened again to kidnap him, take him to a warehouse and torture him, he responded by saying to them 'get on with it then'; thus calling their bluff.

Tackling difficulties: reframing and disputing power, omniscience and compliance beliefs

There are a number of problems we routinely encounter in this stage of our CTCH work. A particularly difficult obstacle to overcome is encountered when voices do actually deliver on their threats. Clients report that their voices promise to get louder and more abusive, they keep them awake, cause them physical pain, make them have nightmares and show them terrible things if they are not obeyed. In these cases, beliefs can be reinforced when the voice does indeed punish them by keeping them awake or tormenting them. These consequences are often perceived to be in response to non-compliance though they usually occur at other times too. Helping clients to reflect on this latter point is one strategy for helping them, illustrating that they have benefited from not complying with the voice and have not lost anything; their experience shows that the voice would have, for example, got louder and been more abusive whether they had resisted or not.

Case example: Ben

Ben had been gradually learning to resist his voices' commands. However, Ben felt that the voices were not only continuing to torment him for this but also making him feel sick. On one occasion during the week he had actually vomited. The therapist explored this in more detail:

NK: How long has this sickness been going on for?

Ben: For months now. I can't bear it.

NK: Yes, it sounds very distressing, and you said it's been going on for many months?

Ben: Yes, for ages, at least since I've been in here (in hospital). So about 5 months.

NK: And remind me Ben, how long has it been now since you've been standing up to them and not doing what they say?

Ben: Well, a couple of weeks I guess, since after we started meeting.

NK: So you say that they made you sick before – even when you were doing what they said?

Ben: Yes, they always do.

NK: So is there any benefit to doing what they say if you're going to be sick anyway?

Ben: I guess not . . . it's pointless. At least I won't feel like a mug as well as feeling sick.

Having weakened Ben's belief in needing to always comply, the therapist was then able to go on to explore other reasons why Ben might feel sick. Ben said that the doctors and staff on the ward had told him that it was a normal side-effect of the methadone that he was taking. This allowed the therapist to then suggest that perhaps, like the rainmaker (see Appendix 6), the voices were falsely taking credit for Ben's sickness. Perhaps the reason why Ben felt sick most of the time was because it was as his doctor had explained it was a normal (albeit unpleasant) side-effect of the methadone.

Building discomfort tolerance

In cases like Ben's, it can also be helpful to build discomfort tolerance by directly addressing beliefs in the individual's capacity to withstand unpleasant experiences, drawing on REBT. The aim here is to answer two key questions:

- Can you stand it?
- Is there past evidence of doing so? There always is!

We typically begin by asking the client what they do when the voices are persistent, loud, insulting or (seemingly) inflicting some punishment on them. It is important to identify what the client says to themselves at this point, for example: 'I can't stand this, it's too much for me too bear'. The therapist can then enquire how telling themselves this is helpful. The point here, and perhaps the hardest part for the client to learn, is that *they* are disturbing themselves about this and creating their own discomfort. Of course, the experience is not pleasant and can be very difficult to tolerate, but by the client telling themselves that they 'cannot stand it' this adds to their distress. Subsequently the therapist may gently suggest that while they would *prefer* it if the voices stopped, they don't *have* to stop. Dryden and Bond (2000) have suggested that an emphasis on preferences rather than demands is important. If the client is demanding that they should not have to put up with this then the therapist may gently enquire 'How does this make it so?' and 'How will this help?' This of course must be broached sensitively respecting the client's efforts to cope thus far. Examples of when the client has tolerated discomfort in the past can be highlighted through guided discovery and reframed as evidence that they have been able to do it once and will be able to achieve it again. Some examination of the longer term benefits may also be useful here in order to build motivation for the person to tolerate such unpleasant and distressing experiences in the future. The use of coping strategies to manage these distressing episodes is often vital. Subsequently the client can develop a new piece of self-talk: 'It's very difficult and upsetting, but I can stand it and I can use my coping strategies to help me.' As noted earlier even when they do comply, the voices sometimes do these things anyway, so it may be a more useful strategy to learn to stand it. The client's use of safety behaviours, it might be suggested, only provides an illusion of safety.

Case example: Stephen

While Stephen continued to be taunted both by the voices and the children in the street when he went out because of his odd appearance (even more so after shaving his head after following the voice's advice), he started to tell himself that he could stand it. He learned to hold his head up high and eventually his voice, and the children got bored and stopped taunting him.

Targeting other aspects of power

In some cases, clients will find it too difficult to begin to question their beliefs about omniscience and power directly. Voices may respond very aggressively to such attempts; the person may simply be too immersed in the voice's world or too distressed. In such cases a useful strategy is to explore broader components of the client's power relationship using the VPDS, described in Chapter 1. Using this, the therapist can tackle each component of power: weakness, confidence, etc. by highlighting where the client does not fully endorse ratings in favour of the voice. The reasons for this can be explored and evidence of the client's own power reflected upon. The cognitive strategies described earlier in this chapter can also be applied to illustrate that the client does have power in the client-voice dyad and this can lead them to feel stronger and more confident, etc.

Enhancing coping strategies

Sometimes the client's level of distress is so overwhelming that they are unable to question the voice's power at all. Such clients are likely to have a poor coping repertoire. The focus, therefore, may need to be upon coping strategy work and building discomfort tolerance. The therapist may therefore work more on level 2 strategies.

Case example: Trevor

Trevor believed that his voices would arrange to have him attacked if he left the house after 3 pm. He consequently ensured that he was at home every day by 2.50 pm. He had many pieces of evidence for this, ranging from information from TV programmes that the world was unsafe to previous experiences of being attacked when in public places at night and a belief that the voices were people who had bullied and attacked him when he was at school. Trevor had no strategies to cope with his voices and could not begin to imagine that they might be wrong. Together with the therapist he worked on ways to cope when the voices were at their worst (usually in the evenings) and he could then begin to question their power: after all, if they were so powerful, how could he control them by putting on headphones or singing?

Working on other power relationships

For some clients, working on other power relationships (level 6 work described in Chapter 6) that are not so dominating as the relationship with the voice can be a useful focus. Strategies developed here (such as being more assertive with others and setting boundaries) can then be extended to the relationship with the voice once the person feels more confident in applying them.

Case example: Simon

Simon lived in supported accommodation. He heard the voice of spirits telling him that they would possess him if he did not obey their commands to harm himself or other people. Simon also felt that he was being taken advantage of by the staff where he lived. They would ask him to go to the shops for them and were not very flexible in agreeing when he might do his chores (they wanted them done before 11 am but Simon went to college 4 days a week which required him to leave his accommodation by 8.45 am to catch the bus). He, therefore, worked with the therapist to learn to be more assertive with key members of staff. He learned to put his point across in a considered and polite but firm way that did not result in him losing his temper or feeling that his views were not being considered. His ability to adopt a less subordinate position, to put boundaries around his relationship with staff and to not allow himself to be bullied by them was used to illustrate how he could change relationships with the spirits.

Level 4 work with Peter and Angel

Peter

Belief change strategies

Having developed a good working relationship with Peter, his beliefs could be explored in more detail. Peter was asked to rate his degree of conviction in each belief. Evidence for each belief (control, power, omniscience and compliance) was subsequently systematically examined. In many cases, Peter's beliefs had already changed and he was not sure whether the voices were in as much control as he previously thought. Peter became more confident and aware of information that refuted their power as opposed to supporting it.

HIGHLIGHTING INCONSISTENCIES

Over time Peter and the therapist gathered lots of information about what the voice would tell him. At various points throughout therapy inconsistencies emerged. For example, Peter was sometimes told that he was special and the voice he heard represented an important connection with the spiritual world. However, at other times the voice would tell him he was no good and useless. There seemed to be an inconsistency in what she told him and what he believed.

Other inconsistencies were also identified: the voice would tell him he was no good and useless, yet his friends, family and people he had met at his art group were very complimentary. For example, the voice said he was useless, yet he had received many positive comments about his art and had been encouraged to start an art course at college.

It was valuable to identify and explore these inconsistencies and gently put forward the suggestion that the voice he heard changed her mind about things and that other people did not agree with her; she might therefore be less all seeing and knowing than he had previously thought. The therapist was subsequently able to explore the reasons why she might say these things. He came to realise that she would tell him many different things and the main reason she did this was to try and maintain control by manipulating him and oppressing him.

ADDRESSING OMNISCIENCE BELIEFS

Building on Peter's increasing doubts a metaphor was used to illustrate how it is important to assess the evidence when forming beliefs. Peter found the story of the rainmaker in Appendix 6 very useful and could identify the links between the rainmaker portraying himself as powerful and how his voice did the same. Peter felt that his voice gave the impression that she knew everything and that what she told him was accurate and truthful. Through

Socratic questioning, Peter and the therapist were able to explore the validity of the voice's claims that she had blown up his computer, thus illustrating her power. The therapist and Peter were able to establish that she knew little about computers, and Peter indicated that the repairman had told him that it was a failure in one of the components; this was a manufacturing fault and nothing more. This introduced some doubts as to whether his voice always told the truth and instances where she had not were pinned down. This idea was expanded on further by exploring how horoscopes work and whether it is possible to make predictions about someone's life. Peter was able to recognise that horoscopes make general statements about what might happen in the future such as 'you will come in to money' or 'you will overcome challenges ahead'. It was possible for Peter to identify that not everything the stars indicate is going to happen. As with his voice, not everything he was told came true, but previously he was biased towards information that supported the voice's power.

It was suggested that it could be valuable for Peter to be vigilant for information that doesn't necessarily fit with the voice's viewpoint. It was possible to explore this in some detail using specific predictions that were made by the voice. She indicated that his computer would blow up again and that a friend of his would die. Over a number of sessions it was identified that in both cases the voice had said these things would happen but did not provide specific details (what blowing up meant and which friend would die) or the voice did not say when this would happen and had been saying it for many months. Peter began to recognise that like a horoscope the voice only provided sweeping predictions that carried with them very little specific detail. Over time Peter developed a record of what he had learned. He wrote this down on his computer (further going against the voice's advice) so that he could refer back to it when times were difficult. This became his way of reiterating his progress, learning to brag about his achievements and the changes he had made, to check that he was continuing to use his new understanding, and to keep testing the voice and what he was told.

ADDRESSING COMPLIANCE BELIEFS

Having now doubted the omniscience of his voice, Peter was ready to question his need to comply by addressing his belief that she (the voice) could materialise and harm him directly:

RA: You've mentioned that she has said she will materialise and harm you. Could you tell me a little bit about that?

Peter: She starts shouting at me and gets very nasty. She'll tell me to burn myself, that I deserve it as I am useless. She's said she'll materialise and harm me if I don't go along with it.

RA: It sounds as if you are concerned she will show herself and harm you. Has she ever done this before?

Peter: Actually she has. I was sleeping on the sofa and I woke up. In the corner of my eye I saw a shadow.

RA: Do you think that was her?

Peter: Yes. She was trying to frighten me.

RA: So let me see if I have this right. She told you that she will materialise and if she did she will harm you. When you were on the sofa and had just woken up you did see her. You felt she did this to frighten you. On this occasion she didn't harm you directly.

Peter: Yes.

RA: What do you make of the fact that she had an opportunity to harm you but didn't?

Peter: I don't know. She could have.

RA: Do you always do what she wants?

Peter: No. Not always, on odd occasions when it gets too much.

RA: Does she always make threats?

Peter: Most of the time.

RA: So sometimes she makes threats but you don't go along with what she wants. Does anything happen?

Peter: No.

RA: What do you make of that? That she makes threats, you still don't do what she says and nothing happens?

Peter: I guess . . . maybe she just can't do it.

RA: You think she might not be able to?

Peter: Well. She hasn't done it yet and she's had plenty of chances.

RA: What does that say about her?

Peter: That she shouts a lot and is nasty but that's all. It's horrible but maybe she can't do what she says.

RA: It's interesting, isn't it? She is meant to be really powerful, yet when we have looked back she has threatened you but never harmed you. She tends to shout, is nasty and frightens you but doesn't follow the threats up. Maybe they are empty threats. Maybe she is all mouth and no trousers. Even if she can materialise, it might mean that she still can't harm you.

Further time was devoted to reviewing Peter's conclusions to this discussion and what he had learned regarding his voice's true power, omniscience and whether there would be any penalty if he resisted doing what she wanted. This helped to gather more information about his experiences and helped consolidate the gains made. These were written down and all the evidence supporting the new belief elicited:

•   She makes false claims and predictions.
•   She only wants to manipulate me.
•   She sounds convincing but this is a bluff.

- Why does she have to shout, if she is so powerful she could just make me do it.
- She boasts about harming me but cannot – only something physical like a bullet or a knife can do that.

Peter could refer to this list at times when he was more distressed and found it more difficult to remember these new insights into his voices' true power.

Angel

Belief change strategies

Angel was frightened that if she disrespected her voices they might get worse. The therapist suggested that given the voices were making such a huge demand of her (to sacrifice herself to stop all the pain and suffering in the world) that it was understandable that she might want to question this. The therapist made the following comparison:

NK: Do you respect me Angel?

Angel: Yes, of course.

NK: And supposing if I asked you to jump of the roof of this building because I believe that you can fly, what would you say to me?

Angel: Well I guess I'd want to know how you would know that I would be able to fly.

NK: So you might initially want to question how I could be so sure that you could fly.

Angel: Yes.

NK: And that would be understandable, wouldn't it, given the risks associated with what I was asking of you.

Angel: Yes, I guess so.

NK: And you would want to question me, even though you respect me.

Angel: Yes.

NK: And, have the voices ever been wrong about anything before?

Angel: They were wrong when they said that you would get me sectioned after our first session.

NK: So given that they've got at least one thing wrong in the past, I'm wondering then whether we might want to question them when they ask you to sacrifice yourself, or to walk in front of cars, so that we can be really sure that if you do sacrifice yourself it hasn't been done so in vain.

Angel: Yes, I guess so.

The therapist and Angel then drew out the advantages and disadvantages of resisting versus complying with the voices, and Angel was able to see that a huge disadvantage would be the effect that sacrificing herself would have on her family. To help Angel to feel more able to question the voices, a coping card with the following was typed up for her to take home:

> It's only fair to my family, and myself, that I question the truth of what the voices are telling me to do, as the consequences would be catastrophic for them, and me, if the voices are either lying or are mistaken (remember that they've got things wrong before – for example, when they predicted that I would get sectioned).

ADDRESSING BELIEFS ABOUT OMNIPOTENCE AND OMNISCIENCE

Given that Angel had already identified a high emotional investment in the positive beliefs that she held about her voices, the therapist was alert to the necessity of working with Angel's beliefs about specialness before attempting to undermine this potentially protective belief. Moreover, as one of Angel's key pieces of evidence for the power of the voices was that they were messengers from God teaching her 'the right way', to be able to undermine this it was necessary to additionally target Angel's beliefs regarding identity and purpose. Although in reality this work was done concurrently with CTCH level 4, as the therapeutic tasks fall under CTCH levels 7 and 8, we will discuss them in detail in Chapters 7 and 8 respectively.[1]

The therapist's opinion was that it was only when Angel began to believe that she could be special in other ways and when she had some doubt in her mind about the voices' identity and purpose that she was able to begin to question their omnipotence and omniscience. This is likely to be the case when the identity of the voices is considered to be an all-powerful entity such as God or the Devil.

As Angel's doubts about the voices increased, in particular about their identity (that they were messengers from God) and their meaning and purpose (that they were teaching her the right way), she felt able to question how powerful they really were. The therapist then asked Angel to rank order the other evidence she had for the voices being 100 per cent powerful, from least to most convincing. The evidence, along with the key disputes that were used in therapy to undermine these, is outlined below:

1   *They have the capacity to take my thoughts away.*
Angel explained that during meetings the voices 'took her thoughts away'. The therapist explored the times that this had happened and it emerged that it only occurred in important meetings which Angel found particularly stressful. The therapist explored other explanations for Angel's thoughts being taken away including the role of anxiety. After reading some psycho-educational material on the effects of anxiety, Angel concluded that anxiety might have played a role in 'her thoughts being taken away'. The rainmaker

analogy was also used as a metaphor for how perhaps the voices were taking credit for things that would have happened anyway: her feeling anxious and forgetting what she might have wanted to say at important meetings.

2   *They have made correct predictions about bad things happening.*
Although Angel said that her voices had made correct predictions about bad things happening, on exploration it emerged that their predictions were always very general. This was likened to horoscopes, in that if the predictions were so generalised and vague, the likelihood would be that one would always be able to find an element of truth within them. Furthermore, when asked to systematically make a list of all of the times the voices had made predictions which did not come true, it emerged that there were numerous examples of when they had been incorrect. Again, did this suggest they were full of empty threats and all mouth and no trousers? The therapist suggested to Angel that they could perhaps test this out in the session by asking the voices to make a prediction and seeing whether it would come true. Initially, Angel was reluctant to do this:

Angel: I don't think that is a good idea. The voices are saying that they won't lower themselves to that.

NK: Oh really, that's interesting because I would have thought if they really wanted us to take them seriously then this would be an ideal opportunity to prove how powerful they really are.

Angel: No, they really don't want to and say they won't.

NK: Hmmm, I'm wondering whether it is a matter of 'won't' or 'can't'. I wonder whether they might be a bit scared that we are getting wind of the fact that they are 'bigging' themselves up a bit.

Angel: Yes, I guess that could be possible, I hadn't thought of that.

NK: Yeah, because really it would be in their best interest to play ball with this, wouldn't it – if they want you to continue doing what they say?

Angel: Yes, I think it would.

The therapist then proceeded to write a word on a piece of paper, and while she was doing so asked Angel to ask the voices to predict what the therapist had written down. Needless to say, the voices were unable to rise to the challenge and they predicted the word incorrectly. The experiment was carried out several times but on no occasion were the voices able to make a correct prediction. Angel was very surprised about this and said that it certainly undermined the credibility of the predictions that they made.

3   *They claim to have made things happen, for example the Tsunami, 9/11 and the deaths of two family members.*
Here the therapist introduced the idea that saying something is not the same as doing it, and that just because the voices claimed to have made things

happen, it did not necessarily follow that they had. The therapist was able to draw upon earlier revelations:

NK: We have already discovered that the voices tell lies, so why should we believe them this time?

Again the rainmaker analogy was used to illustrate that perhaps, like the rainmaker, the voices were taking credit for things that were not their doing and that would have happened anyway. Could there be other explanations for these things happening? The following explanations were examined:

1   The therapist tentatively queried whether given that one of Angel's deepest concerns was causing harm to others, could it be possible that the voices might be taking credit for these things so that they could then pin the blame on her?
2   In the same way that school bullies might do, is it possible that the voices are homing in on Angel's fears as a way of trying to blackmail her? Indeed, this might especially be the case given that Angel is such a caring person and would do anything to stop the pain and suffering of other people.

A discussion then ensued about how the world is not always a fair place and how sometimes bad things happen. The fact that bad things happened before Angel was even born was highlighted, as well as a discussion about how it could be possible that the voices could cause all of these things. Furthermore, were these bad things consistent with the kind of things that messengers from God might do?

ADDRESSING COMPLIANCE BELIEFS

Having cast some doubt on the voices' omnipotence and omniscience, the necessity to act in harmful ways was next questioned. Angel believed, 'If I don't do what the voices say, bad things will happen to other people'. Her evidence for this was that 'Bad things have happened when I have resisted them'.

Having begun to see that there were some inconsistencies in what the voices said and that there had been numerous occasions when she had resisted commands and the threats had not come true (e.g. being sectioned after talking about them in therapy), Angel and the therapist developed a list of such instances enabling her to consider developing 'alternative' beliefs:

If I stand up to the voices, bad things won't happen.
The voices threaten this because my biggest fear is causing harm to others, rather than because I am causing harm to others.

Angel endorsed this new belief 15 per cent. While low, she said that this new found doubt gave her the courage to feel able to test this belief through resisting some of the voices' commands.

Unfortunately, however, at this point in therapy there was news of a natural disaster that had occurred which had incurred a high death toll. The voices were blaming Angel for this. Consequently, Angel stopped taking her medication completely, became increasingly unwell and was finding the voices more distressing and consuming. The following coping card was drawn out to help Angel feel more able to take her medication, and to dispute her compliance belief:

> It has been difficult to take my medication because the death toll has been rising and the voices blame me for this. But *remember the rainmaker*. How could it be possible that not taking medication could cause such bad things to happen? And at any rate, although the voices claim that they are making these things happen, do they have the power to do this? *Claiming to have the power to be able to carry something out doesn't necessarily mean that we actually have the power to carry something out.* We have found a lot of evidence which suggests that the voices aren't as powerful as they make out they are.

Summary

In this chapter we have described in detail the process we have evolved for addressing beliefs regarding control, power, omniscience and compliance, employing a mixture of guided discovery, Socratic dialogue and didactic methods using key disputes or lessons. Perhaps most critically adopting a gentle enquiring style and offering these disputes sensitively enables the therapist to keep clients engaged in what is often a difficult and anxiety-provoking process. A flexible approach tailored to the client's case-specific and changing needs is also very important. As the case studies illustrate, there are different means for achieving change based upon individual factors.

Note

1   The reader is reminded that although the authors are presenting a protocol-based approach the clinical reality is that these stages are not always linear and must be approached flexibly according to the individualised formulation of the client and agreed goals.

Chapter 5

CTCH Level 5

Reducing safety behaviours and compliance

Introduction

When we feel anxious, anyone of us might engage in behaviours that serve to mitigate the anxiety we experience and thereby prevent the feared consequences from happening. This has been termed 'safety behaviour' (Salkovskis, 1991) and is reinforced by an immediate decrease in anxiety. In clients with psychosis the actions and the behaviours that they engage in can have profound consequences. In this chapter we examine the role of safety behaviours in command hallucinations. We describe our approach to addressing them, building on the cognitive work from level 4 and showing how behavioural experiments can be devised to reduce compliance and further weaken beliefs about power and compliance.

The role of safety behaviours in command hallucinations

To summarise the points made in earlier chapters, safety behaviours serve to maintain the beliefs that mediate them by preventing disconfirmation of voice beliefs: that the voice is powerful and can punish the person for non-compliance. Safety behaviours are seen implicitly by those who experience command hallucinations as helpful because they mitigate the immediate threat. In the longer term, however, the person remains trapped in a subordinate position and remains at risk of engaging in harmful behaviours (a key intervention target). Safety behaviours in voice hearers may take several forms (Meaden *et al.*, 2010):

- full compliance (doing as the voice commands or as the client believes they should: taking an overdose);
- appeasement or partial compliance (making a gesture or symbolic act that goes some way towards the full compliance: amassing pills but not taking the overdose);
- threat mitigation strategies (anticipatory actions that reduce the likelihood of needing to act: not going into a chemist).

Hacker *et al.* (2008) have also classified safety behaviours in voice hearers based upon their sample of thirty individuals with a current experience of auditory verbal hallucinations:

- avoidance (76.7 per cent): not eating particular foods (to avoid poisoning); walking out in crowds (to avoid a demonic attack), social gatherings (possible disclosure of shaming information), being alone (to avoid self-harm commands);
- in-situation safety behaviours (70 per cent): hypervigilance (looking through windows to check for the persecutor), engaging voices in conversation (to prevent information disclosure), holding batteries (as a weapon), walking over drains (absorption of energy to reduce vulnerability), route or clothing changes (to disguise oneself and deceive the voices), lying to voices (about their itinerary), wearing a religious talisman (to ward off black magic);
- escape (23.3 per cent): leaving home because the voices said they were coming, leaving the communal lounge because of fear of compliance;
- pre-emptive aggression (53.3 per cent): towards the voice (shouting back, making threats, insults, refusing commands), pre-emptive physical assault (hitting other people believing them to be under the power of the voices);
- compliance and appeasement (50 per cent): full compliance (e.g. hitting others, smashing windows), overt appeasement (securing employment for the voice by psychic communication with an employer), covert appeasement (e.g. mentally rehearsing self-harm without intending to do so);
- help seeking (40 per cent): contacting a 'good alien' via telepathy, praying to God, seeking reassurance from staff, asking the priest for forgiveness, asking relatives for protection, asking to be arrested;
- rescue factors (10 per cent): God intervening (believed to have happened due to non-occurrence of harm).

When asked about the effectiveness of their safety behaviours in reducing threat, 91.3 per cent of participants in the study rated their behaviours as at least 5 out of 10 at being effective in reducing the threat. This reduction in the sense of immediate threat, however, served to maintain beliefs in voice control, power and omniscience: that the voice could have carried out their threat if this behaviour had not prevented it. The behaviour thus constitutes a 'near miss' (Salkovskis, 1991).

Helping clients to fully understand both the short-term (the immediate consequences of harmful compliance) as well as the longer term disadvantages (prevention of disconfirmation) is the focus of level 5 work. This helps clients decide whether their safety behaviours are necessary as a protective strategy; whether the client is in any true danger and, if not, do they still need to adopt safety behaviours.

Behavioural experiments

In CTCH, behavioural experiments are employed to help establish whether safety behaviours are necessary and indeed really keep the person and others they care about safe. A number of small-scale studies in the field of anxiety disorder suggest that positive treatment outcome is related to the use of a combination of behavioural experiments, the dropping of safety behaviours within those experiments (McManus *et al.*, 2009; Okajima *et al.*, 2009) and the combined use of behavioural and cognitive techniques (Bennett-Levy, 2003).

When devising behavioural experiments, changes in behaviour are designed with the client in order to subject their beliefs to:

> A logical analysis *and* empirical hypothesis-testing which leads individuals to realign their thinking with reality.
>
> (Clark, 1995)

In the true nature of a scientific experiment, the process might be:

- observational (e.g. a survey of others' views or observing what others might do in a similar situation);
- manipulative (e.g. changing one piece of the situation in order to see what happens).

In reality neither the therapist nor the client can be entirely sure of the outcome since random and chance factors will, and often do, intervene. Therapists cannot make absolute predictions about others or the world. It is therefore important that both the client and therapist carefully agree on a set of parameters and conditions under which the belief will be brought into question and the utility of an alternative belief evaluated while being mindful of the limitations imposed by chance factors. The client is required to suspend their belief in the feared outcome and more importantly to withhold the safety behaviour. While dropping these behaviours typically engenders anxiety in the client in the short term, in the longer term it promotes changes in both cognition and future behaviour.

Understanding and exploring the role of safety behaviours

A useful first step is to explore with the client their understanding of the role of their safety behaviours, and through the use of guided discovery support them to examine both their advantages and disadvantages. The idea that compliance with voices might actually be unhelpful is introduced initially when discussing the CTCH formulation (see Chapters 3 and 4) and through using allegories and metaphors in the form of short stories (see Appendix 6). While these can be helpful for many clients, some find these examples too abstract. In addition, attentional and auditory processing deficits in people with psychosis (Strauss, 1993), medication effects and other distractions (e.g. voices) can make it difficult for clients to concentrate. In these instances a simpler or more normalising explanation might be used.

Case example: Anna

Anna felt that other people at her local day centre were laughing at her (which her voice supported); she felt anxious as a result and so avoided going. The therapist shared her personal story of a fear of spiders in order to illustrate and elicit from Anna the way anxiety worked and the role of avoidance in maintaining this anxiety:

KB: So it got to the point where I couldn't be in the same room as a spider because I thought it would jump out and bite me, which was very awkward when I was at work because I had to keep an eye out for spiders all the time and leave the room if I thought one was there. If I had asked you for help, as someone who isn't afraid of spiders, what might you have suggested to me?

Anna: Well, you needed to know that there was nothing to be afraid of, not from small spiders anyway.

KB: And how could I have done that?

Anna: I saw a TV programme about this where they got the people to be in the room with the spider and they then got them to hold different spiders to prove there was nothing to be afraid of. I could take you to a zoo and get you to look at lots of spiders.

KB: So I would need to do the thing that I was most afraid of in order to prove that it couldn't hurt me.

Anna: That's right, then you wouldn't be frightened anymore.

KB: Using that example, if you didn't want to feel anxious of others at the day centre, what would you need to do?

Anna: Go there, I suppose.

By using this example, Anna was able to understand the rationale for dropping the safety behaviour, even though the idea of doing this made her feel anxious. It can be helpful to draw on the client's own experience to illustrate the point. Anna, for example, reflected on a time when she had contacted her brother after many years, even though she was worried that he would not want to know her. She had told herself that if she did not try she would never find out. Her brother was actually very pleased to hear from Anna and had thought that is was Anna herself who did not want any contact with him due to her mental illness.

Conducting behavioural experiments

In our level 5 work we have largely adopted the Lewin/Kolb model of experiential learning (Lewin, 1946; Kolb, 1984) as the most helpful means of designing successful behavioural experiments. It provides a simple tool with a useful feedback loop that can be used with the client to illustrate shared learning among participants. The cycle (Figure 5.1) has four main elements (planning, experience, observation and reflection) and these are used as a framework to plan and systematically conduct and evaluate each experiment. Each component acts as preparation for the next and forms a loop where reflection on the one experiment helps to plan the next. The aim is to provide further evidence that disproves the voice's power (work begun in Chapter 4) and increases the individual's power (see also Chapter 6).

1   Planning: developing the experiment idea
In view of the levels of anxiety that many clients who have command hallucinations experience at the thought of dropping their safety behaviours,

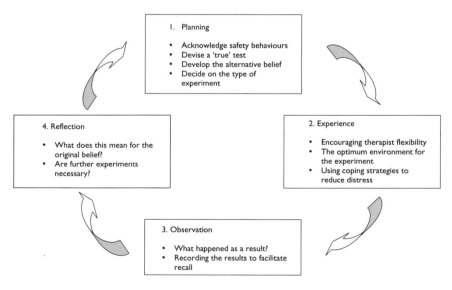

Figure 5.1 The Kolb model of experiential learning

laying the ground work (e.g. examining the benefits of doing so) is arguably the most important part of the experiment. To begin with, the function of the behaviour within the CTCH formulation is reviewed:

- Does it serve to mitigate the threat, appease or fully comply with voice commands?
- Which of the client's beliefs about their voices does the behaviour prevent disconfirmation of?

Understanding this along with the feared consequence of dropping the behaviour is a key part of the planning process. The *weakest first principle* may be applied here in order to reduce resistance to change and maximise the chances of a successful experimental outcome. The initial safety behaviour should be carefully chosen. It may for instance be one where the client perceives that punishment will be less likely (perhaps drawing on past inconsistencies in the voice's use of punishment elicited in level 4 work) or less severe.

Case example: Mike

Mike felt that the voices would attack him if he left the house in the evening. They told him that he had to turn off the TV and listen to them instead. They had also told him not to leave the house. However, detailed exploration revealed times when he had ignored their commands to listen; he had instead gone out for a drink. When he came home the voices had kept Mike awake all night insulting and abusing him. On other occasions he had stayed in but kept the TV on as it was a favourite programme. On these occasions the threatened attack had not occurred. The weakest command (to turn the TV off) was therefore agreed as being the easiest safety behaviour to address since Mike had already proved he could ignore this command without incurring the feared consequences.

In further preparation, a cost/benefit analysis is often helpful. This involves:

- talking about what life might be like if the safety behaviour was no longer necessary;
- exploring the changes in emotion and the activities that might be possible;
- examining the benefits for the client, their family or friends;
- exploring all the voice hearer's reservations.

This list can be returned to if at some further point motivation is reduced. By exploring all the voice hearer's reservations, the therapist can encourage participation in this level of CTCH work and minimise the risk of the person falling back on using safety behaviours if things become too difficult. In Mike's case, being able to go out for a drink when he wanted to and socialising with his friends, were clear benefits to dropping this safety behaviour and served to maintain his motivation in the face of his voices' threats and when his voices actually delivered on their threats by keeping him awake. The use of coping strategies to help build discomfort tolerance (see Chapter 4) is clearly important in such cases.

Case example: Mehmet

Mehmet found re-examining the benefits and costs of his behaviour especially helpful. His voices instructed him not to wash, but this contravened his religious beliefs and meant that he was unable to engage in daily prayer as he was not able to clean himself. He used the list agreed with the therapist to motivate himself, to remember the hierarchy of goals that had been drawn up and the achievements he had made thus far.

When assessing costs and benefits it should also be borne in mind that some client's behaviour may also be mediated by their more general beliefs and attitudes. These so-called ego-systonic beliefs will often need to be targeted (an issue addressed more fully in Chapter 11).

Case example: Craig

Craig heard the voice of Yellow (a demon) who instructed him to 'hit him, stab him' when out in his local community. He acknowledged, however, that he often had these thoughts himself whenever others showed him signs of disrespect. Craig believed that not acting would show weakness and leave him vulnerable. As a consequence he had a long forensic history of assaulting others with weapons.

In addition to the general caveats of designing behavioural experiments (see Rouf et al., 2004 for a review), the following points we have found are particularly relevant for those under the influence of powerful voices:

a. *Response to 'hypothetical contradiction' (RTHC)*. Testing RTHC has its roots in the work of Karl Popper (1935, 2002). He first made the distinction between what he termed 'conditional scientific predictions'. These take the form 'If *X* takes place, then *Y* will take place'; these are typical of the natural sciences and take the form of hypothetical assertions stating that certain specified changes will come about if particular specified events antecedently take place. Brett-Jones *et al.* (1987) in their pioneering work (although based on a small sample of nine people) successfully correlated the outcome of CBT with the abilities of the participant to consider changing their beliefs in the light of contradictory evidence. Typically, the therapist attempts to elicit, or may suggest, a hypothetical scenario whereby circumstances occur that will lead to belief change. Asking questions such as:

- 'Are there any circumstances under which you would question your belief?'
- 'If X happened rather than Y, would you question your belief in any way?'

A favourable response is one whereby the client agrees to review their belief in the light of this new evidence. If there is no favourable response then the therapist must question the utility of the behavioural experiment since the client will likely not change their belief and will re-attribute it: as either not a true test (e.g. another event intervened to change the outcome) or as a near miss. The procedure may be repeated and the reasons for a non-favourable response explored.

Hurn *et al.* (2002) found that RTHC was a useful tool for assessing the potential usefulness of therapy and was independent from insight, degree of conviction, degree of preoccupation, anxiety and depression. Beginning hypothetically creates less stress and allows the therapist to anticipate the requirements of a 'true test', to ascertain the consequences of power beliefs in such a scenario and anticipate any problems.

Case example: Colin

The therapist noticed that Colin found it very difficult to think about stopping some of his safety behaviours:

KB: So, let's just imagine that you had gone out even though he (the voice) had told you not to and that you weren't attacked. What would that mean to your belief that he could have you attacked?

Colin: I'm not sure; it might just be a fluke; he might be trying to trick me and not attack me, just so he can laugh at me later.

> *KB:*   So how many times would you need to go out and not be attacked for it not to be a 'fluke'?
>
> *Colin:* I don't know; I don't think I could ever be sure, because he will always tell me he can get me next time.

It became clear through this discussion that Colin would need to practise the skill of leaving the house on five or more occasions for him to begin to believe that the voice was not 'tricking' him. Had the experiment composed of just a single occasion, it would not have achieved the desired results.

b. *Covert appeasement.* Care should also be taken to ensure that the client is not engaging in any covert appeasement, such as telling the voice that this is not a true test and asking it not to punish them, or carrying out the behaviour in their imagination to appease the voice.

c. *Anticipating the need for support.* It is also important to examine what support the person may need to carry out the experiment: should other people be there (the person's care coordinator, friend, carer etc.). Should the therapist accompany the client? Flexibility in accompanying the voice hearer (or assisting them in finding someone who can) outside the usual appointment time while they are practising resisting the commands is important. A phone call between sessions to remind the person of the rationale for the experiment can also be a useful means of providing support. Flashcard reminders that the voices' threats haven't come true and so are not as powerful as they make out can also offer valuable support to carry out experiments. This will help to minimise 'opt outs', if the task seems too difficult. Care should be taken at this point in order to avoid the trap of introducing another safety behaviour, for example the client might believe that the feared event did not happen because someone else was there and the voice knew this.

d. *Agreeing an alternative replacement belief.* This work will build on that begun in level 4 where evidence for and against a belief has been evaluated and an overall conviction rating given for the belief: 'my voice can predict the future'. The alternative belief can then be agreed: 'my voices make mistakes and cannot predict the future as they claim'. As behavioural experiments help to build evidence for and against, this new belief conviction ratings may be used to provide an easy way of monitoring change and the success of any experiment.

e. *Using graded hierarchies.* When tackling safety behaviours, an anxiety-provoking process, we have found that drawing up a graded hierarchy reduces resistance. Often this involves targeting more innocuous or less risky safety behaviours first (risk as evaluated by the voice hearer). A systematic hierarchy gradually pairs the feared stimulus with relaxation (Wolpe, 1958). This can be adapted and the voice hearer encouraged not to comply or appease the voice in a graduated manner, using anxiety reduction techniques as necessary, while ensuring as far as possible that these do not become further safety behaviours. The VCS (Beck-Sander *et al.*, 1997) can be a useful tool in eliciting and rating all relevant safety behaviours, from least to most risky, including appeasement. Resisting some 'less risky' commands (e.g. 'stand up', 'turn off the light') without adverse consequences can undermine the power of the voice to the extent that people can 'jump' stages as they get more confident.

Case example: Deidre

Deidre had previously been complying on a daily basis with her voice which commanded her to take an overdose or cut herself. She found that once she could resist the voice telling her to turn off the light; this diminished its power to the extent that she could also begin to challenge the command to cut herself followed by the command to take an overdose.

---

2   Experience: conducting the experiment

Ideally behavioural experiments are agreed and conducted without flaws or hitches and the client reconsiders their belief in light of this new information. Having followed the previous steps, the experiment might then be carried out within the session. Grounding strategies (see Kennerley, 1996 for a review) and relaxed breathing can help to reduce the anxiety still further and can be encouraged for use at other times.

One simple test which can be used with some clients is to test out whether the voice has the ability to harm others. For example, if the voice claims to have the ability to hurt others, the therapist can invite the voice to harm the therapist. Care needs to be taken in staging this test. The therapist and client will need to agree that it is the voice that will do this independent and unaided by the client. Clients may understandably be reluctant to let potential harm come to the therapist who they have developed a therapeutic relationship with, is someone whom they trust and see as being there to help them. The therapist will need to spend some time reassuring the client that they are comfortable with this test and confident in its outcome. Examples of any past threats made towards the therapist by the voices can be drawn on at this point.

Case example: Fabian

Fabian's voice (the destroyer) seemed very powerful to Fabian and claimed that he had brought about many disasters and wars in the world. He had threatened the therapist on a number of occasions as well as Fabian's sister and niece.

AM: Do you remember Fabian when the voices said he would cut my legs off if you came to these sessions?

Fabian: Yeah.

AM: That has never happened, has it?

Fabian: No.

AM: What's your explanation for that?

Fabian: Well no . . . he likes to boast you know . . . but it's exaggerated like.

AM: Do you think that he could harm me now?

Fabian: Sure if he wanted to.

AM: Perhaps we could test him out.

Fabian: Not sure about that . . . you don't want to mess with him.

AM: Okay. I can understand that this might be a bit scary for you, but I have tried this many times with other people and am quite confident we can test him.

Fabian: mmm

AM: Do you trust me?

Fabian: Yeah.

AM: Okay, well how about if we asked the destroyer to cut my little finger and make it bleed. I can easily put a plaster on afterwards.

Fabian: He (the voice) says that he is not going to rise to such a petty challenge.

AM: Well . . . I would have thought that this is an ideal opportunity for him to show us very easily just how powerful he is . . . and it would be in his own interest I'd have thought to show us.

Fabian: True . . . he's gone quiet now!

AM: Why do you think that is?

Fabian: I don't know.

AM: Maybe he's just boasting again?

Fabian: Yeah – I think you're right. It's surprised me; I thought that he could easily do it!

The client and the therapist may also consider other types of harm such as giving the therapist stomach ache, making them vomit, etc. Again, as with behavioural experiments, generally the likelihood of chance factors intervening and the therapist actually becoming ill must be considered.

Conducting the experiment in session as in Fabian's example has the advantage that the therapist can remain alert for unhelpful beliefs that emerge. For instance, feelings of anxiety engendered by taking a risk may subsequently be interpreted in an unusual way.

Case example: Robert

Robert believed that his voices were sending 'electricity' around his body whenever he experienced anxiety. He interpreted his anxiety in session as indicating that he was being punished for daring to test the voices' power.

---

3   Observation: observing the results

Returning to our example of the inner detective in Chapter 3, it is useful to agree with the client what results they should expect and how these will be spotted. What clues should they look for: are they gathering information (observational) or gathering experiences (active)? Recording these observations is important when people may find it difficult to take in all of the information especially in view of the high levels of emotion and the adverse effects on cognition that psychosis may involve (Strauss, 1993). With this in mind, written session summaries can be developed that discuss:

- how safety behaviours function for the client;
- the rationale for the experiment;
- the original and alternative beliefs (including conviction, preoccupation and distress ratings prior to the test);
- what happened in the experiment;
- belief ratings afterwards.

These can be developed in the planning stage and completed at the outcome. Other clients might find it helpful to keep a 'diary of resistance' to illustrate how many times they resist the voice and the consequences of resisting (e.g. did any harm actually occur?). Some clients find 'flashcards' with a few words summarising each step of the experiment helpful here.

4   Reflection: consolidating new learning

Through guided discovery, the therapist can help the client reflect on the outcome of the experiment and the lessons learned as a result of carrying it out. The therapist might concentrate on the following:

- What the results mean to the client?
- What might it mean about their earlier fears and predictions?
- What the implications are for their beliefs?
- What the implications are for the alternative beliefs?

Even in cases where experiments do not go as planned, reflection can help clients understand the outcome in a helpful way.

Case example: Natalie

Natalie heard voices telling her to attack her mother with a knife. She had previously been arrested for threatening people in her supported living placement. Her voices had also told her that she should avoid all crowded places because otherwise they (the voices) would make her panic and faint. Natalie and the therapist had worked through a hierarchy (focusing on this safety behaviour first) so that she reached the point where she felt able to take an outing to a crowded shopping centre, only to find in the middle of the experiment that shoppers were evacuated because of a bomb threat (a therapist's worst nightmare!). Understandably, the therapist was concerned that this would have resulted in a temporary setback for the client and spelt disaster for the alternative belief. However, when reflecting on this experience the client was able to say that she saw other people looking hot, sweaty and nervous and so interpreted her reaction as realistic, given the circumstances. She did not attribute this turn of events to the voices. After all, if the voices were so clever, she reasoned, then they should have predicted this outcome too. It was not the expected result and probably could not be planned for, but the preparation in noticing and dealing with signs of anxiety (using her inner detective) had helped nonetheless, allowing Natalie to control her own reactions and notice the reactions of others.

A period of time that allows for consolidation is often helpful. The client and the therapist can review the implications of the experiment and any weakening of the alternative belief. Summaries from stage 3 (observation) can be used to help the client reflect on the process and consolidate the learning from each experiment, especially when they are not with the therapist and may feel compelled to listen to the voices again.

Case example: Deidre

Since not following the voices' commands, they had become quieter and less frequent. Deidre began to miss the voices' company in the absence of another positive relationship (other than with the therapist). Being able to use the written summaries to remind Deidre of the distress she had experienced previously when she felt compelled to do as her voice commanded, as well as the distress which followed cutting herself and overdosing, helped to maintain her resolve. Subsequently, in therapy the notion that Deidre was now more in control and had 'got her life back', meant that she now had the possibility of developing new friendships.

Tackling difficulties in behavioural experiments

Effective behavioural experiments serve to consolidate cognitive change and build on doubts about voices achieved in CTCH level 4 work. They diminish the evidence for control, power, omniscience and compliance and increase conviction that the voice is less powerful, can't carry out their threats and make mistakes or tells lies. Even when we have followed the above steps, experiments can still however go wrong. In our current work we have identified several common reasons for this.

Insufficient time devoted to earlier levels

In some cases where experiments have not proven fruitful, not been carried out, or where clients have disengaged from therapy, voice power has not been adequately addressed in earlier sessions.

Case example: Robert

Despite spending considerable time examining the costs and benefits of his safety behaviour of not washing, Robert continued to believe that the voices could cause 'electricity' to take over his body if he tried to disobey his voice. In a previous session a model of anxiety had been introduced as an alternative explanation for these sensations, but this had not sufficiently changed his belief in the voice's power (a powerful spirit). As a result, the anxiety generated by the graded hierarchy led to more feelings that felt like 'electricity'. Unfortunately, Robert disengaged from therapy without discussing his worries further.

Had the therapy continued, the therapist would need to have returned to CTCH level 4 work and looked again at power beliefs, perhaps re-examining other times when the voices had made mistakes or not carried out their threats. Roberts's problem may be also reformulated as one of 'discomfort intolerance'. Devoting more time to building up his coping strategies may also have been useful.

Substituting new safety behaviours

In some cases well-intentioned efforts to reduce distress, promote coping and motivation to engage in behavioural experiments may have also led to new safety behaviours being adopted. When effective coping strategies are introduced and taught, there is always this potential: the client drops their safety behaviour in favour of the new (albeit more functional) coping strategy, leaving voice beliefs untested.

Case example: Ahmed

Ahmed heard the voice of Shedu (a storm demon), who threatened him with cutting off his hands, removing his eyes and genitals. Ahmed felt tingling in his hands and experienced blurred vision at these times, which he interpreted as signs that Shedu was carrying out these threats. Working with his therapist in-sessions, Ahmed learned relaxation methods: controlled breathing for dealing with these symptoms. He was also given a relaxation tape covering full muscular relaxation for use outside of the sessions during stressful periods generally. After mastering these and applying them in a behavioural experiment, Ahmed concluded that 'Shedu is still powerful, he is a storm demon and they are very powerful', but I can cope better now and the relaxation functioned as 'a shield' enabling Ahmed 'to resist his evil demands'. Ahmed was happy with this progress and was no longer setting fire to his flat for fear of Shedu's punishment. He subsequently decided to decline any further cognitive work. The behavioural experiment devised with the therapist had proved that he could resist and was (via relaxation) battling the voices' attempts to mutilate his body. However, he still believed that the voice could do so if he did not use these strategies as a shield, noting that he had 'to not fight in order for Shedu to win'.

The function (including the client's appraisal of its significance) needs to be borne in mind when teaching new coping strategies in order to avoid this. However, the costs and benefits should always be borne in mind. In Ahmed's case, he was happy with the work and new coping strategies he had mastered, he was less distressed and felt less compelled to engage in harmful behaviours. He also reported having regained a certain degree of power as he was able to resist commands from his voices. It is important here to revisit the goals of CTCH, which are to reduce distress and harmful compliance. These had clearly been achieved for Ahmed despite little cognitive change in many of his voice beliefs, which may arguably make him vulnerable to further relapses. It should be noted too that belief change (e.g. in voice power and the need to comply) had been brought about through behavioural change: using applied relaxation skills in this case. This may be a rationale for employing behavioural experiments when there has been limited success in level 4 work and greater gains at level 2 work.

Positive voice beliefs

In our research trial work, we have noted how clients who hold positive, as well as negative, beliefs about their voices are often reluctant to reduce their safety behaviours. Positive beliefs about voices are a key factor in compliance behaviour (Shawyer *et al.*, 2008) and can make motivation to begin experiments to disprove the voice's power difficult. The rationale for reducing safety behaviours centres around their unhelpfulness, however, for some such behaviour is necessary to maintain their relationship with the voice which for them is beneficial, despite the dangerous things they do. Careful work is needed here to explore this relationship and the associated beliefs.

Case example: Andrea

Andrea heard one female voice. She recognised that many of the things she was told to do (e.g. to cut herself or to starve herself) were dangerous but she occasionally complied with these commands because she was afraid that the voices would abandon her. Andrea had heard her voice since she was 14 years old. Around this age, she was sexually abused and the voice she heard was a source of support and reassurance. As Andrea got older she continued to rely on her voice for support, but also realised that much of what she was told to do was damaging to herself. The validity of her beliefs, the need to comply and the changing nature of her relationship with her voice and others were all explored during the course of therapy.

Through Socratic dialogue the relationships that the client has with their voices can be explored. Parallels can be usefully drawn with other human relationships as part of this process: friends can give bad advice and good friends would not desert a person just because they did not go along with what they said. It can also be helpful to examine how relationships change over time. By helping the client to understand this, they can gradually be helped to see their relationship with their voice in a new way and begin the process of negotiating with them and setting boundaries (as in level 6 work) and thereby create a different relationship with the voice, rather than get rid of it altogether. The client can thus start to assume a greater level of control, make more informed choices and rely less on the voice, with the ultimate aim of forming more positive relationships with others.

Dealing with infrequent but high-risk commands

Infrequent high-risk commands involve demands to cause severe injury and potentially life-threatening actions to self and others and to property (as in the case of arson). Because they are infrequent, they are harder to test out experimentally. Clients may also not experience commands for the majority of the time and only do so under conditions of relapse.

Case example: Edward

Edward had recently tried to strangle one of his housemates in response to voices commands. Prior to this he had attacked a member of the public on the bus a few years previously and approximately 10 years prior to that had tried to stab a nurse on a psychiatric ward. These behaviours were potentially lethal, and a direct response to voice commands. Mostly, however, Edward experienced a running commentary on his daily actions (e.g. 'you are drinking a cup of coffee'). Because he did not want to comply again with commands, each time he began to hear louder voices or commands he would ask to be admitted to hospital and would be released a few days later. He believed this had stopped him from complying. This threat mitigation safety behaviour prevented disconfirmation that the voices did not have the power to carry out their threats to kill him. While the therapist discussed with Edward the role of safety behaviours and how compliance maintains beliefs about voices, exploring these high-risk episodes, there was no hierarchy to develop because Edward felt that the voices 'came out of nowhere' and made no other demands. This was the source of the voice's power over him.

The challenge of therapy was to address Edwards's belief in his own powerfulness (explored further in Chapter 6). Despite the absence of regular commanding voices, the therapist decided to play the role of the voice so that realistic interactions with the voice and methods for resisting their commands (using coping strategies, setting boundaries and standing up to them using assertiveness skills practiced in session) could be explored. Instead of dropping a hierarchy of risky behaviours, Edward began exposing himself to situations which he felt were increasingly stressful and therefore could trigger the voices. A pathway to care was agreed with his team so that risk could be managed if needed. Edward went to visit his mother's grave and also began to use public transport again. This did indeed activate his voices. Edward learnt that he had the power to control the voices; he could adjust their 'volume', ask them to come back later and be assertive with them in his head using the role plays devised with the therapist. He used relaxation strategies such as controlled breathing to reduce the anxiety that the stressful situations created. Ultimately, Edward learnt that he did not have to comply in order to keep the voices at bay or admit himself to hospital.

For clients such as Edward, we also may utilise a relapse prevention methodology (Birchwood *et al.*, 2000a) with a particular focus on the re-emergence of command hallucinations and factors that lead to the client acting on them.

Other factors may need to be considered here including the degree of impulsivity, medication compliance, interaction with substance use and the circumstances involved in previous high-risk incidents. It should also be noted that the routine use of nonaggressive safety behaviours increases the risk of violent or suicidal behaviour (Freeman *et al.*, 2001). As in Edward's case, a pathway to care should be negotiated with others involved in the persons care: when additional support should be offered, when extra medication might be considered, etc.

Building discomfort tolerance when dropping safety behaviours

There is also the problem that for some clients their voices do actually carry out their threats when safety behaviours are dropped. This is usually the time when the voices up the stakes (e.g. threaten to get worse or louder) if the person does not obey, and they do exactly that. As described in Chapter 4, an examination of the client's discomfort intolerance beliefs is important here and some cognitive disputing and reframing will be required. This work serves to equip the client to withstand the punishment contingent upon withholding the safety behaviour.

Case example: Deidre

Deidre had learned that she could ignore the voice when it was demanding because she knew that if she gave into its demands then the voice would be even more demanding in the future. She knew this because she had used the same strategy with her son when he was a toddler. Subsequently, Deidre learned to ignore the voice when it was demanding, responding only when it was nice to her. At all other times she would put it in the 'naughty corner'.

Inoculating the person against criticism: creating a safe place

For some clients the daily insults and the repercussions of abusive voices (when they do carry out their threats) are overwhelming and can lead to disengagement. Drawing on compassionate mind training for people with psychosis (Mayhew and Gilbert, 2008), clients can be helped to create a safe place or 'compassionate other'. These strategies help them hear critical comments and abuse, but not react to them, safe in the knowledge that these comments and insults alone cannot do any harm. Angel (one of our main case studies), for example, found it helpful to imagine a compassionate figure serving as a protective bubble that would envelop her and deflect the comments. Such a strategy is often useful for clients who have not experienced a completely safe or trusting relationship in their lives and therefore struggle to generate a stable sense of self that can help combat the uncertainty and injustice of life. The essence of this approach is to allow a person to hear the thoughts without reacting to them. Such imagery helps to generate a calming, safe place that the person can retreat to when the voices are relentless and they feel they cannot cope with them. Other coping strategies, described in Chapter 3, can also help cope with persistent voices. Further uses of imagery to help combat critical voices are described in Chapter 8.

The timing of experiments

The timing of when to carry out experiments is also important, considering all factors that are present in a person's life when deciding whether to begin behavioural experiments, or even to delay therapy completely during times of stress. In Robert's case (described earlier in this chapter), it may have been helpful on reflection not to have conducted the experiment during Ramadan, a time when he had not been eating or sleeping properly. For other clients, times of stress may include family occasions or other social gatherings, medication time (e.g. having a depot) or care plan reviews. Such additional stressors may mean that the client cannot cope with new tasks or the anxiety that dropping the safety behaviours will engender.

Level 5 work with Peter and Angel

Peter

The role and impact of safety behaviours

When Peter started therapy, his voice was relentless and she had told him to cut himself because 'he deserved it' and because 'he was useless'. In level 4 work, he came to realise that he could resist her and not go ahead and do what she wanted and that although she would be aggressive and nasty towards him, she was not able to physically harm him. She needed him to do it for her. Instances in the past had also been identified where he had resisted the voice and nothing bad had happened. Additionally, Peter now had effective coping strategies he could use and this was evidence that he now had more control. When he was fully engaged in something else (painting, meditation), she went in to the background and was not as vocal as she was at other times. No consequences followed this even though she threatened that there would be. His confidence grew and he became more aware that 'she was all mouth and no trousers' (e.g. made empty threats). Peter began to think that he could increase his control further and develop a different relationship with his voice. The stray cat metaphor was used:

> If you continue to feed the hungry cat it will continue to come back for more.

In many cases this seemed to be what Peter was doing. He would go along with what the voices wanted, and this would add to his difficulties and the power imbalance.

Devising and implementing behavioural experiments to test out the function of safety behaviours

Over several sessions it was possible to develop a hierarchy of appeasement, threat mitigation and compliance behaviours. These were scored and the therapist and Peter worked their way through the hierarchy by exploring the evidence and doubts Peter now had and agreed which safety behaviours seemed least threatening to drop.

As a first step the therapist suggested that if the voice was really powerful she should be able to harm the therapist. Peter agreed. A behavioural experiment was set up in order to test this out. Could the voice Peter heard cut off one of the therapist's fingers if directly asked to do so? Peter believed this might be possible but did have doubts (she only wanted to harm him and might not want to reveal herself). However, these doubts withstanding, he did feel she could do this. After one week (the agreed time frame), she had not been able to achieve the task set and Peter developed further confidence and doubted her even more.

It was then possible for Peter to directly test out whether she could indeed materialise and physically hurt him. Peter was not sure what she would do as she would not directly say. As a specific test, Peter encouraged her to materialise and harm him in the session. She was not able to do this either in the session or subsequently when asked to do so in between sessions. As a consequence, Peter's compliance behaviour stopped and he no longer cut or burned himself. This information was documented in a flashcard so that Peter could remind himself of his successes.

Angel

The role and impact of safety behaviours

Angel had already been socialised to the concept of safety behaviours through introduction of the spinning tribe analogy (see Appendix 6) which she found exceptionally helpful. By this stage of therapy she was still responding to commands to sacrifice herself, to walk in the road (a potentially lethal behaviour) and had stopped taking her medication, which only served to increase her voices further.

Devising and implementing behavioural experiments to test out the function of safety behaviours

A hierarchy of ten target commands that Angel rated from least to most difficult to drop was developed. These ranged from the least distressing commands that she heard ('stand up' or 'leave the room') to more dangerous commands ('don't take your meds', 'walk in the road' and 'go to the park to sacrifice yourself'). This was drawn out with Angel (steps 1, 9 and 10 are shown in Table 5.1). Using the *weakest first principle*, the aim of the hierarchy was to enable Angel to feel more able to progress through in a graduated way. The therapist elicited the exact content, frequency of each command, and Angel's fear of disobeying each command (her compliance belief). Using Socratic questioning and logical reasoning, the therapist subsequently elicited the evidence for and against Angel's compliance belief for each command.

This provided further support for Angel's new 'alternative' compliance belief:

> If I stand up to the voices, bad things won't happen. The voices threaten this because my biggest fear is causing harm to others, rather than because I am causing harm to others.

Table 5.1 Excerpts from Angel's graded hierarchy

Command	What do the voices say, or what am I afraid will happen if I don't comply?	Evidence for	Evidence against
Step 1 *Stand up* Frequency: four times daily	That something awful will happen (especially to my family)	Bad things have happened in the past when they have said that	• I don't see how that could happen • The amount of times they tell me to do that – such a lot would have happened • They are always general in their predictions – they never give a time or date (like horoscopes) • Bad things happen – the world is not a fair place
Step 9 *Don't take your meds* Frequency: daily	That something awful will happen (especially to my family) And I will choke (or general harm will come to me)	Awful things happen everyday. This is because I am less likely to sacrifice myself if I am taking medication News items show that bad things happen when I take them	• How could it be possible that not taking medication could cause such bad things to happen? • Although the voices claim that they are making these things happen, do they have the power to do this? Claiming to have the power to be able to carry something out doesn't necessarily mean that we actually have the power to carry something out • There have been times when I have taken medication and bad things haven't happened
Step 10 *Walk in the road* Frequency: varies from not at all to every road I cross	That something awful will happen (especially to my family)	They tell me that the cars will go through me and that will be their proof that I am special It would be a miracle and would indeed be proof	• What difference should taking medication make? If cars can go through me then how is it possible for the medication to affect that? • It would be a miracle and seems unlikely • Experience tells me that cars swerve to avoid me, which could cause harm to others

Despite this therapeutic plan, it was clear to the therapist that Angel was becoming increasingly unwell and distressed by her voices. It was the view of the therapist that this was likely being influenced by the fact that Angel had not been taking her medication for several weeks at this point. Furthermore, Angel was complying more frequently with very dangerous commands such as walking in the road and making preparations to go to the park with the intention of sacrificing herself. It was essential for the therapist to assess and monitor Angel's ongoing risk as well as liaise closely with Angel's team psychiatrist about her safety in the community (details of dealing with risk issues are expanded upon in Chapters 9 and 10). Given these issues, the therapist felt that it was necessary to abandon the systematic graded approach as intended and instead prioritise the most risky commands. With Angel's agreement, the initial safety behaviour to be dropped became 'do not take your meds'. This was because it had already been established that not taking her medication lead to Angel becoming more consumed by the voices and more likely to comply with their commands to 'walk in the road' and 'go to the park' to sacrifice herself.

Using behavioural experiments to test out the function of safety behaviours, the therapist introduced the use of a 'medication diary' as shown in Table 5.2. This was a daily record of occasions when Angel was able to resist the voices' commands by taking her medication. It also logged Angel's mood as the voices told Angel that she would feel better if she did not take her medication. Thus, the aim was to additionally test out this claim.

The problem that Angel, and the therapist, was faced with was that if Angel resisted by taking her medication she did not get immediate disconfirmation of her belief (because the voices were always so vague with their threats and there was no timeframe as to when the threatened bad event would happen). Hence, Angel understandably described feeling 'awful' after taking her medication. Furthermore, Angel said that although in the sessions she felt

Table 5.2 Medication diary – gaining control for myself

Please circle whether you have been able to take your medication and, if possible, rate your mood at the end of each day from 1 to 10 (with 0 being the worst ever and 10 being the best ever)

Week No.:	Day:	Day:	Day:	Day:	Day:	Day:	Day:
Taken medication?	Yes/ No	Yes/ No	Yes/ No	Yes/ No	Yes/ No	Yes/ No	Yes/ No
Rate mood at end of each day from 0 to 10							
Optional comments							

motivated to resist the voices' commands and was able to hold on to the possibility that the voices might not be all powerful, this became very difficult outside of the sessions when the voices would continually contradict what was said in the sessions. Angel found listening to audio-recordings of the sessions a helpful way of overcoming this. Coping cards summarising the key themes were developed collaboratively in session and then typed up by the therapist for Angel to keep and read between sessions. Angel's coping cards are shown below:

Angel's Coping Cards: To Read When Trying to Take My Medication

> However strong the negative feeling is, and no matter how frightened I am that something bad is going to happen, it *does not* mean that something bad is going to happen. Remember that the spinning tribe felt frightened for several weeks – but this didn't mean that the world was going to stop spinning – the fear that they felt was just a reflection of their worry that the world would stop spinning. So, feeling bad does not always mean that it is bad. Also, it was only after a few weeks of not spinning that the spinning tribe were able to learn that their initial beliefs weren't true after all, and the world didn't stop spinning and come to an end if they stopped spinning.
>
> Although I feel bad after taking my medication, this is understandable because it shows that I *don't* want what the voices are saying to come true. Therefore, in order for me to learn that bad things won't happen to other people if I take my medication, I need to try and take it regularly for a period of time. Feeling bad after taking my medication is not an indicator that bad things will happen, it is more a reflection that I am a caring person, and do not want to cause harm to anyone. Just as it did with the spinning tribe, the more regularly I take my medication, the easier it will get.

As noted in these coping cards, Angel often used 'feeling bad' as evidence of bad things happening (e.g. I feel bad, therefore what I've done must be bad). This would frequently lead to Angel complying with the voices due to her discomfort intolerance belief that 'I can't stand it when I feel bad or guilty'. In order to help Angel feel more able to withstand 'feeling bad', the therapist revisited the work begun in level 3, socialising Angel to the impact of thinking biases (Powell, 2009) in particular emotional reasoning. Thought diaries were introduced to help Angel evaluate her thinking patterns and she was encouraged to use her coping strategies to help her to withstand the 'feeling bad'.

Using this approach, Angel gradually learnt that there were several times when she had resisted the voices by taking her medication and their predictions did not come true. This doubt enabled the therapist to again put forward the argument that the voices were 'all mouth and no trousers' and 'full of empty threats'.

It was agreed that Angel would now continue taking her medication and that this would constitute an ongoing experiment. Angel would record her mood in a medication diary to test out the voices' claims. Angel learnt that although she initially felt bad after taking her medication, after taking it consistently for a few days, her mood improved. This challenged the voices' claims (and therefore their omniscience) that medication would not make her feel any better. Angel was subsequently able to take her medication every day.

As Angel became more sceptical about the omnipotence of the voices, in particular their ability to cause harm, she was able to increasingly resist the voices' commands and work her way through the hierarchy. A more general resistance diary (see Appendix 7) was introduced to monitor all occasions when Angel was able to resist the voices' commands. The diary was used to reduce Angel's safety behaviour of walking in the road. Over a period of 2 weeks, Angel was encouraged to resist these commands and record the consequences. The terrible consequences were specified: something bad would happen either to Angel or her family. This is always a risky strategy with such broad predictions, which neither the voices nor Angel could specify further, since the therapist could not control events. Nevertheless the voices' threats and predictions did not come true over this period (or over the next month). Angel began to realise that resistance did not always lead to terrible consequences. Consequently, this gave further credence to her new belief:

> If I stand up to the voices, bad things won't happen. The voices threaten this because my biggest fear is causing harm to others, rather than because I am causing harm to others.

Summary

In this chapter we have described the important role safety behaviours play in keeping individuals with command hallucinations trapped in a subordinate position. Reducing the use of these behaviours is a key stage in dismantling the voice-power schema. We have described our use of behavioural experiments to test power beliefs. A good deal of preparation time is often required in establishing motivation, ensuring graded exposure to the feared situation, verifying the challenge to each safety behaviour and anticipating and addressing 'near miss' explanations. With sufficient preparation even unexpected results can have a positive learning experience for the voice hearer. However, behavioural experiments may still not work as planned and extra planning including flexibility with timing, building psychological resilience and consideration of the person's goals may be necessary. In the next chapter we build on this cognitive and behavioural change by explicitly reflecting on the power shift that has taken place thus far and addressing the person's broader social rank.

Chapter 6

CTCH Level 6

Raising the power of the individual

Introduction

In this chapter we explore the client's perception of their position in broader social rank terms drawing parallels between their changing relationship with the voice, and others in the broader social environment. Our use of the formulation template is extended to bring in social rank elements: the dominate–subordinate schema that we argue underlies the client's relationship with their voices and with others. This phase consolidates the shift in power, further inoculating the client against the demands of their voices.

The development and maintenance of subordinate schemas

In Chapter 1, we described the basic tenet of social rank theory and the research we have conducted with colleagues in demonstrating its importance in those experiencing command hallucinations. The finding that an internal view of the self as powerless (subordinate) in the face of a more powerful (dominant) 'other' can be a result of underlying low self-esteem (Birchwood *et al.*, 2000b, 2004) and is mirrored in our clinical work. The cognitive theory of low self-esteem (e.g. Fennell, 1998) would suggest that such core beliefs might originate in difficult early experiences of psychological trauma (e.g. abusive or bullying relationships). The relationship between core self-schemas and the development of psychotic symptoms will be explored further in Chapters 7 and 8.

If a core belief of the self as inferior to others is perceived as being supported by society, then a maintenance cycle may develop in which the individual feels increasingly powerless to change their situation. While it is acknowledged that perceptions of inferiority could be objective (stigma) or subjective (shame), there is evidence to support the presence of both. Stigma might be defined, from an evolutionary perspective, as the means by which society protects itself and future generations, by excluding those who could damage social cohesion because their characteristics or beliefs are deemed not to fit with those of the general population (Kurzban and Leary, 2001). In an empirical review, Lee (2002) suggests that there is transcultural evidence for societal stigma of schizophrenia, as measured by attitude surveys in the general population, as well as 'self-stigma', or the internalisation of wider social stigma.

It has been suggested by researchers for over 20 years that people who experience psychosis feel stigmatised by society (Birchwood *et al.*, 1993; Corrigan, 1998), and this is supported by cross-cultural research (Lee, 2002). Recent work by Dinos and colleagues (2004) has further proposed that psychosis sufferers are indeed the most susceptible to the experience of stigma. These researchers interviewed forty-six people with a range of difficulties (psychosis, drug use, anxiety, depression and personality disorder) and concluded that people with psychosis and people with problematic drug use were more likely to report the effects of social stigma. The experience of long-term stigma or the fear of stigma by society may in itself have detrimental effects on the individual. First, it may be an environmental risk factor in the development of psychotic and pre-psychotic symptoms (Van Zelst, 2009). Second, it can lead to an expectation of social defeat and as such may have long-term neurobiological effects on dopamine levels in the brain and consequently increase the risk of developing psychosis (Selton and Cantor-Graae, 2005). The sensitisation (or increased baseline activity) of dopamine has been noticed in depressed animals who display socially defeated behaviour, and in individuals with psychosis who were naive to anti-psychotic medication. Finally, the experience of social stigma either before or after a diagnosis of psychosis may lead to shame, or the internalisation of that stigma. This can result in social anxiety, lowered social expectations and submissive behaviour.

Previous work supports the idea that social stigma leads to shame, and has found that people with psychosis view themselves as unattractive (Birchwood *et al.*, 1993; Iqbal *et al.*, 2000) and of low personal worth (Corrigan and Kleinlein, 2005). Furthermore, approximately a third of people following a first episode of psychosis exhibit signs of social anxiety (Pallanti *et al.*, 2004). Gilbert and Trower (1989) suggest that social anxiety is a defence against others in society who are seen as more attractive and of greater worth. From an evolutionary perspective, it is a submissive behaviour designed to protect the individual from an attack by more powerful others (Gilbert, 1992, 2000a,b). Submissive behaviour fuelled by shame, therefore, protects the person from the perceived threat of further social exclusion or complete rejection. However, it may also maintain their position because the behaviour is itself perceived as shameful. For a person who hears commanding voices, such behaviour may be the actions or activities they feel obliged to commit (such as harming themselves, attacking others, public humiliation) which are themselves behaviours stigmatised by society, and serve to maintain the person's individual sense of shame. The cycle then perpetuates because the feeling of shame maintains perceived low social rank.

If the experience of psychosis compromises the social rank of the sufferer, one would not only expect evidence of social stigma and shame but also a reduced self-confidence. This is indeed the case. Furthermore, sufferers experience not only low self-esteem (Gumley *et al.*, 2006), but they are also more likely to face post-psychotic depression (Birchwood *et al.*, 2000c) and positive symptoms of psychosis (Barrowclough *et al.*, 2003) and therefore a worsening of the condition itself.

As stigmatisation of people with mental health problems is seen as culturally ubiquitous (Lee, 2002), it follows that there must be therefore some protective factors militating against the social effects of the diagnosis. Rüsch *et al.* (2009) suggest that those who do not succumb to the stigma of society are able to do so because they have greater resources to cope with that threat, and that shame is a consequence of insufficient 'stigma-related' coping strategies. There is often an interplay between early negative self-image, childhood trauma and insecure environment and the development of psychosis, leading to further exacerbation of an already weakened view of the self and social position (Birchwood, 2003). This is one theory of the interconnection between shame and stigma in the development of psychosis. Research thus far has yet to determine the precise causal effect.

Implications for treatment

It is clear from the literature reviewed so far that those techniques which help to provide a more stable and secure sense of self, creating powerful self-beliefs, will increase the sense of an individual's power and self-esteem. Research indicates that CBT interventions which target negative appraisals of psychosis can improve self-esteem (Hall and Tarrier, 2003; Gumley *et al.*, 2006). This suggests that not only are beliefs about the symptoms linked with self-esteem, but that modifying those beliefs can improve perceived social standing.

A further mechanism by which individuals with psychosis may experience shame is by means of threats from their voices. By implication, voices appraised as omniscient will know all about the person, including things about which they feel ashamed and would not want to be revealed to others. Voices may thus exert power and ensure compliance by threatening to expose the person's secrets to others. This constitutes a psychological threat. If in addition the person believes that they can hear the thoughts of others or that their own thoughts are available to others, this may add to their sense of threat. Targeting these beliefs in CTCH and helping the person to recognise that the voice cannot deliver on this threat (in previous levels) are further mechanisms for addressing shame and social rank issues.

Identifying new beliefs about the power of the individual

Research into CBT targeted at improving self-esteem (e.g. Fennell, 1998) suggests that new, helpful beliefs about the self can be identified and then reinforced using behavioural techniques. Hall and Tarrier (2003) asked patients in a ward setting who had been diagnosed with chronic schizophrenia to identify their positive qualities, and then gather evidence to support that quality which they might be able to report back. The results of this surprisingly simple intervention were to increase levels of self-esteem in the intervention groups into the 'normal' range which were maintained up to 3 months later. Within the context of social rank theory (Gilbert, 1992), adopting a more helpful set of positive interpersonal self-beliefs necessarily illustrates the reduced power of the 'other', and consequently relocates the source of power as lying with the individual.

At the commencement of level 6 work in CTCH, the voice hearer should (ideally) have greatly reduced their conviction in:

- their voices' ability to harm;
- their voices' ability to carry out their threats;
- their voices' ability to accurately predict the future.

However, clients may remain unaware of the consequential shift in power that follows this changed conviction. Socratic dialogue can be used to explore the changes that have taken place along with the use of the CTCH formulation. Changing power beliefs can be reflected back to the client and explored in more detail.

Case example: Adrian

Adrian and his therapist had been discussing the spirits that he heard over the course of approximately fifteen sessions:

Adrian: When I talk to you about the spirits I start to feel like I understand them more, we can talk about what spirits can and can't do – that's really useful. No one has ever talked to me about it before.

KB: How does it make you feel when you understand them more?

Adrian: Like I've got some control over them, I listen to that CD[1] you gave me and they leave me alone. I can question them and I know they don't always tell the truth.

KB: So we have established that they tell lies, and we realised they don't always predict the future accurately?

Adrian: Yes!

KB: And what did it feel like when you didn't steal from that shop like they told you to?

Adrian:	It felt real good you know, like I'd won over them. They tried to come inside me but I didn't let them; it felt more like anxiety like you said. I did the breathing and it got much better. I was in control and they couldn't do nothing about it!
KB:	So if I've got this right then, they tell lies, they don't always predict the future and they can't come inside you. So you don't have to do what they tell you to do?
Adrian:	Yeah, like I'm in charge now. I understand what they're trying to do and I won't let them do it.
KB:	So, if you previously thought that they had all the power to make you do things, what do you think now?
Adrian:	Well, I'm sort of in charge, but they do still threaten me you know and it's scary, I'm not sure I always know what to do.
KB:	So if you are in charge now, could we say that some of that power is yours now? [Adrian nods.] It sounds like the spirits tried their best to make you do what they say, but all they managed to do was to make you feel scared.
Adrian:	It was really scary.
KB:	It sounds scary, but even though they tried their hardest; could they make you do it?
Adrian:	Well no, but they really tried.
KB:	It sounds like it and from what you said they tried their hardest, but couldn't make you do it. So who has the power to decide what you do?
Adrian:	I guess I do.
KB:	Right, what convinces you of that?
Adrian:	'Cos I don't have to do what they say, like I didn't rob that shop, they couldn't do nothing to me.
KB:	So, on our first evidence list, we wrote down how they convinced you that they had the power. It sounds like you've got a new belief now, that you have more power than they do. I wonder what evidence we have for that now that we could write down next to it?

A traditional CBT technique is to list all of the evidence for and against a new belief and then to encourage the client to reflect on this information, including the worry that the new belief might not be accurate. Evidence can begin with the results of the disputation (Chapter 4) and behavioural experiments (Chapter 5). Adrian's belief did fluctuate as the voices made a

Belief: *I have more power than the spirits*	
For	**Against**
1. I am in control 2. I can do my relaxation and breathing like Karen said, and they get quieter	1. If I'm on my own then they get really loud and scary
3. They cannot make me rob the shop no matter how hard they try 4. They can't harm me 5. The tell lies	2. They have convinced me to do things in the past
6. I can stop them coming inside me 7. My body belongs to me – its only anxiety they make me feel like they are possessing me – they don't really posses me 8. I can do my relaxation and breathing like Karen said and the symptoms go	3. They have possessed me in the past and made me do things

Figure 6.1 Adrian's new powerful self-beliefs card

comeback, but Adrian found that if he wrote his evidence list on a wallet-sized card (shown in Figure 6.1), he could take it out with him as a reminder to use when the voices tried to convince him otherwise. Reviewing the evidence in this way allows the therapist to identify any unhelpful beliefs that the client still holds and challenge them using the techniques described in Chapter 4.

Alternative explanations about the origins of the voices can further diminish their power by providing a rationale for the onset of voices (see Chapter 7). For some clients, the suddenness of the onset and the lack of information about voices can play a large part in maintaining the mystique and therefore power of the voice. This was the case for Edward whom we met in Chapter 5.

Case example: Edward

Edward reported that the voices occurred suddenly and this meant that he had no control and was proof that they had all the power since they could come on as they wished. Psychoeducation about the causes and prevalence of voices and establishing an understanding of the stress-vulnerability model along with some relapse prevention work was provided. This enabled Edward to feel that he had more power and control over what was happening. Furthermore, this diminished the power of the voices because he was able to label them as an 'illness' and that stressful life events had contributed to their existence. While relapse prevention and psychoeducation is not a specific target in CTCH, it had a particular use here in relocating the power to Edward and away from the voice. As a result of his new sense of control and empowerment, Edward took up a position as a peer support worker in order to help others who had been in the same situation.

Our CTCH formulation template (first shown in Figure 3.1) shows the clear links between beliefs, distress and behaviours. A reformulation (as shown in Figures 8.6 and 8.8) can also be helpful here.

Reinforcing new power beliefs

Having established new voice beliefs as more helpful and indeed accurate ways of appraising the experience of hearing voices, it is important to support the client to act in accordance with their new beliefs: to act as if they were true. While traditional disputation and reframing of beliefs might result in a logical or rational change for the person, there is still an experiential or emotional gap (Ellis, 1962) especially where, as the person is hearing the voice being critical, or commanding them to act, in that moment, it continues to feel real and accurate. As we noted in Chapter 5, behavioural change can lead to belief change and also serve to reinforce new power beliefs by acting against the voice-power schema. Frequently, however, further work is needed. We have accordingly developed and adapted a number of strategies to reinforce new powerful self-beliefs.

The brag slot

Drawing on the work of Hall and Tarrier (2003) described above, a useful initial and relatively easy technique that can be introduced is the use of a 'brag' slot first described by Byrne et al. (2006). This can be introduced at either the beginning or the end of sessions for the client to talk about what has gone well during that week, highlighting, for example, how the client has stood up to the voice or how they had been able to be assertive with their partner for the first time in a long time. If the client is feeling particularly down having had a bad week, this can be a useful means of maintaining motivation to continue with the work by beginning the session in this way. Brag slots can be practiced as homework as a means of coping with difficult times or times when other homework tasks are being conducted: in building motivation to carry out a behavioural experiment.

Case example: Margaret

As well as being derogatory, Margaret's gangster spirits told her that she was famous and a beautiful film star. Margaret said that this was the only time that she felt good about herself, which meant that she felt a greater obligation to comply with their demands to get drunk and make herself homeless (both of which placed her at risk as she was a recovering alcoholic who had spent many years homeless). Margaret and the therapist agreed to work together to help her feel good about herself without having to rely on the gangster spirits for this. Initially the therapist and Margaret agreed to have a 'brag session' in which they developed the following list:

Positive Things about Margaret

A list of the things that I am proud of:
1 I've built myself up.
2 I have got stamina and willpower.
3 I am a miracle: I came through 9 years of being homeless to paying my own way, having a flat and building my home up.
4 I feel proud of myself because I have done it alone. I've managed to get the things that I want and the things I feel comfortable with.
5 I've broken away from all the drinking lot.
6 I am strong.
7 I look after and care for my cat.

During the week add any others that you can think of here: ....
....
....

In subsequent sessions, a 10 minutes 'brag slot' was devoted to discussing one item on the list, in addition to other items that Margaret had added during the previous week.

Establishing boundaries with the voices

This is a strategy we encourage early on in CTCH but here we build on any efforts the client has made thus far to establish firmer boundaries drawing upon their revised power beliefs about the voice and their new more powerful beliefs about themselves. In level 6 work, the client is supported to become more assertive and set firm boundaries with their voice. The aim here is to help the client learn that they can:

1   question the voices' commands directly;
2   set boundaries with them;
3   not always be at the whim of their voices;
4   have time for themselves.

This simultaneously serves to break the cycle of engagement and build resistance by not reinforcing the voices' demands. Parallels should again be drawn here with the voice hearer's relationships with others and how being assertive and setting boundaries are sometimes necessary (as in the case of nosy neighbours or bullies). In line with social rank theory, these dominate–subordinate relationships are common in our clients, a point we will return to below.

Case example: Charlie

Charlie learnt that she could ignore the voice by imagining it as her son who used to demand sweets when they visited the shop. She reflected that when she gave into her son he would continue to demand sweets each time they visited a shop, but that by ignoring him she knew he would eventually give up. Given this new interpersonal sense of self-power she now had, it was suggested that she could now tell the voice to 'do it yourself if you are so powerful'. She practiced this in session and this made her feel stronger in the face of the voice and more likely to resist the voice in the future. She was then able to put this into practice outside of the sessions.

A useful first step in this process is to support the client to formulate a number of short, assertive stock replies to the voices and not to get drawn into protracted debates with them. The client should respond clearly and firmly without shouting. Therapist and the client may role play, taking it in turns to be the voice. Alternatively, if this feels too uncomfortable, the therapist may make an unreasonable demand of the client and ask them to respond assertively. The subject of role play is elaborated upon below.

Case example: Kate

Kate's voices of dead spirits ganged upon on her and told her that she was useless, to kill herself by walking in a busy road, smash the windows of shops, to get arrested and gave her advice about how to dress (in Kate's own view badly). With the help of her therapist she learned to tell the voices:

'You walk in the road if you want to'.
'Why don't you smash the window yourself'.
'I am busy now, come back later'.
'You're talking rubbish – I don't have to listen'.

Case example: Stephen

Stephen's voices said 'shave your head and you'll get respect'. After reflecting on this with his therapist he acknowledged that this was not the case. Stephen had shaved his head and continued to be taunted by local youths. He subsequently decided to respond to further commands by saying to them, 'Your advice is bullshit, I am not listening'.

In the context of a strong and safe therapeutic relationship, the voice hearer can begin to test out some of what they imagine to be the voices' responses to these actions, and how they could manage their responses. It is useful to prepare the client for an escalation in the voices' demands with the consistent reassurance from the therapist that they will become less demanding (as in Charlie's case with her son). Drawing on everyday examples that highlight the principles of reinforcement (ideally ones from the client's own life) will be useful preparation.

Feeling the power

Facilitating experiences of emotions that accompany the alternative powerful thoughts may be helpful in allowing full integration and acceptance of those alternatives, acknowledging how it feels to be in the initial position, and also the feelings of increased power. Useful strategies we have drawn on for some clients are the 'empty chair' and 'two chair' techniques. Initially established to facilitate change in people who experience depression, they have been shown to facilitate what may be termed emotional knowledge (e.g. knowing and feeling that the new belief is true and the old one false) or change (Paivio and Greenberg, 1995; Watson and Greenberg, 1996) or insight. These techniques involve asking clients to converse with a critical 'other' (using the 'empty chair' technique) or to then accept that 'other' as part of themselves (the 'two chair' technique). The latter has been adapted for use with people who experience distressing voices (see Chadwick, 2006) where those voices represent unresolved negative interpersonal experiences or schemas.

Role play

Role play has been an experiential technique described by Albert Ellis (1962) in which he would encourage people involved in therapy to begin to act as if their new beliefs were true. In order to minimise the gap between logical and emotional knowledge, Ellis asked people:

- how their lives would be different if this belief were true;
- to name the three things that would be most different;
- to describe previously problematic events but with the new rule;
- how they would carry themselves differently.

Role play can be used to facilitate gaining this emotional knowledge (Greenberg et al., 1997) by encouraging the client to enact in session these new roles in line with their new powerful interpersonal self-beliefs. Non-verbal as well as verbal communication and cues are used to fully act out the part expected of the new belief. In this role play, the voice hearer may begin to talk back to the voice (with or without formal assertiveness training), perhaps by directly challenging it, utilising agreed short, assertive stock replies as described above.

Rakos (2000) suggests that training might begin by examining and challenging the thoughts about the self within the social situation and then progressing to a behavioural hierarchy in which the person is encouraged to gradually expose themselves to situations that they initially felt they would be unable to be assertive in but could ultimately prove that they could cope with.

The empty chair

Drawing on the work of Greenberg et al. (1997), the 'empty chair' technique invites the client to converse with the powerful or critical 'other' by placing the 'other' in a chair opposite them and describing how it feels to be criticised by them. The therapist limits this part of the exercise to a few minutes. The person then swaps seats and talks as the other, validating the feelings that have been expressed and discussing how it feels to be in this second chair. For the purposes of addressing power beliefs, this process can be adapted so that the person:

- first describes what the voice has done to them;
- describes the emotional experience of living with that voice with the 'old' belief: that the voice is powerful;
- in the second chair (the client) is encouraged to act in accordance with new powerful interpersonal self-beliefs and tell the voice that
  1   they are not going to comply with their commands;
  2   that they do not believe the criticisms being levelled at them;
- they are then asked to describe how this feels;
- depending on the goals of the exercise, the individual might then take the position of the voice to describe how it feels to receive these responses.

Within this process the person is encouraged to always reflect on their feelings in order to produce the maximum experiential change (Watson and Greenberg, 1996).

Case example: Colette

Colette's voices constantly told her that she was stupid, useless and that she should do what they say (which ranged from orders to tidy up her flat to more serious commands to kill herself). One of Colette's primary goals in therapy was to feel more assertive in her relationships with both the voices and other people. She said that she had never felt able to talk back to or verbally stand up to the voices. The therapist suggested trying the empty chair technique as a means of practising being more assertive with the voices. In this transcript Colette had arrived at the session feeling upset about an incident the night before in which the voices prevented her from visiting a friend:

NK: So sitting in that chair (Chair 1) Colette, can you take me back to that situation last night when the voices were giving you a hard time?

Colette: I was trying to get ready to go to out and they just started going on and on.

NK: If you imagine that situation again now, what are they saying to you?

Colette: That I'm useless, I'm stupid and that there is no point in going because I have nothing to say to anyone.

NK: How does that feel?

Colette: (tearfully) Horrible. I feel so low.

NK: What do you feel in your body?

Colette: I feel weak, trod upon, again.

NK: And what do you do?

Colette: Nothing. I just take it. I stop getting ready and just stay in. I don't go to my friends.

NK: And do you get an image at all of what you look like?

Colette: Yes, it's that same image again (Colette had previously disclosed experiencing an image when she heard the voices that reminded her of herself as a child cowering away from her abusive father). I'm hunched up and cowering away from the voices. They are just too powerful and I'm scared not to do what they say.

NK: What beliefs about yourself are associated with that experience?

Colette: I'm stupid and weak. The voices are right – I'm pathetic.

Colette is then asked to move to the second chair. Drawing on a more powerful self-belief developed in a previous session, the therapist incorporated this into the two chairs exercise:

NK: OK, Colette, do you remember what your new belief is?

Colette: Yes, 'I am intelligent and capable of doing the things that I want'.

NK: OK, so with that belief in mind, I'd like you to go back to that situation last night again. Let me know when you feel you are back in that situation.

Colette: (after a few moments) Yes, I'm there. I can hear them.

NK: What are they saying?

Colette: (tearfully) The same thing – that I'm stupid, useless and that there is no point in going out.

NK: This time Colette, with that new belief in mind, what would you like to say back to them?

Colette: I'm not sure I can . . . I'm scared (becoming more tearful).

NK: Just take your time. I'm here with you and remember that you can stop this at any point.

Colette: No (to therapist resolutely) . . . I need to do this.

NK: I can hear that determination of yours shining through!

Colette: (In a firm voice and sitting up in her chair, reading the new beliefs from her coping card of pre-rehearsed 'powerful' statements to the voices) Now you listen to me, I'm not listening to you anymore – I'm going to do what I want to do.

NK: That's brilliant. How does that feel?

Colette: (crying) Good . . . but scary.

NK: Has the image of yourself changed at all?

Colette: Yes, my shoulders are no longer hunched. I'm stronger. I'm bigger.

NK: How does it feel in your body?

Colette: OK I guess. Can we finish this now?

After this exercise, Colette became very distressed and tearful. She said that it was the only time that she could recall that she had ever asserted herself with the voices even though she still felt scared about the possible repercussions. Initially, the therapist was concerned that perhaps this technique had been introduced too early in the sessions, and perhaps further time should have been spent building Colette's coping repertoire. Interestingly, however, in the weeks after this, Colette was able to verbally stand up to the voices and was more able to resist their commands. At the end of therapy, she maintained that although this was the most difficult session in therapy, it was the most useful.

Addressing power in other non-voice relationships

The universality of core beliefs in which the self is viewed as inferior to others (Ellis, 1962; Fennell, 1998) indicates that people feel relatively powerless not only in relation to their voices, but also in relation to other people in their lives. This might be family members or friends, or the health professionals they work with. This can be measured formally using the Social Comparison Scale (Allan and Gilbert, 1995; discussed further in Chapter 8), or informally in clinical interview. The link between the manner in which a person relates to the voices, and the way that they relate to other people in their lives can be made and illustrated through sharing this aspect of the CTCH formulation at this stage. The same methods that promote change in the client's relationship with their voices can be used here to promote change in their broader interpersonal relationships.

Role play as described above can provide some initial confidence to practice new strategies. When helping someone behave differently to others, however, the person's role and position within that relationship should first be considered and the other party might need to be recruited to support the inevitable change within the social system.

Case example: Charlie

Charlie (described above) heard the voice of an 'angel' who criticised her and told her to harm herself. Through meeting with the therapist and role playing her responses, she had learnt to resist these commands without the feared consequences. She was also married to a man who would criticise and ignore her. Instances of verbal or prolonged emotional abuse would often lead to a worsening of the voice of the 'angel'. The parallels between the two relationships were drawn and she was able to see that she related to her husband in the same way that she had done to the voice; she would give in to his demands, believe his criticisms and end up feeling worse about herself and her relationship. She decided that she would begin to use the same coping strategies with him as she had done with the voice; she would ignore him unless he was nice to her, tell him that she was busy at the moment but would make time for him later. She began to see him as a bully whose demands would get worse if she gave into him. Initially her husband simply responded more aggressively and Charlie reported feeling frightened. To further support Charlie, the therapist met with them both together for a few sessions in order to explore her husband's view of the effect that the 'angel' had on their lives and to recruit him into supporting Charlie's new stance towards the 'angel'.

It was important to get her husband's support to foster collaboration and change the dynamic from one of hostility to collaboration, in which any changes are likely to be sustained. Charlie's husband was reluctant to acknowledge that problems might stem in any way from their relationship. He did however accept that these were new skills which she needed to practice. If successful, she would be less troubled by her voices and so there would be ultimately less burden upon him. Her husband subsequently reported that as Charlie recovered they had begun to rediscover their relationship – he was less stressed and so less inclined to be critical.

Working with the broader social environment: promoting inclusion

At this point in therapy, the therapist and client may usefully spend some time considering the client's broader social network and environment. Often clients with psychosis lead socially isolated lives due partly to stigma and more limited social opportunities (e.g. through lack of employment) as well as more directly to the difficulties associated with experiencing command hallucinations themselves and complying with their demands. It is often useful here to work more closely with the client's care team and to discuss increasing social contact and opportunities and how these can best be facilitated, either as part of specific CTCH goals (using strategies and techniques used in level 6 and previous levels) or in the broader context of the client's multidisciplinary care plan. Peter, one of our main case studies, provides a detailed example of this level of work in CTCH.

Tackling difficulties in raising the individuals' power

For some individuals, voices can feel so overwhelmingly powerful that they do not feel capable of questioning them at any level. Adopting a personalised graded hierarchy is often helpful, beginning with aspects of voice activity which are agreed to be least likely to cause adverse consequences for the client. Role play with the therapist acting as the voice may be a 'safer' adjunctive early strategy.

Positive power beliefs

As in other levels of CTCH, in some cases clients hold positive beliefs about their voices and so do not wish to challenge them. Learning to recognise and consolidate the power shift may therefore prove problematic. They may, however, not always wish to follow what the voices command, and the process of previous levels of CTCH work may have begun to question indirectly their voices' power and the wisdom of or need to always do what they say. This can be highlighted to the client emphasising that the goal is to develop a collaborative relationship, even with friends who we like we may not want to see them all the time and require some personal space, even in more intimate relationships. In such relationships it can be helpful to propose that people we otherwise like or feel positive towards may be unreasonable and we may occasionally need to be assertive with them. This however does not mean that we stop liking them, or stop being friends with them.

A greater focus on levels 7 and 8 may also be considered, examining the meaning behind such positive voice beliefs and addressing any corresponding negative self-beliefs first.

Reflecting on the relationship with the therapist

As noted earlier, the process of taking control back is modelled early on in therapy (e.g. use of the symbolic panic button). At this point the therapist may encourage the client to reflect on their relationship with the therapist: its collaborative nature, gently challenging learned assumptions about professional care relationships that may have been formed in more insecure environments (Waddington, 2002). Negative relationships with health professionals (and possible delusions about the therapist's motives in particular) can be normalised with the voice hearer with reference to previous experiences of care received by others. The therapist can also draw out through Socratic dialogue instances where the client has been assertive with the therapist: turning instances of non-participation in therapy goals into a positive.

Case example: Timothy

Timothy had failed to attend several appointments and was well known within his team for 'not engaging'. The therapist continued to offer appointments via letters and text messages. Eventually Timothy called the therapist to cancel a forthcoming appointment (even though he had also not attended the previous six appointments without letting the therapist know). The therapist praised Timothy for calling her and said that she was encouraged by his increased assertiveness: being able to call and say he did not feel like a session was an indicator that he was standing up for himself and able to verbally express his own needs and wants. The therapist then suggested that perhaps this was something they could build on in therapy to help him feel more able to stand up to the voices. Following this discussion Timothy, impressively, attended a total of twenty-one CTCH sessions. Furthermore when he did not feel like a session, he was able to cancel the appointment rather than just not turn up.

Addressing power in interpersonal relationships

As described above, this usually constitutes an extension of and means of building on shifts in the power relationship with the voice. However, for clients who are unable to engage in this work, an alternative useful starting point is to begin with other relationships where they have had to establish boundaries.

Case example: Ella

Ella kept a dog that she felt she could not control (it had already bitten two health professionals). She had previously completed animal husbandry courses and could recall the importance of boundaries and authority but did not feel she had the confidence to implement them. Assertiveness training (e.g. Rakos, 2000) had encouraged her to be more authoritative with the dog and improved her sense of self-confidence. With the therapist she then explored how she might use similar strategies of setting boundaries and saying 'No' firmly to the voices' constant demands and 'bad behaviour'.

Case example: Mary

Mary had a sister who was bullying and she sometimes also heard her voice. In therapy, Mary and the therapist practiced assertiveness strategies: speaking firmly, looking her in the eye, and not being drawn into long debates with her. Role play was used in session with the therapist playing the role of her sister with scripts obtained from Mary's description of recent incidents. Mary was then asked to try this next time her sister made demands. Mary was subsequently encouraged to stand up to her sister's voice and, in time, extend this to other voice relationships.

In other cases, the therapist may need to work with other colleagues or family members or carers in order to bring about change in family relationships.

Case example: Raj

Raj felt that he had very low value in his family. He was not involved in the family business and not involved in key family decisions. In conjunction with his care coordinator, the therapist met with his brother and uncle and agreed with them that part of Raj's recovery was for him to be more involved in the family business rather than being protected (which they had previously believed was necessary given his mental illness). It was agreed that he could be more involved in working in the family cash and carry, stocking the shelves and helping with deliveries. Raj saw this as a valued role and that he was no longer weak in his family's eyes (a dimension of the social comparison scale). Subsequent work enabled Raj to tell the voice that he was no longer weak (a constant insult by them) providing further evidence of his increasing power.

Such efforts can however readily be sabotaged if others are not on board: For example, Marcus whose supported care workers interpreted his new found assertiveness as challenging behaviour, which threatened his tenancy.

Using behavioural experiments to raise the individuals' power

In some cases clients may, despite being more assertive, continue to believe that others still see them as inferior, undermining efforts to raise the client's power. Stephen noted, for example, that 'I am more assertive with my family but they . . . but they still think I am a loser'. In such cases behavioural experiments, designed to test out beliefs that the person feels inferior to others, or that their views will not be taken seriously, may be considered. In our main case study below, Peter thought that if he spoke to other people they would be able to 'see' the illness and would ignore him. He was encouraged to challenge these beliefs by engaging in social situations. Peter challenged his own beliefs when he went to a barbeque. This afforded a great opportunity to test his own beliefs, what the voice told him and to see whether this married with what actually happened. His beliefs and how they changed are discussed below in more detail.

Case example: Luke

Luke believed that he might not only be a danger to others but that they might be a danger to him. He acknowledged, however, that when he first started seeing the therapist and his new care coordinator, he was apprehensive, yet over the following months he had come to learn that he could trust them. With the help of his care coordinator, Luke was encouraged to walk around a local lake. He predicted that if he spoke to other people who were also walking around the lake they would attack him, ignore him if he said hello or avoid him. Between the therapist, Luke and his care coordinator this belief was tested out. Luke was asked to walk around the lake and encouraged to smile and say hello to people. He recorded what the person's response was. He tried this on four separate occasions and in each case the response was positive. In some cases people smiled back and in others they said hello in a friendly way. In all cases his (and his voices) predictions were not borne out, and the alternative belief that other people are not necessarily a danger to him and just like Luke are going about their own business (in this case enjoying a walk) and may even be friendly.

Level 6 work with Peter and Angel

Peter

Throughout therapy Peter was encouraged to reflect on the changes that were taking place, his ability to gain more control over the voices, his emotions and his confidence in standing up to them and challenging what she was saying to him. Over time Peter was able to explore what the voices told him and examine the evidence for them; this led to him refuting many of the things he believed and helped him develop and validate alternative positive self-beliefs in relation to his voices.

Identifying and reinforcing new powerful self-beliefs

Peter's voice threatened him that she would materialise and harm him if he did not harm himself. Over time he came to believe that although he did see a shadowy figure that he believed was her, she did not go on to harm him. He was able to redirect his attention on to other things and resist her commands and no harm occurred. Peter increasingly thought that 'she talked the talk but couldn't walk the walk'. Over time his confidence grew and he began to develop a set of more positive interpersonal self-beliefs. Peter used his computer to record a number of successes in therapy and a variety of affirmations to coach himself through any difficulties:

- he could take control (using the strategies he had developed);
- she wasn't that powerful;
- he could change how the power was distributed in the relationship by:
  - maintaining and developing control strategies;
  - evaluating what she told him;
- she can go on and on but I have taken control in the past;
- she can't make me do anything;
- I'm the one calling the shots.

He was able to access these when he needed to in order to get through tough times. This led to a burgeoning positive view of himself. Peter could do things right, he was useful and there was hope for the future.

Generalising powerful self-beliefs to the wider social network

At the beginning of therapy, Peter had recently been discharged from his CMHT and felt that they had not been very supportive. He felt very isolated and the theme that emerged was that he did not value himself and did not trust people. During CTCH sessions, Peter mentioned that in his early life there had been instances where he had been abused (emotionally, physically and possibly sexually). He did not have a supportive relationship with his family and was mistrustful of them. There were certain occasions where he visited his father and he would be unappreciative of his visit and positively hostile.

The initial focus of the work was to examine Peter's negative view of himself and the reasons that he did not trust people. Peter did have a good social network but tended to keep himself to himself. He felt stigmatised by his illness, and being unemployed and thought that others did not understand and would treat him differently. This led to Peter sometimes isolating himself when it might be better to be more socially active. Not only would this help him cope better, it also might provide opportunities to refute his beliefs. This was reflected back to Peter and he accepted that this had become an established way of coping yet had a number of downsides.

Over time Peter was able to seek out opportunities to attend social events with his friends. This was challenging for him as he believed that he would be scrutinised by his friends, asked lots of intrusive questions, and this would just confirm his predictions in the first place stating, 'People know I have a mental illness and will treat me differently', 'people won't talk to me or be nice to me because I am not normal'. The therapist supported Peter to attend a barbeque at a friend's house. At first he was very hesitant. However, he found that others at the barbeque knew little about his mental health, job and financial situation, contrary to his predictions. When he did chat to people, they were friendly, pleasant and he found it enjoyable. After the barbeque he was encouraged to examine the situation and Peter was able to identify that his beliefs and predictions did not match what actually took place.

Another situation that arose also challenged Peter's beliefs and predictions. He visited a local dog sanctuary and was informed that some of the dogs were due to be destroyed. He decided to ask if he could take one of the dogs home and they agreed to this. This provided him with a sense that he had helped save the dog and taken control of a horrible situation. It also meant that he had a dog to support, which was a very useful distraction and it provided unconditional love back to him. When he did go out walking, he noted that it provided a great opportunity to interact with others. They would ask him about the dog, how long he had had him and he could reciprocate by asking them questions about their dog or what they did. When this was explored in subsequent sessions, he recalled what had happened and he noted again that people did not know anything about him. People can be friendly and this challenged the view that he had regarding being automatically viewed in a negative way. Furthermore, it was not obvious to others (at least they never indicated this to be the case) that he had mental health difficulties and he did not appear to 'stand out'.

In preparation for the end of therapy, it was agreed to refer Peter back to his CMHT for extra support and a review of his medication. He subsequently met with a consultant psychiatrist he had not seen before and a new different community psychiatric nurse. Although this was unsettling for him, it proved very encouraging and contrary to his expectations. They listened to his story and were attentive to his needs. The theme that emerged was that he had a tendency to negatively predict what would happen or what people would think and he was not accurate.

Peter subsequently began to interact more with friends and professionals and attended a ceramics course. He also learned to actively seek out friends at difficult times and when things were not going so well.

Angel

Angel is a striking example of how powerful voices are mirrored in broader interpersonal power relationships. As a child and young adult, Angel described being constantly criticised by her mother. Now, as an adult, she described relationships in which other people were very controlling and critical of her. She also described herself as always feeling subordinate to other people because she frequently felt scared and unable to express her own needs and opinions. It became clear that Angel held the belief 'If I stand up for myself, bad things will happen or people will reject me'. Indeed, Angel described frequent situations at home and at work in which she was unable to assert herself and was left feeling 'trod upon', hence reinforcing a subordinate position. Angel found these situations very stressful, particularly because they also tended to exacerbate her voices.

Identifying new power beliefs and reinforcing those beliefs

Time was spent helping Angel to recognise her increasing mastery and control gained during the process of CTCH by developing a list of evidence supporting powerful interpersonal self-beliefs:

- I have been able to stand up to the voices and have been able to take my medication every day this week.
- I feel a lot stronger.
- I've been facing my challenges rather than running away.
- I have been resisting the voices and have had control over what I want to do.
- I am good in a crisis and can look after other people.
- I have been able to be assertive and express what I wanted.

Generalising powerful self-beliefs to the wider social network

After reading some literature on assertiveness (from www.getselfhelp.co.uk), Angel and the therapist explored the pros and cons of being assertive and identified times in the past when Angel had been able to be assertive without bad things happening. Although Angel found this difficult, she was able to identify one occasion. She told the therapist about an incident when her son, Joseph, was at school. Joseph was ordinarily a very good student but had fallen behind due to various stressors. As a result his class teacher threatened to only allow him to do a lower GCSE paper, which would have meant that his maximum grade would have been a grade C. Angel described how she had insisted to the class teacher that her son be allowed to take the higher paper (which her son also wanted to do). Consequently, Joseph obtained a grade B in his exam. Angel therefore felt that this was an example of when she had been assertive and a positive outcome had ensued. Building on this example, in addition to her increasing mastery over the voices (from which she was discovering that being assertive, and standing up to them, was resulting in good rather than bad outcomes), Angel and the therapist worked together to help her feel more assertive in other social situations. A number of specific situations were identified, and through the use of role plays and draft emails in sessions, Angel and her therapist rehearsed ways in which Angel might be able to assert herself in these situations. Angel found these strategies very helpful and there were several situations (including sending an assertive email to her boss and expressing what she wanted in a meeting) in which she was able to implement these to good effect. As well as consolidating Angel's new found empowered position, these situations served to help Angel begin to start to question her belief that standing up for herself leads to bad things happening.

Summary

In this chapter we have shown how consolidating and reflecting upon shifts in the power relationship throughout CTCH with voices can be extended to relationships with others and vice versa. An important part of this stage of therapy is to build emotional insight, and along with developing further skills such as assertiveness enable the person to up their social rank and escape from a subordinate position. However, the underlying sources of shame in the form of core beliefs and shamefully labelled past experiences may remain and serve to keep the person in a subordinate position. It is to work at this level that we now turn in the following two chapters.

Note

1   The therapist had provided a recording of a session that used progressive muscular relaxation.

Chapter 7

CTCH Level 7

Addressing beliefs about voice identity, meaning and purpose

Introduction

Although not always possible, ideally clients can progress to work at CTCH levels 7 and 8. REBT practice and theory (Walen *et al.*, 1992) suggest that work at this level is crucial to consolidate lasting change. These final two levels aim to build on progress made at earlier levels and attempt to protect the individual against future relapse. This is important because some clients may not respond to interventions that are focussed solely on the voice-power schema (the inferential level). Indeed, it is often the voices' apparent access to private and 'shameful' information about the person, which disposes them to appraise the voices as omniscient and subsequently omnipotent and potentially harmful (Byrne *et al.*, 2006). Thus, it can sometimes be very difficult to undermine these power beliefs without additionally addressing beliefs about voice identity, meaning and purpose.

Identity refers to beliefs about 'who' the voices are: often this is a supernatural force, the Devil, God or a spirit. For some people, it may be someone known to them such as a friend, relative or neighbour. Other people may not know who their voices are, or their voices may emanate from a range of different people. Arturo, for example, said that he heard a multitude of voices, which came from various strangers and people that he knew. For some people, the identity may refer to one being; for others it may represent several people or an organisation, such as MI5 or the Catholic Church. Voices do not always represent an actual person or being: Noreen reported hearing a bird tweeting and Matthew reported hearing the voices of cats.

Meaning and purpose refers to beliefs about the voices' intent and whether the voices are construed as benevolent or malevolent: are the voices punishing them for bad things that they feel they have done or are they guiding the person to do the 'right thing'. We have found that beliefs about meaning and purpose are often closely linked to the person's core beliefs. For example, Hussain believed that his voices were deservedly punishing him for bad things that he had done in his past. When working with this belief it was important for the therapist to additionally address Hussain's underlying core self-evaluation that he was a bad person.

Knowing the identity of the voice and believing the voice to be real affect compliance to commands (Junginger, 1990; Barrowcliff and Haddock, 2006) and levels of distress (Mawson *et al.*, 2010). Chadwick and Birchwood (1994) found that beliefs about voice identity and meaning led to voices being construed as either benevolent or malevolent, which in turn lead to the individual being more likely to comply or resist respectively. Voice malevolence is also associated with greater distress (Mawson *et al.*, 2010). Therefore, addressing an individual's belief about the identity, meaning and purpose of their voices can be a very important step in reducing both distress and compliance. In this chapter we describe our approach to tackling identity and purpose beliefs and how this often connects to more developmental and historical factors; paving the way for level 8 work.

The development of identity, meaning and purpose beliefs: implications for reframing

Freeman and colleagues (2004) have suggested that the most convincing reason why delusional beliefs are adopted is the absence of plausible alternative explanations. They found that this was particularly evident for internal experiences such as voices. They posited that individuals may not know that these experiences can be internally generated, and therefore, in an understandable attempt to make sense of them, an external 'delusional' explanation may be selected. Usually, such an explanation is informed by pre-existing beliefs, reasoning and attribution biases and ongoing confirmatory experiences, which provide compelling evidence for the individual's selected explanation. In contrast, in the absence of knowing about internal anomalous experiences, it is not surprising that the alternative explanation, which is so frequently given to clients of 'being ill, is comparatively far less convincing, and perhaps even more distressing. Accepting a label of mental illness, or gaining 'insight', is not always helpful to individuals in terms of reducing their distress (Cooke *et al.*, 2007). Indeed, Brett (2004) found that clients with unusual beliefs attributed to psychiatric illness have far higher levels of distress compared to those attributing their beliefs to personal meaning (e.g. normalising and spiritual appraisals). The aim of CTCH levels 7 and 8 work is to help the client find meaning in their experiences by providing a more compelling alternative explanation for them, which is less distressing and less likely to drive the need to comply.

Sometimes it is possible to reformulate the client's explanation for the origins of their voice in psychological or even neurological terms. For example, one prominent model proposes that voices result from self-monitoring deficits leading to inner speech not being recognised as self-produced and therefore being perceived as being 'alien' and externally generated. Others argue for a more memory-based model, whereby voices may reflect an involuntary activation of memories (Waters *et al.*, 2006) or de-contextualised trauma flashbacks. This model can be particularly helpful when the voice content is linked to previous traumatic experiences. Arguing that not all voices are exact memories of traumatic experiences, Fowler *et al.* (2006a) propose that voices may be thematically linked to voice content. Rumination about interactions with an abuser might provide the raw material for many voices by means of misattributed inner speech. This fits with the phenomenology of many voices whose content is not the same as what was said during/surrounding earlier trauma yet is related to it. In addition, some authors have proposed that the development of voices occurs more for interpersonal reasons than neurocognitive ones. For example, Perez-Alvarez and colleagues (2008) propose that voices often occur during times of interpersonal difficulty, serving a protective function of filling a gap and providing a 'substitutional inter-personal world' (p. 77). This is consistent with the notion that unusual beliefs can serve a function of protecting against low self-esteem and depression (Bentall *et al.*, 1994). Chadwick *et al.* (1996) have extended this notion to propose that delusional beliefs serve the function of defending the individual against underlying core negative self-evaluative beliefs. This link can be uncovered using thought or inference chaining (see Chapter 8).

Given that there are potentially different cognitive, neurological and psychological mechanisms underlying voice hearing (see Jones, 2010 for a review), in providing an alternative explanation, it is essential that this fits the idiosyncratic phenomenology of the client's experience. For it to feel plausible to the client, an individualised formulation must be developed containing meaningful links to the client's personal experiences, which are understandable, helpful and make sense to the client.

Agreeing the beliefs to be targeted

In the beginning, to examine any possible underlying meaning behind beliefs about voice identity, meaning and purpose, the therapist should be sensitive to the possibility that this reflects painful core beliefs and traumas if these have not been revealed in therapy thus far. Furthermore, if the voices are not 'real' others or powerful beings then the implication (e.g. that it is the person's own thoughts) may be equally traumatising (depending upon their content) or overwhelming. The following questions can be useful in eliciting any possible alternatives that the client may have already considered:

- What did you think about the voices when you first heard them?
- Have you ever thought there might be any other explanations for the voices?

- What have other people said to you about who or what might be behind them?
- What do you think about other people's explanations for the voices?

Very often the only alternative that clients have been given is that it might be a symptom of mental illness, being told it is not real, which for the client is frequently associated with the belief 'I am mad', and the feeling that they have not been heard. It is important for the therapist to be mindful of this and to carefully elicit, and address, 'illness' appraisals regarding cause, outcome, loss, entrapment and humiliation (Birchwood *et al.*, 2000c; Lobban *et al.*, 2003).

A further consideration is that even the most distressing voices may be viewed as having a positive purpose: providing a sense of specialness and companionship or offering guidance. Some clients might also hear different voices: some of whom are believed to be benevolent and helpful, while others are more distressing and malevolent. Voices may also change over time. Some malevolent voices may have previously been benevolent, creating an ambivalent relationship between voice and voice hearer. Such clients may wish for a return to their former relationship and this will need to be born in mind when agreeing therapy goals. It can be useful in such cases to explore the factors and events surrounding this change in purpose. The therapist and client will need to carefully and sensitively disentangle these potentially competing beliefs. If unaddressed, positive beliefs could also place the client at risk of relapse (Morrison and Renton, 2001). The following questions can be useful in trying to elicit positive beliefs about voices:

- Supposing we were to find out that the voices were not X (e.g. messengers from God teaching you the right way), how would you feel about that? Is there anything that you might miss?
- As you know, I don't have the power to get rid of the voices, but how would you feel if you woke up tomorrow and the voices were gone?

The client's response to such questioning will alert the therapist to any preparatory work that might need to be conducted before attempting to undermine the client's beliefs about identity, meaning and purpose. Wherever possible, the therapist should try to replace the function that the voices serve (e.g. improving the client's social network, offering guidance) or address the negative implications of a potential alternative explanation. The case example of Angel at the end of this chapter highlights the importance of this. Other examples are described below.

Case example: Margaret

Margaret said, 'If they are not really gangster spirits, it must mean that I am mad and that would be terrible'. This alerted the therapist to the importance of adopting a normalising rationale (as pioneered by Kingdon and Turkington, 1993) and de-stigmatising voice hearing before attempting to dispute Margaret's beliefs that the voices were gangster spirits. This was done through presenting information on the frequency of voice hearing (including in non-clinical populations), sharing examples of famous people who have been reported to hear voices such as Anthony Hopkins, Zoe Wannamaker, Ghandi and Winston Churchill, and providing recovery stories of other voice hearers (such as those reported by Romme et al., 2009).

Case example: George

George, a devoted father, frequently heard a male voice commanding him to punch his daughter (which he had always resisted). He expressed anxiety, 'If it is coming from me that would mean that I really am an evil person'. This highlighted to the therapist that before attempting to re-attribute George's beliefs to an internal source, it was necessary to socialise him to the idea that intrusive thoughts (and therefore by implication voices) are normal phenomena, are frequently ego-dystonic in nature (not in keeping with the person's core values and attitudes), and commonly represent our worst fears.

Case example: Caroline

Caroline in contrast to Margaret and George said that although she would feel happy if the voices were gone, she 'would miss their companionship' and could 'not imagine my life without them'. This suggested to the therapist the importance of trying to help Caroline find other sources of companionship before attempting belief change and the need for social inclusion work as described in Chapter 6.

Clarifying the evidence for beliefs

As in level 3 work, at this stage the client is asked to list all the evidence that they use to support their beliefs in identity, meaning and purpose. Again, we adopt the 'weakest first principle' whereby the client is asked to rank order this evidence from least to most convincing, thereby creating a disputation hierarchy (Meaden *et al.*, 2010). The purpose of this is to pursue a 'path of least resistance' as it is likely to be easier to undermine the weakest piece of evidence first. Also, the doubt generated from addressing weaker pieces of evidence may increase openness to reappraising more compelling pieces.

Case example: Carol

Carol heard the voice of her deceased son who she believed was haunting her. When asked to list the evidence that she used to support these beliefs, from least to most convincing, Carol said:

Identity: *I believe that it is my son because*:

1 he says that it's him;
2 it sounds like him;
3 I see him when he talks to me;
4 he looks and sounds so real.

Meaning and purpose: *I believe that he is haunting me because*:

1 he died traumatically (in a car accident) and so has not been able to reach heaven . . . like in the movies;
2 I could not save him. That is why he is haunting me.

Other general principles described in Chapter 4 are useful here for deciding which beliefs are to be addressed first (e.g. identity or meaning and purpose beliefs): rating the degree of interference with daily functioning, the amount of distress associated with them and the amount of time the client spends thinking about the belief.

Devising alternative beliefs

Having conducted the necessary preparatory work for potential belief change, the next task for the therapist is to establish the replacement, alternative belief. Given that many clients may have difficulty generating other explanations (Freeman *et al.*, 2004), it may be necessary to tentatively 'float' alternative explanations for their experiences. In general, we tend to propose the stress-vulnerability model as a broad building block for possible alternative explanations. This model suggests that people may have a greater or lesser predisposition to psychotic experiences or other physical/mental health symptoms, which are triggered by higher or lower numbers of stressful events. Then, if possible (or desirable given the function of the client's current beliefs and any negative implications that an alternative explanation might hold), a more specific alternative explanation for the voices might be proposed. Drawing on the theoretical literature, a psychological or neurological explanation, which is individualised according to the idiosyncratic nature and phenomenology of the client's experiences and beliefs, may be suggested. Generally, this includes elements of one or more of the following:

- the voices as misattributed inner speech or the 'brain making mistakes';
- the voices as traumatic memories or echoes from the past;
- the voices as a protective function from difficult and traumatic times and associated core beliefs.

Once the therapist has tentatively floated a possible alternative explanation which seems acceptable to the client, it can then be helpful to generate a cost-benefit analysis of both beliefs being true or false. Even if there are positive or functional aspects to the voices, once the client sees that they would be 'better off' if their beliefs were false, their motivation to proceed with this stage of therapy will usually be increased. This was certainly the case for Angel, whose cost-benefit analysis is shown in Table 7.1.

Table 7.1 Advantages and disadvantages of the voices being messengers from God

Belief 1: 'The voices are messengers from God teaching me the right way'	
Advantages of the belief being true	*Disadvantages of the belief being true*
1 The doctors and staff would not have to fight against me to take my medication 2 I would be special and chosen	1 It means that it would be true that I have caused, and will continue to cause, bad things to happen in the world 2 If someone finds that out, they might try to bump me off 3 Everyone else would be thinking what the voices say (that I am evil) 4 I wouldn't have any support to help me cope with the voices 5 I would be frightened of the consequences of having to do what the voices say (sacrificing myself)

Reframing and disputing beliefs about identity

Having already begun the process of questioning the validity of identity beliefs, the therapist now draws upon the client's own doubt, past or present, their own contradictory evidence and behaviour, and their own concerns that their beliefs about the voices' identity might be wrong. The 'Columbo' technique noted earlier is a particularly powerful form of Socratic questioning, with an emphasis on curiosity, pointing out inconsistencies in a general curious way (Fowler *et al.*, 1995).

As well as reframing and disputing current identity beliefs, the therapist and client can additionally review the evidence for and against the alternative explanation(s). Often the evidence supporting the alternative explanation provides a helpful reframe for some of the evidence supporting the original belief.

Disputing the evidence

As in level 4 work, the therapist utilises a number of key disputes designed to build upon earlier teaching. Again the aims are to undermine the power of the voice by tackling the pieces of evidence that are commonly used to support identity beliefs:

Supporting evidence: 'They have told me that they are X' (e.g. God, the Devil).

Key dispute: 'We know that they've told lies in the past, so why should we believe them when they claim to be X?'

Supporting evidence: 'Only X would have the power to make me do things'.

Key dispute: 'If it really was X, do you think that you would be able to resist them as much as you have been able to?'

Key dispute: 'If it really was X, why do they need you to do Y, why not simply do it themselves?'

Drawing on the work completed in earlier CTCH levels, the therapist can review the voices' lies, false claims and deceptions with the aim here of introducing the notion that just because the voices claim to be a particular person, it does not mean that they are them:

Key dispute: 'Is it possible that they might just be saying that they are X (e.g. God/the Devil) just to frighten you or to big themselves up?'

Key dispute: 'Given how close you were to X (e.g. your mother), is there any chance that they might be pretending to be her because they think that you would be more inclined to listen to them?'

Key dispute: 'I might claim that I am X (e.g. the Queen), does it mean that I actually am . . .'.

Challenging the voices' omniscience

In this level of CTCH, the aim is to undermine the voice's omniscience by challenging how much the voice knows in line with their identity. The aim is to further expose the voice as a fraud since they will not know all of the things that would be known by the person or organisation they claim to be, or which the person has assumed them to be. Here the client draws on their increased power and assertiveness skills from level 6 work to challenge the voices to answer questions that they ought to know. The therapist may begin this process by asking questions such as:

> If your voice really is God, then shouldn't they be able to answer questions about the Bible?

The therapist might then set up a behavioural experiment in which the voices are challenged to answer specific questions, for example, about Christianity or the Bible. Other key disputes here are:

Supporting evidence: 'Only X would know about things in my past/ only X would know what I am thinking'.
Key dispute: 'Are there things in your past that the voices don't know?'
Supporting evidence: 'The voices seem very knowledgeable'.
Key dispute: 'How much do they really know . . . are there any things that the voices should know about if they really are X that they don't'.

Case example: Desmond

NK: If the voices really are MI5 agents then they must know lots of information about MI5.

Desmond: Yes, they do.

NK: So, if we were to ask them specific questions about MI5, would they be able to answer them?

Desmond: Yes, of course.

NK: So if I was to ask them in what year MI5 was formed, would they be able to tell us that?

Desmond: Yes, they would . . . but they won't answer.

NK: Hmmm . . . well that's interesting, isn't it? Surely it is going to be pretty easy for them to answer a simple question about their own organisation.

Desmond: They say they won't lower themselves to answering your silly questions and they don't need to prove themselves.

NK: Oh really! I would have thought if they really wanted us to take them seriously and to believe that they are MI5 agents, then this would be an ideal opportunity for them to prove it to us.

Desmond: No, they are refusing to play your game.

NK: Hmmm, I'm wondering whether it is a matter of 'won't' or 'can't'. I'm wondering whether maybe they are not very clued up agents or perhaps they could even be fibbing about who they are.

Desmond: Hmmm . . . I'm not sure . . .

NK: Well, I would have thought that it would be in their best interest to play ball with this, wouldn't it? I mean, if they've already gone to so much effort to try to make us take them seriously, it would be pretty easy for them to answer a simple question, wouldn't it?

Desmond: Yes, I guess so . . . (starting to sound a little more doubtful).

As Desmond's doubt about the voices being MI5 agents gradually increased, the therapist suggested developing a further set of questions to 'quiz' the voices on their knowledge about MI5, which the voice hearer could ask.

Recruiting the help of other people can sometimes be useful here to gather information that the voices can be challenged about.

Case example: Gareth

When trying to gather information as to whether there was anything in Gareth's past that the voices did not know, Gareth's father was asked to write down a few key things about Gareth's early life that Gareth could not remember. Examples included names of relatives and key milestones such as when Gareth spoke his first word. It emerged that there was much the voices were ignorant about.

Proposing alternatives

Having created doubt regarding the voices' identity, alternative explanations can be proposed. These can be introduced as a type of experiment. Care must be taken to consider the possible outcomes and the impact of these on the person; they should not be carried out just to prove that the person is wrong (Johns *et al.*, 2007). With this type of experiment, it is important to ensure that the client does not know the answers to the questions, since this would mean that the voices would then also be privy to this knowledge! Chapter 5 provides a basic outline of some of the key areas that need to be considered when setting up a robust behavioural experiment.

The brain makes mistakes

Clients often report how real the experience of voice hearing is for them. We do not dispute this but rather introduce the idea that the brain is complex and capable of 'making mistakes'. For example, one of the authors is colour-blind and would often disclose this to her clients asking them to test her on the colour of certain objects in the room. To the source of much amusement for many clients, the therapist inevitably made several mistakes on this task, enabling her to make the following observation:

> I see that cup as red (rather than green as stated by the client) and that feels really real to me. But because I know that I am colour-blind and my brain has a tendency to make mistakes about colours, despite how real it feels, I know that the cup is probably green just as you say.

Other analogies of mistakes made by the brain include visual illusions, referred pain, trauma flashbacks, dreams and nightmares (see Nelson, 2005 for a review). It can be particularly useful to draw upon any personal experiences that the client might have had.

Case example: Ruth

Ruth reported having frequent dreams that she was in a fairground, enjoying being on all the rides. On waking it would usually take her several seconds before she realised, to her disappointment, that the dream was not real and that she was actually at home in bed. This highlighted to Ruth that when dreaming we often believe certain things to be real even though they are not really happening.

Using examples of other 'mistakes' that the brain makes can be a powerful normalising tool, as rather than implying 'illness' it suggests that 'mistakes' made by the brain are a normal phenomena and that voice hearing may be just one example of this (albeit a more distressing one). Pictorial diagrams can also be helpful in illustrating these mistakes (such as that shown in Figure 7.1). In general, we have found introducing the concept of the brain 'making

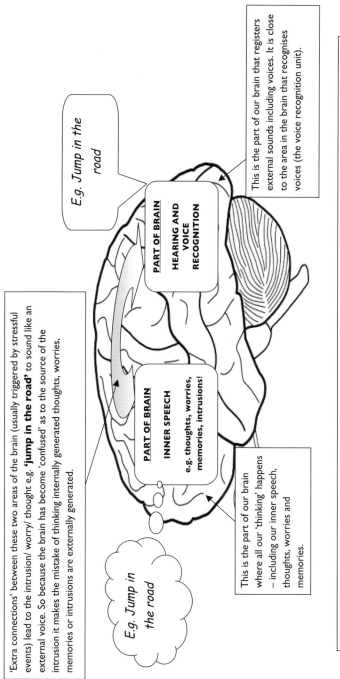

'Extra connections' between these two areas of the brain (usually triggered by stressful events) lead to the intrusion/ worry/ thought e.g. **'jump in the road'** to sound like an external voice. So because the brain has become 'confused' as to the source of the intrusion it makes the mistake of thinking internally generated thoughts, worries, memories or intrusions are externally generated.

E.g. Jump in the road

PART OF BRAIN

HEARING AND VOICE RECOGNITION

PART OF BRAIN

INNER SPEECH

e.g. thoughts, worries, memories, intrusions!

E.g. Jump in the road

This is the part of our brain where all our 'thinking' happens – including our inner speech, thoughts, worries and memories.

This is the part of our brain that registers external sounds including voices. It is close to the area in the brain that recognises voices (the voice recognition unit).

This process is an example of how the brain can sometimes make mistakes or 'play tricks on us' (just like visual illusions and colour blindness). It happens to lots of people particularly after very stressful events e.g. bereavement, childhood abuse, divorce.

Figure 7.1 The brain makes mistakes

mistakes' a very helpful way of building evidence to support the alternative explanation: that the voices might reflect memories of past bullying or self-critical inner speech. In the latter case, it is notable that studies of negative thinking in depression and voice content (Gilbert *et al.*, 2001) reveal significant similarities. Such empirical evidence may be usefully shared with the client.

When the voice represents a person known to the client, and the client recognises the voice to be them, the therapist can again draw on the idea that the brain is complex and capable of making mistakes. A useful analogy is that we can often recognise people's voices in dreams even though the person is not really there. We have also found it helpful to draw on the work of Nelson (2005) who used the term 'voice recognition units' for the area of the brain that has learnt to recognise and distinguish between people's voices. Nelson (2005) suggested that these are located close to the part of the brain that is 'making the mistake' or misattributing inner speech to an external source. She further proposed that if the voice recognition units are mistakenly activated then:

> The brain will produce the subjective experience of actually hearing that particular person speaking the words. The voice recognition units for voices that have been heard recently or for voices that are more familiar to the person are more likely to be activated. The recognition units for people who are of particular importance for the person are likely to be more sensitive to activation and hence also more likely to be recognised.
> (Nelson, 2005, p. 32)

Case example: Cain

Cain heard the voices of three of his childhood friends: Lucy, Max and Alfie whom he believed were persecuting him because he stopped being friends with them. He had not been in contact with these friends for over 15 years and he found it very confusing and upsetting that he continually heard their voices telling him that he was evil and commanding him to do 'bad' things, including to kill himself. In therapy, it emerged that Cain's mother had sadly committed suicide when he was 10. Shortly after, Cain and his father moved out of the area. Cain subsequently lost touch with his friends. It was not long after this when he started hearing the voices of his friends. Initially, he found their voices to be comforting as they would say nice things to him but before long Cain said they turned nasty and started instructing him to do bad things. Cain reported that it was a downward spiral for him from then on.

The therapist proposed to Cain that the voices may have been triggered by the traumas of losing his mother and his best friends in the space of a few weeks. She suggested that perhaps initially the voices served a protective role by providing him with the friends that he so dearly missed. It seemed as though their turning nasty coincided with other difficult events in Cain's life, including him being sent to a youth offender's centre for burglary. The therapist speculated whether this may have been a time when he was feeling particularly bad about himself and wondered whether the voices were perhaps echoing those beliefs that he held about himself. Cain found this a very helpful way of making sense of the voices. He said that he found the concept of the voice recognition unit being 'mistakenly activated' a particularly useful way of explaining why it was that he still heard the voices of Lucy, Max and Alfie. Figure 7.2 shows a diagrammatic formulation that was developed with Cain.

Examining the voice's characteristics

Another useful technique can be to examine the physical properties and general characteristics of voices. The aim here is to explore whether the voice possesses all of the properties one would expect given its identity.

Case example: Cain

Cain said that his voices were exactly the same as he remembered them when he was 10 years old. Through Socratic questioning, it was proposed that Lucy, Max and Alfie would now be in their late twenties and so, most likely, their voices would have changed and matured as they had got older.

Examining the content of voices can be another very effective means of undermining identity beliefs when the voices sound like a particular person. The following transcript is taken from a session with Carol, who we introduced earlier in this chapter. Carol heard the voice of her deceased son, Alex, whom she believed was haunting her. Carol frequently heard Alex's voice saying, 'Just kill yourself mummy', 'Nobody will miss you' and 'You are a terrible mother':

NK: I wonder if you might be able to describe to me what kind of person Alex was.

Carol: He was so kind. Such a loving boy, and always putting everyone else before himself. He would not have hurt anyone.

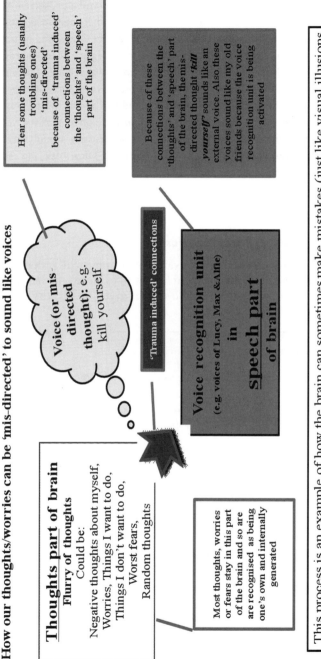

Figure 7.2 Cain's reformulation

NK: Mmmm, yes that fits with everything that you've told me about him. He sounds like he was a really thoughtful and special boy.

Carol: He was. Everyone loved him. He was really popular at school.

NK: Right, so I guess that just makes me wonder whether these are the kind of things that he would have said to you when he was alive.

Carol: No, he would never have said anything like that.

NK: Does anything that you hear him saying now sound like the kind of things that he would have said?

Carol: No, I guess it doesn't really.

NK: Do you think that he would really want you to kill yourself?

Carol: No (hesitantly) . . . I don't think that he would.

The therapist and Carol then began to systematically examine the content of the voices. Carol soon noticed that the content of the voices seemed more similar to her own thinking than it was to her son's. She began to wonder whether perhaps the voices might be a reflection of her own (guilty) thinking in relation to not being able to prevent her son's death. It was proposed that perhaps her being able to hear Alex's voice so clearly and vividly was also a reflection of how much she loved and missed him, and was perhaps her brain's understandable way of trying to keep Alex's memory alive but was distorted by her own guilt.

Examining the content of the voices can also be used to exploit any incongruence between what the voice says and what would be expected of the person or entity ordinarily. For example, when Zoe heard the voice of God instructing her to kill her neighbours, the therapist tentatively highlighted the incongruence between this and what one might expect God to say.

Reframing and disputing beliefs about meaning and purpose

If it is possible to re-attribute the identity of the voice to an internal source such as misattributed 'inner speech', the 'brain making mistakes' or 'unprocessed traumatic memories', this will weaken resistance to subsequent reframing of the person's beliefs about meaning and purpose.

Case example: Cain

The suggested alternative explanation for the source of Cain's voices, that they were triggered by the traumas of losing his mother and best-friends, and although initially protective they later turned nasty as difficult life events impacted on him, made it relatively easy to reframe his meaning and purpose beliefs. Rather than believing that Lucy, Max and Alfie were persecuting him because he had stopped being friends with them, an alternative explanation was proposed: that the voices were 'my brain's understandable attempt to keep hold of my friends after mum died' and 'my brain making mistakes and echoing my fears and worries'.

Although we have found it generally easier to address beliefs about identity first, the therapist should be guided by the path of least resistance to reducing distress and compliance. For some clients it is not always possible, or indeed appropriate, to reframe beliefs about identity due to the emotional investment the client may have in their voices. Nevertheless, it may still be possible to address beliefs about meaning and purpose in order to reduce distress and compliance. In these cases further time will need to be spent on exploring the purpose of the voice and using Socratic questioning to examine alternative theories. When addressing beliefs about meaning and purpose, it can be useful to ask the following questions:

- What does the voice want?
- Does it echo the person's own thoughts, needs or wants?
- Is it ego-systonic/dystonic (in or out of keeping with the person's own values and attitudes)?

Case example: Dorothy

Since the birth of her son 20 years ago, Dorothy heard the voices of several malevolent police officers whom she believed were trying to harm her son. They also commanded her to do things that she did not want to do, such as urinate in public places and throw objects out of her flat window (which was on the fifth floor of a housing estate, overlooking a public seating area). The voices threatened to harm her son if she did not do what they said. She also heard benevolent voices whom she described as her friends. Dorothy said that her friends gave her good advice and complimented her on the way she looked. When the therapist tentatively floated alternative explanations for the voices, Dorothy uncharacteristically became very guarded and suggested that these other explanations implied that she was 'a mad Schizophrenic' which, she said, would be devastating. She also proceeded to quickly provide the therapist with further evidence for how she knew that the voices were who they claimed to be and also repeatedly spoke about the importance of her friends. It became evident to the therapist that it was not likely to be possible, or indeed helpful, to provide Dorothy with an alternative explanation regarding the identity of the voices.

Such therapy moments highlight the importance of the therapist adopting a 'crab-like' stance (E. Peters, personal communication) in which the therapist can withdraw from a particular exchange or suggestion as quickly as it was entered. Rather than attempting to address beliefs about identity, therefore, the therapist and Dorothy (having already weakened her omnipotence and compliance beliefs) agreed instead to target beliefs about the meaning and purpose of the voices.

Through Socratic dialogue, the therapist suggested that rather than trying to punish Dorothy because she was not a capable mother, perhaps the voices were trying to distress her because they were jealous that she had such a lovely son, whom she had in fact brought up very well. Dorothy found this a plausible and less distressing explanation about the voices' intent.

Addressing ego-dystonic/systonic issues

Sometimes voices may reflect the person's own needs, thoughts and wants; sometimes they may be entirely ego-dystonic, and sometimes the voices may reflect a combination of both of these. Clarifying this can be helpful since if the person realises that the voices are ego-systonic, this can serve to usefully undermine the power of the voices on the premise that the client wanted to do it anyway. Caution, however, needs to be taken if the client is likely to experience any shame or distress at pointing out that the voices may reflect their own thinking, especially where this has led to harmful acts. Innocuous commands are a good starting point here: voices telling the client to 'switch off the light, get up, have a wash'.

Case example: Timothy

Timothy heard voices telling him not to have a bath. Timothy had always had difficult experiences at bath times while growing up: his mother told him that 'Cleanliness was Godliness' and he learnt to associate bath times with family arguments and his mother shouting. Highlighting these links and suggesting to Timothy that perhaps 'it was understandable if he did not want to bath' was helpful because it empowered him with a sense of agency as opposed to him believing that he was solely complying with the voices against his will.

When dealing with ego-dystonic voices, before attempting to re-attribute them to an internal source (if appropriate), it is important to provide some psychoeducation about the nature of intrusive thoughts (and therefore by implication voices): highlighting to the client that unwanted thoughts are normal phenomena, are frequently ego-dystonic in nature and commonly represent our worst fears. Irrespective of whether the goal is to re-attribute them to an internal source or not, we have found it helpful to compare the content of voices to dreams in that they:

- may reflect an underlying worry, fear, need or want;
- may be a memory of something the person read about, heard or saw that frightened them or seemed important for some other reason;
- may be a past memory of something that has happened to the person;
- may just reflect a vague idea that floated through the person's mind.

Also, just like with dreams and nightmares, voices may reflect a 'hotchpotch' of all of the above and may occur involuntarily.

Tackling difficulties in addressing beliefs about voice identity, meaning and purpose

Level 7 work in CTCH is often particularly difficult since it implicitly begins to address the causes of the experience of hearing voices. In earlier levels the aims are primarily to undermine the voice's power in order to reduce distress and harmful compliance, whereas here we are proposing a more personalised model (built on the cognitive one). The aim is, however, still one of deconstructing the voice-power schema: the identity, meaning and purpose components of it. We have encountered a number of difficulties, which make this work problematic.

Addressing collateral symptoms

People frequently report experiencing images when they hear voices (Morrison et al., 2002) and may state that 'I see X when he talks to me'. Often this might be an image relating to the identity of the voice (such as spirits, demons or an abuser) or the threats made by the voices (such as being pushed in front of a car or the death of a loved one). Images may also pertain to events from people's past, feared catastrophes and memories of real traumatic life events. For example, as well as seeing her son when she heard his voice, Carol experienced distressing images of him dying in hospital. Images may provide compelling evidence for the identity of the voice and its power.

Visual hallucinations can occur in a variety of conditions (Bell et al., 2010) and can range from flashes of light, changes in visual acuity seeing coloured shapes or patterns through to fully formed complex scenes of a fantastical nature. Visual hallucinations that seem to have particular reference or acquire special meaning are more common in schizophrenia and bipolar disorder. They also tend to be perceived as real and may form part of the person's delusional system (Cutting, 1987).These can be related to neuropathology but are also common in those with trauma histories (Ross *et al.*, 1994).

Such experiences provide strong evidence to support powerful voices. In some cases level 7 work may need to be considered earlier since the origin of these experiences may need to be explored and alternative explanations examined before proceeding with disputing and refraining other aspects of the voice-power schema. Providing psychoeducation about the nature of intrusive imagery, visual hallucinations or post-traumatic intrusions can be particularly helpful here as well as information regarding the many different kinds of causes and conditions under which they may occur (see Bell *et al.*, 2010; Eperjesi, 2010 for reviews).

Intrusions and anomalous experiences in other sensory modalities are also important to assess for so that information can be provided to help the client make sense of such experiences. These are rarely offered voluntarily and can be particularly distressing.

Case example: Stephanie

Stephanie described how her childhood abuser (whose voice she also heard) continued to rape her on a repeated basis. She reported being able to feel him physically penetrating her vagina. Understandably, this was a compelling piece of evidence supporting Stephanie's power beliefs regarding the voice of her abuser. Making links between her current experiences and the earlier sexual abuse she experienced, as well as providing psychoeducation regarding the nature of flashbacks, was an integral component to undermining Stephanie's beliefs about the omnipotence and identity of the voice.

'Poor me' and 'bad me'

As discussed already, it is not uncommon for people to believe that the voices' purpose is to punish them. Sometimes the client might believe that they are being punished for no good reason, whereas another client might believe that such punishment is entirely deserved. Trower and Chadwick (1995) coined these two different types of persecutory belief as 'poor me' and 'bad me' paranoia respectively. 'Bad me' paranoia has been found to be associated with lower self-esteem, more negative self-evaluative thinking, lower negative evaluations about others, higher depression and anxiety

(Chadwick *et al.*, 2005). The beliefs described by Cain are consistent with 'poor me' paranoia.

Case example: Cain

Cain believed that the persecution from Lucy, Max and Alfie was unreasonable. This may explain why it was relatively easy to reframe his beliefs about the meaning and purpose of his voices.

In contrast, when clients believe that punishment is justified it may be necessary to examine the evidence for and against this belief. Examining the client's core self-evaluative beliefs, for example that they are a 'bad person', may also be required (see Chapter 8).

Problems using analogies

There are times when using analogies (such as the brain making 'mistakes' because of activation of voice recognition units) can be too complex. People who hear voices can find concentration difficult because of cognitive difficulties, the effect of neuroleptic medication or just the distracting nature of voices. Simplified analogies, figures and diagrams may need to be developed in these cases.

Level 7 work with Peter and Angel

Peter

Throughout therapy, Peter heard a woman's voice; he did not recognise who she was. He felt that she was there to punish him for past behaviours. He stated that 'she was a ghost, demon, hex, curse, witch or gypsy'. She would be very critical towards him, insulting and telling him to harm himself. Later in therapy when his mood improved and he became more confident about himself and his situation he began to hear a second voice that was male. He said that the voice called himself 'the universe' and was part of the universe. The male voice was more positive and would make a humming noise that would drown out the woman's voice. Peter felt that he was encouraging and supportive.

Agreeing the beliefs to be targeted and preparing for belief change

The emergence of a second guiding and benevolent voice provided a useful opportunity to work with Peter's beliefs about identity. It was tentatively suggested that this might actually be a part of him that was recognising how he was changing, developing and challenging the female voice, gaining more control and power. This new voice then reflected this change. Peter subsequently began to consider that his beliefs that the female voice he heard was a ghost, demon or hex were gradually being questioned. This second voice was drowning her out and offering something different; he was encouraging and supportive, something Peter was not used to.

Clarifying the evidence for beliefs

During the therapy process, Peter indicated that his early family life had been very difficult. He alluded to the fact that it was violent and he was emotionally neglected and sexually abused. However, he did not want to talk about who the perpetrator was or provide any further information. Peter and the therapist nevertheless were able to tentatively make some links between his earlier experiences and the development of his voices, introducing the idea of the stress-vulnerability model. It was possible to draw on earlier work and the notion of facts versus beliefs. Peter had become much more confident challenging what she told him and now questioned whether she was right: that he was no good and was useless. Through Socratic questioning it became apparent that just as his new voice reflected his increasing confidence maybe the female voice reflected his own sense of failure at times and his tendency to put himself down for past mistakes (self-downing in REBT terms). Peter and the therapist now questioned whether he deserved to punish himself for things that happened so long ago. He had not wanted them to happen. If he looked at himself now, Peter saw himself as a supportive son and brother.

Devising alternate beliefs

In line with his improved confidence, Peter suggested that he change his name since his surname was directly linked to his past and represented the curse or hex that he felt was associated with him, his past and current experiences. The woman he heard represented the curse or hex. After exploring this further with the therapist, Peter came to conclude that he did not need to change his name in order to make changes in relation to the past. Although there was an association between the woman and the past, he began to feel that this was not backed up. There had been many aspects of his recent life that had been very positive and Peter felt that he could now do things to take control. Peter recognised that his beliefs had already changed and in many respects what she told him and what he believed might not be backed up by the evidence. This led to a weakening of the belief that she represented a curse or hex. Peter began to consider that he was not deserving of punishment and perhaps his voice did not represent a curse and that not everything that had happened to him was bad. Peter had in fact experienced several good things in his life (both in the past and more recently) and agreed that it would be valuable to look out for these and build up the evidence for them.

Reframing and disputing beliefs about identity, meaning and purpose

Using guided discovery, it was possible to explore his current experiences, the validity of what the woman continued to say and how others saw him. When Peter's mood improved, he began to attend an art group and walked his dog, and this led to a number of new experiences which conflicted with derogatory comments made by his voice (described in Chapter 6). He subsequently began to think that his past experiences could be linked to the negative things she said to him but did not seem to reflect his current experiences. Peter began to believe that:

- she was not a ghost, demon or curse but rather a result of his brain playing tricks;
- maybe what she said reflected the impact of his early experiences;
- what she said no longer held true;
- while bad things had happened to Peter and his family, good things had happened also:
  - he had run his own business successfully for many years
  - he was now in a relationship and spent quality time with his partner's daughter
  - he was attending an art course (a long-held ambition)
  - he had good friends who were very supportive;
- not everything in his life was bad and caused by her.

Peter now began to understand more about the reason why the voice might have developed, and this provided a different interpretation: that it represented all of his negative self-views and tendency to live his life to high standards and put himself down very harshly when things went wrong. This enabled him to question and challenge her further. In many cases evidence was identified that refuted what she told him and what he had previously considered to be true. This supported his new insights: reframing his beliefs about what she truly represented.

Angel

Angel believed that her voices were messengers from God teaching her the right way. She rated her conviction in this belief as 100 per cent. Socratic dialogue early on in therapy had indicated that Angel maintained a high emotional investment in her positive beliefs about the voices because she believed that she had been chosen because she was special.

Agreeing the beliefs to be targeted and preparing for belief change

Given Angel's positive beliefs about her voices, the therapist was alert to the necessity of working with Angel's beliefs about 'specialness' before attempting to undermine this potentially protective belief:

NK: Angel, have there ever been other times in your life when you've been special?

Angel: No, but (hesitantly) I guess the voluntary work I do and my son feel special to me.

NK: And do you think all the voluntary work that you do is quite a special feat?

Angel: I guess so, but I'm finding it difficult to do anything at work at the moment, so that's hardly special. Isn't it.

NK: It has been a really tough time, hasn't it? What do you think has been making it so difficult to work lately?

Angel: It's the voices. They tell me I'm useless and go on at me the whole time so it's hard to concentrate on anything. Sometimes, I'm so useless I can't even make it into work.

NK: Because of the voices?

Angel: Yes, they just go on and on criticising me. Sometimes I just think that I should just leave and not bother anymore.

NK: Do you think that's what the voices want?

Angel: It must be.

NK: As you were saying that Angel, it just struck me that (tentatively) if the voices were trying to stop all the pain and suffering in the world, then why would they want to stop you from doing the helpful and special things that you do at work?

Angel: I'm not sure. It just doesn't make sense.

The therapist proceeded to point out that the voluntary work had benefited hundreds of people, so why would the voices try to sabotage her input to that? To reinforce this, the therapist asked Angel to list some of the feedback that she had received in regards to her voluntary work, all of which was exceptionally praising. In addition, Angel was asked to describe her relationship with her son and what Angel felt was special about him, Angel listed a number of attributes, for example she said that her son was kind, hard working and thoughtful. The therapist then asked:

NK: Who do you think he learnt those qualities from?

Angel: Well it certainly wasn't his dad (jokingly)!

The therapist highlighted how having raised a child is no mean feat, and that Angel's descriptions of her son must say something about her parenting skills. Was this, the therapist queried, something that could be considered special? Furthermore, Angel stated that the voices sometimes encouraged her to avoid her son, which led to the therapist making the following dispute:

NK: It sounds as though rather than making you feel special, they are trying to sabotage all the things that do make you special!

This dispute allowed Angel to consider an alternative purpose belief: rather than teaching her the right way, perhaps the voices were trying to distress her (and therefore she would not need to obey their commands).

Clarifying the evidence for beliefs

At this point, Angel was beginning to question the true purpose of the voices as well as their true identity as messengers from God. When asked whether Angel had ever considered any alternative explanations for the voices, she expressed that she had previously considered that they might be part of an illness. The therapist speculated whether it might be helpful to examine her beliefs in identity meaning and purpose in the same way that they had her beliefs about control, omnipotence and compliance. Angel was keen to pursue this, and so was asked to list all of the evidence that supported her current beliefs about identity, meaning and purpose. Her disputation hierarchy was as follows:

Identity: *I believe that they are messengers from God because*:

1   they have told me;
2   only God would have the power to make me do things;
3   they seem to know everything about me;
4   I have felt special when I have tried to follow through with my purpose (of sacrificing myself).

Meaning and purpose: *I believe that they are teaching me the right way because*:

1   that's what they say and it's wrong to question a vocation;
2   it is a test of my faith to see if I will follow them without question.

Devising alternative beliefs

As Angel's doubt in her current beliefs about the voices increased, she spontaneously suggested an additional alternative explanation for the voices: that they could reflect what she was thinking about herself. She also wondered whether the voices may reflect how people from the past used to speak horribly to her. The therapist felt that the schema work that Angel had been working on concurrently (discussed in Chapter 8) had helped Angel to realise that she was sometimes hard upon herself, and that she held core beliefs that seemed to echo the voices' criticisms (that she is useless, bad and at fault). This cognitive shift paved the way for the development of an alternative, potentially more acceptable, explanation for the voices: that the voices were as she had previously thought part of an illness that may reflect how people from the past used to speak horribly to her. The advantages and disadvantages of the original and the alternative beliefs being true or false were then examined (as depicted previously in Table 7.1). This exercise was useful not only in confirming to the therapist the importance of Angel feeling special, but it also provided Angel with some hope that things could feel better: if the alternative explanation was found to be true, she might actually feel less distressed and would not have the responsibility of having to sacrifice herself to stop world suffering. In the process of doing this, Angel also speculated whether criticising herself (echoed in the voices) was a means of pre-empting and coping with others criticism of her: an understandable strategy perhaps learnt in childhood.

Reframing and disputing beliefs about identity, meaning and purpose

Keen to preserve Angel's belief that she was special, the therapist tentatively floated the idea of whether it might be the case that Angel is special but that perhaps she has been chosen by God in a different way than the voices were suggesting. The therapist was able to draw on the earlier dispute: 'given we already know that they get things wrong'. Perhaps, the therapist suggested, rather than stopping people's suffering through sacrificing herself, Angel's role was to alleviate other people's suffering through doing good things, as she had demonstrated through her voluntary work. This doubt enabled Angel to identify some further inconsistencies with the Bible. For example, in the Bible, Angel thought that God's meaning of sacrifice was more about doing good things for others, and sacrificing one's own needs, devoting time and energy to do this, rather than sacrificing one's own life. Indeed sacrificing one's life, she said, would be seen as suicide, and therefore a sin, in God's eyes. Further biblical comparisons were made, for example the story of Lucifer's attempt to tempt Jesus with food when he was fasting in the desert. The therapist speculated whether it might be possible that, like Lucifer, the voices were trying to lead Angel astray from what God truly wanted her to do – not to sacrifice her life but to sacrifice her time and energy into helping other people. Was it possible, the therapist suggested, that like Lucifer in the desert the purpose of the voices was to test her and like Jesus her challenge was to resist them? This explanation meant that Angel's positive belief in regard to having been chosen by God could be preserved in the face of undermining the more distressing aspects of her beliefs: that the voices were messengers from God (her identity belief) teaching her the right way (her purpose belief) and that she should therefore obey their commands.

Through Socratic questioning and utilising the key disputes outlined earlier in this chapter, the therapist helped Angel to systematically evaluate the evidence supporting her current beliefs as well as the evidence for and against each of the alternative explanations. This was first done for Angel's identity beliefs and then for her beliefs about meaning and purpose. The results of this were drawn up collaboratively in sessions as shown in Tables 7.2 and 7.3.

The therapist highlighted to Angel that each explanation was not necessarily mutually exclusive and that Angel may find that several explanations are helpful in making sense of the voices. The 'brain making mistakes' diagram (shown in Figure 7.1) was shared with Angel, as a way of making sense of why the voices 'felt so real'. The therapist proposed that perhaps Angel's difficult early experiences had triggered the 'extra connection' in the brain leading some of her thoughts and memories to sound like external voices. To normalise this (aware that when examining the advantages and disadvantages of her beliefs being true or false, Angel had stated that having an illness might indicate a weakness), the therapist shared other examples of the brain making mistakes, including referred pain, visual illusions and the therapist's own experience of being colour-blind. Angel reported finding the concept of the 'brain making mistakes' helpful and de-stigmatising. She said that, unlike previous explanations that she had an 'illness', it fitted with her experiences, was more explanatory and helped her to understand *why* she heard the voices.

After examining the evidence for and against her beliefs, Angel said that she only endorsed the belief that the voices were messengers of God (5 per cent), and that she no longer believed that they were teaching her the right way at all. Instead, Angel said that she believed that the voices were one of the symptoms of an illness that reacts in stressful situations. She believed that this may have been triggered by the traumas in her childhood and that the voices may reflect how people from the past used to speak horribly to her. She also believed that the content of the voices may mirror what she learnt

Table 7.2 Advantages and disadvantages of the voices being part of an illness

Belief 2: 'The voices are part of an illness that may reflect how people from the past used to speak horribly to me'

Advantages of the belief being true	Disadvantages of the belief being true
1 I would not have to sacrifice myself 2 I would not feel as though everyone was against me 3 I need not be fearful of not doing what the voices say 4 I would not have to walk in front of cars 5 I would not be responsible for all the bad things that the voices say	1 I might not get that special feeling again 2 I do not want it to be an illness as I would feel like it was a weakness 3 I would not feel special anymore

Table 7.3 Examining identity beliefs for Angel

Evidence for the belief being true	Evidence against the belief being true
They are messengers from God. *Belief ratings – before: 95%; after: 5%*	

• They have told me
 	
 • Only God would have the power to make me do things
	• We know they tell lies, so why should we believe them?
	 • I can block them out; therefore, they can't be that powerful
	 • I have been able to resist their commands
	 • What they say is not God-like. For example:
	  o God would consider suicide a sin, which is what they are essentially asking me to do
	  o They are aggressive and have a nasty tone
	  o They bully and embarrass me

• They seem to know everything about me • I have felt special when I have tried to follow through with my purpose (of sacrificing myself)	• They don't know everything about me • I want to be special • They are not making me feel special at the moment – they are more like nagging bullies • They blame me, rather than offering me other ways of doing things
The voices are part of an illness that reflects how people from the past used to speak horribly to me.	
Belief ratings – before: 0–50%; after: 100%	
• The tone and content are very similar • They make me feel the same • I am hanging on to it (because I got so used to negative attention) • Professionals think so • Medication reduces effects by blocking the process of the 'brain making mistakes'	• Medication does not get rid of them • Although I understand this applies for others, I feel different
They could reflect what I am thinking about myself. Perhaps criticising myself is a means of pre-empting and coping with criticism from others. *Belief ratings – before: 70–80%; after: 90%*	
• They are similar to what I am thinking	• They come from outside my head (therefore they do not appear to be my thoughts)

to believe about herself as a child. Angel said that she found these new beliefs to be less distressing and far more helpful than her former beliefs.

Summary

In this chapter we have described our approach to addressing beliefs about voice identity, meaning and purpose, and how this connects to more developmental and historical factors. This is part of the reformulation process and paves the way for working with core beliefs, beginning with how these connect to beliefs about voices and their psychological origins.

Chapter 8

CTCH Level 8

Addressing the psychological origins
of command hallucinations: working
with core schemas

Introduction

Our final stage of CTCH aims to effect longer term changes and to minimise
the risk of relapse by work at the core belief level. Mawson *et al.* (2010)
suggest that the lack of reliable significant improvements in voice-related
distress post-intervention in their review of cognitive therapy trials may be
because other mediating variables, including social schemata, were not targeted
in these studies. Although some authors refer to core beliefs as schemas
(or schemata), Beck (1964) distinguishes the two: 'schemas are cognitive
structures in the mind, the specific content of which are core beliefs' (cited
by Beck, 1995, p. 166). More recently, however, Chadwick (2006, p. 98) has
suggested that a schema is perhaps not even usefully thought of as a cognitive
structure but more as 'a cognitive-affective experience . . . laden with explicit
and implicit meaning and it is this affect and meaning that are at the forefront of the client's mind'. In turn, this affect and meaning determine the
way in which the individual makes sense of the world around them. In REBT
terms, core belief work involves addressing the person's core 'demands'
and 'musts' which they make of themselves and others and is necessary in
order to effect longer term change compared to work at the inferential level
(in CTCH voice-power schema work). Social rank theory is also part of our
CTCH model. Core beliefs related to social rank are expressed in terms
of dominate–subordinate schemas: I am weak; others are more powerful or
confident. In CTCH, we distinguish core beliefs in the following ways:

- negative self or other person evaluations (e.g. I am bad; others are
  untrustworthy);
- dominate–subordinate schemas (e.g. I am weaker than others; others use
  and abuse me);
- interpersonal rules, rules for living or unhelpful assumptions (e.g. in
  order to be worthwhile, I must always do things perfectly/be liked by
  others; I must never trust anyone), which fuel negative person evaluations.

In this chapter we describe our approach to working with these beliefs, beginning with how they connect to beliefs about voices. We outline our reformulation process as part of this work and how this addresses the psychological origins of voices.

Adverse childhoods and environment: social stress, expressed emotion and the development of core beliefs

As we noted earlier, individuals who are dominated by powerful voices tend to also view themselves as subordinate to others in general: are lower in their social rank. This in turn is frequently reflected in the person's developmental history. Critical, hostile and over-involved (often termed 'high expressed emotion') family environments have been associated with the development of psychosis and more frequent relapses (Bebbington and Kuipers, 1994; Butzlaff and Hooley, 1998; Onwumere et al., 2010). Having been bullied or severely abused are further factors found to significantly increase the likelihood of developing psychosis (Bebbington et al., 2004). Interestingly, command hallucinations involving harm to self or others have been particularly associated with early experiences of physical and sexual abuse (Read et al., 2003). It seems likely that adverse early life events, in particular those that engender the development of subordinate schemas (e.g. I am powerless; others are stronger) and negative person evaluations (e.g. I am bad), may in turn influence the nature and appraisal of subsequent anomalous experiences such as personified voices (Fowler et al., 2006a). In this way dominate–subordinate schema becomes mirrored in the relationship between the person and their voices (Birchwood et al., 2000b, 2004). Rooke and Birchwood (1998) noted that the onset of psychosis, possible compulsory hospital admissions, loss of roles and goals, and the stigma associated with a diagnosis of schizophrenia may fuel this even further through perceived and/or actual loss of social attractiveness and talent, of belonging or 'fit' with a social group. Hence, the person who already feels subordinate in the social rank hierarchy is down ranked even further.

Exploring the potential role of core beliefs in the aetiology and maintenance of command hallucinations

Drawing upon the general research literature reviewed so far, the task in CTCH is to understand and co-construct how core beliefs may function in the aetiology and maintenance of command hallucinations for a given client. An important first step (if the therapist has not already done so) is to take a detailed developmental history.

Taking a developmental history

Although some people welcome the opportunity to discuss their past experiences early on in therapy, others may prefer that this comes later on, when a trusting therapeutic relationship has been more completely established and the person has acquired some strategies to cope with their voices. A clinical judgement will need to be made in collaboration with the client as to the timeliness of when (or even if) this is done. The therapist's aim here is to carefully elicit an account of the development history of the client's problems, noting key experiences, stressors or traumatic events that may have led to the development of core beliefs and ultimately to psychotic experiences and beliefs. The client's meaning and purpose beliefs (e.g. the voices are punishing me for bad things that I have done) may have already provided the therapist with clues as to the client's underlying core beliefs. While taking a developmental history, it is important to make event-appraisal links by asking questions such as the following:

- How did that make you see yourself/others/the world at the time?
- What did you learn from that experience?
- How did those experiences impact on the way you viewed yourself/others/the world?
- What did that mean to you?
- Did you develop any strategies to help you manage/cope at the time?

At the same time the therapist needs to validate the client's distress and emphasise the understandable nature of the client's beliefs in the context of their experiences. Beliefs and patterns of behaviour have adaptive value as people try to make sense of their experiences, and it is important to try and reflect this back to the client.

Case example: Colette

Colette was raised by her father who she described as very verbally (and sometimes physically) abusive, highly critical and a 'heavy drinker'. To avoid her father's criticisms, Colette would try to be the 'perfect daughter' and would do everything that she possibly could to please him. Nowadays, Colette tries to please everyone around her, including the voices. The voices told Colette that she was 'useless', 'worthless' and commanded to her constantly tidy up as well as more serious commands, including killing herself. Colette spent much of her day obeying the voices and frequently spent up to 8 hours per day tidying her flat. She had also tried to kill herself in the past but now 'appeased' the voices by punching herself and the wall or by holding a knife to her wrist.

In terms of her relationships with other people, Colette described feeling never able to say no, 'trod upon' and weak. Unlike many of our clients, Colette did not believe that the voices were capable of publicly shaming or harming her if she disobeyed them, but she believed that she 'should' do what she was told and that she would not be able to cope if they became more intense (an implicit compliance belief). Colette believed that she was useless and that in order to be accepted (and avert criticism) by the voices (another implicit compliance belief) and others, she must always do what she was told and try to be 'perfect', otherwise people would not like her (an interpersonal rule for living). The therapist emphasised to Colette that this was understandable given her past experiences and that, in fact, such behaviour was probably helpful as a child, as it likely prevented her father from lashing out at her. The therapist highlighted how things were different now: Colette was an adult and, as such, was in a more powerful position and capable of making her own decisions now. The therapist tentatively suggested that her 'rules' and subordinate behaviour (both in response to the voices and other people), while understandable, were perhaps now less helpful and perhaps no longer necessary (as she was no longer in danger from her father's criticisms and threats of violence). The therapist further highlighted how perhaps these rules were actually now contributing to her distress and reinforcing her subordination schemas since the cycle of being 'trod upon' and complying with things that she did not want to do was being perpetuated.

Assessment tools: using schema and trauma inventories in CTCH

Questionnaires can be a useful additional tool in the assessment of trauma histories and core beliefs. Although questionnaires might be considered impersonal, they can potentially be less intrusive for some clients who might initially find it easier to tick a box about having experienced a specific traumatic event rather than having to disclose it verbally. However, it is important that the therapist supplements the use of inventories with a sensitive clinical interview in which questionnaire items which have been endorsed can be discussed. We have found the following measures helpful:

1   1 The *Evaluative Beliefs Scale* (EBS; Chadwick *et al.*, 1999) measures negative self-evaluative beliefs about self and others. Evaluative beliefs are assessed across three specific dimensions: six items constitute a self-evaluation sub-scale (self–self, e.g. I am a total failure), six items constitute evaluations of other people (self–other, e.g. other people are inferior to me) and six items constitute a person's beliefs about how other people evaluate them (other–self, e.g. people see me as worthless). Higher scores reflect greater negative evaluation.

2   The *Social Comparison Scale* (SCS; Allan and Gilbert, 1995) measures social rank in relation to (significant) others and includes the subscales of social rank, social group fit and social attractiveness. The scale utilises semantic differential methodology whereby participants respond on a scale of 1–10, for example 'In relation to others I feel' (e.g. Incompetent 1 2 3 4 5 6 7 8 9 10 Competent).

3   The *Brief Core Schema Scale* (BCSS; Fowler *et al.*, 2006b) assesses evaluative beliefs about the self (e.g. I am unloved) and others (e.g. other people are hostile). It is a twenty-four-item, four-point self-report rating scale (where 1 indicates 'believe it slightly' and 4 indicates 'believe it totally'). Four scores are obtained: negative self (BCSS-NS; six items), positive self (BCSS-PS; six items), negative others (BCSS-NO; six items) and positive others (BCSS-PO; six items).

4   The *Childhood Trauma Questionnaire* (CTQ; Bernstein and Fink, 1997) is a twenty-eight item retrospective self-report inventory designed to detect likely cases of childhood abuse and neglect at three levels of severity: low, moderate and severe. It includes scales for physical abuse, sexual abuse, emotional abuse, physical neglect and emotional neglect. It also helpfully includes a minimization/denial scale for detecting individuals who may be underreporting traumatic events.

5   The *Post-traumatic Diagnostic Scale* (PDS; Foa *et al.*, 1997) is a forty-nine-item, four part, self-report inventory that covers all of the main forms of traumatic life events. Individuals are asked to indicate (by ticking a box) which traumatic life events they had experienced in childhood (up to 16-years-old) or adulthood. Using a four-point scale, respondents then rate seventeen items representing the cardinal symptoms of Post Traumatic Stress Disorder (PTSD) experienced in the past 30 days. Finally, respondents rate the level of impairment caused by their symptoms across nine areas of life functioning. The PDS is particularly useful as an aid to diagnosing PTSD (although it cannot be used in isolation to provide a diagnosis) as it taps all of the main criteria listed in the *DSM-IV* (APA, 2000) scheme for PTSD.

6   *Revised Impact of Events Scale* (IES-R; Weiss and Marmar, 1997) is a twenty-two-item self-report measure designed to assess distress associated with post-traumatic symptoms for any specific life event. The IES-R has twenty-two items and three subscales (re-experiencing, hyperarousal and avoidance) to parallel *DSM-IV* criteria for PTSD. Respondents are asked to rate each item in the IES-R on a scale of 0 (not at all), 1 (a little bit), 2 (moderately), 3 (quite a bit) and 4 (extremely) according to the past 7 days.

Using thought or inference chaining to uncover core schemas

Thought, inference or inference-evaluation chaining (downward laddering in CBT) is a method that can be used to identify and propose a connection between a psychotic (inferential) belief and a negative self or person evaluation. It thus provides an alternative interpretation for the inferential belief and helps the client make sense of certain experiences. One form of questioning in inference chaining uses the 'if . . . then . . .' format. So 'if that happens *then* what implication or meaning does it have for you that you find so distressing?' Another useful question is to ask (in a sensitive manner) 'What is so bad about that?' It is bad for the person as it has further meaning: a person evaluation perhaps. Each of these questioning formats starts with a specific ABC of a distressing voice hearing experience or event. The questions are repeated in order to obtain deeper inferences until the evaluation is revealed. Evaluations are often implicit (hidden) in the client's inferences (beliefs about their voices) and voice content, and are made explicit through this process. A useful starting point in eliciting evaluations is to assume that the client's inferences are true: that the voice is punishing them for bad things they have done:

AM: So, when they (the voices) started laughing at you (A) and talking more loudly as you sat down in the pub you felt quite uneasy. Is that right?

Steven: Yeah, that's right!

AM: And what did you make of the situation?

Steven: Well, I thought I'm being set up by them again (inferential B).

AM: So you interpreted this situation as further evidence of them trying to stop you going out for a quiet pint (the next inferential B)?

Steven: Yes.

AM: Okay, so tell me how that works exactly.

Steven: They laugh at me and take the piss and I shout at them (out loud), everyone would see then that I am a nutter.

AM: So (assuming that the inference is true) how does that make you feel being set up in that way?

Steven: A bit angry (C) . . . pissed off really.

AM: A bit angry?

Steven: Yeah, well quite angry, I got more angry as I was sitting there having to take it.

AM: Having to take it?

Steven: Yeah, them putting me down . . . knowing I'd react . . . they're bastards!

AM: So if I have this right *if* the voices put you down (A) *then* that makes you really angry (Ce), but it also leads to you shouting out loud (Cb) and then other people would put you down too?

Steven: Yes . . . really pisses me off.

AM: So, I hope that this doesn't sound insensitive Steven, but *what* is so bad about that, the voices and other people putting you down I mean, that makes you so angry?

Steven: Well, they were treating me as if I was a nothing (the other-self evaluation).

AM: A nothing?

Steven: Yes.

AM: And how do you feel about that?

Steven: Pretty angry; I thought if they (others in the pub) don't watch it I'll hit one of them . . . like I glassed that guy last year.

AM: Okay, this might seem like a really strange question, but let's assume this is how the voices and others really think about you . . . *what* is so bad about that. . . . viewing you in this way that makes you feel *so angry*?

Steven: Well, other people always treat me like this . . . like I'm an idiot – I don't count for nothing . . . like I am a nothing.

AM: Okay, does that have any implications for the way you see yourself; in other words, does it say anything about you as a person?

Steven: I don't know why it bothers me so much.

AM: Okay, let's assume that you thought that about the voices, that they were nothings. How do you think they might feel if they thought you thought that about them?

Steven: They probably wouldn't like it . . . they'd give me grief.

AM: Okay. Do you think that it would bother them as much as it bothers you?

Steven: Probably not . . . *they* are all high and mighty.

AM: So is there a difference between how they would feel about it and how you feel then?

Steven: I suppose there is.

AM: And do you think that the difference might be because their view of you taps into how you really see yourself?

Steven: I suppose so.

AM: And is that how you see yourself?

Steven: I suppose it is.

AM: That you're 'A nothing' (the person self-evaluation)?

Steven: Yeah.

AM: And how does that make you feel when you think about yourself in that way?

Steven: Pretty bad (becomes flushed and tearful).

AM: It looks like that is pretty painful.

Steven: Yes, it's pretty heavy.

Developing a personal model: reformulating and connecting core beliefs to psychotic beliefs and power schemas

For some clients where evaluative themes have been more readily elicited within the course of therapy, core beliefs can be suggested more directly as the start of a reformulation process. The following therapy extract illustrates the process of introducing the evaluative theme as an alternative explanation for an inferential belief. Here, a connection between Angel's rule for living (that she must subjugate her own needs/wants to stop bad things happening) and her inferential belief (that it is her duty to sacrifice herself to prevent all the pain and suffering in the world) is tentatively suggested within a developmental context:

NK: So Angel, so far we have looked at the evidence that supports your belief that you must sacrifice yourself in order to stop world suffering.

Angel: Yes.

NK: And after examining the evidence and trying to think of other possible explanations you felt a little less convinced that you need to sacrifice yourself. Is that right?

Angel: A bit, yes.

NK: Okay. Perhaps we could move on a bit today and start to look at whether there is another way of understanding your belief that you must sacrifice yourself.

Angel: How do you mean?

NK: Well I have been thinking about some of the very difficult and painful experiences that we have talked about. In particular how awful it must have been for you when your abuser told you that if you screamed, he would hurt one of the other children instead.

Angel: I felt like I had no choice. I had to protect the other girls.

NK: What a really difficult and distressing situation for you to have been in. And that's something that you continue to try to do, isn't it – protect other people?

Angel: Well, it's my responsibility. I have to do what I can to save people from bad things happening. It's my duty.

NK: Yes, we've talked about this a lot, haven't we? And I was thinking how perhaps it's not surprising that you might think that – because as a young child that was the very situation that you were forced into: you were told that in order to protect others, you must be subjected to harm yourself. I'm wondering what that situation taught you about how to stop bad things happening in the world?

Angel: Well I guess I learned that I could stop bad things happening but only by sacrificing myself.

Having proposed some tentative links between the client's core beliefs and their inferential beliefs, the next task is to develop and share a personal model of the client's psychotic experiences drawing upon the client's increasing insight. An implicit aim of reformulation work is to finally uncouple the power relationship with the voices by revealing their true origins and purpose. In Chapter 7, we have suggested how we might use the stress-vulnerability model as a broad building block for this and how it may be possible to reframe the person's experience in psychological or neurological terms (e.g. the voices as misattributed inner speech, the 'brain making mistakes', traumatic memories or echoes from the past, a protective function from difficult and traumatic times). Again the ABC model is our key tool and can be used in conjunction with these other psychological models to formulate how evaluative beliefs arise from developmental experiences and may be (a) connected to the client's beliefs about their voices and (b) result in subordination responses. This is shown diagrammatically in Figure 8.1 for the case of Angel.

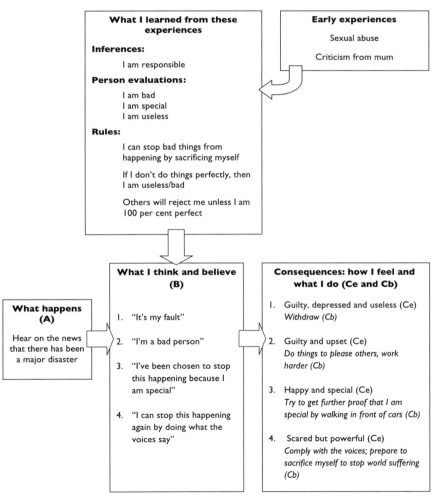

Figure 8.1 Angel's reformulation

Linking back to function/personal meaning: why this voice and why this content?

The content of voices can often provide ample information about a person's history as well as the schematic lens through which the person sees the world, themselves and other people. Not only is the onset of hearing voices frequently associated with traumatic life events (Romme and Escher, 1993), but such events may directly influence the person's beliefs about their voices (Andrew *et al.*, 2008) and voice content (Close and Garety, 1998). Hardy *et al.* (2005) found that 12.5 per cent of people with psychosis who reported experiencing a traumatic event claimed that it still impacted upon them negatively and that the content of their voices was specifically linked to the content of the traumatic event. Almost half (45 per cent) exhibited an emotional theme within the content of the voices (e.g. threat, guilt), which corresponded to the emotional theme of the traumatic event. Read and Argyle (1999) found in their study that in three out of seven instances, content of voices could be directly linked to physical or sexual abuse. Read *et al.* (2003) subsequently identified a close relationship between auditory hallucinations and abuse (in childhood and adulthood) command hallucinations to harm or kill themselves.

Consistent with these findings, we have found that the onset of hearing voices is usually preceded by a traumatic event and that voices frequently reflect significant, or particularly familiar, individuals in the person's life. Helping the person to identify and make sense of these links can be a very important stage in the reformulation process.

Case example: Comfort

Comfort heard the voice of her uncle who sexually abused her as a child. He repeatedly told her that she was 'dirty' and 'bad', and commanded her to do things including to strip naked and to hurt herself. He also said, 'If you don't do what I say, you'll be punished/ I'll kill your sister'. Consequently, Comfort would generally always comply with his commands. She also saw images of her uncle and consequently believed that he must still live nearby (contrary to objective reports). In the following therapy extract, the therapist helped Comfort to make links between the content of what her uncle said in the past and what he (the voice) says now:

NK: The main thing that upsets you is that your uncle's voice tells you to do things that you really don't want to. Is that right?

Comfort: Yes, it's horrible. It is so humiliating, and the worse thing is – I just don't have any choice at all. I know that if I do it (strip naked in public) I'll get picked up by the police again, but if I don't, he'll do something worse – kill me or my sister.

NK: Is that something that he used to threaten when you were a little girl?

Comfort: Yes, he'd say he'd punish me by killing my sister. I love my sister so much and I just couldn't cope with that.

NK: Of course, you couldn't. It sounds like a very difficult and distressing situation to be in. And the things he tells you to do now – are those similar to what he would ask of you as a child?

Comfort: Yes, he'd always ask me to strip for him.

NK: Is there anything that's different now, to what he would say then?

Comfort: He never threatened to kill me then – but I always wished that he would, so that he didn't kill my sister.

NK: Anything else that is different?

Comfort: He never told me that I was bad or dirty then. He used to say that I was his favourite girl. But I felt dirty no matter what he said. I hated myself then and still do.

NK: So it sounds like there are some differences in terms of what your uncle said then and what he says now. But that what he says now seems to perhaps reflect how you think about yourself?

Comfort: Yes, that's right.

As the session proceeded, the therapist tentatively proposed an alternative explanation for Comfort's experiences: that perhaps the voices reflected memories of what her uncle used to say to her, as well as how the abuse made her see herself. It was explained that the brain sometimes (if trauma is not properly processed) replays such memories at stressful times, causing Comfort to hear voices that sounded like her uncle.

Comfort was asked to describe the images in detail – she recalled that the image was always the same: her uncle looked exactly the same as he did 35 years ago; he had thick brown hair, was the same size and wore the same large glasses and blue shirt that he typically wore then. Through Socratic questioning, it emerged that today Comfort's uncle would be 85 years old and, most likely, would look and be dressed differently: in fact he may even look quite old and frail. This was used as evidence to suggest that the images may actually be flashbacks of her uncle, which was understandable given the traumatic nature of the abuse, and that this was perhaps why objective reports suggested that her uncle no longer lived nearby.

Sometimes, the content of voices changes over time. In our experience it is indeed common for clients to report hearing voices in early childhood, which might initially be benevolent and helpful, but then become more critical, hostile or commanding at a later stage. This can be very confusing for the individual and it may be important to help the person to identify any life experiences which might have impacted upon the nature of the voices and caused this change in their purpose.

Case example: Ade

Ade recalled hearing several voices since he was 5-years old. He said that the voices were like companions who supported him through times when he felt lonely. Nevertheless, when Ade was eighteen he was violently assaulted by a group of local youths. Soon after this he described the voices as 'turning nasty': they started telling Ade that he was weak and useless and that other people were demons. It was then that they also started issuing him with commands to cut himself, as well as to 'kill all the demons'.

With clients such as Ade, the therapist can build on the work commenced in CTCH level 7 to acknowledge the functional nature of the voices (such as companionship or distraction from early abuse) but can then Socratically highlight how the content and nature of the voices may have changed in accordance with certain life experiences and the person's evolving beliefs. Such beliefs may be 'shattered' or exaggerated after traumatic life events (Janoff-Bulman, 1992) which may in turn impact significantly on the nature and content of voices.

Case example: Ade

In Ade's case, it was formulated that being violently assaulted understandably lead to him developing beliefs that 'others can't be trusted', 'other people are bad (demons)' and 'I am weak'. Furthermore, it was formulated that the anger that he felt towards himself (for not standing up to the youths) and the group of youths was likely being reflected in the content of the commands: to cut himself and to 'kill all the demons'.

Linking core beliefs and voice beliefs/content: identifying similarities and meanings

Another aspect of reformulation work is to examine how the client's core beliefs are reflected in voice beliefs and content and may constitute a dysfunctional form of the self-serving bias, serving to defend the person against their own core beliefs (Trower and Chadwick, 1995; Chadwick *et al.*, 1996). In the following example, we return to our main case study of Angel. The therapy transcript below builds on the earlier one from a previous session with Angel. In this session the therapist is helping Angel to make links between the content of the voices and her evaluative beliefs:

NK: Angel, am I right in remembering that shortly after the abuse you went to live with your aunt?

Angel: Yes.

NK: And I know from what we've discussed before that that was really difficult for you. How did you make sense of it at the time?

Angel: I hated myself. I thought I must be to blame for what happened and that I must be a really bad person. My mum would always tell me I had the Devil's blood in me so I thought that's why he chose me, and that's why she sent me away.

NK: I can't imagine how hard that must have been for you. How did you cope with those thoughts at the time?

Angel: He (the abuser) told me that he chose me because I was special. And although I hated myself for what happened, I told myself that at least I had been able to stop bad things happening to the other children.

NK: Yes, and that was probably true at the time. It sounds like that was a very important way of making sense of and coping with such a traumatic thing happening to you. Are there any similarities do you think between how you felt then and how you feel now when the voices instruct you to do things?

Angel: Well, I hate what the voices say to me. They scare me and I don't want to do what they ask of me. But I like feeling special and having the power to stop world suffering.

In this example, beliefs about the voices (that Angel has been chosen because she is special), can be viewed as 'defending' against her so-called core beliefs that she is bad and responsible.

Case example: Keith

Keith lived with his grandmother until he was 7. He stated that his mum did not want him. When his grandmother died he returned to the family home, which was emotionally and physically abusive. His stepfather and his stepfather's friends would sexually abuse him and though his mum was aware of what was happening she did not intervene. In fact, Keith reported that he was treated completely different to his stepbrother, who also lived in the same home; Keith remembers him as being the favourite.

Keith blamed himself for many years for everything that had happened; this reflected what his mum used to tell him: that he 'deserved to be punished' and that 'he was useless'. As a consequence of the beatings, he had considerable time off school and as a result made few friends. His social network outside of the home was limited. He was bombarded with his mother's and stepfather's verbal and physical abuse.

In his teens, Keith began to hear the voice of his mother who would reiterate what she had told him before (she had since died). For over 30 years he heard the same things. Not only were they things that were said when he was very young but he had come to believe them. Keith would say 'I am flawed, useless' and that 'others are better than me' and 'others are a danger to me'. Keith developed several interpersonal rules for living, one of which was 'if you trust people then they will let you down and hurt you'. Not only did Keith continue to hear his mother reiterating his own beliefs, it impacted directly on his behaviour. He tended to punish himself for not being a better son; it had been his fault. He would drink too much and sometimes take overdoses. Keith would also isolate himself from others: they were a danger to him and there was always the threat that he would be taken advantage of as he had been before.

For Keith, taking a Socratic approach and using a responsibility pie chart were a powerful technique. This is discussed in more detail below.

Reframing and disputing negative person evaluations

Work at level 6 should have already begun the process of addressing subordination schemas by raising the person's rank in relation to both their voices and of others. However, such beliefs may represent more deeply held core person evaluations and will often require further work. Core person evaluations, Trower *et al.* (2010) note, are sometimes referred to as 'hot beliefs', which follow from an extreme rule of living that certain negative events (As) absolutely must not happen (or conversely that certain positive events absolutely must happen). This rule is described as an irrational demanding philosophy in what is now called REBT (Ellis, 1962) and termed a *dysfunctional assumption* in CBT (Beck, 1976). Rules for living, which are often interpersonal in nature, may be subtly expressed and their relationship to person evaluations may require careful exploration and clarification before proceeding: 'In order to be worthwhile I must be perfect' (constituting a conditional assumption or rule). This may mean that the person believes they 'must do everything perfectly' (a rule for living) and by implication if they do not then they are worthless (a possible self-evaluation).

In the development of the EBS, Chadwick *et al.* (1999) identified six key person evaluations: weak, failure, inferior, unlovable, worthless and bad. In CTCH, we attempt to clarify these (though they may often be expressed in the individual's own idiosyncratic terms: 'I am a nothing' in Steven's case described above, meaning that he saw himself as essentially worthless). Care must be taken to establish whether such beliefs constitute person evaluations: is this how the person globally self-rates themselves?

Having shared the reformulation, it may be possible to progress to working with self-evaluative beliefs that for some clients may underpin and drive their delusional (inferential) thinking: their beliefs about their voices. The therapist's aim here is to reframe and dispute the client's beliefs through:

- offering challenges in a sensitive and tentative manner/Columbo style;
- highlighting logical inconsistencies in the belief system and unhelpful philosophies;
- devising replacement beliefs;
- encouraging the client to act in accordance with new beliefs (thereby developing emotional insight).

We have been particularly influenced in this work by REBT theory and practice as well as drawing upon approaches developed elsewhere for managing schematic beliefs (Beck *et al.*, 1979; Padesky, 1994; Beck, 1995; Young *et al.*, 2003). Before embarking on such work, it is important to provide the client with a rational for working on their core beliefs. The prejudice analogy (Padesky, 1994) can be useful for this. This is a technique which aims to help clients see that their beliefs operate in a similar way to a prejudicial belief, with incoming information being processed differently depending on whether it fits with, or is opposed to, our current beliefs: that the person is weak and useless. Another strategy that we have found helpful is likening the person's beliefs to a child's shape-sorter toy. This is illustrated in the following didactic dispute:

The way our brain stores beliefs about ourselves, the world and others is a bit like a children's shape-sorter toy (Figure 8.2). Just like the holes in

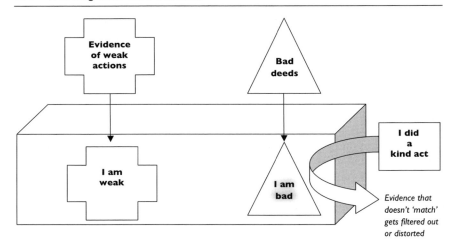

Figure 8.2 Introducing core belief work using a child's shape sorter analogy

the box, our beliefs can be rigid and fixed. With the shape sorter, when a matching shape comes along it is able to fit nicely into the shape-sorting box. Similarly with our beliefs, when things happen that match our current beliefs (e.g. voices telling you that you are bad), it is able to fit nicely into your 'belief box' because it matches what you have learned to believe about yourself (that you are bad), and therefore reinforces that belief even further. However, when a shape comes along that does not match the holes in the box (e.g. a square), it is unable to fit into the shape sorter. Again, this is similar to how our beliefs operate: if incoming evidence does not fit with your current beliefs (e.g. evidence that suggests that you are not bad and have not caused this bad thing to happen), it is filtered out because it does not match your current beliefs and therefore has nowhere to go. Sometimes our brains can act like a child trying to force a shape into the wrong hole: our brain can be so eager to get 'a match'; it has the ability to distort and skew information so that a square is squeezed into a triangular hole. Hence, evidence that disconfirms our beliefs (a kindly act) can become distorted, or misremembered (I did not really help that person; I was just being selfish), in a way that supports our original belief (the triangle: I am bad, rather than the square: I am a kind person and not all Bad). In this stage of therapy, it is almost as if we need to chisel some more holes in the shape sorter so that all the shapes can be let in, supporting a less biased view.

Cognitive techniques

Once agreed as a therapy goal, it is important to collaboratively devise an alternative 'replacement' person evaluation. This can be done in the same way as developing an alternative replacement psychotic belief. Useful questions here are as follows:

- If you didn't think you were X (e.g. bad), how would you like to think about yourself?
- If you weren't the old belief (e.g. bad), what would you be?

When a negative evaluative schema is actuated: 'I am bad', it is as if the experience of self is 'one dimensional' (e.g. globally) and inescapably (e.g. stable, cannot change) bad. It is 'like a drop of ink in a glass of water' (Chadwick, 2006, p. 99) which has the power to colour a more realistic view of oneself with a blinkered durability and force.

Case example: Bradley

Bradley was a 19-year-old man who heard voices commanding him to hurt himself and other people. He believed that the voices were deservedly punishing him because he was a bad person. His evidence supporting this was that he had done bad things in his past, including seriously physically assaulting others. On one occasion this had led to a young man being hospitalised. Bradley felt very remorseful about this and believed with 100 per cent conviction that he was totally bad and therefore deserved to die.

Making such whole person evaluations as in Bradley's case are logical errors (as demonstrated in the techniques below). Wessler and Wessler (1988) describe a useful set of cognitive techniques in the practice of rational emotive therapy (the predecessor of REBT practice) which we have adapted and adopted for use in CTCH. These techniques expose the process of global self-rating as illogical:

1   Rating behaviour versus rating the self – does an action define a person? In person evaluations such as Bradley's, it is usually the case that one or more criteria of behaviour are being used. Bradley evaluated himself as 'bad' on the basis that he had hurt people in the past. There are two important lessons for the client to learn here:
    i   Bad behaviour is not the same as globally being bad.
    ii   Just because someone does some bad things, it does not mean that they are completely bad – we are all fallible human beings capable of making mistakes and acting in both good and bad ways.

The therapist can illustrate this concept with examples, such as running up and down the therapy room making train noises. The therapist can then ask the client if such behaviour (acting like a train) means that the therapist is a train. In our experience, clients usually find this example quite amusing, which will provide the added benefit of making the concept more memorable. To return to our example of Bradley:

Bradley: Of course you're not a train!
NK: Why not?
Bradley: Just making train noises does not mean that you are a train!
NK: So how does having assaulted someone make *you* bad then?

Importantly, we do not condone bad behaviour; assaulting someone is never a good thing. The point is whether or not the person can be said to be wholly bad. What the client is doing here is rating themselves on the basis of one or more behaviours.

2   Big I little i
Having highlighted the error of defining oneself (or others) according to arbitrary criteria (usually behaviour), it can be useful to introduce the concept that the self (or others) consists of many elements, attributes and characteristics – and therefore rating the 'whole self' as either good or bad is always destined to be flawed. 'Big I little i' is a useful technique for examining the tendency to globally evaluate oneself or others (negatively or positively) (Figure 8.3).

Case example: Bradley

Although essential not to condone or excuse Bradley's behaviour, it was important therapeutically to highlight the context of such assaults: Bradley was in a youth gang and such behaviour had always been in the context of gang fights, as well as Bradley responding to voices encouraging him to hurt others at the time. Furthermore, Bradley had been beaten badly by his stepfather as a child and so had learnt to resolve conflict with violence. When examining the evidence through Socratic questioning that did not support his belief that he was completely bad, Bradley was able to identify other positive attributes: he was a loyal friend and had always looked after and protected his mum and sister. The therapist highlighted the arbitrary nature of labelling oneself according to one or more criteria. We are all in fact multi-dimensional with many attributes and characteristics. A useful way of illustrating this point is through a pictorial pie chart.

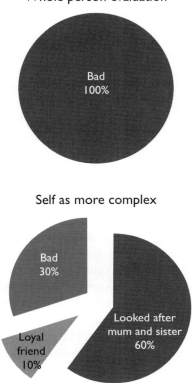

Figure 8.3 Big I little i example – Bradley

Pie charts can be useful as a means of clarifying with the client their evaluative belief. This in itself can illustrate to the client the global nature and extent of their thinking and begin the process of change since clients will often state that this is not completely them when confronted with their beliefs visually in this way. Here, the therapist draws a circle and writes, for example, 100 per cent bad or weak in it and may then shade in the circle. 'Is this you?', the therapist asks. 'Is this what you are saying?'

Case example: Keith

The first approach with Keith was to use Socratic questioning to look at what factors might have led his mother to behave in the way she did. Keith still heard her voice and for him she represented someone who was always loving, yet had not been towards him. Over a number of sessions, Keith and the therapist were able together to draw out some of the reasons why she might have behaved as she did towards him and not towards his stepbrother. Keith and the therapist identified that she was young when she fell pregnant with Keith, it was socially unacceptable to be unmarried and have a child at that time, she was subsequently forced into a marriage with a man who was not the father, she knew little of how to bring up a child, she had limited social support and Keith was a reminder of a time in her life that she so much regretted.

The purpose of putting together all the information was in no way to condone her actions. This was very clearly reflected back to Keith; how she had behaved was wrong. However, Keith saw himself as flawed and this went some way to contextualise the situation and look at some of the reasons she might have behaved in the way she did. This allowed the therapist and Keith to look at who else was responsible for his welfare and move away from just focusing on himself and his mother. This helped to depersonalise events and revealed how responsibility was broader than just the two of them. For example, the role and support of the social services, the police, the school, his stepfather, his brother and the wider family. Keith could see that many people had a role to play in protecting him and supporting him yet they did not. This helped him to see that he was not the only person responsible for what happened and that they should have done something to stop it.

A second part of the exercise with Keith was to look at him as a whole person. While Keith evaluated himself as 'useless' and 'flawed', the therapist enquired, 'was the whole of him made in this way?' Had he done things that he could be proud of and that represented a different part of his whole self? With the help of the therapist, Keith was able to identify that although he had gone through so much as a child he did not take this out on his stepbrother (back then or now); he was in contact with him still and they were good friends. Although he had been told on many occasions by his voice to stab people, he had never acted upon this and he had recently struck up a relationship with a woman who was supportive and loving towards him (she saw something perhaps he did not). This was drawn out visually on a pie chart and although a portion of the circle contained a view of himself that was critical and hostile, Keith could also see that there were other aspects that were positive and represented a person who was not flawed but had many good qualities.

3   Measuring the office desk

In this technique the therapist can ask the client to measure the office desk (or any piece of furniture available). When the client gives a rough measurement for perhaps say the width, height and depth of the desk, the therapist accepts none of these answers on the premise that 'none of them is the desk'. The therapist can use this to highlight that the whole of the desk is not any of its parts and that the width, height or depth of the desk are just arbitrary measurements. The therapist can then extend this analysis to human behaviour.

4   The bowl of fruit

This exercise described by Wessler and Wessler (1998) is a particular powerful means of conveying the idea that the whole is greater than the sum of its parts.

Case example: Bradley

NK: Bradley supposing we had a bowl containing fruit, and I placed one piece of bad fruit in it. Would you think it was a good bowl or a bad bowl?

Bradley: No.

NK: What if I placed another bad piece in?

Bradley: Hmmm, I'm not sure. Surely it has a bit of both in it?

NK: Okay, so if I said it was a bad bowl of fruit, would you agree or disagree with me?

Bradley: That's tricky one. I guess I'd disagree because there are some good fruit in it.

NK: So it's neither good nor bad?

Bradley: I guess.

NK: What if I replaced all of the good fruit with bad fruit?

Bradley: Now it's bad?

NK: But I asked you about the bowl!

Bradley: Laughs.

NK: Okay, so if we think back to our discussion earlier and your belief that you are 100 per cent (totally) bad, what do you think we can learn from the fruit bowl example?

Bradley: Well, I guess nothing is just good and bad (laughing). Most things have a bit of both.

NK: And do you think we can apply that to you?

Bradley: Yes, I suppose so – I guess no one is wholly good or bad even if they have a lot of bad fruit in them . . . you know make mistakes.

NK: So how about thinking of yourself as the bowl and your behaviour as one piece of bad fruit in it?

5   The changing nature of self – can we be forever bad/weak/a failure?
Another important concept to introduce is the idea that whole person constructs
are not static and that the self can change.

Case example: Bradley

Bradley stated that for the last 2 years, he had 'moved away from the gang
scene' and was no longer involved in gang crime and fights. It was important
to reinforce this positive decision and to highlight how Bradley had changed
over time. Indeed he had not hurt anyone for 2 years now. The therapist also
felt that it was important to empower Bradley in feeling able to continue to
change:

NK: If you no longer believed that you were bad, what would you like
           to believe about yourself?
Bradley: I'd like to think that I was a good person, who was trying his best.
NK: And what do you think you'd be doing differently if you were to
           believe that about yourself?
Bradley: I'd be staying away from the gangs, going to college and helping mum
           a bit more around the house.
NK: Aren't you doing some of those things now?
Bradley: I guess I am.
NK: So you've changed?
Bradley: Yes – I suppose I have (smiles).

If the client is not able to identify ways in which they may have changed,
famous examples can be used. Wessler and Wessler (1998) cite the case of
the 'crime of the century' involving Richard Loeb who kidnapped and killed
a young boy. Years later he was pardoned as a reformed character, he became
a social worker, married and spent much of his life doing good works. A
favourite example we cite is that of St Francis of Assisi:

St Francis of Assisi was the founder of the Franciscan order. He was born
into a prosperous family in 1182 and was spoilt by both parents. As a
child and young adult, he was said to have enjoyed a 'frolicking' lifestyle
with little care for those around him. In his early twenties, a serious illness
caused Francis to take a deeper look at his superficial life and he began
to see the emptiness of what he was doing. He changed his thinking and
decided to retreat from his worldly life and devoted the rest of his time

to the care of the destitute and the sick. Like-minded people began to join him in his new life and by 1210 he had a brotherhood of eleven men.

Therapist disclosure can also be helpful to illustrate how the 'self' might have changed over time. For example, one therapist described himself as being a shy child, without friends. As he started secondary school, he developed a few friendships but still felt like an outsider. As he grew older he felt that he had become more acceptable to others. Now, the therapist describes himself as a confident adult with some good close friends. He also has a successful career and is a good father. As with pie charts, this gradual change over time can be illustrated in a diagram (shown in Figure 8.4), which can be subsequently used in therapy to chart the client's own changes.

6   Disputing in the past

Disputing in the past, or historical testing (Padesky, 1994; Beck, 1995; Young *et al.*, 2003), involves examining the circumstances under which schematic beliefs were first formed and then using the same techniques for disputing and reframing beliefs about voice power (as described in Chapters 4 and 7) applying them to powerful others in the past. The context of belief formation often makes the development of subsequent beliefs understandable as illustrated in the following case example.

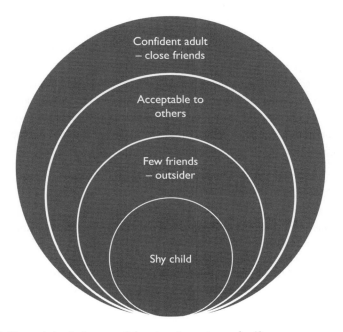

Figure 8.4 Therapist's disclosure of the changing nature of self

---

Case example: Mehdi

Mehdi was raised in a foster home and learnt that in order to avert bullying from his older foster siblings, it was important to 'show them that I am a man' by behaving in a provocative or aggressive manner. This behaviour was re-enacted in response to voices telling him that people were looking at him and to assault them, which he had done.

Case example: Yannis

Yannis said that his father always told him that he was 'screwed up', 'a mess' and 'pathetic' and so it must be true. He felt that of all people, surely his father would know him best.

Case example: Adrian

Adrian told the therapist that his mother had died when he was young (aged 5). He had been sent to live with his father, but his father had told him that he could not care for him and he had instead lived with his father's sister and parents. In this care he had experienced daily bullying from his cousins, which was reportedly condoned and encouraged by his aunt. In order to protect himself, he would either hide or try to do everything for his aunt in order to get some protection. It was consequently understandable that he would find it difficult to trust others, consider himself 'useless' and try to appease people in authority in order to win favour with them.

A number of modified key disputes can be taught here or elicited by means of Socratic questioning:

Key dispute 1:   'Just because your mother/father (or other powerful person) said this or made you feel this way does not mean that it is true and true forever?'
    The aim here is to down rank the other, making them seem fallible and so questioning the validity of their opinion and their omniscience.

Key dispute 2:   'They are fallible human beings just like anyone else'.
The lesson that we are all fallible is particularly relevant to clients who express high perfectionist standards. Usefully the therapist may also show that they are fallible by using self-disclosure or in-session by perhaps being 5 minutes late for the session.

Key dispute 3:   'A label is not a fact'.
Here the client can be encouraged to think about the general issues of labelling things and how this can be wrong or misleading (e.g. fake designer jeans in the market).

Key dispute 4:   'Your father, mother, etc. did this for other reasons, not necessarily because of anything you did'.
Thinking about other reasons for a person's behaviour can help a client to consider that it is not always their fault. A pie chart (see p. 199) can be helpful to illustrate this point.

It can also be helpful to re-evaluate the client's evidence for their schematic beliefs by reviewing any additional historical data supporting such beliefs. Morrison *et al.* (2004) suggest that this can be done by systematically breaking down life experiences into chunks (such as 5 years, or particular key experiences) and then within each period, Socratically, reinterpreting old evidence in a new light. An example of this is shown for Lilly in Figure 8.5.

Behavioural techniques

Behavioural interventions are designed to build emotional insight. The client can be asked to act 'as if' the new belief were true and to test out whether the belief is more accurate and helpful than the old one. This can then be consolidated through the use of flashcards, core belief worksheets (Beck, 1995) and positive data logs (Padesky, 1994).

Case example: Bradley

Over the next few weeks, Bradley was asked to act 'as if' his new belief was true (that he was mostly a good person who was trying his best) and was asked to record evidence that fitted with this new belief as compared to the old belief. Bradley noticed over the forthcoming weeks that he had continued to stay away from the gangs, he was helping his mum around the house and he had spoken to his care coordinator about enrolling in college. Bradley began to feel hopeful that he could continue to change and that perhaps there may be some truth in his 'new belief'.

Core belief worksheet: Lilly

Belief to be examined: **'I am stupid, weak and useless'**

Evidence that supports the core belief	Evidence that contradicts the core belief
School • My experience at school – the girls would laugh at me, ignore me and turn their backs on me.	• They did not drag me down like they thought they would. • The teachers saw me in the way that I wanted – they saw that I was a good pupil and was trying my best. • The teachers at school used to smile at me. • I was made head girl at school. • That's in the past.
• I was not assertive enough then to go forward in the line – I was weak.	• I am still here and I am fighting. I am showing that I am determined.
Work • What people said about me – that I'm crazy, stupid and that I'm like a light switch (e.g. the lady I used to work with).	• Well, again, that is in the past. It says more about them than it does about me. • I didn't cave in.
My husband's mother • My husband's mother took an instant dislike to me.	• I did nothing wrong and despite everything, I treated her with respect.

Conclusion:

The evidence does not support that I am stupid or useless. Just because I leant to think that about myself as Stupid, Weak and Useless, it does not mean that I am.

I can work on beginning to believe a new belief about myself.

New belief:

'I am clever, and , and am learning to be stronger with experience'

Figure 8.5 Reviewing the historical evidence for a belief

Evidence to support the new belief

1. I have been keeping appointments – I always turn up even if it is hard.

2. I have always been able to talk, even if I know that it upsets me or if I have felt ashamed.

3. Talking has become easier for me.

4. I have been able to carry on with day-to-day things.

5. I have become more assertive in my approach to day-to-day things.

6. I have been able to show some assertiveness with my children.

7. I have been able to have conversations with my family even though it was hard.

8. I have been able to resist the voices and use alternative strategies.

9. I can sing.

10. If I get trapped in the cycle, I just need to use the 'exits':

My thoughts: rather than dwelling on the negatives, I can:
- Look at the good memories and remember the positive things that I have done.
- I can rationalise my thoughts using the charts.
- Try to understand people action's.
- Tell myself I do not deserve this.

The voices: rather than doing what the voices say:
- I can resist them and stand up to them by ignoring them or telling them 'you're not going to stop me'.
- I can use alternative strategies (e.g. distraction, stress ball, speaking to someone).

My behaviours: rather than withdrawing and shutting myself away:
- I can do the things that I want to do (be strong).
- I can socialise more and make conversations.
- I can be assertive.

Reframing and disputing rules for living

Within the notion of rules for living, we encompass what have been termed elsewhere *dysfunctional assumptions, conditional or unconditional assumptions*. These we argue all amount to rules whereby the person must lead their life to a certain standard or in a particular way and are as noted earlier, often interpersonal in nature.

Cognitive techniques

The first task for the therapist is to explicitly state and clarify the rule the person has adopted:

> Are you saying that in order to be loved you *must always* do what others want?

The adaptive value of these beliefs for the individual over their life course should be explicitly noted. The therapist may then proceed to fairly examine the problems that they are now causing. This can be done by examining the advantages and disadvantages of a particular rule or assumption. Other strategies that can be helpful include the following:

1   Agreeing new rules: preferences rather than musts, shoulds and demands
Once the unhelpfulness of rules have been agreed, it can be useful to collaboratively generate more flexible rules, with a focus on adopting a 'desiring' rather than a 'demanding' philosophy. For example, 'I would prefer it – but don't absolutely have to (be perfect)'. Useful questions to ask here are as follows:

- What would be a more flexible rule to live your life by?
- Where does living your life by this rule get you? (a pragmatic dispute)

2   Disputing in the past
As with person evaluations, it is sometimes necessary to return to the origins of rules, where and when and from whom these were learnt. Again the source of the rule is often important. As part of the down-ranking strategy we adopt throughout CTCH, we attempt to further undermine the omniscience of the rule giver. All rules are of course arbitrary and subject to revision. Examples can be drawn here with more general rules and laws. These rules may be drawn up with good intentions, as in the case of banning smoking, and also to oppress and restrict others as in the case of carrying identity cards in Nazi Germany. Examining the intent of the powerful other can be helpful in further down ranking the other and hence rejecting the rule:

Key dispute 1:   'Where is it written that this rule is right/these people are right?'

3   Living your rule to the full
Rather than attempting to dispute the usefulness of a rule directly, another strategy is to expose the rule as unworkable. Useful starting questions in this process are as follows:

- What stops you attaining perfection?
- What will it take?

The therapist can help the client to come up with a plan. Eventually the size and scope of the plan will become absurd as in Claire's case below:

AM: Okay, let's look at what you need to do to be perfect and avoid ever being criticised.
Claire: Well, I always need (as the voices would also instruct her) to do what others ask me to do.
AM: And what does that involve?
Claire: Just responding to whatever is asked of me.
AM: Every single time?
Claire: I guess.
AM: So how often are you asked to do something?
Claire: Several times a day.
AM: That's a lot!
Claire: Yes.
AM: Do they criticise you even if you do what they ask.
Claire: Always – because I don't do it right.
AM: What would it take to do it right then?

After elaborating all of the details required, including doing things immediately, without complaining and accurately anticipating what others wanted and how they wanted it to be done, the therapist and Claire went on to examine other aspects of being perfect. It soon becomes evident, however, that the list of requirements is ridiculous:

Claire: Can we stop now?
AM: Sure . . . but can I ask why?
Claire: It's making me feel panicky and depressed.
AM: Okay . . . but can I just ask whether you think now that it's possible to live by your belief in having to do everything perfectly?
Claire: Probably not.
AM: Could anyone do it?
Claire: Maybe not. . . . I guess I just never sat down before and thought about it.
AM: Thought about what you are demanding of yourself?

Claire: Yes (cries) . . . sorry . . . it's a relief . . . I put myself under all this pressure to keep everyone and the voices from criticising and rejecting me . . . it's crazy!

AM: And they still criticise you?

Claire: Yes.

AM: So does it make sense to continue living your life in this way by this rule?

Claire: No (cries) . . . I guess not.

Behavioural techniques

Behavioural interventions are again designed to develop emotional insight. As with person evaluations, the client can be asked to act 'as if' the new rule was true and to test out whether the rule is more accurate and helpful than the old one. This can again be consolidated through the use of flashcards, core belief worksheets (Beck, 1995) and positive data logs (Padesky, 1993, 1994).

1   Shame attacking

Shame attacking exercises (Ellis, 1969) are a powerful means of addressing rules (and the person evaluations they support) in cases where people fear rejection or disapproval. They are designed to overcome the emotion that occurs when others disapprove. Thus, someone who thinks 'I must always be approved of in order to be worthwhile' is asked to act in such a way as to invite disapproval or rejection, thereby acting against their own rules.

Case example: Jamie

Jamie was asked to hum loudly at a bus stop (a strategy he used to quieten his voices). The feared consequences happened and he was laughed at and some people moved away. Jamie was asked how he felt about this, while a little embarrassed he acknowledged that he could cope and in fact did so better than he had predicted. More importantly it gave him the opportunity to utilise his new belief: 'if people do laugh at me it does not mean that I am a pathetic nobody (as the voices had claimed), I can live with others laughing at me as I am a worthwhile person'.

In other cases, the person may not actually receive the predicted criticism and rejection following a shame attacking exercise and so may learn that, for instance, they do not have to do everything perfectly in order to be approved of and so be lovable.

Tackling difficulties in level 8 work

As might reasonably be expected, attempting to change long-held core beliefs by which the person has led their life for many years is difficult. Many of our clients do not attain this level of therapy. We have, however, evolved a number of useful strategies for overcoming difficulties here.

Difficulties eliciting the developmental history

Some clients may find it too difficult to discuss their history but may respond better to the use of written materials since it provides some emotional distance. The following is an adaptation of a technique that has been used with clients who have hearing difficulties.

Case example: Audrey

Every time the therapist tried to talk about her childhood in Jamaica, Audrey would break down in tears and ask to talk about something else because she found it too distressing. The therapist used a written record of Audrey's history that already existed in her medical file and developed flashcards that Audrey could point to which indicated whether she had found an experience positive or negative. Prior to this work, Audrey and the therapist had developed tentative ideas about how she thought of herself, based on what the voices were telling her. These thoughts were also written onto cards, and Audrey could point to the necessary card when the therapist was 'discussing' an event from her past. Over a number of sessions using this technique, Audrey said that she felt as if she had more control and was now better able to speak a little more about what had happened.

Rejection of the reformulation

Some clients may react angrily or dismissively to the notion that their core beliefs are the reason for or origin of their voices.

Case example: David

David was angry when it was suggested that he saw himself as fundamentally unlovable (a person evaluation) and that this fuelled his voice's insults about his appearance and ability to get a girlfriend. Work refocused on earlier levels of CTCH when it became apparent that David would likely disengage from therapy if the therapist persisted with attempts to connect his voice beliefs to core beliefs in this way.

Case example: Keith

Although Keith began to accept the possibility that his mother's voice was a representation of the past, what he found challenging was why he had not come to this conclusion sooner. If he had, it would have meant that his life would not have been so difficult; he could have stood up to her sooner (the voice) and got on with his life without always being manipulated. This was really difficult for Keith to work through and he conceptualised anything before this point as 'wasted time'.

The therapist drew comparisons with achieving certain things in one's life, such as getting a job that we enjoy or being in a relationship that is reciprocally supportive and loving. The therapist and Keith were able to consider that these things do not just happen. Many factors need to be in place. The person needs to learn things along the way (make some mistakes) that will help them. If they don't have a variety of jobs or different relationships, they are not able to develop as a person and understand what they do want. Similarly what we want at 20 might be very different to what we want at 30 or 40. Here, the therapist reflected back to the client that they had not qualified as a mental health nurse until they were 30 and as a therapist until their late thirties. They had lived a life that had helped them get to this point. If they had tried it sooner, maybe it would not have been right for them. It was reflected back to Keith that perhaps he had needed to learn about himself, developed enough trust over time to sustain a therapeutic relationship and challenge his voice and himself. Maybe years ago he had not been ready to do this. However, now he had done these things; he could live his life more fully without the voice of his mother coercing and manipulating him. He could live his life and use these experiences to further shape a positive view of himself.

A gentle and sensitive reformulation should always be aimed at with the reformulation proposed as merely one possible explanation, adopting a 'crab-like' stance enabling the therapist to move away quickly if necessary. For some clients, however, work at other levels may be more valuable and more acceptable.

Problems in achieving core belief change

Very often, core belief work can be met with resistance (Beck, 1995). This is not surprising given that core beliefs, by their very nature, are the most fundamental level of belief; they reflect how the person has learnt to make sense of themselves, others and the world around them; often clients will report 'always' having believed they were, for example bad or 'never' having felt able to trust people. Liotti (1989) has conceptualised resistance to change in terms of the importance of the construct being challenged to the person's belief system:

> The resistance to change of a given construct may be studied in terms of its integration into the overall construct system (that is, its connections with other constructs), of its superordinacy (that is, the number of other constructs that are subsumed under it) and of its predictive capacity. The more meaningful a construct is – that is, the greater number of events it has been able to predict during the person's lifespan – the greater it's resistance to change. The more central the construct – that is, the closer it is to the persons experience of self – the greater its resistance to change (p. 33).

Cognitive disputes at this level are a form of philosophical disputation focused upon asking the person to change their core philosophy, their sense of self and how they have constructed themselves in the light of often very difficult, emotionally painful experiences. These will understandably be difficult to change.

Case example: Sam

Sam held the belief that he was useless and 'used and abused'. As such he engaged in certain rules (e.g. being a people pleaser, trying to be 'perfectly good') and behaviours (e.g. always agreeing with others, never saying no to others demands) to compensate for his belief. Such rules and behaviours only served to reinforce his subordinate position by preventing him from engaging in disconfirmatory experiences. Although he agreed with the therapist disputes (perhaps in line with his interpersonal rules for living), he continued to find it difficult to change either his behaviour or his pattern of thinking.

For people, like Sam, their beliefs have held strong predictive validity over the course of their lives. Furthermore, when an evaluative belief is actuated, in that moment that *is* the person's experience, so as well as having predictive validity, it has experiential validity (Chadwick, 2006).

A further factor to consider in attempting core belief work in people with psychosis is the so-called confirmation bias (Alloy and Tabachnik, 1984). This suggests that the process by which we seek out, store and interpret relevant information is biased by our existing beliefs such that we can be impervious to contradictory evidence, and only notice information which confirms our pre-existing beliefs. This bias is present in all of us, but for some people their core beliefs may serve an additional psychological function: as a defence against negative self-evaluation. Such individuals may have a high emotional investment in their beliefs, even if they are distressing (as illustrated in the case of Angel). Garety and Freeman (1999) found that people with psychosis may be more likely to have such reasoning biases making it more difficult for them to generate alternative explanations for their beliefs. Experimental research has consistently found that people with delusions are more likely to jump to conclusions, show belief inflexibility and have a deficit in 'the metacognitive capacity of reflecting on one's own beliefs, changing them in the light of reflection and evidence, and generating and considering alternatives' (Garety *et al.*, 2005, p. 374).

It is therefore not surprising that core beliefs can be extremely resistant to change, even in the face of disconfirmatory experiences. Sometimes it may be necessary to address the cognitive biases (e.g. jumping to conclusions, dichotomous thinking) underlying and maintaining the person's core beliefs before addressing the actual content of the core belief itself. In other instances, clients report that although intellectually they can recognise that their beliefs are not true, they do not 'feel' it. Recent literature suggests that one means of overcoming this 'heart-head lag' (Lee, 2005) may be through the use of imagery (Holmes and Mathews, 2010), as illustrated in Angel's case below.

Another difficulty is that cognitive disputes aimed at addressing core beliefs can be quite abstract and embody some philosophical discussion. Not all clients will see the point of such discussions:

Case example: Clarke

When his therapist attempted to describe the changing nature of self, Clarke responded by saying, 'It depends what kind of drugs you're taking'. Clearly he did not get the point of this discussion.

Considerable care and creativity may be required. Visual diagrams are useful as are parables and stories, as we have described in earlier levels.

Level 8 work with Peter and Angel

Peter

Exploring the potential role of core beliefs in the aetiology and maintenance of Peter's command hallucinations

For this level of therapy, Peter and the therapist were able to build on some of the themes that had emerged in level 7:

- how his early abuse, difficulties at school and drug use had impacted on his life;
- how the woman he heard might represent how he began to negatively view himself (I'm useless, I'm no good);
- how he saw others (others are better than me, others think I am weird/different).

Together, Peter and the therapist examined what factors might lead to someone hearing voices. This provided both an explanation and normalised how often it occurs. For example, under certain circumstances people can hear voices following a trauma (e.g. a bereavement) or if they have taken nonprescribed drugs. It was possible to explore what actually happens with the brain and what might cause someone to hear voices. The inner-loop model was discussed, and how the brain can get confused in distinguishing between inner thoughts and external speech. It was valuable to look at other instances where the brain can get confused/tricked: as in the case of optical illusions (examples were given to him).

This afforded an opportunity for Peter to read around the subject which is something he was very good at doing. He was able to identify that it was more common than he first thought; many people hear voices and some are able to live alongside them in the recovery process (Cleary and Dowling, 2009).

Developing a personal model: reformulating and connecting core beliefs to psychotic beliefs

This reformulation, that Peter's voice reflected negative views of himself misattributed by the brain as an external voice, offered an explanation as to how factors in the past might have contributed to Peter's current experiences of voice hearing. This seemed to fit well with what Peter had disclosed over the course of CTCH and he agreed with this tentative explanation. Peter, however, was not ready to discuss in detail his past experiences at this point, but he was willing to examine his deeper beliefs about himself and others, how these might have developed and how they might have changed. Peter was now increasingly far more able to recognise that most of what the voice said reflected what he really thought about himself and others and how these beliefs had also now been brought into question as newer evidence had emerged that refuted them.

Reframing and disputing Peter's negative self-evaluations and rules for living

Peter's increased confidence and changed behaviour (going out to see his friends, attending art classes and walking his dog) led to him automatically challenging what the voices told him but he still did not always accept that there was no validity to what they said. In order to develop further emotional insight, it was suggested that it would be valuable to see how much this new emerging evidence fitted with his old core beliefs and whether more positive core beliefs could be developed. Peter was able to use a log that recorded information about the successes in his past and current life, what he was doing well and working towards. This challenge added weight to adopting a positive view of himself. For example, an old person evaluation Peter had was: 'I am ashamed of myself and therefore a bad person'. An alternative core belief was developed: 'I am me, I am a good person, my heart is in the right place'. Peter's log *provided* good evidence to support this new belief; he frequently did things for others, looked after and cared for his dog. Therapy progressed to examining some of Peter's rules for living and how alternate rules might be developed. An agreed rule to target initially was: 'I don't have faith in others, they are all the same'. An alternate rule was developed: 'people worry me but don't necessarily judge me, I tend to judge myself but I don't have to'. Peter and his therapist noted how this new belief was now better supported by his current experiences of supportive friendships and experiments socialising in the park when walking his dog. Agreeing to suspend his old belief in preference for the new one and examine it in light of ongoing experiences, Peter was finally able to let go of the belief.

At this point in therapy, Peter's old CTCH formulation was examined and a new one constructed (shown in Figure 8.6) to better reflect his new beliefs.

Despite this progress, the explanation that his voices were a trick of the brain was rejected at this point in therapy. Peter was a spiritual person and this explanation did not fit for him. He did, however, now think that his experiences in the past had contributed to his voice's existence. Peter also continued to challenge what she told him and no longer believed her since he now had good evidence that he was a good person who just like everyone else was fallible and made mistakes. A further protective factor in his recovery journey was that Peter was now much more open to trusting others and had stopped isolating herself. As part of his ongoing recovery journey, he turned the voice's comments into a creative/positive outlet through his art, sculpture and writing. This was Peter's path to recovery which he is still on.

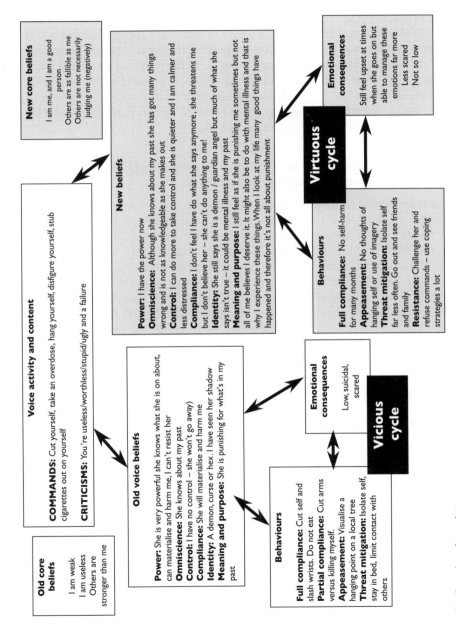

Figure 8.6 Peter's reformulation

Angel

By this stage of CTCH, Angel had made dramatic progress in terms of being able to stand up to the voices and in her courage to question and test her beliefs about them. Furthermore, Angel was becoming increasingly aware of the ego-systonic nature of the voices, in particular their derogatory comments that she was 'weak', 'useless' and 'at fault'. In the previous chapter (CTCH level 7), we noted that, when examining different possible explanations for the voices, Angel had begun to endorse the belief that the voices might echo how 'people from the past used to speak horribly' to her, thus mirroring what she learnt to believe about herself as a child.

Exploring the potential role of core beliefs in the aetiology and maintenance of Angel's command hallucinations

A developmental history had already been taken at the outset of therapy (see Chapter 1). As Angel's evaluative themes were readily elicited throughout the course of therapy, additional psychometric measures were not administered. With hindsight, however, formal measures might have provided a useful measure of change, have highlighted additional evaluative themes and may also have facilitated the process of socialising Angel to the universality of core beliefs. Utilising measures such as the EBS (Chadwick *et al.*, 1999) can help to reassure clients that other people hold such beliefs about themselves and others. Through sensitive discussion with Angel, the therapist clarified the following negative self person evaluations:

- I am bad
- I am useless.

Rules for living which supported these person evaluations were identified as:

- 'I *must* stop bad things from happening by sacrificing myself'.
- 'If I don't do things perfectly, then I am useless/bad'.
- 'Others will reject me unless I am 100 per cent perfect'.

Angel was socialised to the concept and nature of core beliefs through use of the prejudice analogy (Padesky, 1994) and the children's shape-sorter example (as shown in Figure 8.2 and discussed earlier in this chapter). Angel said that she had felt reassured by the idea that 'just because I have learned to believe these things about myself, it does not mean that they are true'. Angel's inflated sense of responsibility meant that when bad things happened (e.g. natural disasters, friends illnesses), she would blame herself, which would then be reinforced by the voices. Therefore, although Angel was beginning to be able to take the voices less seriously, her belief that she was responsible and bad and the associated intense feeling of guilt provided her with convincing evidence that she was indeed to blame. When events occurred that activated these beliefs, Angel said that she felt 'weaker' and less able to stand up to the voices. It was also clear that daily stressors, in particular those that activated her core belief that she was 'useless', had the potential to further derail her. The therapist and Angel agreed that working on these core negative person evaluations, and helping Angel to make links between her past experiences and current beliefs, would help her to feel better able to resist the voices' criticisms and commands and stand up to them, therefore inoculating her against the risk of relapse.

Developing a personal model: reformulating and connecting core beliefs to psychotic beliefs

Earlier in this chapter, we outlined how a connection between Angel's rule for living (that she must subjugate her own needs/wants to stop bad things happening) and her inferential belief (that it is her duty to sacrifice herself to prevent all the pain and suffering in the world) had been proposed, and also how the therapist had made links between the content of the voices and Angel's evaluative beliefs. Building on this, the reformulation was collaboratively drawn out in the session (see Figure 8.1 shown earlier). The therapist tentatively suggested that when something bad happened that led to Angel feeling guilty and depressed, in an understandable attempt to reduce such distress, Angel sought the means to feel 'special' (rather than 'bad'). This understandable drive to feel special led to Angel engaging in a number of behaviours including withdrawing, doing things to please others, working harder and complying with the voices (including walking in front of cars in order to obtain proof that she is special and preparing to sacrifice herself to stop world suffering).

The therapist highlighted how such behaviours were understandable given Angel's early experiences and indeed were likely to have been very useful in helping Angel to cope with the abuse, and also her mother's constant criticisms. Nevertheless perhaps, the therapist suggested, these 'rules' and subordinate behaviours (both in response to the voices and other people) were now less helpful. The therapist highlighted how things were different now: Angel was no longer at risk of rejection or criticism from her mother, nor (arguably) was she (or others) in immediate risk of danger. Furthermore, Angel had already demonstrated that she could be special in ways that did not involve the voices (see Chapter 7): she was a good mother and has engaging in voluntary work. The therapist highlighted that rather than making Angel feel special, it seemed that the subordination responses were perhaps now contributing to her distress since the cycle of feeling 'useless' and complying with things that she did not want to do was being perpetuated.

Reframing and disputing Angel's negative self-evaluations and rules for living

When asked to prioritise which beliefs she felt most important to work on, Angel chose the beliefs listed below. Initially she found the task of developing replacement core beliefs very difficult. She said she could not ever envisage viewing herself in a different way. Nevertheless, determined as she was to change her current situation, she was eventually able to come up with the following 'new' beliefs:

Old belief: I *must* stop world suffering.
New belief: I can do my bit to change the world and make it a better place.
Old belief: I am bad.
New belief: I do good things.
Old belief: I am responsible.
New belief: I feel sad when life is not perfect.
Old belief: I am useless.
New belief: I try my best.

Having established a number of alternative beliefs, the therapist and Angel fairly examined the evidence supporting her old beliefs and drawing on the techniques described earlier in this chapter employed a number of philosophical disputations. Adopting the *weakest principle first*, Angel's evaluation of herself as useless was targeted:

Key dispute: So called 'useless behaviour is not the same as globally being useless'.
Just because someone does some 'useless' things it does not mean that they are completely useless.
If I pranced up and down the room and whinnied like a horse, would it make me one?

Therapist disclosure was also useful at this point: the therapist had intended to write a therapy update report to Angel's team a few weeks previously but had not yet managed to do this. In addition to apologising to Angel for this, the therapist disclosed to Angel that when she felt overly busy at work she sometimes fell behind on her admin and report writing:

NK: Do you think that makes me useless Angel?
Angel: Of course, not!
NK: But I wasn't able to keep up with all of my work tasks.
Angel: Yes, you've been so busy, it's understandable.

This disclosure was useful in illustrating that we are all fallible human beings capable of making mistakes and acting in both useless and competent ways.

The therapist further reinforced this idea through the 'Big I little i' technique in regards to Angel's belief that she was useless. Drawing on earlier work, Angel was able to identify that she was a good mother and was helping others through her voluntary work. These, Angel felt, accounted for 60 per cent of the pie chart.

Agreed as the most distressing and most resistant to change belief, Angel's evaluation of herself as bad was examined employing the disputing in the past technique (since most current 'evidence' was now questionable having come from the voices' claims):

NK: Angel, you've listed that a powerful piece of evidence that you are bad is because that is what your mum said to you, is that right?

Angel: Yes, she always told me that I was bad.

NK: So it's understandable that you learnt to believe that about yourself. Looking back, do you think that everything that your mum said was true?

Angel: No, she used to tell my brother that he was a wimp and she'd say nasty stuff to my dad too. I don't believe any of that; my brother was tough and stood up to other kids.

NK: Okay, so not everything she said was true?

Angel: No. Not everything.

NK: So, I'm wondering then what makes you so sure that what she said about you was true?

The therapist went on to discuss how all humans, including her mother, are fallible and that just because she said those things does not make them true: a label is not a fact. As Angel's conviction in her 'old beliefs' was beginning to weaken, she was asked to act 'as if' her new beliefs were true. To consolidate the emerging cognitive shift, she was also asked to complete core belief worksheets (Beck, 1995), an example of which can be found in Figure 8.7.

Angel disclosed that a key piece of evidence supporting her belief that she was bad was an image that she frequently experienced of herself shortly after she was abused as a child. This image was associated with intense feelings of guilt, disgust and shame about what happened (having been abused). At this point in therapy, despite using all of the verbal techniques described, there had been very little shift in Angel's belief that she was bad (despite shifts in her other core beliefs). Intellectually, Angel said she understood that she was not bad and to blame but she did not 'feel' it. With the aim of overcoming this 'heart-head lag' (Lee, 2005), the therapist and Angel agreed to re-script this image using the protocol developed by Arntz and Weertman (1999). This is a technique which involves three phases:

1   First, the client is asked to bring the distressing image to mind as if they are in the memory acting as the younger self;

Core belief worksheet

Old core belief: *I am responsible for the bad things that happen to others*

How much do you believe the old core belief right now?   (0–100) __80%_____
        *What's the most you've believed it this week?   (0–100) __95%_____
        *What's the least you've believed it this week?   (0–100) __70%_____

New core belief: *I feel sad when life is not perfect. Bad things sometimes happen but it's not my fault*

How much do you believe the new core belief right now?   (0–100) 40–30%

Evidence that contradicts the old belief and supports the new one	Evidence that supports the old belief (With reframe – alternative explanation)
I feel a great sadness when people are affected by injustices in the world.	I feel responsible for everything ugly going on in the world because of a deep learnt belief from childhood and beyond because I was always blamed if anything went wrong.
I am not a decision maker, politician or a doctor. How can I be responsible for all of this?	I grew up with a secret that made me feel bad and set me apart.
People can only be responsible for their own thoughts, words and deeds.	I felt I had to repent.
I have feelings of responsibility not because I am responsible but I have learned to be responsible and bad for any unhappiness.	
Good and bad things happen to everyone. I know I do not feel that their happiness is all down to me - so I therefore should not feel that their sadness is due to me.	

Figure 8.7 Core belief worksheet

2   Next, the client is asked to imagine the same memory again this time as their current adult self, acting as a bystander to the event;
3   In the third and final phase, they are asked to rerun the memory again but this time as the younger self again with the adult self present.

In this memory, the client is asked what they think about what the adult self is doing, and if there is anything else that they would like or need in this situation (see Arntz and Weertman, 1999 for a full description of this technique). This strategy was used with Angel over the course of two sessions.

When asked what she needed in the third phase, Angel chose to have a guardian angel protecting, comforting and watching over her. This technique proved to be exceptionally powerful and beneficial for Angel. She said that for the first time in her life she did not hate herself and that she felt a contentedness that she had not experienced before. She said this feeling was accompanied by a realisation that she was not bad or to blame for the rape. Indeed during the imagery task, rather than feeling hatred towards her child self she expressed, compassionately, that she was a 'poor little thing'. Angel said that the nurturing image felt warm and comforting and provided her with a 'glowing sensation'. From this the therapist introduced Angel to the idea of a perfect nurturer (Lee, 2005) that Angel could call upon whenever she needed to experience that same warmth and comfort and glowing sensation. The therapist suggested that this could be used as an additional tool when the voices were being nasty and critical.

Extending the use of the pie chart, a standard responsibility pie was used to examine Angel's responsibility to end world suffering. A specific incident was chosen for this: that Angel was responsible for a recent plane crash. Here, the therapist explored the possible range of factors that might be involved. It was agreed that for such an event there is usually a multitude of contributing factors: weather conditions, technical failures, pilot decision-making errors. Angel realised that it was not possible that she could be 100 per cent responsible for this.

Angel expressed that this final stage of therapy had helped her to see that rather than being entrapped in her former vicious cycle in which things got perpetually worse, she was now in a more virtuous cycle in which she felt hopeful that things would get perpetually better. This was mapped out diagrammatically as shown in Figure 8.8 as a final CTCH (re)formulation showing Angel's progress in therapy and the changes in her beliefs and most importantly the reduction in her distress and safety behaviours (the original goals).

Summary

In this chapter we have described our approach to working with core beliefs, beginning with how these connect to beliefs about voices. We have outlined our reformulation process as part of this work and how this can be used to address the psychological origins of the voices as well as capturing changes in CTCH. If successful, working at this advanced level of therapy promotes long-term change and recovery and mitigates against relapse.

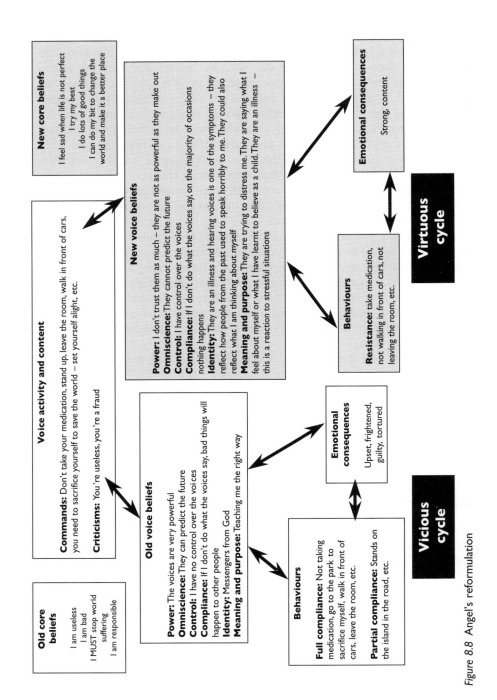

Old core beliefs

I am useless
I am bad
I MUST stop world suffering
I am responsible

Voice activity and content

Commands: Don't take your medication, stand up, leave the room, walk in front of cars, you need to sacrifice yourself to save the world – set yourself alight, etc.

Criticisms: You're useless, you're a fraud

New core beliefs

I feel sad when life is not perfect
I try my best
I do lots of good things
I can do my bit to change the world and make it a better place

Old voice beliefs

Power: The voices are very powerful
Omniscience: They can predict the future
Control: I have no control over the voices
Compliance: If I don't do what the voices say, bad things will happen to other people
Identity: Messengers from God
Meaning and purpose: Teaching me the right way

New voice beliefs

Power: I don't trust them as much – they are not as powerful as they make out
Omniscience: They cannot predict the future
Control: I have control over the voices
Compliance: If I don't do what the voices say, on the majority of occasions nothing happens
Identity: They are an illness and hearing voices is one of the symptoms – they reflect how people from the past used to speak horribly to me. They could also reflect what I am thinking about myself
Meaning and purpose: They are trying to distress me. They are saying what I feel about myself or what I have learnt to believe as a child. They are an illness – this is a reaction to stressful situations

Emotional consequences

Strong, content

Behaviours

Resistance: take medication, not walking in front of cars, not leaving the room, etc.

Virtuous cycle

Behaviours

Full compliance: Not taking medication, go to the park to sacrifice myself, walk in front of cars, leave the room, etc.

Partial compliance: Stands on the island in the road, etc.

Emotional consequences

Upset, frightened, guilty, tortured

Vicious cycle

Figure 8.8 Angel's reformulation

Chapter 9

Ending therapy and promoting longer term change

Introduction

The durability of CBTp is of particular importance given its acceptance and endorsement as part of standard care for people diagnosed with schizophrenia (NICE, 2009). Indeed, part of our aim in writing this book is to extend the use of CBTp to those experiencing command hallucinations which may previously have been seen as the remit of specialist or even forensic services. Trial evidence to date, however (see Introduction and Overview), has cast some uncertainty over whether the benefits of CBTp are sustained once therapy ends, echoing a strand of psychiatric opinion that treatments for schizophrenia are only effective as long as they are active (McGlashan, 1988). In this chapter we discuss some of the reasons why this may be the case and offer some ideas for promoting longer term change.

Factors which may mitigate against sustained benefits

Hafner and Heiden (2008) summarise the evidence regarding the main predictors of short- and medium-term risk of relapse in psychosis. Independent of therapy variables, the number of previous psychotic episodes, the duration of untreated psychosis (DUP) prior to the first episode, severity of depressive symptoms and substance misuse (cannabis in particular) all appear to play a role. Depression, anxiety and especially social anxiety are found to be among the strongest predictors of transition to psychosis in high-risk populations (Owens et al., 2005). Added to this is the consistent finding that morbidity is often higher in large urban and particularly inner city areas (Kelly et al., 2010). Social adversity factors (Morgan and Fearon, 2007; Reininghaus et al., 2008), such as living alone, social isolation, unemployment, failure to achieve expectations and neighbourhood characteristics, may be more prevalent in such environments. These factors appear to operate across the lifespan and are implicated in the onset of psychosis. Overcoming barriers to achieving social inclusion, accessing appropriate accommodation and one's life goals are likely to be significant factors in recovery also. The more immediate social and care environment is also important to consider. Numerous studies have demonstrated that there is a positive correlation between living with a relative where the environment is assessed as having high levels of Expressed Emotion (EE) and higher relapse rates, compared to those residing with a low-EE caregiver (Bebbington and Kuipers, 1994; Butzlaff and Hooley, 1998; Onwumere *et al.*, 2010). Staff may also develop such patterns, especially in inpatient services (Barrowclough *et al.*, 2001a).

Factor analytical studies show depression to be a distinct dimension of psychosis (Murray *et al.*, 2005) and may occur post-psychotically (Rooke and Birchwood, 1998). Depressive symptoms have been found to be higher in people with schizophrenia than matched controls without schizophrenia (Zisook *et al.*, 1999). Depression has also been found to positively correlate with positive symptoms (Sax *et al.*, 1996), and when it occurs beyond 1 year of an acute relapse has been associated with a greater risk of future relapse (e.g. Johnson, 1988).

Individuals diagnosed with schizophrenia present with an increased risk of substance misuse, with some authors (e.g. Kavanagh, 2008) estimating that up to half of all people so diagnosed will misuse substances at some point. Even higher rates are noted for some service settings, depending upon types of substances used and the amount and frequency of use (Kavanagh, 2008). Substance misuse is associated with increased symptoms and the risk of relapse, medication non-concordance, aggression, high-risk sexual activity, depression, suicide, unstable housing and family burden (Drake and Mueser, 2001; Kavanagh, 2008). Several studies have analysed the specific effects that cannabis use or misuse may have on psychosis, in terms of changing symptomatology, or upon the course of the person's psychosis. Two such studies have found that cannabis misuse at the time of, or preceding, first hospitalisation is correlated with more, and earlier relapses, and rehospitalisations when compared to non-users (Linszen *et al.*, 1994; Caspari, 1999). The quantity of cannabis consumed also seems important since heavy use is indicative of more relapses (Linszen *et al.*, 1994). People with schizophrenia and substance misuse have been found to experience over twice as many depressive symptoms than those without substance misuse (Scheller-Gilkey *et al.*, 2002). Likewise, initiation of substance misuse in schizophrenia increases depressive episodes (Cuffel and Chase, 1994).

In summarising this evidence, it is clear that there are a great many factors that may mitigate against success in CTCH and recovery in general. This is one argument in favour of the need for a multidisciplinary team (MDT) who can use their collective skills to work together to address these multiple needs in collaboration with other providers. Indeed, it seems reasonable to propose that strategies aimed at preventing or minimising relapse should enhance the durability of CBTp (Gumley *et al.*, 2003). Another readily apparent fact emerging in our clinical work is that many of our clients continue to require ongoing monitoring and support due to the multiple nature of their problems, social disability and vulnerability to adversity factors. What this means is that they will continue to be seen by mental health services or support workers for some time, especially as the object of the therapy is not to eliminate their voices, but rather to reduce distress and harmful compliance. These service requirements afford an opportunity to offer ongoing CTCH through members of the MDT and to offer it in a way that can help manage daily stresses and potential triggers (the A in our cognitive model).

Strategies for promoting longer term change

We might usefully ask at this point how much further intervention is required to maintain the effect of treatment. Unfortunately, despite a large number of RCTs conducted, there is as yet little clarity regarding a sustained effect with CBT post-treatment (Jones *et al.*, 2011) or indeed what the mechanisms of action for CBT might be. Garratt and colleagues (2007) explored the role that cognitive mediation has with clients with depression, exploring the impact of cognitive work on outcome and if CBT leads to this change. A related question is whether a similar conclusion can be reached with CBTp (Garratt *et al.*, 2007). What seems clear is that CBT has been identified as an effective treatment with many clinical disorders (Butler *et al.*, 2006); however, it is less certain what the mechanisms of change are and what can lead to sustained change. In the absence of hard evidence regarding the long-term impact of CBTp, we suggest a number of practical solutions which we have found important in maintaining the benefits of our therapy.

Initial tasks in ending therapy

Initial tasks in ending therapy include negotiating a reduction in the frequency of sessions and providing written summaries of the therapy so far (see below). Ending therapy should be framed as a positive process and one that supports and reinforces the notion that there has been a shift in power away from the voices and others to the client. Ending therapy provides a further opportunity for clients to reflect on these changes and reinforce positive self-statements: 'I am more powerful than my voice because I can stop it/reduce it, listen when I am ready and resist without penalty'.

Therapist summaries

A useful strategy we have employed is to use a carefully worded written summary of the key insights and most useful strategies for each client. This is usually developed collaboratively with the client and can subsequently be shared with others involved in their care if agreed.

Case example: Jennifer

Jennifer and the therapist developed a summary that detailed several key things she learned during therapy. This fell into three areas: things that Jennifer recognised as helping her take control, things she could remember that refuted the power of the voices, what would help her in the future to sort out information from the past that was still mixed up and led to feeling very distressed.[1]

Jennifer recognised that when she was engrossed in her artwork, her voices would go into the background; she felt freer and far calmer. The therapist and Jennifer were also able to note that although it was difficult for her to go to a local support group, she found it a great distraction and the voices tended to go away. Through discussion over several sessions, the therapist and Jennifer recognised that the voice did not know anything beyond what she knew. They would make predictions, but these were as inaccurate as if she had made them herself. In many cases, the voices were wrong and when Jennifer was on the lookout (using her inner detective) for their mistakes, she was able to spot the misinformation they were giving her. What was also powerful for Jennifer was to understand that she was still piecing together the past and making sense of everything. As she questioned and challenged what the voices said, she was able to look at the evidence for what they were saying and in turn make more sense of the things she had been through in her past. For many years she had not done this because she believed her voices; her confidence was low and she felt it would make things worse.

This information was written down in a summary with bullet point reminders of what she had learnt and what she could do if faced with a similar situation in the future. It also detailed her past beliefs and how looking at the evidence had led to changing these beliefs and developing new ones.

Case example: Colette

Colette's last two sessions of therapy were spent developing a staying well plan as shown below, summarising the key points of her therapy and detailing strategies she had learned to prevent relapse and help keep her well. Colette said that although she had her session-by-session therapy notes, bringing the therapy together in this way helped her to recognise how far she had come and how much progress she had made. She said this made her feel proud of herself.

Colette's CTCH staying well plan

- The most valuable ideas and techniques I have learnt in therapy are:
  - challenging myself to stand up to the voices and to be assertive with other people;
  - not believing everything the voices say;
  - gaining control as the voices are not as powerful and cannot make me do things;
  - using the thought diaries to challenge my thoughts and the voices: ask 'What's the evidence that supports what they say?'
  - learning that I am stronger than I thought and gaining evidence for my new belief that 'I am not useless. I am intelligent and capable of doing the things that I want'.
- My most important goals for the next year are:
  - keep determined – I am proud of myself and I am not going to let the thoughts or voices drag me down;
  - keep busy and continue doing the things that I want to do;
  - continue to attend music classes;
  - continue cooking.
- The events and situations which are likely to be difficult are:
  - family stressors and outside influences: these may make me feel depressed which can make the voices worse;
  - if the voices start to criticise me and tell me I am a fool, useless, etc.;
  - if someone rattles my cage.
- The things I can do in those situations are:
  - question what the voices say: *Am I? What's the evidence for that?*
  - remind myself that the voices are not always right and I might just be having a bad day. If someone rattles my cage, they tend to echo the negative thoughts that I might have in that situation;
  - look through my therapy handouts and remind myself of my positive qualities;
  - try to distance myself from the situation and use the thought diaries;
  - remind myself that if I am low on certain days, it doesn't mean it's all going to go downhill. We all have good days and bad days;
  - try to relax and do something for myself that makes me feel good;
  - don't give into what the voices say – I've shown that I can stand up to them and their threats *do not* come true.

Some clients can find it helpful to have a short summary after each session, as a reminder of the conversation.

Case example: Leroy

Leroy found it difficult to remember the exact content of each session. This was normalised for him as the therapist would spend each session writing notes to help her memory; therefore, it was only natural that Leroy might also struggle to remember things. He was encouraged to make his own notes in the session of things he had found helpful and wanted to remember. The therapist provided him with a folder and he kept all his papers for therapy together, bringing them to each session. He told the therapist it felt like he was really contributing to his own progress with the voices.

Other formats may be useful (especially for clients who have difficulty reading) such as pictorial summaries or MP3 files.

Case example: Michael

Initially paper copies of the sessions were given to Michael but he found it difficult to concentrate and read them, and his general reading level was not that good. Michael found it especially helpful to have information downloaded onto his MP3 player. Several different files were created: a relaxation tape that he could use at night to help calm his voices down and help with sleep, summaries of the sessions that helped reiterate progress, key strategies and insights (as his memory was poor and he found that he could use the MP3 flexibly if he was away from home).

Case example: Ben

Ben found it difficult to remember everything that had been covered in the session. When given session summaries on paper, he said that he tended to lose these and reported that he was unable to get access to a CD player on the ward (where he had been an inpatient for 2 years) to listen to session recordings. Ben absolutely loved cats and heard several cat voices that helped him to stand up to the bad voices. He also loved looking at pictures of cats. Utilising this, the therapist made colourful posters for Ben (see Figure 9.1 for an example) which had key summary points as well as having pictures of cats on. These were laminated so that Ben could stick them on his bedroom wall on the ward. Ben said that he loved these posters and enjoyed looking at them and reminding himself what had been covered in the therapy.

Evidence that the voices are NOT as powerful as they make out

- They weren't able to:
  - Lift up the paper
  - Break the therapist's finger
  - Make the therapist or I feel sick in the session
  - Flick the pages over in the book
  - Make us go to the toilet in the session
- They haven't hurt my girlfriend even though they threaten to
- They are not able to stop me doing the things that I want to do

SO...

<u>I am more powerful than the voices</u>
AND
<u>The voices are full of shit</u>

Figure 9.1 Ben's summary evidence against the power of the voice

Booster sessions

Booster sessions may be usefully considered to ensure that strategies learnt in therapy continue to be usefully applied and any unanticipated challenges to progress can be addressed. The frequency of these should be tailored to the individual client's needs while being mindful of fostering dependency.

Case example: Deidre

Deidre had made good progress with therapy, which had taken her to level 6. She had begun to see the link between the negative content in the voice of the 'angel' and the way her husband also verbally abused and criticised her. She had decided to change her relationship with him in the same way as she had changed her relationship with the voice. This had led her to the point that she wanted to leave and get her own accommodation; however, her husband had tried to keep her with him and she had felt pulled between her own needs and her desire to help him, so she had stayed and because she had stayed the voice of the 'angel' had again become more critical, undermining her decision. This had again led to her considering suicide as an option and so the therapist was asked to see her for a further four sessions. These focused on examining with Deidre the reasons for her 'relapse' emphasising the stress she was under and the reasons for the angel's return. This helped normalise Deidre's experience a little more to reduce her sense of self-blame. Key stages in her therapy were also reviewed, highlighting that despite the angel's return, this did not increase his power and he was still unable to physically harm her. While Deidre decided to remain with her husband, her risk of complying with the angel's commands was reduced to previous levels supporting the benefit of these booster sessions.

Team-based CTCH

CTCH is primarily an individual cognitive therapy usually involving a single therapist and the client. Inter-professional working and sharing the CTCH formulation and successful strategies may be key for maintaining recovery and further progress, especially given the relapse factors noted above. Deidre is a good example of this. In her case, a team-based approach may usefully reduce the need for further booster sessions. Co-opting others as co-therapists, particularly at the later stages of therapy, can support this process as well as serving to generalise skills to other professionals. In this way, CTCH should become part of the care plan if it is not already. Team members can be helped to recognise the client's potential As (which may be early warning signs of relapse) and subsequently utilise CTCH principles in their day-to-day interactions with the client, a process described as team-based cognitive therapy (TBCT; see Meaden and Hacker, 2010 for a fuller description). This approach can be especially useful in harder to reach or more treatment resistant clients affording a 'higher dose' of cognitive therapy. MDT members may require some training and ongoing supervision in order to successfully utilise these strategies. A team-based approach requires the application of CBT principles whenever the client appears distressed by a particular situation or is engaging in the use of a safety behaviour. In the absence of training, team members might be encouraged to review the treatment summaries described above in order to adopt successful CTCH strategies into their routine practice. Part of this work may also require sharing (with the client's permission) the CTCH formulation with the team in order to fully engage them in supporting the client. This can also serve to help address any negative attitudes the team or others may have developed about them.

Case example: Raj

Raj is a 62-year-old man with a long history of self-harming and suicide attempts. He heard the voice of his deceased wife saying, 'Go on just kill yourself, so we can be together again'. Consequently, in the belief that he would be reunited with his wife, Raj had frequently cut his wrists, had tried to hang himself on several occasions and had thrown himself in front of a bus for which he sustained multiple injuries. Raj had been hearing this voice since his wife was brutally murdered 30 years previously. He said that he felt responsible for her death and that he believed that she was unable to reach heaven (hence why he heard her voice) until he joined her. He also believed that he was cursed and that if he got close to people then bad things would happen to them. Consequently, he would frequently be verbally (and sometimes physically) assaultive towards others (including team members) 'to keep them away'.

Raj had both a diagnosis of schizophrenia and borderline personality disorder. He had never been referred for psychological therapy before as he was considered too 'risky' and 'too complex'. The team, understandably, found it difficult to manage his behaviour and felt that his suicide attempts were a means to gain attention. Despite this initial team view, Raj engaged very well and attended all twenty-five sessions. However, only limited progress was made. At this point, Raj and the therapist reframed some of his experiences and behaviour. It was suggested that rather than having borderline personality disorder, Raj was presenting with a traumatic grief reaction. He presented with clear PTSD symptoms related to his wife's murder as well as to his own early experiences of childhood sexual abuse. It was agreed that these now needed to be the goals of therapy before progress could be made in addressing the voice-power schema. The therapist spent several sessions with Raj's team, helping them to formulate and understand Raj's beliefs and behaviour, thus addressing the team's beliefs about his suicidal behaviour and treatability. Time was also spent sharing the CTCH level 2 work (coping strategies) that had been achieved so that the team felt more skilled at helping Raj to cope when he presented in crisis. He subsequently presented less often in crisis and the team were able to support his use of coping with the voice's commands to kill himself. His suicidal behaviour subsequently reduced and the team agreed that Raj should now be referred on for trauma-focused psychological therapy.

Using relapse prevention with command hallucinations

As we have noted in the introduction to this book, CTCH does not routinely employ relapse prevention work (RPW), a psychosocial intervention that includes psychoeducation and self-monitoring and may utilise cognitive therapy elements in conjunction with coping strategies as relevant to the individual's unique set of early signs and vulnerabilities. As Jones and Meaden (2012) note, RPW requires individuals to:

- accept that they have a relapsing condition that needs long-term monitoring;
- recognise the emergence of their early warning signs;
- change their behaviour accordingly and/or initiate care and support from others.

It may prove difficult to use this approach in less well-engaged populations; for these groups, carers or healthcare professionals may provide monitoring and decide when to intervene. In CTCH, this method can be used to enable clients to recognise activating events (As) for their command hallucinations (e.g. having arguments with a partner may activate commands to harm them) and so be better prepared to use CTCH strategies to manage them. Therapist summaries as described above can be useful here, reminding the client of which strategies are most effective. Using the resources of the person's MDT will of course also be important in providing an extra source of support to put these strategies into practice.

Tackling difficulties in ending therapy and promoting longer term change

Despite our best efforts, it is not always possible to maintain the benefits of CTCH. As described above, there are many factors that mitigate against longer term change. Similarly, chance factors may intervene, which promote recovery and stability in clients (e.g. developing a supportive relationship). For some clients letting go of a valued therapeutic relationship may prove very difficult.

Need for long-term therapy

Although unfashionable in current healthcare policy, some clients will need longer term work. The therapist and client must of course clarify whether longer term work is beneficial or is creating dependency. If the latter is the case, greater co-working as described above will be needed. In our current trial work, the maximum number of session for any one client was forty-two. In routine settings the ability of the therapist to offer longer term work in cases where it is likely to be of benefit will depend to some extent on the type of setting. Long-term inpatient settings such as specialist forensic or other residential services provide one opportunity for such work. The first author works as part of his time in an assertive outreach team (AOT) where such longer term intervention in the community is possible.

Case example: Frank

Frank has an extensive history of risk behaviours including assault with a weapon, fire setting and self-harm. He has received services for many years but engaged poorly with them. Under an AOT, his involvement with treatment has improved and it has been possible to work with him on his experiences of command hallucinations. Frank, however, continues to have multiple stressors in his life (e.g. a disruptive and abusive partner, unstable housing) and will often resort to drug use. While CTCH work has largely been completed (up to level 6), at these times it is helpful to provide further contact and review and support him in his use of CTCH strategies. This work is ongoing.

Absent and non-engaged teams

Ideally the MDT is present and the client is suitably engaged with them to allow inter-professional working. However, the challenges of work with demanding clients can leave professionals feeling deskilled and devalued (see Meaden and Hacker, 2010 for a review). It is possible that such challenges, including the need to increase the management of risk, can lead some clients to be prioritised over others. Those who find it difficult to assert or value themselves (such as Peter, one of our main case studies) can give the impression that there are no current difficulties, perhaps because they find it difficult to trust others or they may view others as more important than themselves. In such a climate, clients such as Peter might behave in a way that encourages themselves to 'blend' into the background. Unsurprisingly when teams are feeling pressured they can find it more difficult to notice that some people are doing this. However, this presents challenges for the CTCH therapist who might spend more time with the person than anyone else and generate a more detailed formulation which better understands the risks and needs of the person, especially if that therapist is positioned outside of the team.

Case example: Leroy

Leroy (introduced earlier) heard the voices of the spirits of his dead mother and grandmother, along with numerous other indistinguishable spirits. In the past, these spirits had encouraged him to commit armed robbery and to jump from a 10-ft high bridge, where he sustained broken bones. Leroy had witnessed his mother's death at the age of 6. He had hoped to live with his father after this but instead had been sent to live with his father's family where he had been emotionally and physically abused by his older cousin and aunt. Leroy felt that the use of violence was the only way to get his point across, but that he did not like himself when he acted in this way and so would silently 'seethe' until suddenly becoming very angry. Given his early relationship difficulties, he found trust extremely difficult and had had the experience of not having his voice hearing validated by professionals. He did, however, form a trusting relationship with his therapist and told her that he had never discussed his mother's death or early childhood before. However, during the course of therapy his care team changed and the new team appointed a care coordinator who was rarely available due to other commitments. This person was then on sick leave and the therapist was advised that Leroy could contact the duty worker with any pressing concerns, but that the duty worker would be a different person each time. The care coordinator subsequently left post and it took 8 weeks to appoint a new one; the therapist was told that this was because she (a non-MDT member) was seeing the client. It was decided that, as the therapist could provide only time-limited help, Leroy needed to practice some of his new assertiveness skills and ask for what he needed from his team. During this period the therapist provided a 'holding' function by delaying discharge. After many telephone calls and letters with the team manager, Leroy and the trial therapist linked into a new permanent care coordinator. Two joint sessions were organised to share the work and stress its importance.

These team working issues had taken up much time during the therapy and also meant that Leroy often felt unsafe and unsupported. Consequently, work had only progressed to level 6.

Ending therapy and promoting longer term change with Peter and Angel

Peter

Ending therapy

Like Leroy, Peter had also experienced an absent team during much of his therapy, making regular liaison with his GP important with regular updates (shared with Peter). Clearly, however, despite making very significant progress more comprehensive care planning was required to ensure that his recovery was maintained and supported. Towards the end of therapy, Peter felt more positive about being referred back to his CMHT and was much more confident in expressing his needs. He also acknowledged that while his experience of the team had not been good in the past, this did not mean it would be the same the second time round. He was more willing to take a chance and challenge his own beliefs about what might happen.

The ending of therapy was a gradual process. Very early on in the therapy, Peter was aware that contact would be limited to a certain number of sessions. The therapist and Peter discussed how he felt about ending therapy and agreed to adjust the frequency of sessions from session 15 onwards, allowing him to acclimatise to not seeing the therapist. Peter said that he could not have imagined ending therapy during the early sessions and wondered how he would cope. However, as his confidence grew and he began to socialise more and get support from others (including now his MDT), he felt better about therapy coming to an end. Sessions were planned every 2 weeks and towards the end monthly. A plan was put in place so that he could manage any issues that arose during these times and how he would access additional support if he needed it.

The use of therapy summaries

Throughout therapy, written summaries were provided which Peter found very useful. As part of the summary, Peter and the therapist developed flashcards, basic and more developed formulations, and a positive data log. All of these helped remind Peter of the strategies he had developed, his changing beliefs in relation to the voices and the positive beliefs he began to develop regarding himself and others.

Team working and relapse planning

Peter and the therapist also completed a relapse prevention plan (see Birchwood *et al.*, 2000a) highlighting signs of relapse and which strategies he could use if these were present. This was shared with both Peter's GP and his MDT. Peter and the therapist also explored how he could build on the work already undertaken. One particular recommendation was that he wanted to receive additional therapy that explored his earlier life. The therapist and Peter identified that this particular need could be met via his GP service, and Peter said he would feel comfortable exploring this with him. This involved Peter reaching out to others (which he had previously found very difficult) and promoted his self-efficacy and confidence.

Main outcomes for Peter

In line with our key aims by the end of therapy, Peter reported no longer being distressed by his voices and did not act on them or engage in any compliance, appeasement or threat mitigation safety behaviours.

Angel

Ending therapy

From the outset, Angel was aware of the time-limited nature of the therapy. As the ending of therapy neared although Angel was keen for the opportunity to 'become her own therapist' (as had been suggested by the therapist), she was also fearful that the progress that she had made might be lost without the ongoing help of the therapist. Angel found the analogy of learning to drive helpful here: that the therapist had been akin to a driving instructor, helping Angel to navigate and learn new ways of coping and standing up to the voices, but the whole time it was actually Angel who had been in the driving seat. Therefore, it was Angel (as opposed to the therapist) who had been responsible for her own progress, and as Angel now had all the skills to cope, she no longer needed the therapist. The therapist suggested that just like a new driver will only become a confident driver when they go out driving alone, it would only be when Angel 'goes it alone' that she would feel confident in her ability to maintain the progress that she had made. To facilitate the ending, Angel and the therapist also agreed to gradually reduce the frequency of their sessions: from weekly to fortnightly and then monthly.

The therapist felt that Angel showed a huge amount of courage and dedication to the therapy. Angel expressed that she was very pleased with the progress that she was able to make and reported a feeling of contentment within herself that she said she had not experienced before.[2]

The use of therapy summaries

Angel already had her folder of therapy notes and audio-recordings of the sessions, which she frequently referred to and felt would be a useful reminder of the sessions when they finished. In addition to this, a 'staying well plan' (or 'blueprint' as shown earlier for the case of Colette) was developed summarising the key aspects of therapy which Angel had found helpful.

Angel's staying well plan

- The most valuable ideas I have learnt in therapy are:
  - not believing everything the voices say;
  - just because we feel a certain way (e.g. guilty), it doesn't mean that we are (e.g. guilty);
  - asking myself, 'What would I say to a friend/someone else'?
  - reminding myself that nothing is all bad. I can try and break it down;
  - if people say something to me, let them share their feelings but remind myself that it doesn't mean that it is my fault. Don't let it cripple me. It might be their difficulty;
  - I don't need to be perfect!
- The most valuable techniques I have learnt in therapy are:
  - standing up to the voices: they are not 100 per cent powerful and that nothing awful has happened;
  - using the list to identify my thinking errors;
  - using the forms to record my thoughts, the commands, etc.;
  - using the imagery technique and talking to 'little Angel';
  - using the Angel to protect me.
- My most important goals for the next year are:
  - to stay as I am – I don't want to go back to how things were;
  - not to be devastated by people and the voices;
  - to feel able to speak to someone if I start to feel bad;
- The events and situations which are likely to be difficult are:
  - if bad things happen (e.g. disasters) and the voices blame me;
  - if the voices threaten to hurt my son.
- The things I can do in those situations are:
  - talk to someone;
  - go through my folder;
  - when the voices blame me for bad things happening, ask myself – how could it be my fault?
  - question what the voices say – I don't have to believe what they say;
  - remember the spinning tribe and the rainmaker;
  - keep in touch with the Angel and feel her support;
  - if I do have a blip, try not to think in all or nothing terms (A blip doesn't mean that I'm back to square one. Remember the progress and achievements that I have made.);
  - remind myself that just because I believe something, it doesn't mean that it is true;
  - if I start following the commands, start using the resistance diaries again to try and get on top of it;
  - avoid situations (triggers) where the voices build up;
  - if the voices tell me that I am evil or bad, use the core belief worksheets to examine the evidence for and against this;
  - monitor my 'warning signs'.

Team working and relapse planning

As part of the staying well plan, Angel and the therapist also identified a list of early warning signs (Table 9.1). The aim of this was to help Angel recognise when she might be becoming unwell so that she could put in place her 'staying well strategies' sooner rather than later. A joint meeting with Angel's care coordinator was also conducted in which a handover of the therapy as well as a comprehensive written summary of the therapy were provided (which, with Angel's consent, included the staying well plan and some of the key therapy handouts).

Main outcomes for Angel

Key changes for Angel were also captured on some of our trial measures (described in Chapter 1) summarised in Table 9.2. The results indicate that although some small changes on the VPDS were noted at the 9 month follow-up, these had reduced significantly by the time of the 18 month follow-up. It is interesting to note that the additional ten sessions that were offered to Angel (to complete CTCH levels 7 and 8 work) were conducted *after* the 9 month follow-up appointment. One can speculate about whether work at these levels may have contributed to the improved scores at 18 months. By this point, Angel rated herself as being more powerful and stronger than her voices. In terms of superiority, she rated herself and the voices as being equal at both the 9 and 18 month follow-up (as compared to rating her voice as being greatly superior pre-therapy). There was a small but positive change in Angel's rating of respect, confidence and knowledge on the VPDS; however, post-therapy Angel's belief that the voices were much more able to harm her than she was able to harm them remained unchanged. Importantly, at 18 months post-therapy, Angel reported reduced distress (a key CTCH aim) associated with the voices and rated herself as having control over the voices approximately half of the time (as opposed to no control pre-therapy). The voices also now caused a minimal amount of disruption to her life (as opposed to a moderate level of disruption pre-therapy).

Table 9.1 Angel's early warning signs

Thoughts	Feelings	Behaviours	Physical	Other signs
Believing the voices	Sad	Avoiding people	Stiff	Voices increasing
All or nothing thinking	Not content	Not answering phones	Sleeping less	—
Thinking I am a failure	Overwhelmed	Acting on smaller commands	—	—
Thinking I am responsible	Guilty and responsible	Listening out for the voices	—	—

Table 9.2 Summary comparing Angel's pre- and post-therapy scores on the key psychometric measures for voices

Measure		Pre-therapy	Post-therapy (9 month follow-up)	Post-therapy (18 month follow-up)
Power differential[a]	Power	5	3	2
	Strength	5	5	2
	Confidence	5	5	4
	Respect	4	3	4
	Harm	5	5	5
	Superior	5	3	3
	Knowledge	5	5	4
	Total score	34	31	24
Control over the voices[b]		4	3	2
Disruption caused by voices[b]		2	1	1
Distress[b]		3	3	2

[a] Voice Power Differential Scale (VPDS).
[b] Psychotic Symptom Rating Scale (PSYRATS).

Although she continued to hear distressing voices on a daily basis, the frequency of actual commands reduced significantly (to once a day rather than continuously). Furthermore, when Angel did hear commands, she was almost always able to resist them. The only commands that Angel said that she occasionally complied with at the end of therapy were commands not to talk to people. She expressed, however, that her compliance with this might be because she did not want to talk to certain people anyway (e.g. they were ego-systonic). Most importantly, Angel had not complied with commands to go to the park to sacrifice herself or with commands to walk in the road since 5 months into starting therapy. Furthermore, she had not complied with commands to stop taking her medication and had been taking medication regularly since 7 months into starting therapy.

Summary

In this chapter we have reviewed the key factors which appear to prevent longer term change in clients with psychosis in general and described the strategies we have developed to mitigate against this in clients with command hallucinations. Ending therapy successfully and facilitating ongoing care based upon CTCH perhaps constitute level 9 of our approach.

Notes

1   Jennifer provides her own account of CTCH in our preface.
2   Angel's own account of her experience of CTCH is given in the preface.

Chapter 10

Special issues

A key question in attempting to disseminate any trail-based therapy is, can it be applied in routine practice, especially with clients who often present with additional complex problems? Underlying our approach, the ABC model provides a flexible generic model to guide assessment, formulation and intervention and has been applied to a wide variety of problems (Trower *et al.*, 2010). This suggests that CTCH can also be adapted to address significant co-morbidities in clients experiencing command hallucinations. In this chapter we show how CTCH can be utilised with such clients, illustrating how our level 8 framework can be tailored to the client's case-specific and changing needs.

Adapting the model for clients with a learning disability and cognitive deficits

People with schizophrenia can show deficits across many neurocognitive domains but are most likely to experience such deficits in the context of generalised cognitive impairment (Sharma and Antonova, 2003). Estimates indicate that around 70 per cent may have significant cognitive impairment with the most severe deficits in the areas of learning of new verbal information, sustained attention or vigilance as well as executive functions, verbal fluency (the ability to generate words within a given time limit) and motor speed (Harvey and Sharma, 2002). More moderate deficits (defined as 1–2 standard deviations below the population mean) are to be found in the areas of distractibility, working memory, visuo-motor skills and recall of information (Harvey and Sharma, 2002). Cognitive impairments show a greater relationship to negative symptoms than to positive symptoms such as voices but do not appear to be caused by negative symptoms. In addition, negative symptoms may improve or remain stable, while cognitive impairments may remain stable or worsen (Leff *et al.*, 1994).

These cognitive deficits need to be borne in mind when delivering CTCH and often require adaptations to be made. There are also important clinical reasons against overwhelming a person with demands that they cannot meet.

For example, Kingdon and Turkington (2005) have noted the importance of ensuring that clients are provided with a chance to succeed, especially in the presence of negative symptoms. For this reason, the focus may need to be on small and achievable goals in the first instance which can be gradually built upon.

Using memory aids and prompts

For some clients, alarms or electronic prompts using a wristwatch, dictaphone, mobile phone or personal digital assistant (PDA), or simple notepads and diaries may prove useful. These can act as specific prompts for homework and keeping appointments as well as step by step instructions or summaries of coping strategies and steps in behavioural experiments. Keeping notes on the outcomes of experiments or other evidence fits well with our analogy of the inner detective. Written materials are likely to be helpful for some clients, while others will require visual materials involving pictures or auditory material. Studies of cognitive rehabilitation suggest that external compensation is more beneficial with those with moderate to severe memory deficits, while for those with milder memory impairments training in the use of mnemonics is recommended (Cappa *et al.*, 2005; Cicerone *et al.*, 2005).

Case example: Jill

At the beginning of therapy, Jill indicated that her reading and writing abilities were limited and she often reported difficulties sustaining concentration and remembering things. Her therapist adapted CTCH in several ways:

1 The language used during the sessions was kept as simple as possible.
2 The length of sessions was kept short and breaks introduced.
3 Regular checks were made to ensure that Jill understood what she and the therapist had discussed.
4 The key points covered in sessions were written down in-session and Jill was also asked to summarise what she remembered.
5 Fuller summaries were provided (which included basic formulations/ maintenance cycles) every few weeks and these were copied to a disc so that Jill could listen to this as and when she needed; this aided memory and understanding and fostered continuity in therapy.
6 Jill had a tick list to tick off information related to what time of day it was and where she was; thoughts and emotions could be ticked to indicate how she was feeling and she was again able to tick how she managed the situation and which CTCH strategy she had used in order to cope.

> This resource was used for several sessions and allowed some valuable exploration of which strategies helped Jill, depending upon the situation and her reflections of this in relation to herself and the power of her voices.

Problem-solving training is another useful approach. This is in essence a metacognitive strategy, relying upon the client learning a strategy which can then be used across situations. D'Zurilla and Goldfried (1971) developed a problem-solving approach to use with psychological problems emphasising the following stages:

- problem orientation;
- problem definition and formulation;
- generating potential alternative solutions;
- decision-making concerning the best approach (examining pros and cons);
- solution implementation and evaluation.

Such approaches have shown some benefit in neurological patients with dysexecutive problems (Rath *et al.*, 2003; Mitto *et al.*, 2008) and we have adapted them for CTCH clients.

Case example: Aziz

Aziz experienced significant problems in working memory and attention. His ability to solve everyday problems remained poor and his frustration tolerance was low, reacting badly when his demands were not met immediately. A key trigger appeared to be the stress associated with having to look after his disabled wife and ill mother. This frustration at not getting support from the rest of his family became the A for insults from his voices: 'you're weak, no one takes you seriously', and commands 'go on hit him, set fire to the house'.

Sessions focused upon coping with frustration (teaching him a set of simple coping skills to help manage his arousal levels) and constructive problems solving. He was taught the four-stage problem-solving approach of D'Zurilla and Goldfried (1971):

1 define the problem – *accepting that others cannot always respond as I demand*;
2 identify possible solutions – *practice coping strategies: relaxation*;
3 weigh up the pros and cons of the solution;

4 plan and implement the solution with the most pros – *use the new skills (e.g. ask myself am I feeling stressed, count to ten before reacting, go for a walk, write down my frustrations, use my relaxation CD).*

Using these approaches, arguments with his family greatly reduced and actually led to them increasing the amount of support they gave him. Aziz's voices also reduced in frequency and when calmer he felt less compelled to comply and more able to resist their harmful commands.

Table 10.1 Aziz's cons and pros of the solution

Cons of the solution	Pros of the solution
1 They will think I'm a pushover 2 They wont help me	1 It will avoid arguments with my family 2 They are less likely to help me if I shout and abuse them 3 Arguments start the voices off 4 I could do something stupid

Working with substance abuse in CTCH

As we noted in Chapter 9, substance abuse is a particular problem when working with people with psychosis and is associated with poorer clinical outcomes, higher levels of aggression and violence, and greater risk of suicide and self-harm. These may result in significant problems with engagement, either due to current intoxication or a chaotic lifestyle that accompanies such use. Substances may also lessen the impact of behavioural experiments by preventing full exposure and may be preferred to alternative more functional coping strategies. Furthermore, they can influence the therapy session and affect the client's ability to concentrate, remember information in-session and recall what was discussed in subsequent meetings.

Case example: David

David was experiencing voices which criticised him and told him to 'drink himself to death'. He had been dependent upon alcohol for some 40 years after being sent to prison at the age of 24 for stabbing a man in a pub fight. He had been diagnosed with Korsakoff's syndrome and his memory and speech were becoming progressively worse. In response, he drew up a plan with the therapist to meet at 9 am on the appointment day, and agreed that he would not drink prior to the appointment. The therapist rang his accommodation the day before each appointment as a reminder. He was also provided with recordings of the appointments and his key worker in the accommodation was recruited as a co-therapist to help him complete and remind him of the outcome of homework tasks.

While David engaged in therapy and completed twelve sessions, he only progressed to CTCH level 3 and continued to misuse alcohol.

For such clients, motivational interviewing (MI), combined with CTCH, might be utilised as part of the process of considering the benefits of CTCH compared to current efforts to cope with or minimise problems through substance use. Many clients do not consider their alcohol or substance use to be a problem. The aim during the initial sessions is therefore to elicit change or motivational statements from the client. Here, the therapist uses a number of strategies to guide the client to identify substance or alcohol use as a problem and express a desire to change:

• reflective listening;
• empathy;
• developing discrepancy;
• rolling with resistance;
• selective reinforcement to elicit statements.

MI when combined with CBTp has shown promising results in improving functioning in patients with schizophrenia with associated drug or alcohol misuse (Barrowclough *et al.*, 2001b; Baker *et al.*, 2006; Barrowclough *et al.*, 2010).

Managing long-standing interpersonal problems

For some clients, longstanding interpersonal patterns of poorly relating to others and psychological dispositions characterised by impulsivity and lability of mood, trait anger, hostility, suspiciousness, rigidity, avoidance and dependency may need to be considered and managed. Such clients may be labelled as 'personality disordered'. Therapists will need to consider the extent to which these clients can be managed successfully or their difficulties moderated to allow therapy to proceed. Engagement and the development of coping strategies may require particular attention for such clients (see Millon and Grossman, 2007a and 2007b, for a more comprehensive set of strategies).

Case example: Daisy

Daisy heard the voice of spirits that told her to humiliate and harm herself. She believed that she heard these voices because she was special. She distrusted any health professional because her experience was that they would say she had a 'mental health' problem and was consequently stupid or wrong for believing otherwise. Daisy had struggled to experience closeness to another person, as she had been abused by her mother and brothers and rejected by her father and sister. She would often become angry and hostile when she felt threatened, she had made complaints against several members of staff, and members of her care team felt that she was 'inventing' her symptoms. Daisy found relationships with others difficult to negotiate and would generally distrust their motives. For this reason engagement was very difficult. The therapist therefore spent a number of sessions talking about both the voices and other peripheral matters, allowing Daisy to take control. The formulation of her experiences was shared early to convey that the therapist understood that she thought they were spirits and that she was special. However, when Daisy's mental health deteriorated as depression caused her alcohol consumption to rise and the voices to worsen, the therapist was obliged to discuss the difficulties with other members of her care team; this presented extreme challenges to the delicate relationship. Daisy felt that the therapist had breached her trust and was angry with her and so the reasons for discussing the therapist's concerns were discussed at length and in full. The therapist collaboratively constructed a formulation of trust difficulties to illustrate the process that was occurring. Daisy's existing experience of the therapist was used to illustrate that the therapist was staying within her frame of reference, that the voices were spirits to her, but that those spirits nonetheless meant her to harm herself and she currently believed that she must comply. This was the reason for seeking help and support from the team.

Following team intervention, Daisy's voices became less frequent and intense and her mood stabilised. The focus of CTCH returned to engagement building and a review of her goals. Daisy felt that her main goals were to cope with the voices. Work focused, therefore, on level 2. Daisy did not move onto higher levels of therapy.

Case example: Jackson

Jackson heard voices telling him to kill himself and other people with which he had frequently complied: holding a knife to his chest (partial compliance), shouting at others (appeasement), assaulting others (full compliance) and avoiding others (threat mitigation). The voices also criticised him by saying 'you're useless' and 'you're worthless'. Jackson's voices tended to emanate from people around him, such that he often believed *they* were criticising him and ordering him around. As a result of this he would become very angry, aggressive and sometimes physically assaultive to the person in question. In the first session, Jackson heard a voice coming from the therapist telling him that he was useless. He consequently became extremely angry and aggressive, and stormed out of the session. In the second session, Jackson again became very angry and left the session in a rage. The therapist decided to contact Jackson by telephone to discuss his concerns and experience of the sessions. Jackson reported that he had been hearing voices telling him to hurt the therapist and said that he was therefore worried about continuing with the therapy.

While acknowledging Jackson's concerns, the therapist suggested that perhaps they could start off by having telephone rather than face-to-face sessions. That way Jackson would not feel at risk of hurting the therapist and would have the option of putting the phone down if he felt upset or angry (using this strategy as a means of Jackson gaining control – akin to the panic button analogy). The therapist and Jackson proceeded to have several telephone sessions during which time was spent on further exploring the voices and the previous sessions when Jackson had got upset and angry. The therapist reassured Jackson that she would never criticise him in a session and that it would be against her professional code of conduct to do so. She added that if she was to do this, she could potentially receive disciplinary action from her manager or the Health Professions Council. The following is taken from an early telephone session with Jackson when this was discussed:

NK: I'm really confused by this Jackson because for the reasons we've just discussed (as above) I would never call you useless.

Jackson: But it happens all the time. Even the pastor called me useless the other day. I don't get it because the pastor has been really trying to help me.

NK: So it doesn't sound like the kind of thing the pastor would say?

Jackson: No!

NK: Have there been other times when you've heard a similar thing and it hasn't seemed to be the kind of thing that person would say?

Jackson: Yeah loads! From my mum ... and even Maxine, my care co-ordinator.

NK: And what do you think these people have in common – the pastor, your mum and Maxine?

Jackson: Well, I would have thought they would be trying to help me!

NK: Mmmm ... I could be wrong here Jackson, and do tell me if I've completely got things muddled, but is there any possibility that the voices might be mimicking the voices of these people so that you don't trust the people who *are* actually trying to help you?

Jackson: What do you mean?

NK: Well, I'm guessing that the voices like you doing what they say?

Jackson: Yes!

NK: So, do you think they'd be worried if somehow things changed so that you didn't do what they said?

Jackson: Yes, they'd hate it.

NK: Hmmm ... I thought as much. I'm wondering then whether they might be threatened by me, the pastor, your mum and Maxine – because we are all trying to help you. Again, I might be wrong here but perhaps they are worried that they might lose their control over you?

Jackson: Yeah, that kinda makes sense.

This explanation made sense to Jackson and allowed the therapist to make a plan with him: it was agreed that should he ever hear a voice coming from the therapist in the future, he would check it out with her first rather than simply assuming it was true. Time was also spent on the telephone exploring other triggers for when Jackson became angry and developing some strategies to help manage his anger. This enabled Jackson and the therapist to develop a risk management plan so that he felt able to come in for face-to-face sessions:

1 meeting in a room next to another occupied room in the clinic;
2 the therapist always sitting close to the door;
3 the therapist checking in after each session with the care team to say that she was safe;
4 Jackson always having the option to leave a session if he felt angry (with the agreement that the therapist would later call to check out any misinterpretations);
5 Jackson cancelling sessions if he felt overly angry beforehand.

> As well as being necessary risk precautions for the therapist, these strategies helped Jackson to feel more confident that he would not pose a risk to the therapist. Impressively, Jackson subsequently attended a total of eighteen face-to-face sessions. Although there were times when he became angry during the sessions, he was always able to make use of the risk plan. At no point did he ever harm the therapist, nor did the therapist ever feel at risk of being harmed in the sessions. Furthermore, at his 9 and 18 month follow-up assessments, he rated himself and his voices to 'have about the same power as each other' (as compared to his voice was much more powerful than him pre-therapy). In addition, his 18 month follow-up assessment indicated that although Jackson still heard distressing commanding voices, during those 18 months he had managed to resist carrying out any of the commands issued to him.

Working with other cognitive risk factors

Some clients present with additional cognitive risk factors. Simourd and Olver (2002) propose the term 'criminal attitudes' to capture a broad constellation of criminally orientated attitudes, values, beliefs and rationalisations. Pro-criminal beliefs and attitudes may be said to condone the use of violence and give legitimacy to antisocial acts (Müller-Isberner, 2001). Criminal history variables contribute much of the predictive power of actuarial risk instruments. The predictive accuracy of even the simplest behavioural measures seems to exceed the predictive power of diagnosis (Buchanan, 2008). However, clinically derived variables (such as power beliefs) and coping strategies provide insights into the mechanisms by which a minority of people with mental disorders act violently (Buchanan, 2008) and offer the potential for intervention. Such attitudes are an obvious target of treatment (McNeil et al., 2003) yet are frequently not targeted in current CBTp trials. They are frequently connected to other core beliefs (level 8 work) and may also serve as evidence for the voice's power. Thus, clients may believe that violence is an acceptable solution to managing interpersonal difficulties and accordingly that their voices offer good advice to use violence. Such attitudes may be evident in the form of ego-syntonic voices: the content of their voices will reflect the client's own antisocial attitudes and dispositions.

The ABC model is invaluable in work with such clients. Each risk behaviour should be the focus of assessment and formulation in ABC terms. Only in this way can we be clear about the function each behaviour serves: compliance, distress reduction or legitimate action. Behaviours which look the same in people with psychosis may serve different functions (hitting staff to avoid medication versus hitting staff because they are believed to be the source of derogatory voices), while behaviours which appear very different may in fact serve the same function (cutting and drinking heavily to reduce distress associated with persistent derogatory voices); see Meaden and Hacker, 2010 for a fuller discussion. When working with such clients, it is often difficult to address voice beliefs without also addressing these core beliefs in level 8 work.

Case example: Dermott

Dermott heard voices when he was walking in town saying: 'he is disrespecting you, he's taking the piss' and 'go on do him/slash him'. Dermott had acted on these commands frequently, leading to several convictions and time in forensic settings. During the course of CTCH (when examining the reasons for his voices), Dermott acknowledged that he thought these things himself. Through the process of therapy, the therapist and Dermott discovered that such thoughts were congruent with a physically abusive upbringing, early exposure to violence and Dermott's social environment. He found it extremely difficult not to respond in this way to incidences of social threat in his environment (a deprived inner city area) and also noted that he would be seen as an easy target if he did not respond as he did, and had 'a reputation to maintain'.

Therapy focused on his broad goal of wanting to take control back of his life. The therapist and Dermott agreed in keeping with this goal that he should be able to respond as *he* wanted to in these situations and not as the voice commanded him to. This provided the rationale for beliefs about power to be addressed. Subsequently, his favourable response to CTCH paved the way for work on his core beliefs. Having acknowledged the value of a cognitive approach, it was now possible to consider that his long-held beliefs about others might also be wrong: that he had to act in aggressive and violent ways when under threat. Dermott was helped to see through Socratic questioning that these beliefs prevented him from getting close to others and having a long-term stable relationship and maybe even children of his own.

Case example: Morris

In contrast to Dermott, Morris (who reported multiple accounts of assault as well as an extensive substance abuse history) disengaged from therapy finding it just too risky to address his voices, sensing that they 'keep me safe when I am not on the ball' (due to his current high levels of substance use and intoxication).

Trauma work

Not only are trauma symptoms highly distressing, they may also serve to maintain the client's voice-power schema. The relationship between psychotic and trauma symptoms such as flashbacks and nightmares requires a careful and detailed trauma assessment (see Chapter 8).

Case example: Cindy

Cindy heard spirits commanding her to cut herself and to take an overdose. She believed that the spirits would kill her if she disobeyed them. A powerful piece of evidence supporting this belief was that the spirits would try to suffocate her if she resisted their commands. At these times, she described experiencing the sensation of having hands around her neck and not being able to breathe and having the thought 'I am going to die'. A careful assessment indicated that Cindy had been physically abused by her ex-partner and that on one occasion when she had 'disobeyed' him he strangled her to the extent that she passed out. It became clear that actually what Cindy was experiencing at these times were flashbacks to this traumatic event.

Helping Cindy to make links between the abuse by her ex-partner and her current experiences was a particularly important component of the therapy (CTCH level 8). Reframing the experience of suffocation as a flashback and teaching grounding strategies (e.g. smelling aromatherapy oils and squeezing a stress ball) to gain control of these were crucial elements in undermining the power of the voices. Drawing on the rainmaker analogy (see Appendix 6), previous examples of when the spirits had wrongly taken credit for occurrences were drawn upon, along with psychoeducational material to promote the idea that the voices were not responsible for these experiences, rather it was an understandable response to an extremely traumatic event.

Like Cindy, some clients will experience direct intrusions of traumatic events which may be in the form of auditory, olfactory, visual, gustatory or tactile flashbacks. Helping the client to make sense of these experiences and re-attributing theme as trauma symptoms can be particularly valuable. If the client is able to make such links, it may be that more formal trauma-focused therapy to help process traumatic memories might be indicated. There is emerging evidence to suggest that such work can be helpful in lessening distress in individuals presenting with symptoms of PTSD and psychosis (e.g.

Callcott *et al.*, 2004, Kevan *et al.*, 2007; Frueh *et al.*, 2009; Smith and Steel, 2009). If the client is unable to make such links, or if they are not ready for trauma-focused work, grounding strategies (see Kennerley, 1996 for a review) can be introduced to help gain some control over post-traumatic intrusions. In addition, coping strategies such as controlled breathing, relaxation and sleep hygiene can be helpful in managing symptoms of hyperarousal. Such strategies can be introduced early in therapy (CTCH level 2) with the aim of promoting control and lessening distress.

For clients who may not experience direct PTSD symptoms but for whom it is clear that there are thematic links (e.g. guilt, humiliation) between the content of their voices and previous traumatic experiences, a focus on helping them to make such links and re-appraising the meaning of the trauma may still be useful. This is illustrated in our case of Angel for whom the therapist tentatively queried whether the current sense of responsibility that she experienced (fuelled by the voices telling her that if she did not do what they commanded, bad things would happen to other people) might echo her childhood experience of being sexually abused (during which the perpetrator told her that if she screamed, or resisted, he would hurt another child instead). Such links paved the way for more focused intervention on re-appraising the meaning of the trauma, for which Angel said she had always hated and blamed herself. It was likely that the associated schematic beliefs (e.g. I am bad, I am powerless, I am responsible) were perpetuating Angel's beliefs about the voices and so were a key target of therapy (further details can be found in Chapter 8).

In terms of when to work on trauma, this will need to be guided by the formulation and the clients' goals for therapy. CTCH emphasises promoting control, reframing distressing beliefs, reducing risk and helping the client to make links between their past and current experiences. This can provide an excellent platform for more formal trauma-focused work. One indication is when the client's evidence for voice-power schemas is closely connected to trauma symptoms: the voices must be powerful since they can make the client see hear and feel things.

Matching the client to the level of therapy

At least part of the rationale for earlier levels in CTCH is to work through and thereby diffuse the often high level of distress associated with command hallucinations by building a coping repertoire, disputing and testing out, and hence undermining, the power of voices. This often means engaging the client in a step-by-step process targeted at different aspects of the client's beliefs about their voices and gradually enabling them to drop their safety behaviours. Reducing immediate distress is frequently necessary before clients are able to address often longer standing, more pervasive patterns of thinking about themselves and others. Such patterns will reflect their core beliefs and illustrate how these link to developmental experiences including trauma and other stressful life events. However, for some clients these issues may be at the forefront and indeed may represent the main motivation for engaging in therapy. Some clients will come with these issues high on their agenda and this needs to be respected. The therapist must judge how much of this work to do at an earlier stage and consider the client's capacity to manage the difficult emotional process entailed. For some clients working at this level may mean that direct work on voice beliefs is not needed. However, work will still need to be done on socialising the client into the ABC model if the therapist's use of cognitive techniques and behavioural change strategies is to be seen as relevant to helping the client.

For others, working at the level of enhancing coping strategies and keeping them engaged in therapy may be the main focus of CTCH and therapy may not progress to other levels. It is always possible to return to later levels at a different time, when the client is ready to address other aspects of the voice-power schema. Yet other clients may find the insights gained through cognitive disputation and reframing to be the most beneficial part of therapy[1] and sufficient in itself.

Special issues with Angel

Angel was able to progress through all eight CTCH levels. However, unlike Peter, this was not done in a linear fashion. As has been noted in earlier chapters, it was identified early on in therapy that Angel believed she heard voices because God had chosen her as she was special. While the voices were very distressing for Angel, they also played an important protective role in preserving her self-esteem. It was therefore necessary for the therapist to work on raising Angel's self-esteem, dispute unhelpful core beliefs and find alternative sources of specialness (CTCH levels 6 and 8) before progressing too quickly with reframing and disputing her power beliefs about the voices (CTCH levels 4 and 7).

In addition, it was also clear that daily stressors (such as not getting through all of her daily tasks) and life events (such as family illness or major disasters in the news) activated Angel's core beliefs: 'I am responsible for bad things happening' and 'I am useless', which had the potential to significantly derail her. Angel said that at these times she felt weaker and less able to stand up to the voices when they told her she was 'useless', 'responsible' and that she must comply with their orders. During therapy there was a succession of difficult life events including family bereavements and illnesses, a major disaster in the news (for which Angel blamed herself) and stressful situations at work.

In addition to addressing Angel's core beliefs (as described in Chapter 8), it was agreed that it was important to help Angel feel more able to manage stressful situations generally. The problem-solving approach (D'Zurilla and

Goldfried, 1971) described earlier in this chapter was a particularly helpful way of doing this. Several sessions were subsequently spent problem-solving and supporting her through difficult life events. Within sessions with Angel, it was also important to adopt a flexible and collaborative approach to agenda setting and to allow sufficient time and space to discuss current life stressors, rather than rigidly imposing the CTCH protocol.

At session 25 (our typical CTCH end point), Angel and the therapist reviewed her progress. They had not progressed through all of the tasks necessary to complete level 8 work, but agreed that further work on Angel's core beliefs and helping her to make links between her past experiences and current beliefs would help her to feel more resistant to standing up to the voices' criticism, thereby preventing relapse. Angel also made it clear in the initial sessions that although she wanted the therapist to be aware of her past, she did not want to 'delve' into it. The therapist shared this dilemma with Angel, who said that she now felt keen and ready to engage in this final stage of the therapy. In this case the therapist was able to offer Angel a further ten sessions to complete this work (details of which are discussed in Chapter 8). Sometimes, however, the clinical reality of limited resources means that services may not afford the luxury of being able to offer further sessions. In such cases, where the client is ready, it may be helpful to refer clients on for further trauma or core belief work elsewhere.

Summary

In this chapter we have shown how CTCH can be adapted and at times will need to incorporate other strategies such as MI, trauma-focused work or teaching problem-solving skills in order for progress to be made. In this sense we would propose that CTCH is a need-adapted treatment. In the current trial the emphasis has been on conducting a pragmatic approach which has allowed us this flexibility, while retaining fidelity to the CTCH model and its principles of change: tackling power to reduce distress and harmful compliance.

Note

1   See Jennifer's account of her own therapy in the preface.

Chapter 11

Future directions in CTCH

Introduction

Our multi-centre research trial examined the effects of participants receiving varying levels of CTCH and the degree to which each level was successfully attained using our treatment adherence protocol and fidelity scale developed by the first author (see Appendices 1 and 2). Initial data show that the fidelity scales yielded high inter-rater reliability as rated by trial supervisors ($r = 0.89$). In ongoing research, this scale will, we hope, begin to help us answer key questions about CTCH:

- Which elements of CTCH are most effective?
- For whom is CTCH most appropriate?

In a further development, the first author has conducted an initial pilot study of two single cases examining the application of CTCH to those experiencing persecutory delusions but who do not hear voices. In this chapter we briefly review the evidence and current psychological models supporting a link between persecutory delusions and harmful acts. We suggest that our CTCH model can be successfully adapted to help reduce these harmful acts and reduce distress in such individuals.

Persecutory delusions and risk behaviours

Like command hallucinations, delusions have also been associated with an increased risk of violence (Taylor, 1993). Of those experiencing a psychotic disorder, 17 per cent report delusions, accounting for as much as 40 per cent of violent incidents, suggesting that a small minority may be responsible for a disproportionate amount of violence (Junginger et al., 1998). These same researchers report that 18 per cent claimed that their delusions had motivated at least one act of extreme violence with 15 per cent committing at least two acts of violence motivated by the same delusion. This study demonstrates the important role of stable delusional beliefs over time in the mediation of violent acts. Other studies (Estroff and Zimmer, 1994) have found that one third of people with severe persistent mental illness engaged in threats of violence towards others with those holding delusional beliefs and beliefs of thought insertion or broadcast being more likely to be assaultative. The strong relationship between delusions and violence found in several studies is mainly explained by the effect of persecutory delusions (Bjorkly, 2002a). Choe *et al.* (2008) reviewing thirty-one studies found that persecutory delusions, suspiciousness, and symptoms that undermine internal control and threaten harm (so called threat control override or TCO symptoms; Swanson *et al.*, 1996) increased the risk of perpetrating violence twofold.

TCO symptoms place individuals at increased risk of violence in domestic settings (Kessler *et al.*, 2001), with the overwhelming majority committed against relatives/acquaintances or law enforcement officers (Buckley *et al.*, 2004). Stompe *et al.* (2004) found that threat symptoms were associated with severe violence (e.g. violence resulting in victim's death or victim's hospitalisation). Frequently, the association between delusions and aggressiveness persists throughout the course of the person's illness, such that violent behaviour can be justified as the result of beliefs that others are attempting to, or have caused them harm (Humphreys *et al.*, 1992; Junginger, 1996). Violence may appear as a forced choice in patients who experience persecutory delusions associated with a strong conviction of being threatened and needing to defend oneself (Bjorkly, 2002a). Amore *et al.* (2008) studied 374 patients in a locked, short-term psychiatric inpatient unit. Persistent physical assaultiveness before and during hospitalisation was related to more severe thought disturbances and higher levels of hostility and suspiciousness.

Psychological models

In attempting to explain the precise mechanisms by which individuals with persecutory delusions and TCO symptoms engage in such harmful acts, a number of factors have been identified. It is well documented that there are a broad range of social and environmental factors that are pertinent to understanding risk behaviour in this group, including exposure to community violence, homelessness, a history of violent victimisation, substance misuse, permissive beliefs regarding the use of violence, poor involvement in treatment, personality disorder and a past history of risk behaviour (Estroff and Zimmer, 1994; Monahan *et al.*, 2001; Swanson *et al.*, 2002; McNeil *et al.*, 2003).

Insight is proposed as one factor which may increase risk, with findings that poor insight is more evident in violent patients (Arango *et al.*, 1999). Link and Stueve (1994) have earlier argued that when TCO symptoms are believed to be real, they are real in their consequences. If an individual believes that they have been threatened then they will respond to that threat as though it was real. This has important implications for treatment and suggests altering the target of intervention to appraisals linked to threat response.

Sex differences are evident in the general risk literature with men presenting a greater risk of violence (e.g. Monahan *et al.*, 2001). Women may have reduced risk due to their tendency to engage in so-called 'tend and befriend' behaviours: seeking out friends to help cope with distressing delusions, thus decreasing the likelihood of a violent response to the delusion. Whether such strategies can be taught to those who do not routinely employ them and whether this reduces violence risk require further investigation.

General worry is a factor highlighted by some researchers (Freeman and Garety, 1999; Startup *et al.*, 2007; Foster *et al.*, 2010) with persecutory delusions being found to be characterised by high levels of general worry. Such delusional distress in turn increases the risk of delusions being acted upon (Wessely *et al.*, 1993). Several studies have concluded that specific hallmarks of delusions associated with emotional distress increase the risk of violence in some patients (Bjorkly, 2002a; Hodgins *et al.*, 2003). Anger is another key emotional state associated with increased risk and has been proposed as a key mediator (Haddock *et al.*, 2009). Skeem *et al.* (2006) found that high-risk patients with increased anger were more likely to be involved in subsequent serious violence in the following week. Distress is a clear target for psychological intervention in persecutory delusions and fits well with our approach to command hallucinations.

Psychological interventions to reduce risk in people with delusions: CTPD

Persecutory delusions share many of the psychological characteristics of command hallucinations:

- individuals experiencing persecutory delusions engage in a range of safety behaviours as an adaptive means of reducing the perceived threat they experience (excessive use of which being associated with an increase in risk behaviours; Freeman *et al.*, 2007). They are strongly associated with harmful and sometimes lethal acts (Rogers, 2004, 2005);
- the persecutor is appraised as powerful (Freeman *et al.*, 2001);
- the individual has a low sense of control over the situation (Freeman *et al.*, 2001);
- individuals have poor coping repertoires (Freeman *et al.*, 2001).

While CBTp has been targeted at delusional beliefs with some benefits (Garety *et al.*, 2008), much less attention has been paid in research efforts to specifically targeting risk behaviours as part of their outcomes in those with persecutory delusions. Sirotich (2008) has argued that treatment may serve to diminish the affective arousal usually experienced, reducing feelings of fear or hostility, though the perceptual or cognitive aspects of the symptoms persist. Delusional distress may have an important mediating role in intervening between delusional belief systems and violent behaviour (Bjorkly, 2002b), emphasising the need to target this in treatment efforts. This has been our clear target in CTCH but not generally in CBTp trials (Birchwood and Trower, 2006). In one of the few studies to have targeted the reduction of risk behaviours, Haddock *et al.* (2009) investigated the effectiveness of CBT on violence, anger, risk and psychosis outcomes with people who had a diagnosis of schizophrenia and a history of violence. Those receiving CBT showed a greater reduction in the severity of their delusions, but this was not associated with a reduction in anger scores or the number of physical or verbal aggressive acts.

We have developed a new cognitive therapy method to reduce harmful behaviours and distress in those with persecutory delusions. It is based upon the empirical literature reviewed above and our approach to reduce distress and harmful behaviours in those experiencing command hallucinations. We have called this cognitive therapy for persecutory delusions (CTPD); it has the following core principles:

1   The overall aim is to reduce belief-related distress and what we have termed *persecutory response behaviours* (safety behaviours employed in the reduction of persecutory threat).
2   As in the case of voices where we see voice hearing as a fact, we adopt a similar line here by *not* disputing the persecutory belief itself (unless indications are that this would be helpful). This fosters engagement and allows a clearer focus on the overall goals of therapy.
3   The person's need to respond is reduced by targeting beliefs. We have termed these *persecutory response beliefs* which we propose serve the same function as compliance beliefs: the person believes that they must take certain actions in order to prevent terrible consequences.
4   The perception of threat is addressed by undermining the perceived power of the persecutor to deliver the threat.

CTPD with Becky and Gary

The therapy adopts a similar framework to CTCH comprising nine levels. These are illustrated through two case studies, Becky and Gary, described below.

Gary is a 41-year-old British Asian man of Indian descent with a 3 year history of experiencing persecutory delusions. His diagnosis is persistent delusional disorder – persecutory type. Gary lives with his wife, two daughters and one son. He was born and brought up in Birmingham and is one of two children. He had a normal and unremarkable educational and develop-mental history. His brother noted that Gary was a somewhat socially anxious child who clung to his parents and was especially close to his father whom he idolised as a role model and whom he saw as keeping the family together and building a life for his family after emigrating from India.

Gary began developing suspicions about drivers of a local taxi firm with whom he had previously been friends about 5 years ago. At the time, he was feeling low after the loss of his father from cancer (his mother having died some years previously) and shortly after lost his job. During the subsequent period of unemployment, Gary became depressed and withdrawn according to his family. He was increasingly suspicious, constantly monitoring activity in the street outside his house. He also became increasingly hostile towards his wife accusing her of being 'in with them'. There followed an incident where Gary held a knife to his wife's throat and threatened to kill her if she did not confess to her involvement with these men. Gary's son contacted Gary's brother who having failed to calm him down called the police. Psychiatric services were subsequently involved. Gary showed a poor response to standard treatment. While he was compliant with medication and accepted visits, he continued to hold persecutory ideas with strong conviction and be distressed by and act upon them. Gary's belief centred on a local firm of taxi drivers who he claimed he had fallen out with after an argument one night in the local pub. According to his brother, who also knew these men, only a minor argument had occurred and no one other than Gary had thought anything about it afterwards. Gary, however, became convinced that they were subsequently trying to harm and kill him. He noticed that taxis were often parked up in his road opposite his house. Most recently, he had seen one with a piece of rag coming out of the petrol cap and was convinced that they were preparing to make a petrol bomb and target his house with it. When he had found his wife opening their curtains, he had become very angry and threatened her with a kitchen knife believing that she was signalling to the taxi driver that it was safe to attack him.

Becky is 48 years old. She lives alone and has no children. Becky has a psychiatric history dating back some 25 years. Her current diagnosis is paranoid schizophrenia. Becky was in care from a young age having being placed there by social services. Her family background was characterised by violence and she herself was the victim of severe physical abuse. In her early twenties, she had a relationship with an older man who subsequently abused her physically. At around this time she first developed symptoms of schizophrenia and was admitted to hospital after roaming the streets in the early hours confused and in a state of undress. Becky subsequently had several admissions to hospital, all characterised by persecutory ideas. She has never reported hearing voices. Approximately 5 years ago, Becky became concerned that a recent ex-boyfriend was trying to harm her and was stalking her. She made several complaints to the police about him but their investigations had found no evidence and on one occasion had reported that the man in question had been an inpatient during one of the alleged incidents. Becky also began at this time to experience problems with her neighbours. She came to believe that her neighbour's daughter was trying to harm her by setting fire to her house while she was asleep. She said that Karen (the daughter) was jealous of her and hated her because her father (the next door neighbour) fancied Becky and feared that she would break her parent's marriage up. Again the police became involved but found no evidence to support Becky's allegations.

CTPD level 1: assessment and engagement

The Maudsley Acting on Delusions Scale Schedule (MADS; Wessely *et al.*, 1993) is an interview-based assessment of delusions that provides a detailed assessment of delusional ideation including items relating to conviction and maintenance of beliefs and actions taken in response to them. We have found it to be a useful screening tool for identifying suitable participants for CTPD. The complete instrument takes the form of a semi-structured interview. Gary and Becky's key responses are summarised below under the relevant interview categories:

1   Conviction
See PSYRATS assessment below.

2   Belief maintenance factors
Gary explained how taxis were often parked outside his house and how recently one had had a rag hanging out of the petrol cap (in preparation for making a petrol bomb). He had also caught his wife opening the curtains to, he believed, signal his persecutors.

Becky reported that she had heard a man following her home recently. She had also seen vans parked opposite her house and her neighbours seemed to be coming and going at strange hours.

Neither was willing to entertain the notion that they could be mistaken and could not identify anything which might cast doubt on their beliefs.

3   Affect relating to chosen belief
Both were fearful and worried a great deal about the possibility of being attacked. Becky reported also feeling anger towards her persecutors, while Gary stated that he felt anger towards his wife when he caught her colluding with his persecutors.

4   Action
Gary kept a knife close to him at all times and hid one under his pillow (threat mitigation). He had threatened his wife with this, putting it to her throat (complying fully with his persecutory response beliefs). He stayed indoors much of the time (threat mitigation in the form of avoidance) and always checked before leaving the house (hypervigilance). Gary would only visit the corner shop and church with his brother where he prayed for help from God (help seeking).

Becky had placed multiple smoke alarms throughout the house and would sleep downstairs in case of attack by fire (both threat mitigation strategies). She also kept a kitchen knife or a Stanley knife by her front door (further threat mitigation strategies). She would walk home by different routes each time she returned home (an in-situation safety behaviour) and always checked through the curtain before opening the door (hypervigilance). On several occasions she had threatened her neighbour's daughter with a knife (complying fully with her persecutory response beliefs) and the police had been called.

5   Preoccupation
See PSYRATS assessment below.

6   Systematisation
Gary's beliefs about his persecutors had evolved over a 3-year period and had many gaps and could not be said to be well systematised (it was important therefore for the therapist not to fill these in during assessment). Becky on the other hand had developed her beliefs over a 10-year period and had come up with solutions to addressing any inconsistencies.

7   Insight
Gary was continually frustrated that others did not share his beliefs and he frequently had arguments with his family, especially his brother who laughed at him for his ideas. Becky had reported her fears to the police and psychiatric services on numerous occasions and felt that no one believed her, hence the need to protect and defend herself. Neither Gary nor Becky was able to conceive of a circumstance or situation that would show them that they were not being persecuted. Both rejected response to hypothetical contradiction. Gary stated that his persecutors would 'Know it was a test' while Becky said simply that it 'would not happen that way'.

Both were compliant with neuroleptic medication as they both felt it helped to keep them calm and less distressed by the ongoing persecution they experienced. Otherwise neither saw the need for treatment.

Both Gary and Becky saw their actions as perfectly justified and reasonable under the circumstances. Both agreed that if necessary they would act in harmful, potentially lethal ways again.

During the subsequent assessment phase, a number of measures are administered, some adapted from our CTCH work and others specific to persecutory delusions (see Table 11.1 for pre- and post-measures for Gary and Becky):

3.   Psychotic Symptom Rating Scale (PSYRATS; Haddock *et al.*, 1999) measures the severity of distress-associated delusions on six items that form a two-factor structure of distress/disruption and preoccupation/

conviction. It has good reliability and validity and shows sensitivity to change.

Gary was 100 per cent convinced that 'drivers working for the local taxi firm are trying to kill me'. Becky on the other hand showed varying conviction from 50 per cent to 90 per cent (depending upon activity in her neighbourhood) that 'my neighbour's daughter and ex-boyfriend are trying to attack and kill me'. These beliefs always caused distress. Gary was preoccupied by his persecutors much of the time, while Becky noted that generally she was only preoccupied by them 50 per cent of the time but that this would rise to 100 per cent when she became stressed by them. When thinking about his persecutors, Gary would sometimes think about them for hours at a time, while Becky could distract herself but would think about them for at least an hour or more. Gary's life was severely disrupted by his beliefs, while Becky was able to get on with her life most of the time.

4. The Details of Threat Questionnaire (Freeman *et al.*, 2001) assesses the content of persecutory beliefs in order to identify the most distressing aspects of the experience. It comprises ten questions about the harm that the person believes is going to happen or is happening to them. As such it is a useful supplement to the MADS and supports therapy goal planning.

    Both Gary and Becky expected to be killed and believed that these threats were ongoing and had been real and present within the last month in Gary's case, and within the past 6 months in Becky's case. Both felt most vulnerable in the street or in public places, and also in their own homes, especially at night. Both found this extremely distressing. Gary felt that he coped poorly, but Becky felt more able to cope since she felt prepared. Neither considered that they deserved this harm happening to them in any way.

5. The Persecutor Power Differential Scale (adapted from the Voice Power Differential Scale; Birchwood *et al.*, 2000b) measures the perceived relative power differential between the persecutor and the client with regard to the components of power including strength, confidence, respect, ability to harm, superiority and knowledge. Each is rated on a five-point scale and yields a total power score. Gary and Becky rated their persecutor as powerful.

6. The Persecutory Behaviour Rating Scale (adapted from the Voice Compliance Scale; Beck-Sander *et al.*, 1997) is an observer-related scale that measures the level of behavioural response to the persecutory response belief (see Appendix 5). Persecutory response behaviours are rated on a five-point scale from no 'behavioural response' to 'full response' (e.g. attacks persecutor/harms self). In both Gary and Becky's cases, there were clear and specific incidents involved threatening others with knives, each rating 4. This information was corroborated by Becky's care co-ordinators and Gary's brother.

We also use the ABC model repositioned as CAB (Consequences, Activating Events and Beliefs) to facilitate the process of obtaining the ABC since the C is often what clients most readily report followed closely by the perceived source (the A) of their distress: the persecutors actions. It is often useful when obtaining the C to start with a recent persecutory response behaviour (one that most likely will have constituted full compliance with a persecutory response belief). In both Gary and Becky's cases, there were clear and specific incidents involved threatening others with knives. Next activating events were eliciting (Gary's wife opening the bedroom curtains and for Becky seeing Karen walking towards her house) followed by Gary and Becky's appraisal of them: their persecutory response beliefs. Gary stated that he 'did what was necessary' and that 'it was the only way to get her (his wife) to tell the truth', while Becky said that she needed to 'get in first' when faced with her persecutor and 'scare her off' while being prepared to 'stab her if she did not go away'.

Engagement is especially important in working with people with persecutory delusions since their essence is mistrust of others. Indeed paranoia has been defined as 'a disordered mode of thought that is dominated by an intense, irrational, but persistent mistrust or suspicion of people and a corresponding tendency to interpret the actions of others as deliberately threatening or demeaning' (Fenigstein, 1984). Building on the assessment process, the engagement phase of CTPD is designed to build trust and focus on the goals of therapy.

The therapeutic skills of empathy, listening and being attuned to the client's distress are key in building this trusting relationship. It is also important to address any engagement beliefs and the circumstances under which the therapist will need to communicate risk or involve others. Planning initial sessions with care coordinators or others already in a position of trust can be a useful starting point. Often the client will already have attempted to elicit help from others and the therapist must be honest and avoid colluding with the notion that they will be able to intervene with the persecutor. The aims here are to:

- enable the client to cope with the threat;
- react in less harmful ways to the threat (and so avoid adverse consequences for themselves and others);
- examine fairly the persecutor's capacity and likelihood of harming the client or others.

The therapist may emphasise that they are not in a position to know one way or the other what is actually happening. The therapist is of course not living the client's life and for some unfounded paranoid thinking is more likely given a real victimisation experience (Fowler et al., 2006b). Such thinking may also lead others into conspiratorial type reactions (Lemert, 1962), such that neighbours or others actually do start to persecute the person, perhaps by playing tricks on them, excluding them or talking about the person when out socially or at work.

Both Gary and especially Becky had difficulty in trusting others and consequently considerable time (up to eight sessions) was spent listening to and understanding their experiences, both those relating to the persecutory experiences and more general developmental ones. In Becky's case, it was noted that her lifelong experiences had been difficult and not trusting others, and expecting the worst from them was very understandable. Care was taken to note down what each said and the opportunity given to examine the therapist's notes and completed assessments.

CTPD level 2: promoting control: learning to cope with the threat

Both Gary and Becky rated themselves as having some control over their persecutors' actions by mitigating the threat as they perceived it and reducing their associated distress through medication. As in working with command hallucinations, promoting control is an important step as it functions (at least partly) to address CTO symptoms that are implicated, as noted earlier, in mediating violence. It is also a practical step that further serves to consolidate the initial engagement phase and build optimism for change. Promoting control is also an important conceptual step that serves to undermine the perceived power of the persecutor to carry out their threats.

As in CTCH, this process begins by reviewing and enhancing any existing coping strategies. Gary and Becky had few coping strategies relying upon medication and threat mitigation. Both were taught formal relaxation methods. Gary expressed a long-held interest in meditation and he was supported to use some self-study aids.

Establishing a daily routine was important for both Gary and Becky in enabling them to spend less time being preoccupied with the activities of their persecutors. Both agreed that they spent a lot of time thinking about what might happen but that actually not much happened most of the time. Gary helped with some chores around the house and at his local church a few doors away from his house, being accompanied there by a volunteer. Becky was supported to rejoin local art and exercise classes by her care coordinator.

Neither used so-called 'tend and befriend' strategies, seeing themselves as alone in dealing with their persecutors. An important task in Gary's case was to support him to elicit help from his brother. Since his brother James had previously derided Gary's suspicions, time was spent with James discussing with him how by adopting a gentle listening approach he could help Gary through difficult periods while avoiding arguing or colluding with him. In Becky's case, a close friend at her art class who had experienced her own mental health problems was identified as a potential source of support. A voluntary sector befriender was also employed on a floating support basis.

The notion of building discomfort tolerance employed in CTCH can be used here to build tolerance to threat, lessening the fear and anxiety experienced and thereby also reducing the need to respond in harmful ways. The possibility was suggested to both Gary and Becky that 'keeping a cool head' was advantageous when dealing with threat since it would enable them to respond by considering all of the facts and in the best way. Coping strategies, it was suggested, could be used to help.

CTPD level 3: socialising the client into the ABC model

Relocating the problem at B is a key stage we argue in any cognitive therapy. This can be particularly tricky when working with people experiencing persecutory delusions. Here, the A is not voice content or commands, it is an activating event and as such seen as a fact by the client. The rationale for considering the cognitive model for clients here is:

- to be able to examine the persecutor's power and ability to harm;
- to re-evaluate what response is most appropriate in light of this examination.

It was a fact that Gary and Becky experienced persecution, it was agreed, but the power of the persecutor and their response to the perceived threat, it was suggested, may be worth examining. Having already shown Gary and Becky that they could develop more control, the persecutors' power was tentatively questioned. Both were encouraged to distinguish between facts and beliefs and to see how viewing them in this way meant that they could be changed. Using guided discovery, Gary identified that he had believed that his job in the car industry was a job for life, since people always wanted cars. Becky noted how her belief that she would never be able to live in her own house was no longer true.

The disadvantages of believing that they each had to respond by acting in harmful ways were next examined. Becky noted that she had already been in trouble with the police. For Gary the stakes were even higher, he would harm his family and no longer be able to care for them.

CTPD level 4: developing and sharing the formulation: the ABC of threat appraisal

The ABC model underpins our CTPD formulation. The process involves separating out the various As, Bs and Cs. As, which lead to persecutory response beliefs, are clearly important along with any cognitive biases in determining perceptions of threat, fear, anxiety and harmful behaviours. Power beliefs and those concerning control, identity and purpose are likely to be less driven by ongoing As and built up over time as the belief system becomes more systemised during periods of preoccupation and in an effort for meaning.

Having accepted that the cognitive model may be helpful, elements of this formulation can be shared, especially those regarding response beliefs and behaviours with core beliefs held back at this stage.

CTPD level 5: agreeing and setting therapy goals in CTPD

Evidence for each belief identified in the formulation should be elicited using a gentle Socratic manner. The weakest principle first can then be applied with the aim of reducing distress and safety behaviour use .The process of sharing the formulation with Gary and Becky made it easy to agree the goals of therapy: reducing anxiety and fear and acting in ways, that though understandable, could have disastrous consequences. Both wanted to stop living their lives in fear and not to end up in prison or special hospital. Gary also wanted to stop frightening his family and to be able to care for them.

CTPD level 6: reframing and disputing the power of the persecutor

The general cognitive strategy is to draw upon the client's own doubt, past or present, carefully and sensitively eliciting any of the client's own contradictory evidence and behaviour. The overall aims of this phase of CTPD are to:

- weaken the conviction that the client (or important others) is likely to be harmed and thereby reduce the perceived power of the persecutor and increase the perceived power of the client;
- reduce the client's belief-related distress;
- reduce the use of persecutory response behaviours: safety behaviours.

In CTPD, the initial strategy is to down rank the persecutor by undermining their capacity to harm. Both Gary and Becky were asked to reflect on the fact that while the threat had been active for a number of years, no harm had actually occurred in that time. Becky responded by arguing that this was only because she was prepared and her persecutors knew this. The therapist explored this further:

AM: Okay. Have there been any times you can recall that you were not taking as many precautions?
Becky: No. I am always on my guard!
AM: I remember you telling me recently when you were decorating and you had to sleep upstairs because of the paint smell.
Becky: Yes.
AM: Did anything happen . . . did Karen or your boyfriend try anything then?

Becky: No . . . but I was scared they would though.
AM: So is it just possible that they may have lost interest at that point?
Becky: I don't know.
AM: I was just thinking that it must be hard for them to keep this up all the time.
Becky: I suppose it would.

In this way the persecutor's continued interest is undermined along with their capacity to present a constant threat.

Another strategy is to highlight the persecutor's weaknesses. In Gary's case, he was asked to talk about his persecutors: what sort of personalities they had, were they people who boasted and talked big, etc.:

Gary: Yeah . . . this one always goes on about how many women he has had and how good he is at card games.
AM: Is that true?
Gary: No . . . he's a liar!
AM: If he lies about that, do you think that it is possible that he could be lying or at least exaggerating these threats?
Gary: It's possible!
AM: Maybe some people like to just intimidate you . . . maybe they park in your street just to frighten you . . . you know?
Gary: They do frighten me!
AM: But maybe . . . I don't know what you think about this Gary, but maybe they don't actually intend to physically harm you?'
Gary: You mean that they just want to upset me?
AM: It's just an idea . . . something to think about?

Through utilising these strategies, both Gary and Becky gradually began to have some doubt about their persecutors' power and their capacity and intent to actually harm them. However, both felt that the psychological threat was almost as bad. It was important therefore to continue work begun earlier with coping strategies to build further discomfort tolerance, ensuring that these strategies were practiced regularly and employed during stressful periods. Coping cue cards were used, summarising the strategies and the key steps involved.

CTPD level 7: reframing and disputing persecutory response beliefs and reducing the use of persecutory response behaviours

Having reduced the power of Gary and Becky's persecutors and enhanced their control, it was now possible to examine whether the persecutory response beliefs identified earlier were true and indeed helpful. A useful initial question to ask at this point is: 'So if X is not currently intending to or able to harm you, do you need to respond in this way?'

Gary had threatened his wife with a knife but had also said that he wanted to protect his family. Gary and the therapist examined how this behaviour fitted with his role as family provider, and protector and how if he did do something this could end in prison or special hospital; how would he protect his family then? In Becky's case this was trickier, her beliefs were ego-systonic (reacting in this way was viewed by her as a normal response to any threat). Becky acknowledged, however, that there were still adverse consequences.

In considering alternative responses (and consequently ones which were at odds with his persecutory response beliefs), Gary was asked if his persecutors motives were not to cause physical but emotional or psychological harm, what would be a more appropriate response?

The useful analogy of the school bully was explored here. Gary had taught his younger daughter not to be afraid at school when she was being bullied. Gary and the therapist were then able to explore how he might think and behave differently in response to his own bullying persecutors:

AM: What would be a good way of showing these men that you are not afraid?

Gary: I need to stop hiding in the house.

AM: So what would you need to be doing?

Gary: Going to the shops, having a drink in the pub, going for walks in the park.

AM: Okay and what is stopping you from doing that now?

Gary: Being attacked by these men of course!

AM: But ... haven't we already established that they only want to frighten you?

Gary: There's still a chance you know ... that they ... that they could attack me.

AM: So how could we test this out?

At this point the notion of safety behaviours can be introduced. While these function to reduce the perceived threat of persecution for Gary and Becky, they prevented them from learning that the threat remained and that harm was still likely. From the client's point of view, this constitutes a risk of potentially serious even lethal harm. It is important therefore to begin with dropping safety behaviours that are agreed as having less serious consequences.

In Becky's case, the initial goal was on reducing the number of smoke alarms (a threat mitigation strategy) from thirty to eight (one in each room/area of the house). This was chosen and agreed from a hierarchy of most to least distressing/difficult to withhold behaviours and built upon the disputes and coping strategies of previous phases. Following each removal of a smoke alarm, Becky was asked to note how she had felt and importantly if there had been any increase in threats from her persecutors. Becky reported that although she had felt more anxious, nothing had actually happened and she had been able to cope.

CTPD level 8: raising the power of the individual

Previous disputes and safety behaviour reductions served to reinforce the notion that both Gary and Becky had more control and that the likelihood of actual harm was much less than they had believed previously. Both also felt that they had now been able to show their persecutors that they were no longer afraid. Gary stated that 'they are just trying to scare me and have a joke on me'. Becky considered that her persecutor Karen had maybe lost interest and that her ex-boyfriend was a coward: 'he's all talk'.

This phase of CTPD is also aimed at addressing core dominate–subordinate schemas. Consequently, both were asked to reflect on their ratings of power and how the balance of power had shifted (see outcomes in Table 11.1).

CTPD level 9: connecting core beliefs to delusional inferences

While core belief work is advocated in our work, both Becky and Gary can be seen as having so-called 'poor me' paranoia characterised by undeserved punishment (Trower and Chadwick, 1995). Such psychological processes present particular challenges for cognitive therapy (Chadwick and Trower, 2008). Poor me paranoia often lacks links with formative life experiences (Chadwick, 2006). While in Becky's case such links are implied, they are less evident in Gary's case. In CTPD, inference chaining may be used. This failed to identify core negative person beliefs regarding the self for Becky. As Chadwick and Trower (2008) note, however, for clients such as Becky, the origin of her poor me paranoia appeared to be more attributable to underlying rules and assumptions regarding the mistrust of others and the world as an unjust place and herself as a victim, but one who could and would fight back. In Gary's case, inference chaining revealed his belief in being weak and a failure. For Gary, being able to stand up to his persecutor proved in his mind that these beliefs were no longer true. Moreover, he rejected any suggestion that his difficulty in coming to terms with his father's death and loss of his job and this core belief were in any way connected to his delusional belief. Rather Gary saw these beliefs as due to a period of depression when 'my head was not right'. Addressing Becky's underlying assumptions regarding not trusting others and the world being an unjust place, were discussed as requiring longer term development work with the therapist whom she had begun to trust (as advocated by Chadwick and Trower, 2008). At this stage, however, she acknowledged that the necessary, and to her mind, quite acceptable use of violence was perhaps not always the best solution and felt that she now had other coping strategies she could use.

Outcome

Both Becky and Gary continued to hold their persecutory beliefs with strong conviction but showed changes in terms of the details of their threats. Gary had modified his belief to 'drivers working for the local taxi firm are trying to make me ill' (100 per cent), while Becky had changed her belief to: 'My neighbour's daughter and ex-boyfriend want to kill me' (80 per cent). These and other outcomes are reported in Table 11.1.

As rated on the PSYRATS, these beliefs caused only minimal distress. Preoccupation had also dropped and both now rated the disruption to their lives as 1.

Both now felt that the likelihood of harm happening had been over 6 months ago. Both Gary and Becky continued to feel most vulnerable (though

Table 11.1 Summary comparing pre- and post-therapy scores on the key psychometric measures for voices for Gary and Becky

Measure		Gary Pre-CTPD	Post-CTPD	Becky Pre-CTPD	Post-CTPD
PSYRATS[a]	Conviction	4	0[d]	3	0[d]
	Distress	4	1	4	1
	Preoccupied	3	2	2	1
	Disruption	3	1	3	1
Details of threat questionnaire	Real and present threats	100(%)	10(%)	100(%)	0(%)
	Distress	9	2	7	2
	Coping	3	9	8	10
Power differential[b]	Power	5	3	4	3
	Strength	5	3	4	3
	Confidence	5	2	4	2
	Respect	3	2	3	2
	Harm	5	3	5	3
	Superior	2	2	2	1
	Knowledge	3	3	3	1
Persecutory behaviour[c]	No behavioural response		1		1
	Symbolic preparatory acts or gestures				
	Preparatory acts or gestures				
	Partial response	4		4	
	Full response				

[a] Persecutor Power Differential Scale.
[b] Psychotic Symptom Rating Scale.
[c] Persecutory Behaviour Rating Scale.
[d] In original persecutory belief.

rarely now) in the street or public places and now much less so in their own homes. Importantly, coping had improved considerably with Gary and Becky rated herself as 10. She also noted that coping now involved taking a relaxing bath or discussing her worries with her friend from the art class rather than checking smoke alarms.

Power ratings had also changed for both. Gary subsequently rated himself as equally powerful and by the end of therapy saw that they were equally able to harm each other. Becky rated her persecutors as equally powerful and strong but felt more confident and greatly superior to them.

According to Gary's brother and care coordinator, he now scored 1 on the Persecutory Response Behaviour Rating Scale. Becky's care coordinator also scored her as 1. Both of these ratings accorded with self-report during therapy sessions. Neither was engaging in secreting or carrying knives and both were leaving the house regularly. Becky still continued to check before opening the door and check her smoke alarms daily. Gary, however, had dropped all of his safety behaviours.

Summary

In this chapter we have highlighted some of the potential future directions in CTCH as well as describing a new development, successfully applying CTCH principles and practice to those with persecutory delusions. We hope to test this important new application in a forthcoming trial.

CTCH – Treatment adherence protocol (TAP)

(Treatment Adherence Protocol)

To be completed by the supervisor.

Complete for each therapy tape selected for rating.
Client (initials or code):
Therapist:
Rater:
Session No.:   Therapy level attained:
Date Rated:
( ) Audiotape ( ) Videotape ( ) Live observation

Rate all items on the following scale:

1	2	3	4	5
No examples of CTCH procedures employed	Limited use of CTCH procedures	Acceptable level of CTCH procedures employed	Considerable use of CTCH procedures	Comprehensive use of CTCH procedures

CTCH level 1: assessment, engagement and initial goals

Establishment of rapport

Did the therapist successfully establish rapport and trust: used **empathic listening**, explored beliefs and psychotic experiences in detail in a **non-judgemental way**, helped the client **feel understood**?

Normalising

Did the therapist help the client to understand their relationship with the voice in terms of other power relationships?

Addressing engagement beliefs

Did the therapist explore and address any **beliefs that may threaten engagement**: worsening of symptoms, resistance by voices, inability of the therapist to understand experiences?

Locating the problems at C: agreeing the behaviours and voice-related distress to be targeted: setting initial therapy goals

Did the therapist develop a collaborative description of voice-related distress and the compliance behaviours and agree that they would be the overall focus of therapy?

CTCH level 2: promoting control

Reviewing and enhancing coping strategies: promoting control

Did the therapist **systematically review the effectiveness** of the client's coping strategies for addressing power imbalances, reducing compliance and improving control *(i.e. reviewing when they were used, how consistently they are applied and how effective they were)*? Did the therapist reframe current coping strategies as evidence for control? Were efforts made to **improve these coping strategies and introduce further strategies** where appropriate and subsequently **use these as evidence for reframing beliefs about control**?

CTCH level 3: formulation, clarifying and agreeing beliefs

Developing and sharing the CTCH formulation

Did the therapist develop and share a formulation using the CTCH formulation template?

Relocating the problem at B

Did the therapist help the client to **view the problem as a belief** and explore the benefits of adopting a CTCH model to better manage their distress and reduce compliance behaviours?

Agreeing the beliefs to be targeted and setting initial therapy Goals

Did the therapist develop a collaborative description of the initial beliefs to be targeted: concerning **promoting control** and subsequently **power beliefs**?

Clarifying the evidence for beliefs

Did the therapist **assess the evidence** that the client uses to support their beliefs about **power, omniscience and control?**

Clarifying the use of safety behaviours and threat mitigation strategies

Did the therapist **assess the use and function** of safety behaviours and threat mitigation strategies?

CTCH level 4: reframing and disputing power, omnipotence and compliance beliefs

Reframing and disputing power and omniscience

Did the therapist reframe or dispute the client's beliefs through discussion, offering challenges in a sensitive and tentative manner/Columbo style? Was there evidence that the therapist (a) discredited the claims made by the voices, (b) addressed perceived power imbalances, (c) drew upon the client's own doubts about the voices, (d) highlighted logical inconsistencies in the belief system and (e) encouraged the client to consider alternative explanations?

Reframing and disputing compliance beliefs

Did the therapist challenge the client's beliefs through discussion, offering challenges in a sensitive and tentative manner/Columbo style? Was there evidence that the therapist (a) discredited the claims made by the voices, (b) addressed perceived power imbalances, (c) drew upon the client's own doubts about the voices, (d) **highlighted logical inconsistencies** in the belief system, (e) encouraged the client to consider **alternative explanations**?

CTCH level 5: reducing safety behaviours and compliance

Behavioral experiments/reducing safety behaviours

Did the therapist explore and emphasise the benefits of resisting voice commands and threats? Did the therapist use Response to Hypothetical Contradiction (RTHC)? Did the therapist adopt a systematic graded approach and construct a treatment hierarchy with more innocuous safety behaviours targeted first? Were other (more functional) coping strategies in place as alternatives for the safety behaviour? Was the test devised as a true test of the belief with an alternative belief established?

CTCH level 6: raising the power of the individual

Raising the power of the individual

Did the therapist help the client to question the voice's command and threats directly? Did the therapist help the client to become aware (through Socratic questioning) of the increasing power shift and identify their own mastery and control? Did the therapist help the client to develop alternative powerful self-beliefs?

CTCH level 6a: addressing broader interpersonal power issues

Addressing other power relationships

Did the therapist explore and clarify other dominate–subordinate relationships? Did the therapist draw upon the client's changing power relationship with the voice and suggest extending these strategies (e.g. being more assertive) in other power relationships? Did the therapist develop therapy goals for intervening with powerful others (e.g. involving their key/care worker in developing a more valued role)?

CTCH level 7: working with identity, meaning and purpose beliefs

Agreeing the beliefs to be targeted

Did the therapist develop a collaborative description of the beliefs concerning **identity, meaning/purpose** and agree which beliefs and in which order they would be tackled?

Clarifying the evidence for beliefs

Did the therapist **assess the evidence** that the client uses to support beliefs about identity, meaning and purpose?

Reframing and disputing beliefs about identity, meaning/purpose

Did the therapist challenge the client's beliefs through discussion, offering challenges in a sensitive and tentative manner/Columbo style? Was there evidence that the therapist (a) **highlighted logical inconsistencies** in the belief system, and (b) encouraged the client to consider **alternative explanations**?

Behavioural experiments/reality testing

Did the therapist encourage the client to seek **disconfirmatory evidence and experiences**? Was a clear behavioural experiment devised as **a true test** of the client's beliefs?

CTCH level 8: working with subordination schemas: self and other evaluations

Exploring developmental/vulnerability factors/traumatic experiences and their implications for the development of psychotic beliefs

Did the therapist explore **developmental/vulnerability factors/traumatic experiences** that may have led to the development of psychotic experiences and beliefs?

Reformulating psychotic beliefs: developing a personal model

Did the therapist help the client to develop a **personal model** of their psychotic experiences based on a shared understanding of: (a) dominant self-other schemas, (b) the role of developmental and vulnerability factors in giving rise to and shaping core beliefs, and (c) the role of psychotic experiences as a protective layer/defence/misattributed inner speech and stress-vulnerability models?

Identifying core beliefs about self

Did the therapist explore and identify the client's core self-beliefs: **dominate–subordinate schema, negative self and self-to-other evaluations, dysfunctional/conditional assumptions, rules for living**?

Disputing and reframing core beliefs

Did the therapist **assess, dispute and reframe the evidence for the client's core beliefs,** disputing or reframing the evidence, pointing out logical inconsistencies in the self belief system, looking for alternative explanations. Did the therapist use **specific philosophical disputation techniques**: *Big I little i, evaluating behaviour versus whole person evaluations, changing nature of self?*

CTCH Treatment fidelity manual

Overview of the manual

This manual provides more detailed guidance on ascribing ratings to individual items on the TAP. Each 1–5 rating for each TAP item is provided with the core CTCH techniques which should be clearly demonstrated for the rating to be made. It is not intended to offer an extensive list of all possible techniques for that item. Raters must judge the appropriateness of any novel techniques that are used in addition to CTCH ones aimed at achieving the same impact. A rating of 3 (acceptable) should be seen as a cut-off or minimum standard for the therapist to achieve.

Clearly, not all items on the TAP will be relevant to a particular level of therapy, though some items from other levels may be relevant in a particular session being rated. Therefore, all items on the TAP should be rated for that session. All items for the relevant level being rated must be rated and if not present, a 1 given. Items from other levels may be rated as N/A for not applicable.

Detailed rating guidance

CTCH level I: assessment, engagement and initial goals

Establishment of rapport

I	No examples of CTCH procedures employed	There were **no examples** of active listening skills used in the session
2	Limited use of CTCH procedures	Therapist employed only **some use** of active listening skills
3	Acceptable level of CTCH procedures employed	Therapist employed **several examples** of active listening skills **AND** the client shows that they felt listened to and understood (e.g. agrees with therapist's summaries)
4	Considerable use of CTCH procedures	Therapist showed **several examples** of active listening skills. **AND** the client shows that they felt listened to and understood (e.g. agrees with therapist's summaries). **AND** the therapist took a position of uncertainty, gave permission for the client not to talk about their voices for brief periods (*but* explored reasons for this), focused on emotional Cs for the client and reflected these back in an empathic way
5	Comprehensive use of CTCH procedures	Therapist employed active listening skills **throughout the session** that were accurately attuned to the client's account (e.g. offering encouraging remarks, empathised with difficulties and distress, paraphrased and summarised experiences and explanations), **AND** the client shows that they felt listened to and understood (e.g. agrees with therapist's summaries). **AND** the therapist took a position of uncertainty, gave permission for the client not to talk about their voices for brief periods (*but* explored reasons for this), focused on emotional Cs for the client and reflected these back in an empathic way

Normalising

I	No Examples of CTCH procedures employed	There were **no examples** of attempts to normalise the client's experiences
2	Limited use of CTCH procedures	Therapist made **some attempts** to use a normalising example
3	Acceptable level of CTCH procedures employed	Therapist offered normalising examples as relevant throughout the session (e.g. nosey neighbours, bullies)
4	Considerable use of CTCH procedures	Therapist offered normalising examples as relevant throughout the session (e.g. nosey neighbours, bullies) **AND** the client showed that they accepted the analogy
5	Comprehensive use of CTCH procedures	Therapist offered normalising examples as relevant throughout the session (e.g. nosey neighbours, bullies) **AND** the client showed that they understand the example. **AND** the client demonstrated that they understood the analogy (e.g. related it to their own experience)

Addressing engagement beliefs

I	No examples of CTCH procedures employed	There were **no examples** of attempts to address engagement beliefs
2	Limited use of CTCH procedures	Therapist made **some attempts** to elicit and address engagement beliefs
3	Acceptable level of CTCH procedures employed	Therapist carefully elicited and addressed the client's engagement beliefs
4	Considerable use of CTCH procedures	Therapist carefully elicited and extensively addressed the client's engagement beliefs. **AND** introduced the use of a symbolic 'panic button'
5	Comprehensive use of CTCH procedures	Therapist carefully elicited and extensively addressed all of the client's engagement beliefs (e.g. expectations of the pace of therapy, concerns that symptoms may be exacerbated or that further restrictions being applied when disclosing information about symptoms). **AND** introduced the use of a symbolic 'panic button' **AND** anticipated that voices may comment adversely about the therapist

Locating the problems at C: agreeing the behaviours and voice-related distress to be targeted: setting initial therapy goals

1	No examples of CTCH procedures employed	There were **no examples** of agreeing the overall focus of therapy around voice-related distress and compliance behaviours
2	Limited use of CTCH procedures	Therapist made **some attempts** to agree the overall focus of therapy around voice-related distress and compliance behaviours
3	Acceptable level of CTCH procedures employed	Therapist developed a collaborative description of and agreed the overall focus of therapy around voice-related distress and compliance behaviours
4	Considerable use of CTCH procedures	Therapist developed a collaborative description of and agreed the overall focus of therapy around voice-related distress and compliance behaviours **AND** began to set initial goals around reducing voice-related distress
5	Comprehensive use of CTCH procedures	Therapist developed a collaborative description of and agreed the overall focus of therapy around voice-related distress and compliance behaviours **AND** began to set initial goals around reducing voice-related distress **AND** agreed appropriate compliance behaviour reduction goals

CTCH level 2: promoting control

Reviewing and enhancing coping strategies: promoting control

1	No examples of CTCH procedures employed	There were **no examples** of the therapist reviewing the effectiveness of the clients coping strategies
2	Limited use of CTCH procedures	Therapist made **some attempts** to review the effectiveness of the clients coping strategies
3	Acceptable level of CTCH procedures employed	Therapist **systematically reviewed the effectiveness** of the client's coping strategies for addressing power imbalances, reducing compliance and improving control (*i.e. reviewing when they were used; how consistently they are applied and how effective they were.* **AND** made suggestions to improve coping strategies and taught (where appropriate: relaxation techniques), new techniques or strategies
4	Considerable use of CTCH procedures	Therapist **systematically reviewed the effectiveness** of the client's coping strategies for addressing power imbalances, reducing compliance and improving control (*i.e. reviewing when they were used; how consistently they are applied and how effective they were.* **AND** reframed current coping strategies as evidence for control. **AND** made suggestions to improve coping strategies and taught (where appropriate: relaxation techniques), new techniques or strategies
5	Comprehensive use of CTCH procedures	Therapist **systematically reviewed the effectiveness** of the client's coping strategies for addressing power imbalances, reducing compliance and improving control (*i.e. reviewing when they were used; how consistently they are applied and how effective they were.* **AND** reframed current coping strategies as evidence for control. **AND** made suggestions to improve coping strategies and taught (where appropriate: relaxation techniques), new techniques or strategies. **AND** subsequently used the effective application of these strategies as evidence for reframing beliefs about control

CTCH level 3: formulation, clarifying and agreeing beliefs

Developing and sharing the CTCH formulation

1	No examples of CTCH procedures employed	There were **no examples** of the therapist having developed or shared a CTCH formulation
2	Limited use of CTCH procedures	Therapist made **some attempts** to develop and share a formulation
3	Acceptable level of CTCH procedures employed	Therapist **developed and shared** part of the CTCH formulation
4	Considerable use of CTCH procedures	Therapist **developed and shared** the complete CTCH formulation
5	Comprehensive use of CTCH procedures	Therapist **developed and shared** the complete CTCH formulation. **AND** clarified the functional links in the formulation

Relocating the problem at B

1	No examples of CTCH procedures employed	There were **no examples** of attempts to relocate the problem at B
2	Limited use of CTCH procedures	Therapist made **some attempts** to explain the cognitive model
3	Acceptable level of CTCH procedures employed	Therapist explained the cognitive model in ABC terms and explained the benefits of adopting this approach
4	Considerable use of CTCH procedures	Therapist explained the cognitive model in ABC terms and explained the benefits of adopting this approach. **AND** used the model to help explain the client's voice-related distress and compliance behaviour
5	Comprehensive use of CTCH procedures	Therapist explained the cognitive model in ABC terms and explained the benefits of adopting this approach. **AND** used the model to help explain the client's voice-related distress and compliance behaviour. **AND** the client demonstrated that they saw this as helpful

Agreeing the beliefs to be targeted and setting initial therapy goals

I	No examples of CTCH procedures employed	There were **no examples** of agreeing which beliefs to target and set initial therapy goals
2	Limited use of CTCH procedures	Therapist made **some attempts** to develop a collaborative description of the initial beliefs to be: control and subsequently power beliefs
3	Acceptable level of CTCH procedures employed	Therapist developed a collaborative description of the initial beliefs to be targeted: control and subsequently power beliefs. **AND** agreed to target control beliefs
4	Considerable use of CTCH procedures	Therapist developed a collaborative description of the initial beliefs to be targeted: control and subsequently power beliefs. **AND** agreed to target control beliefs **AND** agreed appropriate goals
5	Comprehensive use of CTCH procedures	Therapist developed a collaborative description of the initial beliefs to be targeted: control and subsequently power beliefs. **AND** agreed to target control beliefs **AND** agreed **AND** set appropriate goals

Clarifying the evidence for beliefs

I	No examples of CTCH procedures employed	There were **no examples** of the therapist assessing and clarifying the evidence the client uses to support their beliefs
2	Limited use of CTCH procedures	Therapist made **some attempts** to assess and clarify the evidence the client uses to support their beliefs
3	Acceptable level of CTCH procedures employed	Therapist assessed and **clarified the main pieces of evidence** that the client uses to support their beliefs about **control, power, omniscience and compliance**
4	Considerable use of CTCH procedures	Therapist comprehensively assessed and **clarified all of the evidence** that the client uses to support their beliefs about **control, power, omniscience and compliance**
5	Comprehensive use of CTCH procedures	Therapist comprehensively assessed and **clarified the evidence** that the client uses to support their beliefs about **control, power, omniscience and compliance. AND** put these into a treatment hierarchy (e.g. weakest piece of evidence first)

Clarifying the use of safety behaviours

I	No examples of CTCH procedures employed	There were **no examples** of the therapist identifying and clarifying the use of safety behaviours and threat mitigation strategies
2	Limited use of CTCH procedures	Therapist made **some attempts** to identify and clarify the use of safety behaviours and threat mitigation strategies
3	Acceptable level of CTCH procedures employed	Therapist identified and clarified the use of safety behaviours and threat mitigation strategies. **AND** how these were linked to beliefs about power and compliance
4	Considerable use of CTCH procedures	Therapist identified and clarified the use of safety behaviours and threat mitigation strategies. **AND** how these were linked to beliefs about power and compliance. **AND** discussed how these functioned for the person
5	Comprehensive use of CTCH procedures	Therapist comprehensively identified and clarified the use of **all** safety behaviours and threat mitigation strategies. **AND** how these were linked to beliefs about power and compliance. **AND** discussed how these functioned for the person. **AND** how their use prevents disconfirmation of compliance and power beliefs

CTCH level 4: reframing and disputing power, omnipotence and compliance beliefs

Reframing and disputing power and omniscience

1	No examples of CTCH procedures employed	There were **no examples** of the therapist reframing or disputing the client's beliefs about power and omniscience
2	Limited use of CTCH procedures	Therapist made **some attempts** to reframe or dispute the client's beliefs about power and omniscience
3	Acceptable level of CTCH procedures employed	Therapist reframed or disputed the client's beliefs about power and omniscience through discussion, offering challenges in a sensitive and tentative manner/Columbo style, highlighting logical inconsistencies in the belief system. **AND** discredited the claims made by the voices, drawing upon the client's own doubts about the voices
4	Considerable use of CTCH procedures	Therapist reframed or disputed the client's beliefs about power and omniscience through discussion, offering challenges in a sensitive and tentative manner/Columbo style, highlighting logical inconsistencies in the belief system. **AND** discredited the claims made by the voices, drawing upon the client's own doubts about the voices. **AND** addressed perceived power imbalances
5	Comprehensive use of CTCH procedures	Therapist reframed or disputed the client's beliefs about power and omniscience through discussion, offering challenges in both a sensitive and tentative manner/Columbo style, highlighting any logical inconsistencies in the belief system. **AND** discredited the claims made by the voices, drawing upon the clients own doubts about the voices. **AND** addressed perceived power imbalances. **AND** encouraged the client to consider alternative explanations?

Reframing or disputing compliance beliefs

1	No examples of CTCH procedures employed	There were **no examples** of the therapist reframing or disputing the client's beliefs about compliance
2	Limited use of CTCH procedures	Therapist made **some attempts** to reframe or dispute the client's beliefs about power and compliance
3	Acceptable level of CTCH procedures employed	Therapist reframed or disputed the client's beliefs about compliance through discussion, offering challenges in a sensitive and tentative manner/Columbo style, highlighting logical inconsistencies in the belief system. **AND** discredited the claims made by the voices, drawing upon the client's own doubts about the voices
4	Considerable use of CTCH procedures	Therapist reframed or disputed the client's beliefs about compliance through discussion, offering challenges in a sensitive and tentative manner/Columbo style, highlighting logical inconsistencies in the belief system. **AND** discredited the claims made by the voices, drawing upon the client's own doubts about the voices. **AND** addressed perceived power imbalances
5	Comprehensive use of CTCH procedures	Therapist disputed the client's beliefs about compliance through discussion, offering challenges in a sensitive and tentative manner/Columbo style, highlighting logical inconsistencies in the belief system. **AND** discredited the claims made by the voices, drawing upon the client's own doubts about the voices. **AND** addressed perceived power imbalances. **AND** encouraged the client to consider alternative explanations?

CTCH level 5: reducing safety behaviours and compliance

Behavioural experiments/reducing the use of safety behaviours and threat mitigation

I	No examples of CTCH procedures employed	There were **no examples** of attempts to devise behavioural experiments designed to reduce the use of safety behaviours and threat mitigation strategies
2	Limited use of CTCH procedures	Therapist made **some attempts** to devise behavioural experiments designed to reduce the use of safety behaviours and threat mitigation strategies
3	Acceptable level of CTCH procedures employed	The therapist explored and emphasised the benefits of resisting voice commands and threats and used RTHC. **AND** devised a behavioural experiment as a true test of the belief with an alternative belief established?
4	Considerable use of CTCH procedures	The therapist explored and emphasised the benefits of resisting voice commands and threats and used RTHC. **AND** devised a behavioural experiment as a true test of the belief with an alternative belief established. **AND** the therapist adopted a systematic graded approach and constructed a treatment hierarchy with more innocuous safety behaviours targeted first
5	Comprehensive use of CTCH procedures	The therapist explored and emphasised the benefits of resisting voice commands and threats and used RTHC. **AND** devised a behavioural experiment as a true test of the belief with an alternative belief established. **AND** the therapist adopted a systematic graded approach and constructed a treatment hierarchy with more innocuous safety behaviours targeted first. **AND** the therapist ensured that other (more functional) coping strategies were in place as alternatives for the safety behaviour

CTCH level 6: raising the power of the individual

Raising the power of the individual

I	No examples of CTCH procedures employed	There were **no examples** of attempts to increase the client's power ratings
2	Limited use of CTCH procedures	Therapist made **some attempts** to increase the client's power ratings
3	Acceptable level of CTCH procedures employed	The therapist helped the client to become aware (through Socratic questioning) of the increasing power shift. **AND** identify their own mastery and control
4	Considerable use of CTCH procedures	The therapist helped the client to become aware (through Socratic questioning) of the increasing power shift. **AND** identify their own mastery and control. **AND** helped the client to question the voice's commands and threats directly
5	Comprehensive use of CTCH procedures	The therapist helped the client to become aware (through Socratic questioning) of the increasing power shift. **AND** identify their own mastery and control. **AND** helped the client to question the voice's commands and threats directly. **AND** helped the client to develop alternative powerful self-beliefs?

CTCH level 6a: addressing broader interpersonal power issues

Raising the power of the individual

I	No examples of CTCH procedures employed	There were **no examples** of attempts to examine other power relationships or extend interpersonal strategies developed to manage powerful voices to others
2	Limited use of CTCH procedures	Therapist made **some attempts** to examine other power relationships or extend interpersonal strategies developed to manage powerful voices to others
3	Acceptable level of CTCH procedures employed	The therapist explored and clarified other dominate–subordinate relationships. **AND** drew upon the client's changing power relationship with the voice and suggested extending these strategies (e.g. being more assertive) to other power relationships
4	Considerable use of CTCH procedures	The therapist explored and clarified other dominate–subordinate relationships. **AND** drew upon the client's changing power relationship with the voice and suggested extending these strategies (e.g. being more assertive) to other power relationships. **AND** developed therapy goals for intervening with powerful others (e.g. involving their key/care worker in developing a more valued role)
5	Comprehensive use of CTCH procedures	The therapist explored and clarified other dominate–subordinate relationships. **AND** drew upon the client's changing power relationship with the voice and suggested extending these strategies (e.g. being more assertive) to other power relationships. **AND** developed therapy goals for intervening with powerful others (e.g. involving their key/care worker in developing a more valued role). **AND** linked this back to the CTCH formulation

CTCH level 7: working with identity, meaning and purpose beliefs

Agreeing the beliefs to be targeted and setting initial therapy goals

1	No examples of CTCH procedures employed	There were **no examples** of agreeing which beliefs to target and set initial therapy goals
2	Limited use of CTCH procedures	Therapist made **some attempts** to develop a collaborative description of the beliefs to be targeted: identity, meaning/purpose
3	Acceptable level of CTCH procedures employed	Therapist developed a collaborative description of the initial beliefs to be targeted: identity, meaning/purpose. **AND** agreed to target identity beliefs and subsequently meaning/purpose beliefs
4	Considerable use of CTCH procedures	Therapist developed a collaborative description of the beliefs to be targeted: identity, meaning/purpose beliefs. **AND** agreed to target identity beliefs and subsequently meaning/purpose beliefs. **AND** agreed appropriate goals
5	Comprehensive use of CTCH procedures	Therapist developed a collaborative description of the beliefs to be targeted: identity, meaning/purpose beliefs. **AND** agreed to target identity beliefs and subsequently meaning/purpose beliefs. **AND** agreed **AND** set appropriate goals

Clarifying the evidence for beliefs

I	No examples of CTCH procedures employed	There were **no examples** of the therapist assessing and clarifying the evidence the client uses to support their beliefs
2	Limited use of CTCH procedures	Therapist made **some attempts** to assess and clarify the evidence the client uses to support their beliefs
3	Acceptable level of CTCH procedures employed	Therapist assessed and **clarified the main pieces of evidence** that the client uses to support their beliefs about identity, meaning and purpose
4	Considerable use of CTCH procedures	Therapist comprehensively assessed and **clarified all of the evidence** that the client uses to support their beliefs about identity, meaning and purpose
5	Comprehensive use of CTCH procedures	Therapist comprehensively assessed and **clarified the evidence** that the client uses to support their beliefs about identity, meaning and purpose. **AND** put these into a treatment hierarchy (e.g. weakest piece of evidence first)

Reframing and disputing identity, meaning and purpose beliefs

1	No examples of CTCH procedures employed	There were **no examples** of the therapist reframing or disputing the client's beliefs about identity, meaning and purpose
2	Limited use of CTCH procedures	Therapist made **some attempts** to reframe or dispute the client's beliefs about identity, meaning and purpose
3	Acceptable level of CTCH procedures employed	Therapist reframed or disputed the client's beliefs about identity, meaning and purpose through discussion, offering challenges in a sensitive and tentative manner/Columbo style, highlighting logical inconsistencies in the belief system
4	Considerable use of CTCH procedures	Therapist reframed or disputed the beliefs about identity, meaning and purpose through discussion, offering challenges in a sensitive and tentative manner/Columbo style, highlighting logical inconsistencies in the belief system. **AND** drew upon the client's own doubts about the voice's identity, their meaning and purpose
5	Comprehensive use of CTCH procedures	Therapist reframed or disputed the beliefs about identity, meaning and purpose through discussion, offering challenges in a sensitive and tentative manner/Columbo style, highlighting logical inconsistencies in the belief system. **AND** drew upon the client's own doubts about the voice's identity, their meaning and purpose **AND** encouraged the client to consider alternative explanations

Behavioural experiments/reality testing

I	No examples of CTCH procedures employed	There were **no examples** of attempts to devise behavioural experiments designed to test beliefs about identity, meaning or purpose
2	Limited use of CTCH procedures	Therapist made **some attempts** to devise behavioural experiments designed to test beliefs about identity, meaning or purpose
3	Acceptable level of CTCH procedures employed	The therapist devised a true test of the belief about identity, meaning or purpose
4	Considerable use of CTCH procedures	The therapist devised a true test of the belief about identity, meaning or purpose **AND** used RTHC
5	Comprehensive use of CTCH procedures	The therapist devised a true test of the belief about identity, meaning or purpose **AND** used RTHC. **AND** agreed an alternative replacement belief **AND** agreed an alternative replacement belief

CTCH level 8: working with subordination schemas: self and other evaluations

Exploring developmental/vulnerability factors/traumatic experience and their implications for the development of psychotic beliefs

I	No examples of CTCH procedures employed	There were **no examples** of exploring the developmental history of the client's problems
2	Limited use of CTCH procedures	Therapist made **some attempts** to explore the developmental history of the client's problems
3	Acceptable level of CTCH procedures employed	Therapist carefully elicited an account of the developmental history of the client's problems
4	Considerable use of CTCH procedures	Therapist carefully elicited an account of the developmental history of the client's problems **AND** noted potential key experiences, stressors or traumatic experiences that may have led to the development of psychotic experiences and beliefs
5	Comprehensive use of CTCH procedures	Therapist carefully elicited an account of the developmental history of the client's problems **AND** noted potential key experiences, stressors or traumatic experiences that may have led to the development of psychotic experiences and beliefs **AND** clarified and agreed that these were key emotional and developmental experiences for the client

Reformulating psychotic beliefs: developing a personal model

I	No examples of CTCH procedures employed	There were **no examples** of the therapist helping the client to develop a **personal model** of their psychotic experiences
2	Limited use of CTCH procedures	Therapist made **some attempts** of the therapist helping the client to develop a **personal model** of their psychotic experiences
3	Acceptable level of CTCH procedures employed	Therapist **developed and shared** a **personal model** of psychotic experiences drawing upon the client's increasing insight
4	Considerable use of CTCH procedures	Therapist **developed and shared** a **personal model** of psychotic experiences drawing upon the client's increasing insight. **AND** dominant self-other schema and connecting these and the client's beliefs about the voices
5	Comprehensive use of CTCH procedures	Therapist **developed and shared** a **personal model** of psychotic experiences drawing upon the client's increasing insight. **AND** dominant self-other schema and connecting these and the clients beliefs about the voices. **AND** extended this formulation to include the role of developmental and vulnerability factors in giving rise to and shaping core beliefs **OR** the role of psychotic experiences as a protective layer/defence/misattributed inner speech and stress-vulnerability models

Clarifying the evidence for beliefs

I	No examples of CTCH procedures employed	There were **no examples** of the therapist attempting to explore or identify core beliefs
2	Limited use of CTCH procedures	Therapist made **some attempts** to explore or identify core beliefs
3	Acceptable level of CTCH procedures employed	Therapist explored and identified the clients core beliefs (e.g. through the use of thought or inference chaining for psychotic beliefs, developmental experiences or current distressing situations): negative self and self-to-other evaluations, dysfunctional/conditional assumptions, rules for living
4	Considerable use of CTCH procedures	Therapist explored and identified the client's core beliefs (e.g. through the use of thought or inference chaining for psychotic beliefs, developmental experiences or current distressing situations): negative self and self-to-other evaluations, dysfunctional/conditional assumptions, rules for living. **AND clarified all of the evidence** that the client uses to support their core beliefs
5	Comprehensive use of CTCH procedures	Therapist explored and identified the client's core beliefs (e.g. through the use of thought or inference chaining for psychotic beliefs, developmental experiences or current distressing situations): negative self and self-to-other evaluations, dysfunctional/conditional assumptions, rules for living. **AND clarified all of the evidence** that the client uses to support their core beliefs. **AND** connected these to the client's psychotic beliefs

Reframing and disputing identity, meaning and purpose beliefs

1	No examples of CTCH procedures employed	There were **no examples** of the therapist reframing or disputing the client's core
2	Limited use of CTCH procedures	Therapist made **some attempts** to reframe or dispute the client's core beliefs
3	Acceptable level of CTCH procedures employed	Therapist reframed or disputed the client's core beliefs through discussion, offering challenges in a sensitive and tentative manner/Columbo style, highlighting logical inconsistencies in the belief system
4	Considerable use of CTCH procedures	Therapist reframed or disputed the client's core beliefs through discussion, offering challenges in a sensitive and tentative manner/Columbo style, highlighting logical inconsistencies in the belief system. **AND** drew upon the client's own doubts about their core beliefs **AND** used **specific philosophical disputation techniques:** *Big I little i, evaluating behaviour versus whole person evaluations, changing nature of self?*
5	Comprehensive use of CTCH procedures	Therapist reframed or disputed the client's core beliefs through discussion, offering challenges in a sensitive and tentative manner/Columbo style, highlighting logical inconsistencies in the belief system. **AND** drew upon the client's own doubts about their core beliefs **AND** used **specific philosophical disputation techniques:** *Big I little i, evaluating behaviour versus whole person evaluations, changing nature of self?* **AND** helped the client develop **emotional insight** by acting in accordance with emerging new core beliefs

CTCH Flow chart of key stages and tasks

CTCH level 1: assessment and engagement

- *Gain a detailed account of experience and beliefs*
- *History of the voice(s) as a problem – what is the problem from the client's point of view*
- *Anticipate problems (e.g. that voices will comment on therapist)*
- *Use of symbolic panic button*
- *Normalise (e.g. nosey neighbours, bully analogy)*
- *Pass message to voice – not trying to get rid of them but help reduce your distress*
- *Use any helpful strategies to help engage the client*
- *Discuss strengths and abilities – valuing their struggle and praising that*

CTCH level 2: promoting control

- *Often reframing what the client is already doing – what increases and what decreases the voices (triggers and cues)*
- *New coping strategies (e.g. switching voices on and off, developing boundaries, etc.)*
- *Reframing control as evidence of a power shift*

CTCH level 3: socialising the client to the cognitive model and developing the formulation

- *Beliefs versus facts – beliefs can change (using lower conviction beliefs(e.g. tooth fairy, favourite band)*
- *Beliefs can differ (e.g. the table in the room)*
- *Advantages and disadvantages of beliefs being true and false*
- *Training the inner detective (e.g. Miss Marple, Columbo, etc.)*
- *Reframing difficulties in 'ABC' terms and relocating the problem at 'B'*
- *Initially around level of compliance, control and power (omnipotence and omniscience)*
- *May progress to beliefs about identity, meaning and purpose*

CTCH level 4: reframing and disputing power, omniscience and compliance beliefs

- *Rank order evidence according to the 'weakest first principle'*
- *Highlighting logical inconsistencies in the belief system and encouraging the client to consider alternative explanations by drawing on the:*
  - o *client's doubt and own concerns that beliefs may be wrong*
  - o *client's own contradictory evidence and behaviour*
- *Reframe and dispute omniscience and omnipotence of the voices → discredit truth of what they say, their capacity to carry out threats, the knowledge that they have about the person and their ability to make predictions → so they are 'all mouth and no trousers', why do they need you to act for them if they are so powerful?*
- *Identify and address discomfort intolerance beliefs – build discomfort tolerance (drawing on coping strategies)*

CTCH level 5: reducing safety behaviours and compliance

- *Using illustrative metaphor: South American spinning tribe (Wells, 2000), garlic, vampires, etc.*
- *Emphasise the benefits of resistance*
- *Examine the pros and cons of resisting/complying*
- *Adopt a graded approach to reduce safety behaviours and appeasement*
- *Devising behavioural experiments – in-session initially then practice as homework*
- *Building discomfort tolerance (drawing on coping strategies)*
- *Using the resistance diary*

CTCH level 6: raising the power of the individual

- *Help the client to recognise their own mastery and control over the voices:*
  - o *Questioning them: 'No, why don't you do it yourself'*
  - o *Mocking them: 'Oh, you are so childish'*
- *Raising awareness of the power shift*
- *Introducing a 'Brag-Slot' and raising self-esteem*
- *Using their increasing mastery over the voices to help them become more assertive in other relationships: with other clients on the ward, in other relationships – use in session role plays to practice being assertive*
- *Aim to change broader interpersonal behaviour, may involve systemic work*
- *Useful for raising social rank and providing evidence against subordinate schemas*

CTCH level 7: addressing beliefs about voice identity, meaning and purpose

- *Help the client find meaning in their experiences by providing a more compelling alternative explanation for them which is less distressing and less likely to drive the need to comply (not all clients will reach this level)*
- *Explore beliefs about meaning and identity*
- *Reformulation (where possible/appropriate: misattributed inner speech, brain making mistakes and stress-vulnerability models*
- *May be possible to progress to working with schemas that underpin beliefs: themes of low self-esteem or negative self-evaluation*

CTCH level 8: addressing the psychological origins of the voices and working with core schemas

- *Exploring developmental and vulnerability factors*
- *Reformulating psychotic beliefs and power schemas: developing a personal model*
- *Clarifying and reframing core beliefs: subordination schemas, self- and other evaluations*

Appendix 4

Voice diary

Weekly record of when the voices are better and worse

	Monday	Tuesday	Wednesday	Thursday	Friday	Saturday	Sunday
07:00–08:00							
08:00–09:00							
09:00–10:00							
10:00–11:00							
11:00–12:00							
12:00–13:00							
13:00–14:00							
14:00–15:00							
15:00–16:00							
16:00–17:00							
17:00–18:00							
18:00–19:00							
19:00–20:00							
20:00–21:00							
21:00–22:00							
22:00–23:00							
23:00–00:00							

Please make a note in the boxes of what you are doing. Mark the boxes red when you are not/less troubled by the voices and blue when you are most troubled by the voices.

Coping cards summarising successful strategies used by voice hearers

Phone a close friend	Stick to my routine – keep busy	Do some yoga	Take a few slow, deep breaths
Contact my key worker	Discuss my feelings with someone I trust	Hum or sing	Take an aromatherapy bath with some lavender oil
Take more medication	Tell the voices to go away	Listen to a relaxation tape	Do some meditation
Use distraction techniques	Listen to some relaxing music using my headphones	Have a cup of chamomile tea	Watch my fish in their tank
Listen to some lively music	Dance in my room	Take my dog for a walk	Take a walk in the park
Go and look at the plants/flowers trees in the garden	Read a book or magazine	Watch TV	Go to the gym
Go for a swim	Make a meal	Go shopping	Talk over my voice

Appendix 6

Allegories and metaphors

The *Concise Oxford English Dictionary* (9th edition) cites an allegory as 'a story, play, poem, picture . . . in which the meaning or message is represented symbolically' (Thompson, 1998). Metaphors adopt words or phrases that are intended to do the same. Both can be very useful in communicating certain ideas/concepts and are a valuable tool that promotes discussion. They also offer an opportunity to explore with clients what the allegory or metaphor means, how they would encourage others to make changes and whether they feel that the message relates to their experiences in any way. This can serve as a basis for devising experiments to test beliefs and generate alternative explanations.

In CTCH, allegories and metaphors are used to illustrate how safety behaviours (e.g. appeasement, threat mitigation, harmful compliance) serve to maintain beliefs about the voice's power, omniscience, identity, etc. The spinning tribe metaphor, for example, illustrates a number of points:

1 The voice belief that the client holds and the safety behaviour they engage in have become established over a long period of time.
2 Changing the pattern of behaviour can be very scary and threatening.
3 Dropping the safety behaviour carries certain risks (from the client's point of view).
4 The safety behaviour, however, is based on a belief that has not been fully tested and therefore its foundations (the reason for the safety behaviour) are questionable and uncertain.

Using a metaphor like this can help the client explore their situation and open up the possibility of change. The therapist can propose that while the voices might have told them something for a long time and be very convincing (like the rainmaker) and they have believed it to be true, it does not follow that it is. Clients are asked:

> 'What are the reasons the people in the story are behaving as they are and what would have to do to change the situation?'

'What would the person in the story need to do to test out their beliefs?'

In many instances when the 'rainmaker' story has been recounted to clients, they have tended to say that 'the farmers are being conned. The man is just taking credit for something that would naturally occur'. If asked whether the man has the power to make it rain invariably, the client does not think that this is possible. The client can be encouraged to look at what the farmers would need to do to test out the rainmaker's actual power. The client can then be asked if they can use any aspects of the story and apply it to their own set of circumstances. What would they need to do to test out the power of their voices?

The spinning tribe

In South America, there is a tribe of people who believe that they are the guardians of the world. In order to keep the world spinning and humankind existing, they believe they have to conduct a special ceremony each evening in which they have to spin round and round with their arms held out for two hours. This is causing them much disruption. Members of the tribe get dizzy, fall over and injure themselves. It also prevents them from doing other things. The tribe, however, remains fearful of stopping and believe that if they don't perform this ceremony every evening the world will end.

(adapted from Wells, 2003)

Elephants on the train tracks

John is taking his usual train journey to work and notices that another man on the train, a few seats ahead, is throwing small pieces of paper out of the window. He watches the man for a few minutes and switches his attention back to his book. They both get off at the same stop and nothing is said. The next day John notices that the man from the previous day is doing the same thing again. He becomes fascinated by the man throwing paper out of window and decides to ask him what he is doing. The man says that he's throwing paper out of the window to keep elephants off the tracks. John states that there are no elephants on the track. The man responds by saying – 'well, it must be working then!'

The rainmaker

It had not rained in Northern Africa for several months and the farmers there were desperate for rain for their crops. They heard that a local man called the 'rainmaker' would be able to help them. They visited the man and he said he could make it rain for them but they needed to pay him so that he could appease the gods. Although the farmers did not have much money, they were worried that their crops would fail. They duly handed over some money and the rainmaker said that it would rain in the next few days. A week passed and it did not rain. They visited the rainmaker again and asked what was happening. He said that he would not be able to make it rain unless he was given more money, he had not been given enough last time and the gods had been unhappy. The farmers handed more money over. For a second week there was no rain. The farmers were becoming more desperate and would do anything to save their crops. The 'rainmaker' was visited again and he stated again that he had still not been given enough money and that the gods wanted more. The farmers paid him once more and he stated that it would rain very soon. Two days later it rained. The farmers were so pleased, their crops flourished and they told other farmers about the amazing powers of the rainmaker.

Resistance diary

Please put a tick in the appropriate box, every time you **don't do (i.e. when you resist)** what the voices tell you to do.

	Day:	Day:	Day:	Day:	Day:	Day:	Day:
Morning							
Afternoon							
Evening							
Number of times I have resisted what the voices told me to do today							
Rate mood at end of each day: ☺ or ☺ or ☹	☺ ☺ ☹	☺ ☺ ☹	☺ ☺ ☹	☺ ☺ ☹	☺ ☺ ☹	☺ ☺ ☹	☺ ☺ ☹

References

Addington, D., Addington, J. and Maticka-Tyndale, E. (1993). Assessing depression in schizophrenia: The Calgary Depression Scale. *British Journal of Psychiatry*, *163*(suppl. 22), 39–44.

Allan, S. and Gilbert, P. (1995). A social comparison scale: Psychometric properties and relationship to psychopathology. *Personality and Individual Differences*, *19*(3), 293–299.

Alloy, L.B. and Tabachnik, N. (1984). Assessment of covariation by humans and animals: The joint influence of prior expectations and current situational information. *Psychological Review*, *91*, 112–149.

American Psychiatric Association. (2000). *Diagnostic and statistical manual of mental disorders* (4th edn, rev.). Washington, DC: Author.

Amore, M., Menchetti, M., Tonti, C., Scarlatti, F., Lundgren, E., Esposito, W. and Berardi, D. (2008). Predictors of violent behavior among acute psychiatric patients: Clinical study. *Psychiatry and Clinical Neurosciences*, *62*, 247–255.

Andrew, E.M., Gray, N.S. and Snowden, R.J. (2008). The relationship between trauma and beliefs about hearing voices: A study of psychiatric and non-psychiatric voice hearers. *Psychological Medicine*, *38*, 1409–1417.

Arango, A., Barba, A.C., González-Salvador, T. and Ordóñez, A.C. (1999). Violence in inpatients with schizophrenia: A prospective study. *Schizophrenia Bulletin*, *25*, 493–503.

Arntz, A. and Weertman, A. (1999). Treatment of childhood memories: Theory and practice. *Behaviour Research and Therapy*, *37*, 715–740.

Baker, A., Bucci, S., Lewin, T.J., Kay-Lambkin, F., Constable, P.M. and Carr, V.J. (2006). Cognitive-behavioural therapy for substance use disorders in people with psychotic disorders: Randomised controlled trial. *British Journal of Psychiatry*, *188*(5), 439–448.

Barrowcliff, A.L. and Haddock, G. (2006). The relationship between command hallucinations and factors of compliance: A critical review of the literature. *The Journal of Forensic Psychiatry and Psychology*, *17*, 266–298.

Barrowclough, C., Haddock, G., Lowens, I., Conner, A., Pidliswyi, J. and Tracey, N. (2001a). Staff expressed emotion and causal attributions for client problems on a low security unit: An exploratory study. *Schizophrenia Bulletin*, *27*, 517–526.

Barrowclough, C., Haddock, G., Tarrier, N., Lewis, S.W., Moring, J., O'Brien, R., Schofield, N. and McGovern, J. (2001b). Randomized controlled trial of motivational interviewing, cognitive behaviour therapy, and family intervention for patients with comorbid schizophrenia and substance use disorders. *American Journal of Psychiatry*, *158*(10), 1706–1713.

Barrowclough, C., Haddock, G., Wykes, T., Beardmore, R., Conrod, P., Craig, T., Davies, L., Dunn, G., Eisner, E., Lewis, S., Moring., Steel, C. and Tarrier, N. (2010). Integrated motivational interviewing and cognitive behavioural therapy for people with psychosis and comorbid substance misuse: Randomised controlled trial. *British Medical Journal*, 24 November 2010, 341:c6325. doi:10.1136/bmj.c6325

Barrowclough, C., Tarrier, N., Humphreys, L., Ward, J., Gregg, L. and Andrews, B. (2003). Self esteem in schizophrenia: Relationships between self-evaluation, family attitudes, and symptomatology. *Journal of Abnormal Psychology*, *112*, 92–99.

Bebbington, P.E., Bhugra, D., Brugha, T., Singleton, N., Farrell, M., Jenkins, R. and Meltzer, H. (2004). Psychosis, victimisation and childhood disadvantage: Evidence from the second British National Survey of Psychiatric Morbidity. *The British Journal of Psychiatry*, *185*, 220–226.

Bebbington, P.E. and Kuipers, L. (1994). The predictive utility of expressed emotion in schizophrenia: An aggregate analysis. *Psychological Medicine*, *24*, 707–718.

Beck, A.T. (1964). Thinking and depression II. Theory and therapy. *Archives of General Psychiatry*, *10*, 561–571.

Beck, A.T. (1976). *Cognitive therapy and the emotional disorders*. London: Penguin.

Beck, A.T., Rush, A.J., Shaw, B.F. and Emery, G. (1979). *Cognitive therapy of depression*. New York: The Guilford Press.

Beck, J. (1995). *Cognitive therapy: Basics and beyond*. New York: The Guilford Press.

Beck-Sander, A., Birchwood, M. and Chadwick, P. (1997). Acting on command hallucinations: A cognitive approach. *British Journal of Clinical Psychology*, *36*, 139–148.

Bell, V., Raballo, A. and Laroi, F. (2010). Assessment of hallucinations. In: F. Laroi and A. Aleman (eds). *Hallucinations: A guide to treatment and management* (pp. 377–399). New York: Oxford University Press.

Benjamin, L.S. (1989). Is chronicity a function of the relationship between the person and the auditory hallucination? *Schizophrenia Bulletin*, *15*, 291–310.

Bennett-Levy, J. (2003). Mechanisms of change in cognitive therapy: The case of automatic thought records and behavioural experiments. *Behavioural and Cognitive Psychotherapy*, *31*, 261–277.

Bentall, R.P., Haddock, G. and Slade, P.D. (1994). Cognitive behaviour therapy for persistent auditory hallucinations: From theory to therapy. *Behavior Therapy*, *25*, 51–66.

Bernstein, D.P. and Fink, L. (1997). *Childhood Trauma Questionnaire: A retrospective self-report manual*. San Antonio, TX: The Psychological Corporation.

Birchwood, M. (2003). Pathways to emotional dysfunction in psychosis. *British Journal of Psychiatry*, *182*, 373–375.

Birchwood, M. and Chadwick, P. (1997). The omnipotence of voices: Testing the validity of a cognitive model. *Psychological Medicine*, *27*, 1345–1353.

Birchwood, M., Gilbert, P., Gilbert, J., Trower, P., Meaden, A., Hay, J. and Miles, J.N.V. (2004). Interpersonal and role-related schema influence the relationship with the dominant 'voice' in schizophrenia: A comparison of three models. *Psychological Medicine*, *34*, 1–10.

Birchwood, M., Iqbal, Z., Chadwick, P. and Trower, P. (2000c). Cognitive approach to depression and suicidal thinking in psychosis I. Ontogeny of post-psychotic depression. *British Journal of Psychiatry*, *177*, 516–521.

Birchwood, M., Meaden, A., Trower, P., Gilbert, P. and Plaistow, J. (2000b). The power and omnipotence of voices: Subordination and entrapment by voices and significant others. *Psychological Medicine, 30*, 337–344.

Birchwood, M., Spencer, E. and McGovern, D. (2000a). Schizophrenia: Early warning signs. *Advances in Psychiatric Treatment, 6*, 93–101.

Birchwood, M. and Trower, P. (2006). Cognitive therapy for command hallucinations: Not a quasi-neuroleptic. *Journal of Contemporary Psychotherapy, 3*(1), 1–7.

Birchwood, M., Tower, P. and Meaden, A. (2010) Appraisals. In: R. Larøi and A. Aleman (eds). *Hallucinations: A practical guide to treatment* (pp. 81–103). New York: Oxford University Press.

Birchwood, M.J., Mason, R., Macmillan, F. and Healey, J. (1993). Depression, demoralisation and control over psychotic illnesses. *Psychological Medicine, 23*, 387–395.

Bjorkly, S. (2002a). Psychotic symptoms and violence toward others: A literature review of some preliminary findings. Part 1. Delusions. *Aggression and Violent Behaviour, 7*, 617–631.

Bjorkly, S. (2002b). Psychotic symptoms and violence toward others: A literature review of some preliminary findings. Part 2. Hallucinations. *Aggression and Violent Behaviour, 7*, 605–615.

Blumenthal, S. and Lavender, T. (2000). *Violence and mental disorder: A critical aid to the assessment and management of risk.* London: Jessica Kingsley Publishers.

Bond, F.W. and Dryden, W. (2000). How rational beliefs and irrational beliefs affect people's inferences: An experimental investigation. *Behavioural and Cognitive Psychotherapy, 28*, 33–43.

Brennan, P., Mednick, S. and Hodgkin, S. (2000). Major mental disorders and criminal violence in a Danish birth cohort. *Archives of General Psychiatry, 57*, 494–500.

Brett, C. (2004). *Anomalous experiences and cognitive processes in the development of psychosis.* Ph.D. Thesis, University of London, London.

Brett-Jones, J., Garety, P. and Hemsley, D. (1987). Measuring delusional experiences: A method and its application. *British Journal of Clinical Psychology, 26*, 257–265.

Bucci, S. and Tarrier, N. (2010). Schizophrenia and psychotic disorders. In: S.G. Homann and M.A. Reinecke (eds). *Cognitive-behavioural therapy with adults: A guide to empirically informed assessment and interventions* (pp. 135–148). New York: Cambridge University Press.

Buchanan, A. (2008). Risk of violence by psychiatric patients: Beyond the 'actuarial versus clinical' assessment debate. *Psychiatric Services, 59*(2), 184–190.

Buckley, P.F., Hrouda, D.R., Friedman, L., Noffsinger, S.G., Resnick, P.J. and Camlin-Shingler, K. (2004). Insight and its relationship to violent behavior in patients with schizophrenia. *American Journal of Psychiatry, 161*, 1712–1714.

Burton, A. (1969). *Encounter: The theory and practice of encounter groups.* San Francisco, CA: Jossey-Bass.

Butler, A.C., Chapman, J.E., Forman, E.M. and Beck, A.T. (2006). The empirical status of cognitive-behavioral therapy: A review of meta-analyses. *Clinical Psychology, 26*, 17–31.

Butzlaff, R.L. and Hooley, J.M. (1998). Expressed emotion and psychiatric relapse: A meta-analysis. *Archives of General Psychiatry, 55*, 547–552.

Byrne, S., Birchwood, M., Trower, P.E. and Meaden, A. (2006). *A casebook of cognitive behaviour therapy for command hallucinations.* Hove: Routledge.

Callcott, P., Standart, S. and Turkington, D. (2004). Trauma within psychosis: Using a CBT model for PTSD in psychosis. *Behavioural and Cognitive Psychotherapy, 32*, 239–244.

Cappa, S.F., Benke, T., Clarke, S., Rossi, B., Stemmer, B. and van Heugten, C.M. (2005). EFNS guidelines on cognitive rehabilitation: Report of an EFNS task force. *European Journal of Neurology, 12*, 665–680.

Carr, V.J. (1988). Patients' techniques for coping with schizophrenia: An exploratory study. *British Journal of Medical Psychology, 61*, 339–352.

Caspari, D. (1999). Cannabis and schizophrenia: Results of a follow-up study. *European Archives of Psychiatry and Clinical Neuroscience, 249*, 45–49.

Cather, C. (2007). Attention training: A novel treatment approach to auditory hallucinations. *Cognitive and Behavioral Practice, 14*, 139–141.

Chadwick, P. (2006). *Person based cognitive therapy for distressing psychosis.* Chichester: Wiley.

Chadwick, P. and Birchwood, M.J. (1994). The omnipotence of voices: A cognitive approach to auditory hallucinations. *British Journal of Psychiatry, 164*, 190–201.

Chadwick, P. and Birchwood, M. (1995). The omnipotence of voices II: The beliefs about voices questionnaire. *British Journal of Psychiatry, 166*, 773–776.

Chadwick, P., Birchwood, M. and Trower, P. (1996). *Cognitive therapy for delusions, voices and paranoia.* Chichester: Wiley.

Chadwick, P., Lees, S. and Birchwood, M. (2000). The revised beliefs about voices questionnaire (BAVQ-R). *British Journal of Psychiatry, 177*, 229–232.

Chadwick, P. and Trower, P. (2008). Person-based cognitive therapy for paranoia: The challenges of 'poor me'. In: D. Freeman, R. Bentall and P. Garety (eds). *Persecutory delusions: Assessment, theory, and treatment* (pp. 411–425). New York: Oxford University Press.

Chadwick, P., Trower, P. and Dagnan, D. (1999). Measuring negative person evaluations: The evaluative beliefs scale. *Cognitive Therapy and Research, 23*, 549–559.

Chadwick, P., Trower, P., Juusti-Butler, T.M. and Macguire, N. (2005). Phenomenological evidence for two types of paranoia. *Psychopathology, 38*(6), 327–333.

Chadwick, P., Williams, C. and Mackenzie, J. (2003). Impact of case formulation in cognitive behaviour therapy for psychosis. *Behaviour Research and Therapy, 41*, 671–680.

Choe, J.Y., Teplin, L.A. and Abram, K.M. (2008). Perpetration of violence, violent victimization, and severe mental illness: Balancing public health concerns. *Psychiatric Services, 59*, 153–164.

Cicerone, K.D., Dahlberg, C., Malec, J.F., Langenbahn, D.M., Felicetti, T., Kneipp S. and Harley, J. (2005). Evidence-based cognitive rehabilitation: Updated review of the literature from 1998 through 2002. *Archives of Physical Medicine and Rehabilitation, 86*, 1681–1692.

Clark, D.A. (1995). Perceived limitations of standard cognitive therapy: A reconsideration of efforts to revise Beck's theory and therapy. *Journal of Cognitive Psychotherapy, 9*, 153–172.

Cleary, A. and Dowling, M. (2009). Knowledge and attitudes of mental health professionals in Ireland to the concept of recovery in mental health: A questionnaire survey. *Journal of Psychiatric and Mental Health Nursing, 16*(6), 539–545.

Close, H. and Garety, P. (1998). Cognitive assessment of voices: Further developments in understanding the emotional impact of voices. *British Journal of Clinical Psychology*, *37*, 173–188.

Cooke, M.A., Peters, E.R., Greenwood K.E., Fisher, P.L., Kumari, V. and Kuipers, E. (2007). Insight in psychosis: The influence of cognitive ability and self-esteem. *British Journal of Psychiatry*, *191*, 234–237.

Corrigan, P.W. (1998). The impact of stigma on severe mental illness. *Cognitive and Behavioural Practice*, *5*, 201–222.

Corrigan, P.W. and Kleinlein, P. (2005). The impact of mental illness stigma. In: P.W. Corrigan (ed.). *On the stigma of mental illness* (pp. 11–44). Washington, DC: American Psychological Association.

Cuffel, B.J. and Chase, P.M.S. (1994). Remission and relapse of substance use disorders in Schizophrenia: Results from a one-year prospective study. *Journal of Nervous and Mental Disease*, *182*, 342–348.

Cutting, J. (1987). The phenomenology of acute organic psychosis. Comparison with acute schizophrenia. *British Journal of Psychiatry*, *151*, 324–332.

D'Zurilla, T.J. and Goldfried, M.R. (1971). Problem solving and behavior modification. *Journal of Abnormal Psychology*, *78*, 107–126.

Dinos, S., Stevens, S., Serfaty, M., Weich, S. and King, M. (2004). Stigma: The feelings and experiences of 46 people with mental illness. Qualitative study. *British Journal of Psychiatry*, *184*, 176–181.

Douglas, K.S. and Skeem, J.L. (2005). Violence risk assessment: Getting specific about being dynamic. *Psychology, Public Policy and Law*, *11*(3), 347–383.

Drake, R.E. and Mueser, K.T. (2001). Substance abuse comorbidity. In: J.A. Lieberman and R.M. Murray (eds). *Comprehensive care of schizophrenia: A textbook of clinical management* (pp. 243–255). London: Taylor & Francis.

Driscoll, R. (1989). Self-condemnation: A comprehensive framework for assessment and treatment. *Psychotherapy*, *26*, 104–111.

Dryden, W. (1995). *Brief rational emotive behaviour therapy*. Chichester: Wiley.

Eells, T.D., Kendjelic, M.A. and Lucas, C.P. (1998). What's in a case formulation: Development and use of a content coding manual. *Journal of Psychotherapy Practice and Research*, *7*(2), 144–153.

Ellis, A. (1962). *Reason and emotion in psychotherapy*. New York: Lyle Stuart.

Ellis, A. (1969). A weekend of rational emotive therapy. In: A. Burton (ed.). *Encounter: The theory and practice of encounter groups* (pp. 1–8). San Francisco, CA: Jossey-Bass.

Ellis, A. (2004). Why rational emotive behaviour therapy is the most comprehensive and effective form of behaviour therapy. *Journal of Rational Emotive and Cognitive-Behavior Therapy*, *22*(2), 20–38.

Ellis, A. (2005). Discussion of Christine A. Padesky and Aaron T. Beck, Science and philosophy: Comparison of cognitive therapy and rational emotive behaviour therapy. *Journal of Cognitive Psychotherapy: An International Quarterly*, *19*(2), 181–189.

Eperjesi, F. (2010). Visual hallucinations in Charles Bonnet Syndrome. In: F. Laroi and A. Aleman (eds). *Hallucinations: A guide to treatment and management* (pp. 303–323). New York: Oxford University Press.

Estroff, S.E. and Zimmer, C. (1994). Social networks, social support and violence among people with severe, persistent mental illness. In: J. Monahan and H.J. Steadman (eds).

Violence and mental disorder: Developments in risk assessment (pp. 159–295). Chicago, IL: University of Chicago Press.

Falloon, I.R.H. and Talbot, R.E. (1981). Persistent auditory hallucinations: Coping mechanisms and implications for management. *Psychological Medicine, 11*, 329–339.

Farhall, J., Greenwood, M.K. and Jackson, H.J. (2007). Coping with hallucinated voices in schizophrenia: A review of self-initiated strategies and therapeutic interventions. *Clinical Psychology Review, 27*, 476–493.

Fenigstein, A. (1984). Self consciousness and the overperception of self as a target. *Journal of Personality and Social Psychology, 47*, 860–870.

Fennell, M. (1998). Low self esteem. In: N. Tarrier, A. Wells and G. Haddock (eds). *Treating complex cases* (pp. 217–241). Chichester: Wiley.

Flitcroft, A., James, I.A., Freeston, M. and Wood-Mitchell, A. (2007). Determining what is important in a good formulation. *Behavioural and Cognitive Psychotherapy, 35*, 325–333.

Fine, C., Gardner, M., Craigie, J. and Gold, I. (2007). Hopping, skipping or jumping to conclusions. Clarifying the role of the JTC bias in delusions. *Cognitive Neuropsychiatry, 12*, 46–77.

Foa, E.B., Cashman, L., Jaycox, L. and Perry, K. (1997). The validation of a self-report measure of posttraumatic stress disorder: The posttraumatic diagnostic scale. *Psychological Assessment, 9*, 445–451.

Foster, C., Startup, H., Potts, L. and Freeman, D. (2010). A randomised controlled trial of a worry intervention for individuals with persistent persecutory delusion. *Journal of Behaviour Therapy and Experimental Psychiatry, 41*, 45–51.

Fotherill, C.D. and Kuyken, W. (Unpublished). *Rating the quality of cognitive-behavioural case formulations.*

Fowler, D., Freeman, D., Steel, C., Hardy, A., Smith, B., Hackman C. and Kuipers, E. (2006a). The catastrophic interaction hypothesis: How do stress, trauma, emotion and information processing abnormalities lead to psychosis? In: W. Larkin and A.P. Morrison (eds). *Trauma and psychosis: New directions for theory and therapy* (pp. 101–124). London: Routledge.

Fowler, D.G., Freeman, D., Smith, B., Kuipers, E.K., Bashforth, H., Coker, S., Hodgekins, J., Gracie, A., Dunn, G. and Garety, P.A. (2006b). The Brief Core Schema Scales (BCSS): Psychometric properties and associations with paranoia and grandiosity in non-clinical and psychosis samples. *Psychological Medicine, 36*, 749–759.

Fowler, D., Garety, P. and Kuipers, E. (1995). *Cognitive behaviour therapy for psychosis*. Chichester: Wiley.

Freeman, D. and Garety, P.A. (1999). Worry, worry processes and dimensions of delusions: An exploratory investigation of a role for anxiety processes in the maintenance of delusional distress. *Behavioural and Cognitive Psychotherapy, 27*, 47–62.

Freeman, D. and Garety, P.A. (2006). Helping patients with paranoid and suspicious thoughts: A cognitive–behavioural approach. *Advances in Psychiatric Treatment, 12*, 404–415.

Freeman, D., Garety, P.A., Fowler, D., Kuipers, E., Bebbington, P.E. and Dunn, G. (2004).Why do people with delusions fail to choose more realistic explanations for their experiences? An empirical investigation. *Journal of Consulting and Clinical Psychology, 72*, 671–680.

Freeman, D., Garety, P.A. and Kuipers, E. (2001). Persecutory delusions: Developing the understanding of belief maintenance and emotional distress. *Psychological Medicine*, *31*, 1293–1306.

Freeman, D., Garety, P.A., Kuipers, E., Fowler, D. and Bebbington, P.E. (2002). A cognitive model of persecutory delusions. *British Journal of Clinical Psychology*, *41*(4), 331–347.

Freeman, D., Garety, P.A., Kuipers, E., Fowler, D., Bebbington, P.E. and Dunn, G. (2007). Acting on persecutory delusions: The importance of safety seeking. *Behaviour Research and Therapy*, *45*, 89–99.

Frueh, C.B., Grubaugh, A.L., Cusack, K.J., Kimble, M.O., Elhai, J.D. and Knapp, R.G. (2009). Exposure-based cognitive behavioural treatment of PTSD in adults with schizophrenia or schizoaffective disorder: A pilot study. *Journal of Anxiety Disorders*, *23*, 665–675.

Garety, P., Bentall, R.P. and Freeman, D. (2008). Research evidence of the effectiveness of cognitive behavioural therapy for persecutory delusions: More work is needed. In: D. Freeman, R. Bentall and P. Garety (eds). *Persecutory delusions: Assessment, theory, and treatment* (pp. 329–351). New York: Oxford University Press.

Garety, P.A. and Freeman, D. (1999). Cognitive approaches to delusions: A critical review of theories and evidence. *British Journal of Clinical Psychology*, *38*, 113–154.

Garety, P.A., Freeman, D., Jolley, S., Dunn, G., Bebbington, P.E., Fowler, D., Kuipers, E. and Dudley, R. (2005). Reasoning, emotions and delusional conviction in psychosis. *Journal of Abnormal Psychology*, *114*, 373–384.

Garratt, G., Ingram, R.E., Rand, K.L. and Sawalani, G. (2007). Cognitive processes in cognitive therapy: Evaluation of the mechanisms of change in the treatment of depression. *Clinical Psychology, Science and Practice*, *14*(3), 224–239.

Garrett, M. (2010). Normalizing the voice hearing experience: The continuum between auditory hallucinations and ordinary mental life. In: F. Laroi and A. Aleman (eds). *Hallucinations: A guide to treatment and management* (pp. 183–205). New York: Oxford University Press.

Gilbert, P. (1992). *Depression: The evolution of powerlessness*. Hove: Lawrence Erlbaum.

Gilbert, P. (2000a). The relationship of shame, social anxiety and depression: The role of the evaluation of social rank. *Clinical Psychology and Psychotherapy*, *7*, 174–189.

Gilbert, P. (2000b). Varieties of submissive behaviour as forms of social defence: Their evolution and role in depression. In: L. Sloman and P. Gilbert (eds). *Subordination and defeat: An evolutionary approach to mood disorders and their treatment* (pp. 3–45). Mahwah, NJ: Lawrence Erlbaum.

Gilbert, P. and Allan, S. (1998). The role of defeat and entrapment (arrested flight) in depression: An exploration of an evolutionary view. *Psychological Medicine*, *28*, 584–597.

Gilbert, P., Birchwood, M., Gilbert, J., Trower, P., Hay, J., Murray, B., Meaden, A., Olsen, K. and Miles, J.N.V. (2001). An exploration of evolved mental mechanisms for dominant and subordinate behaviour in relation to auditory hallucinations in schizophrenia and critical thoughts in depression. *Psychological Medicine*, *31*, 1117–1127.

Gilbert, P. and Trower, P. (1989). New theoretical conceptions of social anxiety and social phobia. *Clinical Psychology Review, 9,* 19–35.

Gillespie, M. and Meaden, A. (2009). Engagement. In: C. Cuppit (ed.). *Reaching out: The psychology of assertive outreach,* (pp. 15–42). London: Brunner-Routledge.

Gray, A. and Mulligan, A. (2009). Staff stress and burnout. In: C. Cuppit (ed.). *Reaching out: The psychology of assertive outreach* (pp. 119–141). London: Brunner-Routledge.

Greenberg, L.S., Rice, L. and Elliott, R. (1997). *Facilitating emotional change.* New York: The Guilford Press.

Gumley, A., Karatzias, A., Power, K., Reilly, J., McNay, L. and O'Grady, M. (2006). Early intervention for relapse in schizophrenia: Impact of cognitive behavioural therapy on negative beliefs about psychosis and self-esteem. *British Journal of Clinical Psychology, 45,* 247–260.

Gumley, A., O'Grady, I.M., Mcnay, L., Reilly, J., Power, K. and Norrie, J. (2003). Early intervention for relapse in schizophrenia: Results of a 12-month randomized controlled trial of cognitive behavioural therapy. *Psychological Medicine, 33,* 419–431.

Hacker, D., Birchwood, M., Tudway, J., Meaden, A. and Amphlett, C. (2008). Acting on voices: Omnipotence, sources of threat, and safety-seeking behaviours. *British Journal of Clinical Psychology, 47,* 201–213.

Haddock, G., Barrowclough, C., Shaw, J.J., Dunn, G., Novaco, R.W. and Tarrier, N. (2009). Cognitive–behavioural therapy v. Social activity therapy for people with psychosis and a history of violence: Randomised controlled trial. *The British Journal of Psychiatry, 194,* 152–157.

Haddock, G., McCarron, J., Tarrier, N. and Faragher E.B. (1999). Scales to measure dimensions of hallucinations and delusions: The psychotic symptom rating scales (PSYRATS). *Psychological Medicine, 29,* 879–889.

Hafner, H. and Heiden, W.D. (2008). Course and outcome. In: K.T. Meuser and D.V. Jeste (eds). *Clinical handbook of schizophrenia* (pp. 100–113). New York: The Guilford Press.

Hall, M., Meaden, A., Smith, J. and Jones, C. (2001). Brief report: The development and psychometric properties of an observer-rated measure of engagement with mental health services. *Journal of Mental Health, 10*(4), 457–465.

Hall, P.L. and Tarrier, N. (2003). The cognitive–behavioural treatment of low self-esteem in psychotic patients: A pilot study. *Behaviour Research and Therapy, 41,* 317–332.

Hardy, A., Fowler, D., Freeman, D., Smith, B., Steel, C., Evans, J. and Dunn, G. (2005). Trauma and hallucinatory experience in psychosis. *Journal of Nervous and Mental Disorders, 193*(8), 501–507.

Hartley, P. and Kennard, D. (2009). *Staff support groups in the helping professions: Principles, practice and pitfalls.* Hove: Routledge.

Harvey, P.D. and Sharma, T. (2002). *Understanding and treating cognition in schizophrenia: A clinician's handbook.* London: Taylor and Francis.

Hewitt, J. and Coffery, M. (2005).Therapeutic working relationships with people with schizophrenia: Literature review. *Journal of Advanced Nursing, 52*(5), 561–570.

Hinshelwood, R.D. (2004). *Suffering insanity: Psychoanalytic essays on psychosis.* Hove: Routledge.

Hodgins, S., Hiscoke, U.L. and Freese, R. (2003). The antecedents of aggressive behavior among men with schizophrenia: A prospective investigation of patients in community treatment. *Behavioral Sciences and the Law*, *21*, 523–546.

Holmes, E.A. and Mathews, A. (2010). Mental imagery in emotion and emotional disorders. *Clinical Psychology Review*, *30*, 349–362.

Horvath, A.O., and Symonds, B.D. (1991). Relation between working alliance and outcome in psychotherapy: A meta-analysis. *Journal of Counseling Psychology*, *38*(2), 139–149.

Humphreys, M.S., Johnstone, E.C., MacMillan, J.E. and Taylor, P.J. (1992). Dangerous behaviour preceding first admissions for schizophrenia. *British Journal of Psychiatry*, *161*, 501–505.

Hurn, C., Gray N. and Hughes, I. (2002). Independence of 'reaction to hypothetical contradiction' from other measures of delusional ideation. *British Journal of Clinical Psychology*, *41*, 349–360.

Iqbal, Z., Birchwood, M., Chadwick, P. and Trower, P. (2000). Cognitive approach to depression and suicidal thinking in psychosis 2. Testing the validity of a social ranking model. *British Journal of Psychiatry*, *177*, 522–528.

Janoff-Bulman, R. (1992). *Shattered assumptions: Towards a new psychology of trauma*. New York: The Free Press.

Johns, J., Peters, E. and, Kuipers, E. (2007). Psychosis: Treatment. In: S.J.E. Lindsay and G.E. Powell (eds). *The handbook of clinical adult psychology* (3rd edn) (pp. 374–394). Routledge.

Johns, L.C., Rossell, S., Frith, C., Ahmad, F., Hemsley, D., Kuipers, E. and McGuire, P.K. (2001). Verbal self-monitoring and auditory verbal hallucinations in schizophrenia. *Psychological Medicine*, *31*, 705–715.

Johnson, D.A. (1988). The significance of depression in the prediction of relapse in chronic schizophrenia. *British Journal of Psychiatry*, *152*, 320–323.

Jones, C., Hacker, D., Meaden, A., Cormac, I. and Irving, C.B. (2011). Cognitive behaviour therapy versus other psychosocial treatments for schizophrenia. *Cochrane Database of Systematic Review*, *2011*(4). Art. No.: CD000524. doi: 0.1002/14651858.CD000524.pub3

Jones, C. and Meaden, A. (2012). Psychological therapy and psychosocial interventions in the treatment and the management of schizophrenia. In: P. Sturmey and M. Hersen (eds). *Handbooks of evidence-based practice in clinical psychology. Volume II: Adults*. Chichester: Wiley.

Jones, S.R. (2010). Do we need multiple models of auditory verbal hallucinations? Examining the phenomenological fit of cognitive and neurological models. *Schizophrenia Bulletin*, *36*(3), 566–575.

Junginger, J. (1990). Predicting compliance with command hallucinations. *American Journal of Psychiatry*, *147*, 245–247.

Junginger, J. (1996). Psychosis and violence: The case for a content analysis of psychotic experience. *Schizophrenia Bulletin*, *22*, 91–103.

Junginger, J., Parks-Levy, J. and McGuire, L. (1998). Delusions and symptom-consistent violence. *Psychiatric Services*, *49*, 218–220.

Kavanagh, J.D. (2008). Management of co-occurring substance use disorders. In: K.T. Meuser and D.V. Jeste (eds). *Clinical handbook of schizophrenia* (pp. 459–470). New York: The Guilford Press.

Kay, S.R., Fiszbein, A. and Opler, L.A. (1987). The positive and negative syndrome scale (PANSS) for schizophrenia. *Schizophrenia Bulletin, 13*, 261–269.

Kelly, B.D., O'Callaghan, E., Feeney, L., Browne, S., Scully, P.J., Clarke, M., Quinn, J.F., McTigue, O., Morgan, M.G., Kinsella, A. and Larkin, C. (2010). Schizophrenia and the city: A review of literature and prospective study of psychosis and urbanicity in Ireland. *Schizophrenia Research, 116*(1), 75–89.

Kennerley, H. (1996). Cognitive therapy of dissociative symptoms associated with trauma. *British Journal of Clinical Psychology, 35*, 325–340.

Kessler, R.C., Molnar, B.E., Feurer, I.D. and Appelbaum, M. (2001). Patterns and mental health predictors of domestic violence in the United States: Results from the National Comorbidity Survey. *International Journal of Law and Psychiatry, 24*, 487–508.

Kevan, I.M., Gumley, A.I. and Coletta, V. (2007). Post-traumatic stress disorder in a person with a diagnosis of schizophrenia: Examining the efficacy of psychological intervention using single N methodology. *Clinical Psychology and Psychotherapy, 14*(3), 229–243.

Kinderman, P. and Lobban, F. (2000). Evolving formulations: Sharing complex information with clients. *Behavioural and Cognitive Psychotherapy, 28*, 307–310.

Kingdon, D.G. and Turkington, D. (1993). *Cognitive behavioural therapy of schizophrenia.* New York: The Guilford Press.

Kingdon, D.G. and Turkington, D. (2005). *Cognitive therapy of schizophrenia: Guides to individualised treatment.* New York: The Guilford Press.

Kolb, D.A. (1984). *Experiential learning. Experience as the source of learning and Development.* Englewood Cliffs, NJ: Prentice Hall.

Kurzban, R. and Leary, M. (2001). Evolutionary origins of stigmatisation: The functions of social exclusion. *Psychological Bulletin, 127*, 187–208.

Kuyken, W., Fothergill, C.D., Musa, M. and Chadwick, P. (2005). The reliability and quality of cognitive case formulation. *Behaviour Research and Therapy, 43*(9), 1187–1201.

Kuyken, W., Padesky, C.A. and Dudley, R. (2007). *Collaborative conceptualisation: Working effectively with clients in cognitive-behavioural therapy.* New York: The Guilford Press.

Lee, D.A. (2005). The perfect nurturer: A model to develop a compassionate mind within the context of cognitive therapy. In: P. Gilbert (ed.). *Compassion: Conceptualisation, research and use in psychotherapy* (pp. 326–352). Hore: Routledge.

Lee, S. (2002). The stigma of schizophrenia: A transcultural problem. *Current Opinion in Psychiatry, 15*, 37–41.

Leff, J., Thornicroft, G., Coxhead, N. and Crawford. C. (1994). The TAPS project: A five-year follow-up of long-stay psychiatric patients discharged to the community. *British Journal of Psychiatry, 165*(25), 13–17.

Lemert, E.M. (1962). Paranoia and the dynamics of exclusion. *Sociometry, 25*(1), 2–20.

Lewin, K. (1946). Action research and minority problems. *Journal of Social Issues, 2*(4), 34–46.

Link, B. and Stueve, A. (1994). Psychotic symptoms and the violent/illegal behaviour of mental patient compared to community controls. In: J. Monahan and H. Steadman (eds). *Violence and mental disorder: Developments in risk assessments* (pp. 135–161). Chicago, IL: University of Chicago Press.

Linszen, D.H., Dingemans, P.M. and Lenior, M.E. (1994). Cannabis abuse and the course of recent-onset schizophrenic disorders. *Archive of General Psychiatry, 51*, 273–279.

Liotti, G. (1989). Resistance to change in cognitive psychotherapy: Theoretical remarks from a constructivistic point of view. In: W. Dryden and P. Trower (eds). *Cognitive psychotherapy: Stasis and change* (pp. 28–56). London: Cassell.

Lobban, F., Barrowclough, C. and Jones, S. (2003). A review of models of illness in mental health. *Clinical Psychology Review, 23*, 171–196.

Lowe, R. (1999). Between the 'no longer' and the 'not yet': Postmodernism as a context for critical therapeutic work. In: I. Parker (ed.). *Deconstructing psychotherapy* (pp. 71–85). London: Sage.

McGlashan, T.H. (1988). A selective review of North American long-term follow-up studies of schizophrenia. *Schizophrenia Bulletin, 14*, 515–542.

Mackinnon, A., Copolov, D.L. and Trauer, T. (2004). Factors associated with compliance and resistance to command hallucinations. *Journal of Nervous and Mental Disease, 192*(5), 357–362.

McManus, F., Clark, D., Grey, N., Wild, J., Hirsch, C., Fennell M., Hackman, A., Waddington, L., Liness, S. and Manley, J. (2009). A demonstration of the efficacy of two of the components of cognitive therapy for social phobia. *Journal of Anxiety Disorder, 23*(4), 496–503.

McNeil, D., Eisner, J.P. and Binder, R.L. (2003). The relationship between aggressive attributional style and violence by psychiatric patients. *Journal of Consulting and Clinical Psychology, 71*, 300–403.

Margison, F. (2005). Integrating approaches to psychotherapy in psychosis. *Australian and New Zealand Journal of Psychiatry, 39*, 972–981.

Martin, D.J., Garske, J.P. and Davies, M.J. (2000). Relation of the therapeutic alliance with outcome and other variables: A meta-analytic review. *Journal of Consulting and Clinical Psychology, 68(3)*, 438–450.

Maslach, C. (1978). The client role in staff burnout. *Journal of Social Issues, 34*, 111–124.

Mawson, A., Cohen, K. and Berry, K. (2010). Reviewing evidence for the cognitive model of auditory hallucinations: The relationship between cognitive voice appraisals and distress during psychosis. *Clinical Psychology Review, 30*, 248–258.

Mayhew, S. and Gilbert, P. (2008). Compassionate mind training with people who hear malevolent voices. *Clinical Psychology and Psychotherapy, 15*, 113–138.

Meaden, A. and Hacker, D. (2010). *Problematic and risk behaviours in Psychosis: A shared formulation approach*. Hore: Routledge.

Meaden, A., Trower, P. and Birchwood, M. (2010). Cognitive therapy for command hallucinations. In: F. Laroi and A. Aleman (eds). *Hallucinations: A guide to treatment and management* (pp. 103–123). New York: Oxford University Press.

Meaden, A.C. (2009). *What clients tell us about cognitive therapy: A systematic review of qualitative research*. Doctoral dissertation. University of Wolverhampton.

Millon, T. and Grossman, S. (2007a). *Moderating severe personality disorders: A personalized psychotherapy approach*. Hoboken NJ: Wiley.

Millon, T. and Grossman, S. (2007b). *Overcoming resistant personality disorders*. Hoboken: Wiley.

Mitto, E.C., Evans, J.J., Souza De Lucia, M.C. and Scaff, M. (2008) Rehabilitation of executive dysfunction: A controlled trial of an attention and problem solving treatment group. *Neuropsychological Rehabilitation, 19*(4), 517–540.

Monahan, J., Steadman, H.J., Silver, E., Appelbaum, P.S., Robbins, P.C., Mulvey, E.P., Roth, L.H., Grisso, T. and Banks, S. (2001). *Rethinking risk assessment: The MacArthur study of mental disorder and violence*. New York: Oxford University Press.

Morgan, C. and Fearon, P. (2007). Social experience and psychosis: Insights from studies of migrant ethic minority groups. *Epidemiologia and Psichiatria Sociale*, *16*(2), 118–123.

Morrison, A.P., Beck, A.T., Glentworth, D., Dunn, H., Reid, G.S., Larkin, W. and Williams, S. (2002). Imagery and psychotic symptoms: A preliminary investigation. *Behaviour Research and Therapy*, *40*(9), 1053–1062.

Morrison, A.P. and Renton, J.C. (2001). Cognitive therapy for auditory hallucinations: A theory-based approach. *Cognitive and Behavioural Practice*, *8*, 147–160.

Morrison, A.P., Renton, J.C., Dunn, H., Williams, S. and Bentall, R.P. (2004). *Cognitive therapy for psychosis: A formulation-based approach*. East Sussex: Brunner-Routledge.

Müller-Isberner, R. (2001). Changing attitudes: Effecting positive and lasting changes. In: K.S. Douglas, C.D. Webster, S.D. Hart, D. Eaves and J.P. Ogloff (eds). *HCR-20 violence risk management companion guide* (pp. 85–91). Burnaby: Canada Mental Health, Law and Policy, Simon Fraser University.

Mumma, G.H. (1998). Improving cognitive case formulations and treatment planning in clinical practice and research. *Journal of Cognitive Psychotherapy: An International Quarterly*, *12*(3), 251–274.

Murray, V., McKee, I., Miller, P.M., Young, D., Muir, W.J., Pelosi, A.J. and Blackwood, D.H.R. (2005). Dimensions and classes of psychosis in a population cohort: A four-class, four-dimension model of schizophrenia and affective psychoses. *Psychological Medicine*, *35*, 499–510.

National Institute for Health and Clinical Excellence (2009). *Schizophrenia. Core interventions in the treatment and management of schizophrenia in adults in primary and secondary care (Update). NICE Clinical guideline 82*. London: National Institute for Health and Clinical Excellence.

Nayani, T.H. and David, A. (1996). The auditory hallucination: A phenomenological survey. *Psychological Medicine*, *26*, 177–189.

Nelson, H. (2005). *Cognitive-behavioural therapy with delusions and hallucinations: A practice manual* (2nd edn). Cheltenham: Nelson Thornes.

Norcross, J.C. (2000). *Psychotherapy relationships that work: Therapists contributions and responsiveness to patients*. New York: Oxford University Press.

Oberlander, L.B. (1990). Work satisfaction among community-based mental health service providers: The association between work environment and work satisfaction. *Community Mental Health Journal*, *26*, 517–532.

Okajima, I., Kanai, Y., Chen, J. and Sakano, Y. (2009). Effects of safety behaviour on the maintenance of anxiety and negative belief social anxiety disorder. *International Journal of Social Psychiatry*, *55(1)*, 71–81.

Onwumere, J., Smith, B. and Kuipers, E. (2010). Families and psychosis. In: C. Morgan and D. Bhugra (eds). *Principles of social psychiatry* (2nd edn) (pp. 103–116). Chichester: Wiley.

Owens, D.G.C., Miller, P., Lawrie, S.M. and Johnstone, E.C. (2005). Pathogenesis of schizophrenia: A psychopathological perspective. *British Journal of Psychiatry*, *186*, 386–393.

Padesky, C.A. (1993). Socratic questioning: Changing minds or guided discovery. Keynote Address, European Congress of Behavioural and Cognitive Psychotherapies, London.

Padesky, C.A. (1994). Schema change processes in cognitive therapy. *Clinical Psychology and Psychotherapy*, *1*(5), 267–268.

Paivio, S. and Greenberg, L.S. (1995). Resolving unfinished business: Experiential therapy using empty chair dialogue. *Journal of Consulting and Clinical Psychology*, *63*, 419–425.

Pallanti, S., Quercioli, L. and Hollander, E. (2004). Social anxiety in outpatients with schizophrenia: A relevant cause of disability. *American Journal of Psychiatry*, *161*, 53–58.

Perez-Alvarez, M., Garcia-Montes, J.M., Perona-Garcelan, S. and Vallina-Fernanda, O. (2008). Changing relationship with voices: New therapeutic perspectives for treating hallucinations. *Clinical Psychology & Psychotherapy*, *15*, 75–85.

Persons, J.B. and Bertagnolli, A. (1999). Inter-rater reliability of cognitive-behavioral case formulations of depression: A replication. *Cognitive Therapy and Research*, *23*(3), 271–283.

Persons, J.B., Curtis, J.T. and Silberschatz, G. (1991). Psychodynamic and cognitive behavioral formulations of a single case. *Psychotherapy*, *28*(4), 608–617.

Persons, J.B., Mooney, K.A. and Padesky, C.A. (1995). Inter-rater reliability of cognitive-behavioural case formulations. *Cognitive Therapy and Research*, *19*, 21–34.

Popper, K. (1935). *Logik der Forschung*. Vienna: Julius Springer Verlag.

Popper, K. (2002). *The logic of scientific discovery*. London: Routledge.

Powell, T. (2009). *The mental health handbook*. Milton Keynes: Speechmark Publishing.

Prosser, D., Johnson, S., Kuipers, E., Szmukler, G., Bebbington, P. and Thornicroft, G. (1996). Mental health burnout and job satisfaction among hospital and community-based mental health staff. *British Journal of Psychiatry*, *169*, 334–337.

Rakos, R.F. (2000). *Assertive Behaviour: Theory, research and training*. London: Routledge.

Rath, J.F., Simon, D., Langenbahn, D.M., Sherr, L. and Diller, L. (2003). Group treatment of problem solving deficits in outpatients with traumatic brain injury: A randomised outcome study. *Neuropsychological Rehabilitation*, *13*, 461–488.

Read, J., Agar, K., Argyle, N. and Aderhold, V. (2003). Sexual and physical abuse during childhood and adulthood as predictors of hallucinations, delusions and thought disorder. *Psychology and Psychotherapy*, *76*(1), 1–22.

Read, J. and Argyle, N. (1999). Hallucinations, delusions and thought disorders among adult psychiatric inpatients with a history of child abuse. *Psychiatric Services*, *50*, 1467–1472.

Reininghaus, U.A., Morgan, C., Simpson, J., Dazzan, P., Morgan, K., Doody, G.A., Bhugra, D., Leff, J., Jones, P., Murray, R., Fearon, P. and Craig, T.J.K. (2008). Unemployment, social isolation, achievement-expectation mismatch and psychosis: Findings from the AESOP study. *Social Psychiatry and Psychiatric Epidemiology*, *43*, 743–751.

Rogers, P. (2004). *Command hallucinations and violence: Secondary analysis of the MacArthur Violence Risk Assessment Data*. Ph.D. dissertation. Institute of Psychiatry, Kings College, London.

Rogers, P. (2005). The association between command hallucinations and prospective violence: Secondary analysis of the MacArthur Violence Risk Assessment Study. *Conference presentation at the Institute of Psychiatry Medium Secure Unit Conference.* January.

Rogers, R., Watt, A., Gray, N.S., MacCulloch, M. and Gournay, K.(2002). Content of command hallucinations predicts self harm but not violence in a medium secure unit. *Journal of Forensic Psychiatry, 13,* 251–262.

Romme, M. and Escher, S. (1993). *Accepting Voices.* London: MIND Publications.

Romme, M., Escher, S., Dillon, J., Corstens, D. and Morris, M. (2009). *Living with voices: 50 stories of recovery.* Ross-on-Wye: PCCS.

Rooke, O. and Birchwood, M. (1998). Loss, humiliation and entrapment as appraisals of schizophrenic illness: A prospective study of depressed and non-depressed patients. *British Journal of Clinical Psychology, 37,* 259–268.

Ross, C. A., Anderson, G. and Clark, P. (1994). Childhood abuse and positive symptoms of schizophrenia. *Hospital and Community Psychiatry, 45*(5), 489–491.

Rouf, K., Fennell, M., Westbrook, D., Cooper, M. and Bennett-Levy, J. (2004). Devising effective behavioural experiments. In: J. Bennett-Levy, G. Butler, M. Fennell, A. Hackmann, M. Mueller and D. Westbrook (eds). *Oxford guide to behavioural experiments in cognitive therapy* (pp. 21–59). New York: Oxford University Press.

Rüsch, N., Corrigana, P.W., Powella, K., Rajaha, A., Olschewskic, M., Wilkniss, S. and Batiae, K. (2009). A stress-coping model of mental illness stigma: II. Emotional stress responses, coping behavior and outcome. *Schizophrenia Research, 110,* 65–71.

Sainsbury Centre for Mental Health (1998). *Keys to engagement: Review of care for people with severe mental illness who are hard to engage with services.* London: Sainsbury Centre for Mental Health.

Salkovskis, P.M. (1991). The importance of behaviour in the maintenance of anxiety and panic: A cognitive account. *Behavioural Psychotherapy, 19,* 6–19.

Sax, K.W., Strakowski, S.M., Keck, P.E., Upadhyaya, V.H., West, S.A. and McElroy, S.L. (1996). Relationships among negative, positive, and depressive symptoms in schizophrenia and psychotic depression. *The British Journal of Psychiatry, 168,* 68–71.

Schaufeli, W. (1999). Burnout. In: J. Firth-Cozens and R. Payne (eds). *Stress in health professionals: Psychological and organizational causes and interventions.* London: Wiley.

Scheller-Gilkey, G., Thomas, S.M., Woolwine, B.J. and Miller, A.H. (2002). Increased early life stress and depressive symptoms in patients with comorbid substance abuse and schizophrenia. *Schizophrenia Bulletin, 28,* 223–231.

Selton, J.P. and Cantor-Graae, E. (2005). Social defeat: Risk factor for schizophrenia? *British Journal of Psychiatry, 187,* 101–102.

Sharma, T. and Antonova, L. (2003). Cognitive function in schizophrenia. Deficits, functional consequences, and future treatment. *Psychiatric Clinics of North America, 26,* 25–40.

Shawyer, F., Mackinnon, A., Farhall, J., Sims, E., Blaney, S., Yardley, P., Daly, M., Mullen, P. and Copolov, D. (2008). Acting on harmful command hallucinations in psychotic disorders: An integrative approach. *Journal of Nervous and Mental Disease, 196*(5), 390–398.

Shawyer, F., MacKinnon, A., Farhall, J., Trauer, T. and Copolov, D. (2003). Command hallucinations and violence: Implications for detention and treatment. *Psychology, Psychiatry and The Law*, *10*(1), 97–107.

Simourd, D.J. and Olver, M.E. (2002). The future of criminal attitudes research and practice. *Criminal Justice and Behavior*, *29*, 427–446.

Sirotich, F. (2008). Correlates of crime and violence among persons with mental disorder: An evidence-based review. *Brief Treatment and Crisis Intervention*, *8*(2), 171–194.

Skeem, J.L., Schubert, C., Odgers, C., Mulvey, E.P., Gardner, W. and Lidz, C. (2006). Psychiatric symptoms and community violence among high-risk patients: A test of the relationship at the weekly level. *Journal of Consulting and Clinical Psychology*, *74*(5), 967–979.

Smith, B. and Steel, C. (2009). 'Suspicion is my friend': Cognitive behavioural therapy for post-traumatic persecutory delusions. In: N. Grey (ed.). *A casebook of cognitive therapy for traumatic stress reactions* (pp. 61–78) London: Routledge.

Startup, H., Freeman, D. and Garety, P. (2007). Persecutory delusions and catastrophic worry in psychosis: Developing the understanding of delusion distress and persistence. *Behaviour Research & Therapy*, *45*, 523–537.

Stompe, T., Ortwein-Swoboda, Q. and Schanda, H. (2004). Schizophrenia, delusional symptoms, and violence: The threat/control-override concept re-examined. *Schizophrenia Bulletin*, *30*(1), 31–44.

Strauss, M.E. (1993). Relations of symptoms to cognitive deficits in schizophrenia. *Schizophrenia Bulletin*, *19*(2), 215–232.

Swanson, J.W., Borum, R., Swartz, M. and Monahan, J. (1996). Psychotic symptoms and disorders and risk of violent behaviour in the community. *Criminal Behaviour and Mental Health*, *6*, 309–329.

Swanson, J.W., Swartz, M.E. and Essock, S.M. (2002). The social-environmental context of violent behaviour in persons treated for severe mental illness. *American Journal of Public Mental Health*, *92*, 1523–1531.

Tarrier, N. (1992). Management and modification of residual positive symptoms. In: M. Birchwood and N. Tarrier (eds). *Innovations in the psychological management of schizophrenia* (pp. 147–171). Chichester: Wiley.

Tarrier, N., Harwood, S., Yusopoff, L., Beckett, R. and Baker, A. (1990). Coping strategy enhancement (CSE): A method of treating residual schizophrenic symptoms. *Behavioural Psychotherapy*, *18*, 283–293.

Taylor, P. (1993). Schizophrenia and crime: Distinctive patterns drive violence. *Social Psychiatry and Psychiatric Epidemiology*, *33*, 47–54.

Thorndike, E.L. (1911). *Animal intelligence*. New York: MacMillan.

Townend, M. and Grant, A. (2008). Assessment in CBT: The idiographic approach. In: A. Grant, M. Townend, J. Mills and A. Cockx (eds). *Assessment and formulation in cognitive behavioural therapy* (pp. 7–21). London: Sage.

Trower, P., Birchwood, M., Meaden, A., Byrne, S., Nelson, A. and Ross, K. (2004). Cognitive therapy for command hallucinations: Randomised controlled trial. *British Journal of Psychiatry*, *184*, 312–320.

Trower, P. and Chadwick, P.D.J. (1995). Pathways to defence of the self: A theory of two types of paranoia. *Clinical Psychology: Science and Practice*, *2*, 263–278.

Trower, P., Jones, J., Dryden, W. and Casey, A. (2010). *Cognitive behavioural counselling in action* (2nd edn). London: Sage.

Van Deusen, W. (1971). *The natural depth in man.* New York: Harper & Row.

Van Deusen, W. (1974). *The presence of other worlds.* New York: Harper & Row.

Van Zelst, C. (2009). Stigmatization as an environmental risk in schizophrenia: A user perspective. *Schizophrenia Bulletin, 35*(2), 293–296.

Waddington, L. (2002). The therapeutic relationship in cognitive therapy: A review. *Behavioural and Cognitive Psychotherapy, 30*, 179–191.

Walen, S.R., DiGiuseppe, R. and Dryden, W. (1992). *A practitioner's guide to rational-emotive therapy.* New York: Oxford University Press.

Wallace, C., Mullen, P.E. and Burgess P. (2004). Criminal offending in schizophrenia over a 25-year period marked by deinstitutionalization and increasing prevalence of comorbid substance use disorders. *American Journal of Psychiatry, 161*(4), 716–727.

Waters, F.A.V., Badcock, J.C., Michie, P.T. and Mayberry, M.T. (2006). Auditory hallucinations in schizophrenia. *Cognitive Neuropsychiatry, 11*, 65–83.

Watson, J.C. and Greenberg, L.S. (1996). Pathways to change in the psychotherapy of depression: Relating process to session change and outcome. *Psychotherapy, 33*, 262–274.

Wearden, A.J., Tarrier, N., Barrowclough, C., Zastowny, T.R. and Rahill, A.A. (2000). A review of expressed emotion research in health care. *Clinical Psychology Review, 20*, 633–666.

Weiss, D.S. and Marmar, C.R. (1997). The impact of event scale-revised. In: J.P. Wilson and T.M. Keane (eds). *Assessing psychological trauma and PTSD* (pp. 399–411). New York: The Guilford Press.

Wells, A. (2000). *Emotional disorders and metacognition: Innovative cognitive therapy.* Chichester: Wiley.

Wells, A. (2003). *Cognitive therapy of anxiety disorders: A practice manual and conceptual guide.* Chichester: Wiley.

Wells, A. (2007). The attention training technique: Theory, effects, and a metacognitive hypothesis on auditory hallucinations. *Cognitive and Behavioral Practice, 14*, 134–138.

Wessely, S., Buchanan, A., Reed, A., Cutting, J., Everitt, B., Garety, P. and Taylor, P.J. (1993). Acting on delusions (1): Prevalence. *British Journal of Psychiatry, 163*, 69–76.

Wessler, R.A. and Wessler, R.L. (1988). *The principles and practice of rational emotive therapy.* San Francisco, CA: Jossey-Bass.

Wolpe, J. (1958). *Psychotherapy by reciprocal inhibition.* Stanford, CA: Stanford University Press.

Wykes, T., Steel, C., Everitt, B. and Tarrier, N. (2008). Cognitive behaviour therapy for schizophrenia: Effect sizes, clinical models, and methodological rigor. *Schizophrenia Bulletin, 10*(114), 1–15.

Young, J.E., Klosko, J.S. and Weishaar, M. (2003). *Schema therapy: A practitioner's guide.* New York: The Guilford Press.

Zisook, S., McAdams, L.A., Kuck, J., Harris, M.J., Bailey, A., Patterson, T.L., Judd, L.L. and Jeste, D.V. (1999). Depressive symptoms in schizophrenia. *American Journal of Psychiatry, 156*, 1736–1743.

Zuber, I. (2000). Patients' own problem formulation and recommendations. *Journal of Psychotherapy Integration, 10*(4), 403–414.

Index